What People A~~re Saying about~~ T0244013

## DEATH: Friend or Enemy?

In this instructive and illuminating book, the author explores many different life paths and journeys within the context of lessons learned and her deep understanding of the nature of death as transition to another realm as well as the context of multiple lives. The book is well researched and highly readable, while readers have the opportunity of gleaning significant insights that can shed light on their own current journeys.
**David Lorimer**, Global Ambassador and Programme Director, the Scientific and Medical Network Editor, Paradigm Explorer Chair, Galileo Commission

In Ann Merivale's book *DEATH: Friend or Enemy? Views from the Other Side*, we need to suspend what we believe to be true and then look deeper. Therein lies the fable, the parable. Look deeper. Now you see the laws of heaven, the metaphysical. But don't stop there. Yes, there it is! That mystical moment where the depths within you are revealed as truth. Ann's book takes you on this journey, but it depends on how you open your eyes, and how willing you are to receive the gifts within the text that reveal the vastness of this wonderful work.
**Stephen Paul Chong**, educator, trainer, and author of *The Afterlife: A Journey To*

It is common to refer to the afterlife as the 'great unknown'. Yet there have always been reports of these 'death realms', or bardos — those other realities beyond the physical — and now a growing number of discoverers and reporters confirm what the old texts have told. From near-death experiences, mediums, soul voyages in past lives, and shamanic work, there is a wealth of experience being brought back and shared that describes maps of spirit worlds; meetings with masters, guides, and spirits; and infinite possibilities. More than anything else, however, today's explorers bring back stories, and Ann Merivale, as her previous books attest, is a great gatherer and teller of these tales, having the ability to voyage through the portals of imagination into what is known as the Akashic Records, where the patterns of Karma reveal each soul's adventures and entanglements, losses and learnings across many lifetimes.

All her chapters show that death is not an enemy to be fought and avoided at all costs, but the natural portal of return to spirit, only seeming fearful when mind has been seduced into the illusion of matter as exclusive reality and has consequently forgotten the whole and greater nature of our self. Yes, there are 'heavens' and 'hells' of our own creation, as many environments as there are imaginations to create them, and the hell realm of one who has closed themselves to any care for others can seem a long torture, but light and beings of light are always close, and no-one can stay apart from their beauty forever. As Sofia Tolstoy says in her chapter, "If … you are already knowledgeable about spiritual matters … you will appreciate both that death is only a temporary separation and that there is invariably a good reason for it, whenever it occurs."

**Kris Misselbrook**, Soul Voyager, Cathar Bonhomme, and Secretary of the Quakers in France

# DEATH:
# Friend or Enemy?

Views from the Other Side

# DEATH:
# Friend or Enemy?

## Views from the Other Side

### Ann Merivale

6TH
BOOKS

London, UK
Washington, DC, USA

# CollectiveInk

First published by Sixth Books, 2025
Sixth Books is an imprint of Collective Ink Ltd.,
Unit 11, Shepperton House, 89 Shepperton Road, London, N1 3DF
office@collectiveinkbooks.com
www.collectiveinkbooks.com
www.6th-books.com

For distributor details and how to order please visit the 'Ordering' section on our website.

Text copyright: Ann Merivale 2023

ISBN: 978 1 80341 689 2
978 1 80341 690 8 (ebook)
Library of Congress Control Number: 2023918380

A CIP catalogue record for this book is available from the British Library.

Design: Lapiz Digital Services

UK: Printed and bound by CPI Group (UK) Ltd, Croydon, CR0 4YY
Printed in North America by CPI GPS partners

We operate a distinctive and ethical publishing philosophy in all areas of our business, from our global network of authors to production and worldwide distribution.

# Contents

This book is dedicated to my pioneer therapy teacher, Dr Roger Woolger (1944–2011). Many felt that he had died 'prematurely'. I, however, feel sure that he is now being even better employed on the other side.

## Previous Books

*Karmic Release*
ISBN 81-862822-66-6

*Souls United: The Power of Divine Connection*
ISBN 978-0-7387-1528-5

*Discovering the Life Plan: Eleven Steps to Your Destiny*
ISBN 978-1-84694-821-3

*Delayed Departure: A Beginner's Guide to Soul Rescue*
ISBN 978-1-78279-011-2

*Life Without Elgar: A Tale of a Journeying Soul*
ISBN 978-1-78179-526-1

*Thicker Than Blood? A Fresh Look at Adoption,
Fostering and Step Families*
ISBN 978-1-78279-836-1

*Enchanted Islands: Tales from the Galápagos*
ISBN 978-0-9932970-0-7

*Woman through the Ages*
ISBN 978-1-78904-967-1

# Acknowledgements

Despite its imperfections, Wikipedia is still my constant companion on the computer (and I do respond to their annual requests for donations).

I am ever grateful to my husband, David Pearson, for his constant support for my work and for sometimes listening to my reading of chapters and making valuable editorial comments.

Talks by the musicologist Richard Wigmore have frequently been helpful to me (especially for Beethoven and Schubert).

As for my previous book *Woman through the Ages*, I'm ever grateful to Donald Macleod with his Radio 3 programme *Composer of the Week*.

I also owe a big debt to Cate Haste for her excellent and insightful biography of Alma Mahler, *Passionate Spirit: The Life of Alma Mahler*.

I'm grateful to my psychotherapist friend Jenny Ward for advice on the thorny question of suicide and also for information on the psychologist James Hillman.

It was another friend, Lynne Smith, who told me about the episode of the television programme *Flog It* in which attention was drawn to my beloved Kathleen Ferrier, the truly wonderful contralto singer.

In Lanzarote I was extremely grateful to my very good friend Peg Holden Peters for her arm to hang on to over the tricky bits; to her wonderful son, Janjo, for driving us around for a couple of days; and to both of them for improving on my title for Chapter 21.

Also for Chapter 21, I'm very pleased to have been able to purchase in Lanzarote's César Manrique Foundation the beautifully illustrated book *César Manrique: In his Own Words*, which has both English and German translations side by side on each page. Though I did occasionally deviate from it, a 'thank you', too, to Jonathan Allen for the English version.

For Chapter 23 I'm indebted to Celia Hindmarch for her excellent and comprehensive book *On the Death of a Child*.

I am further repeatedly indebted to my daughter Alice Pearson for coming to my rescue when (partly due to my now semi-useless left hand) I made a blunder with my typing.

I am equally indebted to that wonderful daughter for driving me and my husband, together with Bramble, her boisterous puppy, and in poor conditions, to and from Laugharne so that I could immerse myself for a couple of days in the Dylan Thomas ambience.

Also for Chapter 24, I'm most grateful to Caitlin Thomas for her two extraordinary books (both published after her death in 1994), *Leftover Life to Kill* (now out of print, but I secured a secondhand copy from World of Books) and *My Life with Dylan Thomas: Double Drink Story*. And to their granddaughter, Hannah Ellis, who edited for the centenary of his birth, in 2014, a book with numerous contributors, *Dylan Thomas: A Centenary Celebration*.

For Chapter 25 I'm indebted to Van Gogh's sister-in-law, Johanna, for getting his letters into print in three volumes.

Robert Kanigel's superbly written biography *The Man Who Knew Infinity: A Life of the Genius Ramanujan* proved invaluable for Chapter 26.

As was, finally, a visit to the Holst Victorian House in Cheltenham. There the staff were exceedingly helpful and, besides CDs of some of Holst's music that I didn't know, I was able to purchase a copy of Tony Palmer's brilliant film *Holst: In the Bleak Midwinter* and also a copy of Michael Short's comprehensive book *Gustav Holst: The Man and his Music*.

It's hard to express the extent of my gratitude to Frank Smecker of Collective Ink, who not only helped me enormously with the cover, but also came to the rescue when this 'oldie' was struggling with the technology.

And last, but by no means least, though we differed on some things, such as English versus American spelling of certain words, I'm truly grateful to my editor, Mollie Barker, for picking up some appalling blunders that my multitudinous re-readings had missed.

# Introduction

*He [Shostakovich] liked to think that he wasn't afraid of death. It was life he was afraid of, not death. He believed that people should think about death more often, and accustom themselves to the notion of it. Just letting it creep up on you unnoticed was not the best way to live. You should make yourself familiar with it. You should write about it: either in words or, in his case, music. It was his belief that if we thought about death earlier in our lives, we would make fewer mistakes.*

*Not that he hadn't made a lot of mistakes himself.*

*And sometimes he thought that death was indeed the thing that terrified him the most.*

Julian Barnes, *The Noise of Time*

In his book *The Antidote: A Bracing Detox for the Self-Help Junkie* the journalist Oliver Burkeman comments that "it may be hard to swallow the idea that we should spend more time contemplating death, but there are some powerful and pragmatic arguments for doing so". He quotes, among others, Ernest Becker, an American born in 1924, who died in 1974 from cancer of the colon, a year before the publication of his 'magnum opus', *The Denial of Death*. As a very young man Becker came up against death firsthand while helping to liberate a Nazi concentration camp. This caused him to write about the human tendency to avoid facing up to the fatality of death and to overcome the haunting fear of it by denying its reality.

It's partly the fear of death, now endemic in Western society and of course recently accentuated by Covid-19, that first gave me the idea of writing a book such as this in about 2015. 'Coincidentally', the notion came more or less simultaneously to Mark Young, my friend and practitioner who runs the Ripon Natural Health Centre, but at the time we were both busy with other things and consequently discussed the matter only briefly. So, now that I myself am well into my eighties and Mark is still extremely busy, I feel that we have little time left for dealing with such an important topic.

Buddhists, Hindus, indigenous people of, for instance, the Americas, Western Gnostics have all for thousands of years taken for granted that every soul has countless lives on Earth, so for them losing one life, however 'prematurely', obviously makes the loss appear less tragic than most present-day Westerners believe it to be. Christian teaching on the matter of reincarnation dates only from the Council of Constantinople in AD 553, at which, on account of the influence of Theodora (his by then late wife), the rather weak Emperor Justinian endeavoured to make a change. For she, not having liked the idea of returning to Earth as anything other than an empress, had been keen for the previously commonly held doctrine to be suppressed! Yet the suppression of belief in reincarnation was never totally successful, as there have always been movements of 'Gnostics', such as the Cathars, who retained this knowledge. (The Cathars' beliefs, as you will see in Chapter 4, were distorted and their barbarous and unjust persecution is one of the great shames of the Church.)

How could we possibly learn all that we want or need to in just a single lifetime? And how otherwise could it be fair that some are born with the proverbial silver spoon in their mouths while others incarnate into dire poverty? I am personally convinced that anyone who cares to research these spiritual matters seriously enough will easily find sufficient proof to convince them that they themselves had many previous lives.

Nowadays, however, the Churches have much less influence on the Western world than they did for about a couple of thousand years. The desire for 'scientific proof' of everything has caused atheism or agnosticism to become increasingly common and therefore many people no longer believe in either the immortality of the soul or any sort of afterlife. In contrast, I myself was brought up strictly in the Catholic Church and it took me many years to 'escape' onto a path that, while retaining my admiration for Jesus, I see as more spiritual. Since its focus is supposed to be on 'making it to Heaven', it seems to me nonsensical that the Church teaches nothing at all about what happens when we die! And one of my big quibbles with all church funerals is the prayer "Grant him/her eternal rest". (Can anyone seriously believe that someone such as Bruce Kent, the great activist for the Campaign for Nuclear Disarmament (CND), who was still campaigning a month before his death at the age of 92, would be content to be just lazing around? And anyway doesn't the notion of resting for the whole of the remains of eternity sound intensely boring?)

Unlike other Catholics of my acquaintance who like the idea of 'mystery', I have *always* wanted to know what might happen when I died and have fortunately over the last 30 years or so been able to make up for this lacuna in my religious education by a great deal of reading. This has been combined, too, with much experience of taking people who've come to me for Deep Memory Process, known as DMP (past-life regression therapy), through their deaths in previous lives and listening with interest to their stories. Here I hasten to add that I haven't in this book made use of any of my clients' individual experiences. It was in fact originally intended to be a work of fiction — my first (also my last, since this is my final book) — but now I feel that it might be up to you, the reader, to decide whether or not the book is *totally* fictitious.

Mark, my above-mentioned practitioner and friend, has always described me as a "storyteller" and it is indeed through stories that I decided to illustrate some of the numerous possible post-death scenarios that I've encountered and, through my many years of working in this field, sometimes written about. Certainly *some* of the characters whose tales I've recounted are fictional. The two women in Chapter 20, for instance, are loosely based on a couple of acquaintances that I had in the past, while those in Chapter 22 are entirely fictional. (I mention the latter since I wouldn't want any reader who fancied having some DMP themselves to go chasing a Woolger graduate named Isobel in the Manchester area!) Many of the others, however, are well-known deceased personalities and that's where it will be up to you to decide for yourselves whether or not I was simply letting my imagination run wild or whether I was actually channelling them. Some of the non-fictional characters came to me of their own accord, while with others I decided over a period of several years that I fancied writing about them.

With respect to the latter, following some brief shamanic training, I have over many years sometimes used a drumming CD to communicate with the other side, but I have no way of vouching that what has come through to me is a hundred per cent genuine. However, I don't believe that veracity matters at all for the purposes of this book, as my aim is a general one of education about the afterlife.

In the cases of the famous characters, who should mostly be instantly recognisable, I've done a little bit of exploration of their actual lives while they were on Earth, but I should like to point out that, even if some genuine channelling has on occasion occurred, what has come through my figurative pen will inevitably be coloured firstly by my own special interests in the historical figure concerned and secondly by my knowledge of the sorts of things that *can* happen on the other side.

Returning for a moment to the Catholic Church, one thing for which one can give it credit is its custom of praying for departed souls. Like the Buddhists, whose tradition is to pray for somebody daily for 49 days after death, most Christians appreciate that prayers sent from Earth can help souls on their way. This is needed particularly when the person concerned fails to realise that they have died — a thing that can occur easily, for instance, in the case of a sudden accident. It's sometimes said that generally, when people die, they find what they expected to find; for example, a Christian will meet Jesus, a Buddhist the Buddha, and so on. When it comes to atheists, however, they will usually find 'nothing' and it may take some time for them to be 'woken up' to the reality of life continuing on the other side. Fortunately they do all 'wake up' eventually, but prior knowledge can speed up the process, as can having people who care about them either praying for them while still on Earth or looking down and offering help from a higher level.

One thing that I haven't attempted to touch upon is the different levels that exist on higher planes. These, it is commonly agreed, are seven in number and for those interested in the topic there are plenty of books available. Which of them one goes to in between incarnations depends upon one's level of development. The stories I'm recounting here, however, are related not to that subject but rather to the soul concerned looking back upon their last life and deciding what they learn and what they still need to remedy.

An important point to make at this juncture is that, although it is generally believed among those who have studied such matters that 'God', or whatever name one cares to give Him/Her, decided at some point to split into countless numbers of different 'souls', these have not all had by any means the same number of lifetimes (either on Earth or elsewhere). Hence the terms 'old soul' and 'young soul' that are in common spiritual parlance. Since, however, we are all equal, the latter term is by no means derogatory. (As the renowned clairvoyant Edwin Courtenay commented to me many years ago: "We need the young souls around for their energy!")

As an example: in Chapter 20, which has contrasting stories of two women who got stuck for a while after their physical deaths in what is known in Tibetan as the *Bardo* (between islands), Fiona is clearly an older soul than Beryl. Although she made mistakes in her lifetime (as we all do — otherwise we wouldn't still need to be here), Fiona was, as a nurse by profession, well-educated and knowledgeable and consequently knew full well that she had died. Beryl, on the other hand (appropriately nicknamed 'Mrs Misery'), was probably a much younger soul and so, since she'd had very little education and since Earth's etheric body looks exactly the same as the physical one, she was unable to appreciate the fact that she had left her own physical body.

When one reads about near-death experiences (NDEs), as in the entirely fictional Chapter 15, the normal pattern appears to be that, upon leaving the body, the departing soul is whooshed through a tunnel towards the light, where he or she can meet the person (normally a spirit guide) who is best able to talk with him or her about what they've either learnt or should have learnt during the life that's just ended. The usual pattern is then to discuss the available choices for what is to happen next. Obviously, in the case of NDEs, the choice was made to return to Earth — otherwise the person concerned wouldn't have been able to recount the experience — but my personal experience of regression to previous deaths (both my own and those of numerous clients) differs little from the stories that I've read about NDEs.

I have a few recurring themes in the book. One of these is music, simply because it has been my own abiding passion this time round, but a particular question that has greatly interested me throughout my years of working as a therapist and counsellor is that of relationships. This is of course very often a thorny topic and for that very reason, solutions have to be found before we can clear all our karma and thus be able finally to return to the Source whence we originally came all those aeons ago. 'Soul mate' relationships come in here, as well as 'thorny' ones, and I have in all my writing adhered to the threefold definition given by Edgar Cayce (known as the 'sleeping prophet'). These are firstly 'twin souls', who are literally two halves of the same being, since it's thought that all souls divided into two right at the beginning and occasionally meet up again on Earth before becoming ready for the final reunion. (Such relationships can be either blissful or, again, 'thorny', depending upon the level of spiritual development.) Secondly, 'companion soul mates' (often the most comfortable), that is, people who've been together many times in varying relationships — spouses or siblings, for instance — and consequently know one another well. And thirdly, 'karmic soul mates', which involve people who come together in order to pay a debt. This could be something as drastic as one having previously killed the other, but even in such cases the partnership can be either contented or positively idyllic.

Another theme that intrigues me is that of genius and some of my characters have undoubtedly thus been labelled. So what makes a 'genius'? Does it really make any sense to believe that a person can simply be *born* with a great gift for, say, music or art — especially if it's not in their genes? Isn't it much more logical to think that they must have honed the gift over many lifetimes? Another point here is that when we, for instance, listen to some truly beautiful music or read a wonderful piece of poetry, it can be easy for us to imagine that the person from whom it came was charming, delightful and so on, yet this is very clearly far from being always the case! Where there is light there must always be dark and while leaving readers to draw their own conclusions, I'd just like to point out that emerging *de profundis* ('from the depths') can lead to a kind of ecstasy.

I'll now conclude by mentioning that I have personally always been terrified by the notion of scary rides and consequently never liked the idea of being whooshed through a tunnel! I was therefore delighted to hear from the distinguished shamanic practitioner Simon Buxton, in a workshop he led on the topic of 'Death, Dying and the Beyond', that one has a choice. He encouraged us to practise dying from time to time, saying that we could visualise how we would like to be transported to the other side. My choice was of a boat coming over a tranquil lake to collect me (hopefully containing one or two people dear to me who have already passed on). Hence my choice of cover image, with the rising sun symbolising the new life that lies ahead.

# 1

# A Spiritually Minded Nurse

*In the Gita, the Lord has assured that the person who dies with the Pranava (Om) filling his last breath is sure to be liberated. The sound 'Om' will not help when the mind is flitting from one desire to another, weeping over the imminent departure from the world and at the outcome to come. In such a case, how can the sound help? The glory of Om has to be apprehended throughout life if it is to stand out before the mind at the moment of departure.*

Sathya Sai Baba

My name in my last life was Susie (short for Susan of course, which is what my parents always called me, but I always preferred the less formal-sounding nickname). I was born into a Conservative family of the landed gentry of North Yorkshire, that is, "with a silver spoon in my mouth", as the saying goes, but the 'silver spoon' never suited me! In fact you could well say that I was born a rebel, but now that I've thankfully come Home again, I've been able to see clearly that that last incarnation was one that I myself had chosen as a challenge: to overcome the hurdles of wealth and C/conservatism (in both senses!) and find my true nature as someone who cared much more about helping *people* than about conserving the family name and fortune.

I had an older brother (Kenneth), born four years before me, who, fortunately from my parents' point of view, *was* interested in following in their footsteps and he of course inherited the estate when my father died. I didn't really have that much contact with my parents as a child, as we always had nannies and a cook and so on, and they were on the whole loving and caring towards the two of us. Since Kenneth was that much older, we didn't play together very much and he, naturally, always preferred the company of other boys in the area. This didn't bother me, as I was happy with my own company, loved being outside whenever the weather was nice enough and enjoyed reading; one thing that my parents did do was keep us well supplied with good children's books. Thanks to a nanny of whom I was particularly fond, I learnt to read quite early and on dreary winter days nothing gave me greater pleasure than to be curled up with a book in front of a big roaring fire.

Another good thing about my childhood was that my family always kept dogs. Some of them were used for hunting — a thing that I always abhorred but would have been scolded for speaking my mind about — but there was always at least one pet dog that I loved dearly and who was my constant companion when I wasn't at school. The primary school wasn't very far from our estate. I was often taken there in a pony trap, which I loved, and I made good friends among my fellow pupils, always for some reason being very popular. I was a good student, too, but never hesitated to speak my mind when I saw fault in something that a teacher said. This caused me to be appreciated by the more self-confident teachers but irritating to others.

My family, like others in the area, was Anglican and church every Sunday morning was therefore obligatory. Though I did like some of the hymns, mostly I found the services rather boring and, as for the sermons, the older I grew, the less and less sense they made to me. "If this God they talk about," I would say to myself, "really did create all of us and truly loves us, as the vicar claims, how could He condemn any of us to 'eternal damnation'?" But it felt safer to keep my thoughts to myself and only many years later did I have the good fortune to stumble upon many books and spiritual journals which supported my own intuitive way of thinking.

When I reached the age of 11, I was — inevitably — despatched by my parents to boarding school. Kenneth was by then well ensconced at Rugby School and excelling in sport, but for me, as a "mere girl", they didn't fancy spending as much, since any education I received would "only be needed to equip me for being a good wife to a fellow member of the landed gentry". (Upon leaving school I would of course have been expected to return home and go to lots of balls attended also by young, well-bred, eligible gentlemen!) I didn't absolutely hate the minor girls' boarding school that my parents chose and Anna, with whom I'd been quite good friends at the primary school, went to the same one, which helped both of us not to feel too lonely during the first term. I didn't shine at sport but quite enjoyed badminton and sometimes, as part or all of a biology lesson (a subject that fascinated me anyway), we were taken on pleasant country walks searching for wildflowers and being taught the names of birds and trees (as though I didn't know them all already!). So biology was one of the subjects I chose to do for A-level when I turned 16, along with maths and English. My grades were perfectly respectable and, encouraged by a particular teacher who understood me quite well, I looked into the question of training as a nurse as soon as I'd left school.

My parents, however, had quite *other* ideas. "Oh no, Susan dear! After the end of your final school summer holidays, it will be the start of the débutante season and you can stay with Aunt Grace in London, get presented to the Queen (what a thrill!) and attend some of the debs' balls. Who knows? You might that way even meet a suitable man to marry and that could save us from having to put on so many balls here."

"But Mama," I protested, "I have no great desire either to meet the Queen or to find a husband — at least for the time being. I want to do something really useful with my life and nursing is surely a very respectable profession for a young woman?!"

The argument carried on for several weeks and I really had to dig my heels in, but determination won out in the end and I was finally permitted to apply to train in Manchester. (London, they said, would have been all right for a short time if I'd agreed to the débutante idea, but for a three-year nursing course the capital would have been too far away for them to keep a close eye on me! Incidentally, I was pleased when, in 1958, Queen Elizabeth II decided to abolish the deb tradition, as it seemed nonsensical to me, as well as a waste of public money! Unlike the rest of my family, I was never a great royalist, but I did have to admire Elizabeth for certain things she did and when Prince Philip crossed over in 2021, shortly before his hundredth birthday, he was greeted here with immense acclaim for all the very good things he'd done in that lifetime.)

I greatly enjoyed my time of training in Manchester, even though it was very hard work and I sometimes found the night shifts a trial, and I made some good friends. Early on, a particular friend I had, named Elizabeth, took me along to a meeting of a group of people with spiritual interests and there I was introduced, among other things, to the work of the prophet Edgar Cayce. This accorded with a great deal that I'd always felt intuitively, and it explained, for instance, why I had so often had moments of 'déjà vu' on going to new places and also why I felt that I had been born into the 'wrong' family. ("It was for your learning," Malcolm, the leader of the group explained. "Escaping from that very narrow-minded environment will help you onto a more spiritual path and stand you in good stead for future lifetimes, if you need to have them.")

Though I was never very keen to, I did dutifully go home about once a month, and very occasionally my parents came to visit me, sometimes staying overnight in a posh hotel fairly close to the hospital. Kenneth married Eve, the daughter of a nearby farmer, before I'd finished my studies and they took over the spare wing of our house, which suited everybody perfectly. Eve and I got on reasonably well but had absolutely nothing in common and once she'd got pregnant the first time she was too absorbed in her forthcoming new role to be bothered with seeing much of me. My mother would invariably ask me questions such as "Has a nice young doctor asked you out yet, Susan? Or do you and your friends sometimes go to dances? Now that Kenneth is well settled, your father and I are really looking forward to organising a wedding for our daughter!"

These questions irritated me so much (as though matrimony was the only important thing for a woman!) that on one occasion I plucked up the courage to reply "Oh no, Mother! I don't think I'm destined to have a family this time round. I've probably had more than enough tedious lives of childbearing in the past!"

"What on earth do you mean by that, my girl?" she retorted. "You haven't suddenly become a Buddhist or something, have you? You're surely well aware that we Christians know that we all only have *one* life! That's one of the reasons why it's so important to find the right man while you're still young. Spinsterhood would be a dreadful fate!"

"Not if one's doing something worthwhile and fulfilling," I replied. "What would have happened to *you* last year, when you had to go into hospital for your hysterectomy, if there hadn't been any nurses to look after you?"

My mother just gave me a despairing look and then I said "I think I'd better go and give Sally a walk. She must miss me while I'm away."

I missed the dogs, too, of course in Manchester, but there was nothing to be done about that — at least for the time being.

Once I'd qualified, I worked happily in Manchester for some years, still enjoying the friendship and support of fellow spiritual seekers. I was transfixed by Yogananda's *Autobiography of a Yogi* and also became very interested in other great Indian Masters, such as Vivekananda. Once, my friend Elizabeth suggested I go on holiday to India with her; I gave it some serious thought, but somehow felt that I had no need to go there. "I feel that I know it sufficiently already," I told her. "Perhaps I've had many previous lifetimes there."

"I expect you have," she replied. "Never mind, I dare say Angela will be happy to accompany me."

In due course I somehow got drawn to the capital. "I think there will be even more opportunities there," I explained to my by now only mildly protesting family. Kenneth and Eve were engrossed in their own young family of two and still on the spot should our parents be taken seriously ill, so I felt quite free to get a job wherever I pleased. A good one came up straight away, at Guy's Hospital, and there I felt I learnt a great deal, but when further new horizons called I took up a post in a convalescent home, where I could live in rather than always having to find a small flat to rent.

One of the first friends I made in the home was a fellow nurse named Gwen and we soon found ourselves to be on the same wavelength spiritually. After a few months of working there I happened to buy a raffle ticket and the result was that, to my surprise and delight, I won a baby pig! I knew well from my upbringing on a Yorkshire estate that pigs were not only friendly but also highly intelligent, so I felt that Harry, as I instantly named him, could be a good substitute for owning a dog. I brought him home in my car to the nursing home from the farm where he'd been born and there he quickly made friends with the patients, who were more than happy to have him wandering at will into their rooms. There were always plenty of scraps in the kitchens to keep him satisfied, but sadly, once he'd grown really big, I was summoned to the principal's office, where I was told "I'm very sorry, Miss Diggle, but that pig of yours is just going to have to go now." I was heartbroken, but when I phoned the farmer from whom I'd got Harry, he kindly agreed to come and take him back in his van. He settled happily there among other piggy friends but always seemed delighted to see me again when I went to visit on my days off.

My parents, whom I did always continue to visit fairly regularly, both died when I was in my early sixties and I inherited quite a lot of money. I didn't really feel that I needed it, my salary always having covered my needs quite comfortably, but on the other hand I rather fancied retiring to somewhere much more rural and so finally buying a house of my own seemed sensible. Gwen was more or less the same age as me but was planning on retiring to the outskirts of London, where she had family. She was, however, more than happy to travel around the countryside with me when we were both free. Although I was a dutiful aunt, never failing to send Christmas and birthday presents to my nephew and niece, I felt no desire to retire to Yorkshire, where I didn't feel I belonged, and Kenneth and Eve's way of life and their values differed so strongly from mine. So Gwen and I concentrated our house hunting further south, realising as we did so that prices fell as one went further west. One fine day, having gravitated towards south Shropshire, whose hills were a great attraction, I fell in love with England's smallest town, Bishops Castle.

At around this time, too, we became founder members of a spiritually minded group of people that we decided to name 'Amadea'. The idea behind it matched our ideals perfectly: it was to form a sort of 'alternative retirement home', where the younger members would look after the older ones and then be looked after themselves later when their needs became greater. All the other members fancied living in Devon and so yearly meetings were held there for a while. I didn't really know Devon, but warmer climes certainly had their appeal and anyway the thing that appealed to me most was the ethos behind it all. At one of the meetings in Devon I made friends with a couple named Ann and David, both in their late sixties, who lived in East Yorkshire where he was a professor at Hull University. Together the whole group looked at a few properties that were for sale in Devon, but one of the problems with the idea was that, while some members fancied living in a big house totally as a community, others preferred the notion of continuing to have greater independence, with a group of much smaller abodes all centred on a larger house. Another problem was that, everyone being non-materialistic and spiritually focused, whenever a property came on the market, the cash for it couldn't be raised until most people involved had sold their own homes.

Nobody got totally dispirited with the ideal, but, while nothing definitive was happening, I returned to Bishops Castle and fell in love with a house that had just come up for sale. It was totally unsuitable for an older person, having three floors with a somewhat rickety staircase, but it had a small garden (*ideal* for a small dog!) and so I just went ahead and bought it anyway. I retired at 70, moved there as soon as was feasible and soon acquired a darling little whippet, whom I named Lucy. The townspeople were all very friendly and I was soon made to feel that I belonged and got involved in various worthwhile activities. Gwen found herself a pleasant place to move to, but we kept in close touch and visited one another regularly. The Amadea meetings continued as well, even though no progress was made, but I suddenly heard that a piece of land had been purchased at the very end of my street by someone who wanted to build an eco-hamlet.

So I went and talked to this individual, invested several thousand pounds in the project, and put something about it into the Amadea newsletter. This was in the year 2000 and when my friend Ann read this, she was keen to get involved because she knew that she would soon be inheriting some money from the sale of a Somerset estate previously owned by her grandparents and then two maiden aunts, of whom the younger one had just died. So she and David rushed down to Bishops Castle, where I put them up for a couple of nights, and they had a good talk with the man administering the eco-hamlet project. (I'll call him Wayne.) He encouraged them to buy a plot, saying that they could employ their own architects and that they couldn't possibly lose out since the land was likely to double in value.

Anyway, to cut a long story short, the whole thing dragged on for four years. This didn't at first bother my friends too much, since David had yet to retire, and they made many more weekend visits, all of which made them increasingly sure that they fancied living out the rest of their days in Shropshire. They always brought their Cavalier King Charles spaniel with them, too, which delighted Lucy and me, and sometimes they met there with the two architects they'd chosen, whose ideas were in total alignment with their own. Another thing that happened was that I developed both cancer and problems with my eyes, but I don't care to dwell on any of that, since so many people of similar age to mine then had even worse afflictions.

By the spring of 2004, however, the crunch came for my friends, as David had by then retired and there was still no real progress with the eco-hamlet development. Wayne (who had himself done a tiny bit of architectural training) had just decided that he wanted to design most of the houses himself. The last straw came when he informed Ann and David that he was sacking their architects because their latest design didn't conform precisely to his requirements. That was when Ann commented that the 'eco-hamlet' had turned into an '*ego*-hamlet' and they decided to pull out. (Fortunately they didn't lose out financially, as Wayne didn't dare to deviate from his initial assurance about the land doubling in price! Other interested people pulled out, too, at that point and I asked for my money back and donated it to other causes dear to my heart.)

With their money now safely in the bank, and retaining a good friendship with their bitterly disappointed architects, Ann and David then gave themselves a week to decide on another part of Shropshire in which to live. They very quickly settled on Ludlow, which had, as they said, various advantages over Bishops Castle, such as a railway station.

I myself saw no reason for leaving my lovely house, and the three of us kept very much in touch. They bought a copy of the

# DEATH: Friend or Enemy?

AA book of *50 Walks in Shropshire* and whenever one of these walks took them anywhere in my vicinity, they would drop in, either with or without notice. I loved having visitors and always kept my fridge and larder well stocked, so that I could produce a meal at any time. I also always had a good stock of dog biscuits, even after my beloved Lucy had died, and everybody around me had insisted that, on account of my deteriorating health and poor eyesight, there was no way that I should replace her. Whenever Ann and I met, we always conversed on spiritual subjects and at one point I confided to her that I felt quite ready to go at any moment.

Life, however, often has unexpected things awaiting one around the corner and — obviously before my time had actually come — I developed Alzheimer's. This didn't really bother *me* because my memory went and so I forgot (among other things!) that I was supposed to be dying. But it did bother my family and close friends and so my brother got together with Gwen and one or two people in Bishops Castle and, since Bishops Castle was too small to have a nursing home, they decided to get me moved into a nice one in Ludlow. I had plenty of visitors there (including Ann and David of course) and they always found that I didn't know where I was. I had, however, retained my innate hospitable instincts and so I would always say such things as "How *lovely* to see you! *Do* put the kettle on and there are biscuits in the tin." Ann, who is someone who always likes to find reasons for things, felt (quite rightly, as I can now see from my new perspective over here) that, since I wasn't yet leaving my body, my new purpose was to give the carers someone obliging to look after. She reckoned that I made a pleasant contrast to the many cantankerous patients who made their lives difficult!

One day when Ann and David came to call, they gave me the sad news that their dog, Apu, had died and they brought me a nice photo of him lying on my knee in their house. (Incidentally,

18

for the benefit of any sceptics who thought it likely that people with Alzheimer's wouldn't always tell the truth, I kept pinned to my wardrobe in the nursing home a photo of my pig Harry walking with me down a London street!) Before getting themselves another dog, they decided to pay a long-awaited trip to Australia and New Zealand, so I didn't see them again for a good couple of months. Nobody who came to visit was ever quite sure whether I would recognise them, but as soon as Ann and David arrived back, I asked about their trip and when they were going to get another dog.

After that my body really started to pack it in more seriously and, as often happens when one is nearing the end, I tended fairly regularly to float in and out of it, often meeting with loved ones who had gone on before and were waiting to greet me. These dear ones of course sometimes included dogs that I had owned and loved and when such meetings occurred it wasn't always easy for me to know which plane I was on. So, once when Ann and David visited, saying that they hadn't yet begun seriously to hunt for another dog, I told them that I had 14 and they could go and choose one. Then, the next time they came, I asked "Did you go and have a look at those dogs?" This made them feel sure that I *was* nearing the end, but at that point they were about to go off on holiday to their beloved Geneva (which was where they had originally met).

I did in fact cross over while they were away. It was *wonderful*! I slipped away so easily and painlessly, and the 14 dogs that I'd owned at various stages of my life were indeed among those awaiting me. Ann was sorry to have missed my funeral, but (as Gwen assured her!) it wouldn't have been at all to her taste. Kenneth organised the whole thing and I myself didn't hang around for long, as it was very conventional Conservative Anglican, which I found distinctly boring. But since funerals are designed more for the living than for the dead, that really didn't bother me and at least the service was held in the Bishops Castle church, of which I was rather fond. Then they took my ashes up to Yorkshire and buried them under one of my favourite trees — the one that I used to love climbing when I was about eight. I thought that was rather a nice idea! I can't see much point in tombstones, unless relatives feel they need them as a focus on which to put flowers when they want to commemorate an anniversary or something.

Well, that's an account of my most recent lifetime on Earth. Now I thought you might be interested to hear a bit of what I've been up to since. As I just said, leaving that rather sick body was no problem at all. I simply slipped out painlessly and was immediately greeted by my guardian angel (whom I instantly recognised) and he carried me in his arms to a wonderful warm light, which was bright without being dazzling to my tired eyes. There was quite a crowd awaiting me and Lucy, together with some of the dogs that my family had owned, ran up and started licking me excitedly. I could see my parents and grandparents in the background, but the first person to speak to me was my main guide, whose name I prefer to keep to myself, but I knew him to be a very old friend. His greeting was very encouraging. He started by saying: "Blessings on you, Susie. It's great to have you back here again and I'm sure you can feel quite proud of yourself for all your attainments this time round! You'll no doubt be tired now after those unpleasant physical ailments and a good rest awaits you, but first of all I'd like you to meet a few more people and have a little discussion about how you achieved your purpose."

"I'm not sure that I like to use the word 'proud'," I replied. "It implies some self-satisfaction, when all I really did was what I felt called to do."

"Trust you to be modest!" he said. "Anyway, my dear, I'm happy to inform you that you've now completed your karma on Earth and so higher realms await you, if you so wish. The choice will be yours. If you remember, the only reason you needed to go back was on account of one karmic debt that you had to your parents from a fairly recent previous life. You were in the same sort of challenging situation as this time, when they didn't share your values, but that time you dealt with it by abandoning them as soon as you could and didn't get in touch even when they were dying. As Susan, however, you were always very loyal and they did appreciate your visits, even though they never fully came to terms with the life you, so rightly, chose for yourself. Here they come now to greet you."

"Hullo, Susan. Welcome! Let's have a hug," said my mother.

"Yes, hullo, Susan dear," said my father, always more formal and less able to show his affection. "We've been watching how you were getting on ever since we came back here and I have to say that we've both ended up feeling very proud of you for doing what we can now see was the best thing for a heart as big as yours. We're now learning that wealth and stature are much less important in life than really helping others and so, when we reincarnate, we shall do so into rather less privileged circumstances."

"Good for you!" I replied. "Now let me greet all the grandparents. I particularly appreciated Grandpa Diggle teaching me how to train a dog. The two of us had some affinity there; and as for Grandma, I never forgot her Victoria sponge cakes!"

"Yes, my cakes were indeed renowned as the best in the vicinity. It's really lovely to see you again."

"Oh, look who's coming now!" exclaimed my father.

"It's Harry, my darling Harry! How lovely to see you! How are you doing over here?"

It's easier to understand piggy language on the higher planes than it is on Earth and in any case, as I'd quickly remembered, we all communicate by telepathy, so language is never a barrier. Harry told me that he'd been having a whale of a time playing with the dogs and he commented: "You see, we animals all get on fine over here. We never fight or eat one another, but live in harmony, sometimes greeting our human friends when they cross over, and waiting until it's time to reincarnate in a different form. I rather fancy being a horse next time."

"I'm sure you'd make an excellent horse," I replied, "but now I think my guide wants me to move on, so we can talk more another time, when I've finished my convalescence in a heavenly hospital."

"Yes, Susie," my guide interjected, "the heavenly hospital awaits you, but just before I accompany you there, I have another nice surprise for you: here comes Peter, your twin soul, fairly freshly arrived from Australia."

"Hullo, Susie, my dearest other half! I haven't been waiting for you for *very* long, since my last life came to an end just a few months ago in Earth time. I was watching over you in the nursing home, appreciating the love and kindness that you were spreading there and hoping that you weren't going to suffer too much as your life was ending."

"No, Peter, most of the physical discomfort was over by the time I was leaving Bishops Castle and at the end I was sometimes given morphine, which helped considerably. But how wonderful to see you again! Are we going to stay together for a while now?"

"Yes, we can certainly do that — we even now have the option of fusing completely before returning to the Source as a single entity — but I dare say you'll fancy staying a bit closer to Earth for a while, maybe serving as a guide to someone dear to you."

"Yes, I think I'd like to be a guide to my niece Josie, to whom I always felt quite close. But what have you been up to since we were last together?"

"Well, do you remember that we agreed to incarnate on different continents, where we could each complete our karma? I've just had a life in Australia, where I was also born into a family that didn't share my ideals. They were in fact rather racist, despising Aboriginals, and that triggered me into resolving a small karmic debt, incurred when I'd failed adequately to defend an Aboriginal who got attacked by a white man. I spent a lot of my life working among various Aboriginal communities, became very interested in their art and worked quite hard to promote it, organising exhibitions and so on."

"How very interesting! I look forward to hearing much more about it. But right now I understand that a hospital bed awaits me."

"It does indeed, my dearest. Relax, enjoy the healing and I'll see you anon."

The beautiful hospital truly was a wonderful experience. Drugs were unheard of in it and I was treated with aromatherapy, coloured light and much more. Once I felt myself again and as though I was in the fullness of youth, Peter arrived the moment I thought of him and we nattered endlessly about our different experiences and did a lot of travelling and exploring different realms. From time to time my thoughts turned back to Earth and the friends I'd left behind there. One of these was Ann, whose first book I'd enjoyed reading before I became too unwell. It was on the subject of some of her own previous lives, demonstrating how healing for the present life could come through Deep Memory Process, otherwise known as regression therapy. Since returning here I've watched the progress with further books of hers coming out. So now I feel immensely privileged to be the first contributor to this, her final book!

I'll just end, however, with a little word of warning. The lifetime that I've recounted was, I feel, a happy and fulfilling one, but that, as you of course know only too well, is far from always being the case, so you had better grit your teeth for some of what will ensue. But do, *please*, persevere with the reading because it's important to have a fairly full picture of the innumerable possibilities that can await those who come to the end of their lives. My hope is that readers will learn from some of what they find herein and thus avoid making the same mistakes. So, blessings on you all and maybe we'll meet up at some point. Because it must be remembered that whether rich or poor, sick or healthy, loving or unloving, *we are all one*!

# 2

# An Indian Beggar

*Whenever you can, try to be of service to all you meet. Keep in your heart that you are your brother's or sister's keeper; never their judge. Be as happy as you can one day at a time. Remember that wealth will not bring you happiness. It can only bring you a more comfortable life. You must discover happiness in whatever situation you find yourself. For happiness comes from within, in knowing who you are.*

Aron Abrahamsen, *Holiday in Heaven*

(Aron, who had worked with Edgar Cayce, told the author in a past-life reading that she had come this time "partly as a writer — to disseminate information on the spiritual life".)

My name in my last life was Meena, and I was born into an extremely poor family on the outskirts of Puttaparthi in Andhra Pradesh, the birthplace of the great avatar Sathya Sai Baba. Despite His almost constant presence in the area, however, and the wonderful things that happened there continually (and still are happening), I had the most miserable life imaginable. I was one of five children. My oldest brother managed to get away to Bangalore (now known officially as Bengaluru), where he eventually obtained a job as a rickshaw driver, but he barely ever earned enough even to support his wife and two children, let alone have a spare rupee for his birth family. He visited only once in a blue moon and had no interest in getting glimpses of Sai Baba. ("Well, what has he ever done for *us*?" he would ask.)

When I was born, the third in the family, my mother was so malnourished that she had difficulty in breastfeeding me, so

I'm told that as a baby I often cried relentlessly with hunger. We never had a proper abode — just a sort of makeshift tent, which gave only minimal protection from sun, rain and wind — and so the whole family often suffered intensely, especially during the summer, when there were never very many people around anyway to beg from, and during the monsoons. When the summer heat was at its worst, Sai Baba normally went to his ashram in Whitefield, on the outskirts of Bangalore, or up into the mountains at Kodai Kanal, and the devotees would follow Him. That was of course up until 24 April 2011 when He was still in His body. Since His departure, which naturally brought an enormous amount of grief, people have still come to Puttaparthi in their thousands. These are not only the long-time devotees, who want to worship at his *Samadhi* (the huge marble tomb in the Sai Kulwant Hall, where He always appeared twice daily, sometimes giving discourses), but also others who've come to hear of Him in one of various ways. Sometimes it's because of Him having appeared to them in a dream, telling them to come, and then they had to find out who He was! (Here I'd better explain that I didn't know any of these things while I was alive; it's only since I died in 2021 that I've been able to look back down to see what's going on.)

My father, who'd never been able to be of any use to us, died when I was only 10, and my mother was by then too weak to go out onto the streets herself, so it was up to us four children to do all the begging. My brother Raju died at 15, so then we were just three girls and none of us was strong or healthy. Members of the thronging crowds, who came from every corner of the globe to see Sai Baba, from time to time of course gave us food, and occasionally rags and/or blankets, but — especially during the season when there were few visitors — we often had to resort to combing through rubbish tips for tiny morsels that were just about edible. We never had a single rupee between us, the main reason being that Sai Baba's instructions to the devotees were *not* to give money to beggars. He had various social, medical and educational projects going in the area and it was to those that the visitors were encouraged to give money.

With few exceptions, I spent all day every day sitting on the pavement outside the high wall of the ashram, often holding out my hand hopefully. My sisters did more or less the same, in different spots of the village. We usually did best at festival times, when an abundance of food was served and there were huge numbers of devotees around, many of whom were generous to the beggars. They spoke many different languages, but very few knew even a single word of Telugu, so little communication was possible. I could, however, often tell from the conversations of passers-by when something exciting had happened inside the Hall, such as a healing or the manifestation of a ring, medallion or japamala. I yearned for such a gift myself, as I'd heard enough to know that, whatever it was, it would be sure to bring blessings on whoever received it. Occasionally Sai Baba Himself would be driven past and whenever that happened He would always wave or even wind down the window and give me a smile. That smile was quite indescribable; it was the only thing in the world that gave me the tiniest inkling of what Love could be. I yearned, too, for some of His *vibhuti* (the ash that He manifested so often for so many people and whose healing powers were immense).

As I got older I developed a disease in my hands, which I now know is called Dupuytren's contracture. It tends to be hereditary and my grandfather had also had it for a few years before he died. It causes the fingers to contract, especially those furthest from the thumb, and eventually, opening the hand fully becomes impossible. I was doubly unfortunate in that I got it in both my hands, and that hindered me in many simple tasks, such as washing my few clothes in the Chitravatri River. One day while I was sitting in my usual post, a European woman walked past and when I held out my two hands to her, she looked at them and gave a sort of jolt. Then I noticed that she had the same problem with her left hand! (What I discovered only after I'd died was that her disfigurement wasn't Dupuytren's but had been caused by breaking her wrist — something *very* unusual.) Anyway, she looked at me with great compassion and I could sort of hear her thinking "Goodness, that woman's disability is even greater than mine, poor thing!" Then she went away and came back shortly with some bananas to give me. I did have a bit of difficulty peeling bananas but could just about manage it and they are a good thing to have when one is very hungry; that same woman subsequently came back several times during her stay to give me more. Compassion is *such* an important thing to feel and Sai Baba was of course the epitome of it.

Change came with the onset of the Covid-19 coronavirus around the beginning of 2020. It soon became so widespread that the ashram had to be closed to visitors and one of the accommodation blocks was rapidly turned into a Covid ward. I had to admire those volunteers who took up care of their own accord, some of them postponing their flights home to their different countries in order to do so. The drastic reduction of people on the streets of Puttaparthi hit my family very hard indeed and my mother died in no time. At one point my older brother did return home just briefly, bringing with him some bagfuls of out-of-date tinned food (along with a tin opener) that he'd managed to wheedle out of a few shopkeepers in Bangalore. Before a year had passed one of my sisters died from Covid and I myself caught it not long after. I had never known good health, but the suffering the virus caused me was *unbelievable*! One day a kind white woman who heard me coughing in the street, doubled up in pain, went back into the ashram to fetch a friend and between the two of them they carried me into N1, the block normally reserved for Europeans but which was now being used as a Covid ward. They brought me water frequently, but I was quite unable to eat.

My death came quickly and was *such* a relief. I shot through a tunnel like lightning and fell straight into the arms of Sathya Sai Baba!

"You've suffered enough, my dear Meena," He said, "and have in this lifetime that's just ended paid off a big karmic debt incurred a couple of centuries ago."

"How on earth did you know my name?" was all I could think of to say.

"I know the names of *all* My children," came the simple reply. "Now would you like to greet your parents, your deceased brother and sister and then go on to watch a film of the life that induced your recent suffering?"

"Yes please," was all I could think of to say next and then those four members of my family appeared instantly.

"It's lovely to have you join us, Meena," they all said more or less in unison. "And don't worry about the film. We've all seen ours already and they all showed each of us in a very poor light, but we were all treated with great compassion and understanding. The only judgement made here is by ourselves and there has scarcely ever been a soul on Earth who hasn't done evil things in the past. That's how we all learn over time — a long, long time!"

Then Sai Baba returned momentarily. "Now, Meena," He said, "it's time for one of your guides to take you to the hall where the Akashic Records are kept. It's a vast library in which books are stored that give every soul's entire past-life history. In your case, however, since you are illiterate, a film has been made specially so that you can watch it on a screen and hear voices rather than having to read it. You will no doubt find it shocking and hard to believe that the main character, a wealthy raj named Vijay, who lived in an enormous palace in the north of India, is really you, but probably memories of that lifetime will gradually come back to you. This will enable you to appreciate the reasons why Meena had to undergo such suffering. But never fear: you've now paid off that karmic debt and there won't be any reason for you not to have a much more comfortable life next time."

Hardly had He finished speaking when a beautiful woman appeared, who introduced herself as Shivani. "I was your grandmother in a lifetime you had a long time ago and we had a very close bond," she said. "I've had no reason to incarnate again recently and so I've been watching over you. Now are you ready for me to escort you to the 'cinema'? Don't worry about the scenes that you find distressing. Just resolve never to behave in such a way again."

"OK, I'm ready now. I'll be glad when it's over!"

"When it's over, your etheric body will be able to have a nice long rest. Then, once you feel fully recovered from the Covid, which came on top of a lifetime spent in a very weak body, you'll be in a position to make some good decisions for the future. Just follow me."

I followed Shivani for what seemed like mile after mile of breathtakingly beautiful scenery. I was indeed very tired, yet we travelled completely effortlessly, just floating, as it were, and in due course I espied an enormous building decorated with wonderfully carved pillars. We went inside and there I was overwhelmed by what I saw: people dressed in an array of the most dazzling colours imaginable, some of which I'd never seen before (and we Indians go in for colour, even though I myself as Meena had never possessed anything but drab rags). After a short time a charming-looking older man called us over, saying: "You must be Meena. I heard that you were on your way. We've prepared a film of your life as Vijay, which caused you to be reborn into very poor circumstances. Are you ready to watch it?"

"Yes, I am."

"Well, sit down, both of you, in these comfortable chairs and I'll ask Ananda to start it off for you."

Then a screen suddenly appeared out of nowhere in front of our eyes and the first scene was of an enormous, very beautiful palace, which did indeed look familiar to me. Then I heard an angry voice exclaiming: "Don't you remember that I ordered you to expel *all* the beggars in my domain? I've just been trying to have a pleasant walk in my rose garden and passed no fewer than three of them!"

"I'm sorry," said a manservant who walked out into the palatial hall of the building. "I did order them to go, but getting back in doesn't pose a problem for them. I think they must feel that, since you're obviously extremely wealthy, you should be able to spare them a little food at least."

"Well, in that case, I command you instantly to have a big strong gate with a good lock put at the entrance to the grounds. And if that doesn't suffice, we'll just have to get the walls built even higher. These people are the scum of the Earth and I simply cannot *bear* the sight of them!"

By this time the Raj himself had appeared on the scene. He was corpulent, middle-aged and dressed in the very finest robes.

"Now, when you've given my orders about the gate, send my concubine Priya to me. She was very unsatisfactory last night and so, if she doesn't do better today, I shall have no choice but to dismiss her."

"Where could she go if you did that?" protested the manservant. "She came from a very poor family, as you know, and I'm sure they couldn't afford to welcome her back."

"Well, that's her problem, not mine. I just desire women to give me pleasure and so, if they cease to do so, I have no choice but to dismiss them."

"But Priya is a lovely young woman and very helpful. She takes a great deal of trouble looking after your second wife's two young children, especially when she's unwell, which, as you must know, she has been a great deal recently."

"My second wife? I don't have much to do with her at the moment. I prefer both my first and third wives, but neither of those is either as beautiful or as seductive as most of my concubines. Now, mind your own business and do those two things I bade you straight away."

The manservant left the hall. The scene then moved to a bedroom into which the Raj Vijay entered and there he sat down in a very large, well-cushioned chair. Before very much longer an extremely attractive young woman with long, ebony, braided hair entered the room and said: "You sent for me, my lord?"

"Indeed I did. Your performance last night was very unsatisfactory and now I want to give you one last chance to remain in my household. Come back here at nine o'clock this evening dressed in flimsy chiffon and we'll see what happens."

"I'm sorry if I displeased you, but I was very tired from looking after your wife Ishani's two boys all day. They have a great deal of energy and you know that Ishani is very unwell at the moment. I'm very concerned about her. Have you sent for a doctor? This city has some very good ones."

"I can't be bothered with doctors. It's *her* fault if she hasn't been looking after herself properly. What do *I* care? Anyway those boys are nothing but a nuisance at the moment!"

"Do you not feel *any* paternal love, then?"

"Paternal love? I have no interest in any sort of love that doesn't involve sexual satisfaction!"

"In that case I have no desire ever to sleep with you again. If none of your wives satisfy you, you'd better just send for another of your concubines."

"Right — you're out on your neck. And immediately! I'll call for one of my drivers to dump you in the middle of the city."

"What could I do for employment in the middle of the city? And who will look after those boys of yours tomorrow?"

"Neither of those questions is any concern of mine!"

At this point in the film I burst into tears and implored them to pause it. "I think I've seen enough now," I said. "And I *do* remember being that dreadful man and am mortally ashamed of all his actions. How can I obtain forgiveness?"

"You are forgiven already, Meena dear. The only reason for showing you some of that film was so that you could see the reasons for your having agreed to live the life of a beggar. Now all you have to do is appreciate that you've learnt the lesson and paid off the bulk of your karma. You still just have a few small debts to pay, such as fathering those two sons again and really caring for them. You will also need to come back for a new, caring relationship with Priya, but those things can be done in future lifetimes. Right now the main thing you need to do is rest and get your health back."

Shivani then escorted me to a beautiful hospital, explaining to me as we went that it was the etheric double of the Sri Sathya Sai Super Speciality Hospital, designed by two English architects and situated close to the Puttaparthi airport. I told her that I had indeed heard of it and believed that it specialised in both eye and heart problems; also that all the treatment performed there was free, unlike in other hospitals in India. She replied: "Yes, you're quite right. All the Sathya Sai hospitals on Earth give free treatment, but here on this plane money doesn't exist anyway, so there would be no question of payment. Also, the methods of treatment are further advanced than those at present used on Earth. You see, blueprints for *everything* are conceived first on higher planes and then, once their efficacy has been established, they are gradually transmitted to Earth by reincarnating souls who have learnt them here while in between lifetimes. Also, some of the healing methods used here, such as crystals and colour, were practised thousands of years ago in places such as Atlantis and Egypt. Nowadays there are many people on Earth who are dissatisfied with some of the aspects of Western medicine and choosing to return to more natural things, but it is a slow process as people aren't always open to learning. Homoeopathy, for instance, has in recent years been given a bad press in parts of Europe and consequently some of its great benefits — *and*, I hasten to add, its complete lack of side-effects — are, sadly, ignored. You will be given a chance to sample all of that and you will also be fed plenty of delicious, nutritious food — something that poor Meena missed out on completely. (Of course Vijay, the Raj of whom you've just been reminded, did over-indulge in everything, including food, so she has now paid off that piece of karma.) Now we've arrived, so I'll ask one of the nurses to find you a nice, comfortable bed. Your family will also be able to visit you during your stay here."

"That will be nice!"

"Yes, indeed. Now I'll bid you farewell for the time being and return to collect you when you've made a good recovery."

My stay in that wonderful hospital, with members of my birth family dropping in from time to time, was a truly marvellous experience. I was fed and cared for *so* well and none of the treatment I received caused me any pain at all. After what felt like a few weeks in Earth time, Shivani came back and rejoiced at how well I looked. "Now that you've got some strength and have been fattened up a bit," she said, "it's time for you to shed your etheric body and carry on for a while in your mental body. Your etheric body will simply disintegrate but, having been made so much healthier, it won't leave severe scars on your soul. Besides, your sincere repentance about that lifetime as the selfish Raj will help your spiritual development enormously. So what do you fancy doing next? Would you like, for instance, to take a guided tour of some of the realms to which you now have a 'passport' and then think seriously about the nature of your next incarnation?"

"That sounds a lovely idea," I replied, "but what do you mean by 'passport'? Am I not free now to go anywhere I please, since travel here is done so easily?"

"It's not quite as simple as that. You see, where souls can go in between incarnations depends upon their level of development. It's only very advanced souls who can be granted entry to the highest realms. But don't let that worry you! You have plenty of time at your disposal and will be able to attend lots of interesting classes to increase your learning. There is a plethora of first-class teachers here, many of whom were very big names while they were on Earth, and some of them will welcome you so long as you make it clear that you will be a serious student."

"That I shall certainly be; as Meena in Puttaparthi I had of course no education at all and I should love to extend her very limited horizons."

"Of course, let's set off on a tour straight away. Which continent or country would you like to begin with?"

"I think I'd like to start with a tour of Europe. So many Europeans used to walk past me and many of them seemed to be more caring than a lot of the Indians."

"That's probably because in India beggars tend to be just part of the scenery, whereas in most parts of Europe, which is wealthier, they come as more of a shock and people find seeing so many of them very upsetting. Shall we start with Britain, which forced its language onto India as well as stealing a great deal of our wealth?"

"Why not? But I'm sorry to hear that! I thought many Indians were glad to have English as a lingua franca, when we have so many different ones that inter-state communication can be difficult. Also, wasn't it good that the British built a railway system in our great country? I remember that from the Raj's life, of course, not my most recent one."

"That's like saying that it's good if you have a workman come to your house to do something for you and he takes away all your belongings, but leaves his ladder behind!"

"I see your point, but yes, I'd certainly like to see something of England. I've heard that it's very green and lush compared with India."

"That is indeed true, but we might as well start with London and a few of its most famous sights. By the way, you'll have to appreciate that, though we'll be able to see all the people we pass in the streets, they won't be able to see us. Also, you'll find that we can walk straight through them, as well as through doors and walls, which can feel strange until you've got used to it."

Strange it certainly was, but quite wondrous to see all those magnificent buildings and, when we left the city for the countryside, I was struck dumb by its beauty. From London and its surrounds we went first westwards, where the scenery became more undulating and even more attractive, and then flew across the Channel and down the River Seine to Paris, which I really loved. As we travelled I said to Shivani: "You know, while I was in hospital I reflected on what I might like to happen in my next incarnation and it occurred to me that I'd like to marry Priya, have her as my sole wife and treat her very well to make up for throwing her out before. Besides being very beautiful, she's a really good and caring person and would doubtless make a good mother. Ah, that's a thought! We could even have those two sons, whom the Raj treated so badly as a father. She already has a strong bond with them and in that way I could kill two karmic birds with one stone."

"What a good idea! As a matter of fact, I had anticipated it, so I made some enquiries and found out that Priya is incarnate at the moment. She's very near the end of quite a long, very worthwhile life in which she worked as a nurse in Sri Lanka. I'm sure she'd be glad to meet you again and learn how you've reformed. Did you know that it was possible for the incarnate to meet up at night with people who are discarnate?"

"No, I didn't. How can that happen?"

"Well you see, during our spells in physical bodies on Earth, we tend to leave our bodies when we're asleep. It's useful because, although we don't remember anything about it when we wake up, it helps us to keep in touch with Home. So if, prior to her death, you'd like to talk with Priya about how you'd like your next incarnation to be with her, you'll only need to think about her very strongly and then she'll come."

"How lovely! I'll start doing that straight away."

"Yes, you could begin making a plan tonight and then, while she's finishing off her present life, you could use the waiting time profitably by attending classes."

"I'd love that and I'll tell you what I think I'd like the two of us to do during an incarnation in which she would be my only wife: I'd like us to work together in Puttaparthi on one of the many projects that Sai Baba instigated there. We wouldn't necessarily have to be born there; we could discuss it and decide jointly where we'd most like to incarnate."

"That's right. People go from all over the world to be of use in the Puttaparthi area. You might even fancy qualifying as, for instance, a doctor who could serve for a time in the Super Speciality Hospital."

"I certainly like that idea! Thank you very much, Shivani, for your advice and guidance."

"It's my pleasure. But now we need to part for the time being, as I have other duties to which I'm being called. I could take you straight away to a class in some sort of medicine, but would you like to take a look at one other country en route?"

"How about Italy? The Raj always fancied seeing Rome!"

"Rome it shall be and after that I'll introduce you to Dr Reddy, who is right now giving classes in cardiology."

"That sounds very interesting. I'm beginning to get really excited!"

"Yes, I'm sure you'll do well and will be very happy. So I'll shortly be bidding you farewell for the time being, but we shall undoubtedly meet again."

# 3

# A 'Covid Doctor' Who Makes New Friends

*God has created me to do him some definite service; he has committed some work to me which he has not committed to any other. I have my mission — I may never know it in this life, but I shall be told it in the next.*

Cardinal John Henry Newman

My name is George, and in my last life I made up my mind at a very early age that I wanted to be a doctor. It was a struggle initially, however, as I started out with two quite big handicaps: being black and coming from a working-class background. I was born into an Afro-Caribbean family in Liverpool and was blessed with two parents, who were both very loving, and two younger sisters who always looked up to me. Both my father and my mother worked very hard in local factories to support us all. My widowed maternal grandmother, who was also very loving, lived nearby and was happy to look after the three of us while my parents were out at work. She taught me many things, such as how to treat people with respect even when it wasn't reciprocated, how to tie my shoelaces and how to make Creole bread. She wasn't very literate, but as my studies in school progressed, I taught her to read some longer words than she was used to. I also helped my sisters, Amina and Benita, with their reading. There were about two years between each of us and we grew up feeling very close.

It was difficult for us to afford family holidays, but sometimes our parents took us out on day trips at weekends. The one that sticks out most in my mind was when I was eight and we went to visit the Liverpool Slavery Museum for the first time. Some of that is of course horrific and depressing, but my parents encouraged us to focus more on the bits that tell the stories of black people who did great things. "You see," my father said, "this shows that race need never be a barrier to worthwhile achievement."

"Well," I replied, "do you know what I'd *really* like to do when I grow up?"

"What's that, son?"

"I'd like to be a doctor so that I could make people better."

"That's a wonderful idea," said my mother. "Just keep that ambition firmly in your head and there's no reason at all why you shouldn't succeed. Doctors are people who will always be needed. None of us can hope to remain well all our lives!"

Fortunately I was quite academic and did well at school, particularly in mathematics and the sciences. (My sisters were bright too, but Amina, who had a very vivid imagination and loved writing stories, did best at English, while Benita loved geography and said she wanted to travel the world when she was old enough.) I was blessed with a caring science teacher, to whom I confided my ambition, and he gave me a great deal of encouragement. Once I'd reached the age for deciding about A-levels, I was advised to take maths, physics, and chemistry, which suited me down to the ground, and I got good grades in all three and then applied to study medicine at university, with Manchester as my first choice. They accepted me and my family were pleased, as Manchester isn't too far from Liverpool.

I thoroughly enjoyed my studies, hard work though it all was, fell in love with a Jamaican nurse named Amelia, married her when I was 25 and she 24, and then worked in a series of northern hospitals, ultimately deciding to specialise in infectious diseases. I did a lot of study of infectious diseases of the past and when Covid-19 struck the UK and people were getting more or less hysterical over the numbers of deaths, I was intrigued to discover that the 'flu epidemic of 1918 had killed 250,000 in this country — a figure that Covid still hadn't reached by 2021.

Amelia didn't want to give up nursing completely in order to raise a family, but we managed nevertheless to squeeze in having two lovely children and got a mortgage on a nice house on the outskirts of Liverpool. Amina did a degree in English followed by a postgraduate certificate in education (PGCE) and found that she quite enjoyed teaching, but she still aspires to be a full-time novelist. (She has a partner, but says that her books are her babies!) Benita, on the other hand, achieved her ambition to travel the world and makes a reasonable living from journalism. Grandma died peacefully a couple of years ago, but my parents are of course very proud of all of us. Our paternal grandparents are still out in the Caribbean, but we've all managed the odd visit to them, as well as to Amelia's parents, which has helped us to appreciate our roots still further.

When Covid was really at its height, I was called upon not only to care for people who were desperately ill in hospital but also to do research into the different variants that gradually reached our shores from other countries. Finally, at the age of 58, I caught the virus very badly myself. Amelia and our two sons, Jacob and Roger, who were by then in their early twenties and both studying medicine, were absolutely devastated. I wouldn't be being honest if I didn't tell you that my suffering while I was ill was very intense indeed. I was given the very best possible care, with all the most up-to-date equipment, ventilators and so on, but even the most experienced doctors were unable to save me. When I did finally leave my body, it was a massive relief!

Nobody, however, shared my relief. The local newspapers were full of articles about the "tragedy of the untimely death of a specialist doctor who had been doing so much wonderful work for so many patients". The funeral was intensely moving, with medical people flocking to it from all over the place and heart-warming tributes made by colleagues as well as family members. I tried really hard to embrace all those close to me, whispering into their ears that they had nothing to worry about, as I was now absolutely fine and we could meet up again at night, but it was all in vain.

*\*\**

"What those Westerners don't understand, George," said the guide who greeted me in the Bardo, "is that there is always a good reason for *everything*! You've been called back Home because you're even more needed here than you were on Earth. What they say at funerals about 'eternal rest' is just nonsense. Once you've had some convalescence, you'll be put to work even harder than you were on Earth. That's because, once we've left our physical bodies, we no longer need rest. Do you realise that you *volunteered* for this?"

"No, I certainly didn't. When was that?"

"It was when you were making your most recent life plan. You see, you'd not only been a skilled doctor several times in the past but had also been a victim of the famous 1918 'flu epidemic. So these gave you knowledge from both sides, making you especially well qualified to help Covid-19 victims. More recently, on one of your nightly sorties from your body, you renewed your pledge. And so now here you are! Welcome. We all know full well how tough your departure will be for your family, who will naturally miss you dreadfully, but they're all evolved souls who know subconsciously that loss is one of life's important lessons and that it is only temporary."

"Yes, in fact Amelia and I discussed the possibility of one of us dying from Covid on account of our work. You no doubt know that she's a nurse and that we've recently been working quite closely together. We agreed that it would be something we'd just have to face up to if it happened. All my family were at my bedside when I crossed over and I felt much loved, which was wonderful!"

"You only got the love that you deserved so well and you always gave as much as you received. Now the thing that you most deserve and need is a really good rest. Your guardian angel will therefore escort you to one of our hospitals, with which you are of course already familiar, and then, when you feel fully recovered from the horrible disease, you can be gainfully employed here, both with caring for people who are in a similar condition to yours right now and with research into all the variants of Covid that are currently springing up in different parts of the globe."

"I look forward to that!"

My recovery was reasonably speedy, Amelia and I met up regularly at night and we often discussed our sons' futures. We were very proud of both of them! Jacob was now following quite closely in my footsteps, while Roger was beginning to get interested in such things as acupuncture and so it looked as though he might in due course go down a more alternative route. Amelia herself was still busy caring for Covid victims who'd been admitted to hospital and had so far been fortunate in avoiding catching the virus herself. ("Well," she commented, "we don't want our boys to be orphaned in their twenties and, besides, I need to keep an eye on your parents and sisters, all of whom are finding it difficult to come to terms with having lost *you*.")

I didn't lose any time in getting engrossed in the work, in which, as my guide had explained when I first arrived on the other side, I was already well qualified. I enjoyed the research particularly, as finding cures for Covid and curbing its spread felt very urgent. I felt deeply for the people still on Earth who were beginning to feel more and more fed up with it and kept asking: "When will it ever end?" It was truly marvellous to be able to work so hard without ever getting tired! Over the course of several months in Earth time I came across various previous friends and colleagues and renewing our acquaintance helped all of us to feel inspired to achieve success. Often, when a new discovery was made, one of us would talk to someone on Earth who was involved in the work and came to see us at night, or we'd whisper something into someone's ear. They always imagined it to be their own idea and that was fine. For are we not all one?

Then, on 12 March 2022, we had a new arrival, who introduced himself as Christian Merivale, explaining that he was the oldest of our scribe's three younger brothers. He told us that he'd been unwell in numerous ways for very many years and that, although it had finally been the combination of a heart attack and pneumonia that had killed him, it had been Covid that had sent both him and his dear wife Jane into hospital. "I was in and out of intensive care," he said, "for several days, which was very hard for all my family, but I knew when my body simply couldn't take any more and we'd already agreed with our two children that Jane could go and live near Belfast with our wonderful daughter Katharine and her husband. Being very strong Christians, neither of us was afraid of death and poor Jane had been so burdened for so long with caring for me that my departure was in a way a blessed relief for her. My five siblings half expected me to bounce back, since I'd done that so many times before, but, sad though they are, they all knew that my passing made a lot of sense really and now they're going to have a good time when they all meet up in Somerset for my funeral at the end of the month. Such family reunions are now a *very* rare occurrence, what with everybody being widely scattered between England and Ireland! My two children well understand that I want my body to be buried in the church graveyard near to those of my grandparents and two maiden aunts."

"Somerset?" interjected a doctor, who said that he recognised Christian from his own work on Earth. "I thought you lived in Devon!"

"We did indeed live in lovely Devon for quite a while, initially when I was in farming, but then I went into the Church and after completing theological studies in Durham I was Vicar of Hawes for a while, before being drawn back to warmer climes, where I became a hospital chaplain in Truro. I really loved that work — found, to my own surprise, that I was really good at going to people's homes in the night to tell them that their spouse had died — but ill health forced me to retire early and then we moved to Somerset and remained for many years in the vicinity of the Merivale family home near the village of Shepton Montague, which my grandparents had bought after my grandfather's retirement. Eventually, however, not being very happy with the house we had, we sold it and found a place to rent in an idyllic spot back in our beloved Devon. There I had many dealings with Exeter hospital even before my fatal illnesses and having over the years learnt a great deal about sickness and drugs I feel sure that I could be of assistance to all of you here. I'm familiar with various alternative forms of medicine, too, and was blessed with a wonderful Christian herbalist, who helped me enormously over many years."

"That will be great! But remember that you will yourself need a spell as a patient before returning to work full time."

"Yes, as a matter of fact I *do* remember; it's strange, but I feel that I've been here before. Can this possibly mean that 12 March wasn't the first time that I've died? This immediately gives me a problem, as it appears to conflict with my Christian Faith!"

"Don't worry about that now. You've got plenty of time to learn new things and rethink everything. As your oldest sister has already written in other books of hers, the early Christians all understood about reincarnation. But it's not one's beliefs that matter most each time round. What's really important is how we live our lives: whether we're kind and generous and always ready to help other people. You were all of those things and more and now it's great to have you Home for a while."

Christian was then escorted off to one of our heavenly hospitals for care and rest, but then — two weeks to the day — another lovely man crossed over. He was more or less exactly the same age as Christian, 20 years or so older than myself, but still on the young side to die by present-day standards. He introduced himself as Orlando and told us that his dear wife Grace would of course miss him terribly, but that she was a very strong soul and would cope admirably.

"We met at Bristol University and achieved a Golden Wedding anniversary several years ago. We had many close friends from those good times, but one of them, Annabel, sadly died of breast cancer at only 55. Cancer was of course the pandemic before *the* pandemic, and it, not Covid, is in fact what's just caused my death. It hit my oesophagus first and I did well for a while with a plastic substitute — amazing some of the things they can do nowadays, isn't it? — but then they found it had spread to other parts of my body and was soon labelled as 'terminal'. So my departure came as a blessed release in a way, since Grace and the rest of the family were in the process of bracing themselves for several months of acute physical suffering. I died at home, with only my dear wife present, and it couldn't have been more peaceful. It was mid-morning and my gasping breaths just gradually grew slower and slower, finally stopping about half an hour after I'd become physically unconscious. But being unconscious doesn't mean that one doesn't know what's happening, does it?"

"It certainly doesn't!" I replied. "I remember being very aware when the doctor switched my ventilator off and already rejoicing at the thought of going Home! But how was it for your wife?"

"She was marvellously accepting! She just carried on sitting there, fascinated and dumbstruck, within an arm's length yet not touching me, which was *exactly* the right thing to do. The only sad thing about it is that she's now chastising herself for not recalling that hearing is the last sense to go and consequently feeling that she should have talked with me instead!"

"Don't worry about that. The two of you will be able to talk when she leaves her body at night — that's what I did with my bereaved family — and then she'll remember that communication between loved ones can be telepathic, even while still on Earth."

"That's a great comfort! You know, life can be strange, because nobody had ever foreseen that I would be the first to go — especially as I was somewhat younger than Grace — but we'd both been believers all our lives and knew that the Lord would take care of us, whatever happened. I, incidentally, was a strong Anglican, while she was brought up Baptist but turned Quaker later on."

"Did that not cause any difficulties between you?" I asked.

"Not at all! One of her school friends had been a good Catholic and the two of them had always tolerated each other's differences. Grace and I had enough in common generally to stop us bothering about minor religious differences. At university we had a good friend whose father was the head of the Bristol Royal Infirmary and he gave me a lot of encouragement when I was thinking of going into hospital administration. I, too, had a successful career in that, so you might perhaps value my services in your 'heavenly Covid hospital'. I was always something of a workaholic; I retired quite late and then only gradually."

"Yes indeed," chipped in a guide of Orlando's, "your services will be more than welcome over here, but you'd better forget the workaholism for a while. Right now you need to rest, as cancer takes a great deal out of one, and you'll be wanting to attend the memorial service that's to be held in Manchester for you in the near future."

"Memorial service rather than funeral?" I asked.

"Yes, that's right," Orlando replied. "You see, my many years of work in the hospital scene inspired me to donate my body to medical science. It may be two years before the bits are returned to Manchester for a tiny woodland burial in the new Green Burial Ground and so I asked that the vicar do a minimal committal service with anyone from the family who wants to come. The memorial service will be in about three weeks' time, I think…"

"Giving you the chance of a rest in our cancer hospital before returning briefly for it!"

"Rest? That's true: I haven't yet had time to think about how weary I am! A cancer hospital will be very interesting; I've visited hospices on Earth."

"Yes, they do a wonderful job! Over here we have oncologists, you know, as well as specialists in infectious diseases, like me. With cancer, however, prevention is even better than cure and it looks as though one of my sons is becoming particularly interested in that. But going back to your memorial service, I imagine it will be well attended, since you were a public figure in Manchester, weren't you?"

"Yes, there should be a good hundred, I expect, and some of them will be from my choir. I was always a keen singer. Grace fully appreciated the importance of music to me and I know she'll be doing a good job fulfilling my wishes, even though in the end I only left her half a page of rough notes. She knows that I want the service to include that wonderful passage from Elgar's 'Dream of Gerontius' and I thought that animating my notes would give her something interesting to do when I'd gone! Not that she's *ever* been at a loose end. Our son Jack is big brother to a couple of girls whom we adopted from Sri Lanka when they were only tiny babies and it's partly thanks to that that Grace has for many years been involved with helping refugees."

"An even more important job at the moment, what with this ghastly war in Ukraine."

"Yes indeed and believe it or not, though she and her husband are now in their eighties, one of our other best friends has recently offered one floor of their home to a Ukrainian refugee family!"

"That's really good to hear. Covid has been a huge challenge for the whole world and caused massive suffering to countless numbers of people, but to my mind this war is even worse because it's basically been started wilfully by just one man who's lost his senses. One good thing, however, that both of these 'plagues' have caused to happen is the way in which so many people have come together, absolutely united in their desire to put a stop to it all."

"I couldn't agree more and let's hope that all the prayers now being made will soon be answered."

"Prayers *are* invariably answered, but divine timing doesn't always coincide with human desires."

"Too true! Anyway, my fears for Grace now are alleviated by the knowledge that she is and will continue to be well supported by our family, especially by the two girls, who are very close by. Blanche, who's married and works for the local 111 telephone helpline for the health service, and her 'twin' sister (not by blood) is closer still, as she runs a nursery in our house. In fact, while I was in the process of departing, the only sounds were from Pansy's toddlers, playing happily and unusually quietly together in the next room."

"How lovely!"

"It was. And, when I wasn't working, I used to enjoy helping out in the nursery. Now they'll only have Grace as a 'grandparent figure', but the children always love her, too."

"So your dear wife will cope as well with widowhood as anybody could. Ah, here comes your guardian angel to escort you to the cancer hospital, which I know you'll *love*. It's been great to talk to you and I look forward to meeting you again."

"Thank you. So do I."

Orlando went off to join Christian and then, barely more than another two weeks later, lo and behold who should appear but a 51-year-old Zambian Catholic priest, who told us that he also had a connection to the Merivale family! He explained, however, that it wasn't to our scribe, but to her younger sister Alexandra, who had in her youth worked as a nurse in Zambia and known him as a baby. "You see," he said, "Alexandra is extraordinarily good at keeping in touch with people and in the year 2000, when I was due to be ordained as a deacon in Toulouse, she had the very kind idea of doing some fundraising in order to bring both my mother and my sister, who's her goddaughter, to Europe for the occasion. I'm sure you can imagine how much we all appreciated it."

"Yes, what a generous soul she must be!"

"Indeed she is."

"And what did you do after you'd been ordained as a priest?"

"Well," he replied with a modest smile, "I was eventually appointed to be in charge of the African missionaries in Tanzania."

"Quite an onerous job, then, and you must have been very highly thought of."

"Maybe, but the main thing is that I really loved the work and so I hope to be able still to be of use over here."

"Never fear: there are always endless opportunities on this side for caring people! Did you ever see our scribe's sister again and does she know that you've now crossed over? She would no doubt be very sad, as you're even younger than I am. It's always hard for people on Earth to lose anyone who's very dear to them!"

"To answer your first question: yes, I later had the privilege of doing a year's study in Dublin, and Alexandra and her husband Bernard came to meet me there, which was lovely. In reply to the second question, thanks to modern technology, she heard about my departure within just a few days and, what's more, my family were able to inform her about the funeral."

"I believe you were yet another Covid victim. Is that right?"

"Yes, I told her a few months ago that I'd narrowly survived it, but it seems that it sometimes leaves blood clots, and I suffered with my legs a great deal before I died."

"You're quite right. That's one of the things that I've been studying, so your personal experience of that could also be useful to us."

A fairly short while passed in Earth time and then Orlando popped back and said to us: "Guess what: my dear daughter Blanche has now got Covid! She will recover reasonably quickly, but my wife, wise as always, reckons that, since her work is all to do with advising sick people who dial 111 rather than calling immediately for an ambulance, it will be useful learning for her."

"Yes indeed, there is always a reason for everything. Blanche, once she's recovered, will have a better understanding of what the people she's advising are going through. But now it's perhaps time for us all to get back to work. Orlando, are you quite sure that you've had a long enough rest in hospital? It seems virtually no time since we saw you off there!"

"Oh yes, quite sure, thanks. It was lovely being there and I observed some methods of healing that were quite new to me, but I already told you that I was a workaholic and it's great to be part of such a good team."

"Well, as I said before, you're incredibly welcome over here, but there's no obligation to work full time. Since you told us that you were musical and sang in a choir, you might care to join one over here now."

"What a lovely idea! I'd certainly welcome that."

"They would welcome your talent, too."

# 4

# A Cathar

*Montségur, Montségur,*
*It's not just a name or a place*
*Montségur, Montségur,*
*Your freedom lives on always in us,*
*Montségur,*
*Your truth lives on always in us,*
*Montségur, Montségur.*

Rai d'Honoré, *Troubadour Songs*

*Bon jorn*, I'm happy to meet you! I'm a Cathar and my name is immaterial, though you can call me Amadon if you like, as that's the name by which I was known in the thirteenth century. Although I'm no longer on Earth, I'm telling you that I *am* a Cathar rather than 'was', because once a Cathar, always a Cathar. I was forced to leave my body in 1246, just two years after the infamous massacre at Montségur, and unlike some of my friends and my daughter, who ascended en masse there, I died alone. I had, however, lived for 58 years, which was quite a good age in those days, and I'd achieved quite a bit and been given the honour of becoming a *Parfait*. My dear wife Esperta, who sadly didn't live to find out where and how I'd died, but was of course able to communicate with me at night when she left her body while sleeping, never aspired to become a *Parfaite*. She was always gainfully employed running the household and making use of her herbal skills to treat people in our neighbourhood when they fell sick. Our daughter Blancha, on the other hand, did become a *Parfaite* and, before her death, she sometimes travelled with me and we performed ceremonies together. Our son Clariüs minded our little bit of land, growing the medicinal herbs for his mother as well as most of our food. He in due course had a family of his own, but they stayed close to Montségur and we were always well united. We also had another beautiful daughter, Clemencia, born in between the two of them, but she fell gravely ill and left us at the age of only five. The loss was very hard to bear, but we knew full well that that was a thing we all had to learn through our many lifetimes and that we'd meet again in due course.

Now I'd like to tell you how it came about that I'm able to recount my story here. Well, Ann our scribe has a wonderful guide for this book, whose portrait was drawn for her by a clairvoyant artist named Deborah Thorpe, quite some time before she was free to embark upon the writing. His name is Amos and in one of his many lives on Earth he was a slave taken from West Africa, who, once he'd gained his freedom, campaigned vigorously against slavery.

Ann had arranged to return in May 2022 to south-west France for a meeting at the house of her good friends Kris and Steve, in the little village of Samouillan. Kris (now a Quaker Cathar!) had been a friend or relative of hers in previous lives and a therapy colleague for 20-odd years in their present life. Geoff, another friend and colleague, had arranged to join them there following a visit to the Buddhist monastery at Lavaur, not so far away, to which he goes regularly.

One night prior to leaving home for this trip, Ann decided, before going off to sleep, to communicate with Amos about it. Kris had already booked a couple of nights in bed-and-breakfast accommodation in Montségur for the three of them and while they were talking, Ann heard Amos telling her firmly: "When you're in Cathar country, you'll come across someone who'd like his story to be told." This came as something of a surprise to her, but fortunately — and partly thanks to the encouragement of Dr Woolger, who is now incidentally also doing useful work here on the other side — she'd become much more able to trust what she heard in her head. So, on their first day of working together, she told Kris and Geoff about what she'd been told, explaining that she would be completely open to what transpired and commenting that the communication might come through either of them rather than directly to her. Or that it might, she imagined at the time, even come through the renowned David Lorimer, who actually lives in the area and with whom they'd arranged a lunch date in Mirepoix.

As we all know, however, things in life by no means always work out according to plan and just as they were about to depart for the Ariège it became sadly clear that Steve (who'd been looking forward to a peaceful couple of days tending his beloved *potager*) was not well enough to be left on his own. So a doctor's appointment was hastily made, following which Kris had to rush him into Toulouse hospital. This was of course not only worrying, but it also obviously put paid to the two nights in Montségur. Ann wasn't *too* distraught by this, as she'd been to Montségur before with some of the 'Woolger crowd' (back in the days when she was still *just* able to walk to the top of it), but she did wonder how finding her Cathar story would be possible. When, however, something is ordained to happen, even the most adverse conditions can't prevent it!

So the next morning the indomitable Kris, despite having had to wait six hours in the hospital, decided that, before returning there, they could still do the two-hour drive to Mirepoix and back in order to keep the lunch date. (Ann was relieved when Geoff volunteered to share the driving!) The two men's minds were naturally too preoccupied with the Samouillan dilemma to give any more thought to Ann's mission, but she kept on retaining her trust. As they were coming close to Mirepoix, Kris (prompted, I have to say, by myself and despite protests from Geoff, who had his eye on the time!) suddenly remembered his idea of making a small detour to Vals to have a quick look at the *Eglise rupestre*, the little church of Notre Dame built into the rocks.

The moment that Kris drove round the corner Ann felt increasingly strong goosebumps (always a sign that something important for her writing is about to occur). This church was built with three storeys, had been started in the tenth century and was completed in 1887. Once the three of them were inside at the bottom, admiring the mediaeval bit, Ann sat down and I suddenly appeared very clearly in her head. I was dressed in rags because, way back in 1246, I'd been visiting some fellow Bonshommes in Vals and since they had sensed that some Inquisitors were around, I'd left my white robe hidden in their house and put on the disguise that I often used whenever there was a chance of danger. Before Ann and her friends returned to the car, I just had time to explain to her that some of us Cathars had occasionally used that little church as a refuge and had put a door there with a bolt on it. The suspicious Inquisitors had tried in vain to get in while I kept quiet. At some point later that day I further told Ann about my dear wife Esperta, who kept the home fires burning, as you say in your language, and she then saw her, too, in her head, dressed in green and of the build typical of a middle-aged woman.

After their enjoyable lunch date in Mirepoix, where Ann was delighted to meet David Lorimer for the first time, the three of them went straight to Toulouse hospital, where they found poor Steve all tied up with cannulas through which stuff was being pumped into his body (*very* different from the sort of medicinal tools they used in my day!), but obviously being well cared for. They then returned, still somewhat anxiously, to Samouillan, where Kris whipped up a delicious meal before they went off to bed. At one point in the night Ann responded to a call of nature and then lay awake for a while. So I used this opportunity to give her the rest of my Vals story. It was very simple: when they'd failed to gain entrance to the little church inside which

I'd bolted myself, the persecutors came back later with the wherewithal for barricading me in permanently. There was no wind in Samouillan that night and the two men were probably both asleep in their individual rooms, so Ann was initially baffled by the noise of banging. But then she gradually saw the full story, just as she was accustomed to do when undergoing a regression to one of her own previous lives.

It became clear to her that I'd lingered in that body only for the comparatively short time during which I'd had food and, especially, water with which to sustain it. I can tell you that the thirst was absolutely *terrible* and Ann herself got a little of the sense of it the next day, when (again prompted by me) she found herself getting unusually thirsty. She of course was instantly able to assuage it, there being no shortage of water in the house, but it made her feel intense compassion for me while I was dying, as well as anger with the Church of the time that had instigated the persecution.

Now I must tell you that I'm not recounting my tale because I want you to feel sorry for me. On the contrary, many of us Cathars suffered even greater torture when they were dying! My reason for coming through in this way is because of my conviction that the time is now right for our message to be told again and *without* the distortions put upon it by the Church over the intervening centuries. The truly sad thing about the Church (and this is of course not exclusive to Christianity but has also occurred throughout history with other religions as well) is that very many of its members have strayed from the original teachings of their founder. Not that Jesus Himself really ever did want to found a church! He was one of the many Masters who have over thousands of years incarnated on Earth with the purpose of leading people back to the simple but vital dictums of Truth, Right Conduct, Service, Love and Non-Violence. Where things have gone so wrong — and those good people nowadays who so abhor war and the mindless destruction of such a beautiful planet are at present coming to appreciate it more and more — is when desire for power has dominated.

We Cathars were of course not the first to be so unjustly persecuted. It all dates back to long before my time. The Moors, for instance, had invaded Spain in AD 711, and in fact approximately two-thirds of the ancient Christian world had been conquered by Muslims by the end of the eleventh century. These included the important regions of Palestine, Syria, Egypt, and Anatolia. Although it can be said that African Muslims literally civilised the wild white peoples of that era, they weren't following Muhammad's teachings of Peace and Love any more than was the Church when, in 1096, it ordered the first of a long series of Crusades aimed ultimately at recovering the Holy Land from Islamic rule.

The paradox here is that a Church council both promulgated peace and officially sanctioned war! Tied to this idea was the notion that war to defend Christendom was not only a justifiable undertaking, but also a holy work and therefore pleasing to God. At least the peace movement at that time was designed to protect those in distress and a strong element of that first Crusade was the idea of giving aid to fellow Christians in the East, but they ignored the fact that Moorish advances in mathematics, astronomy, art and philosophy had helped propel Europe out of the so-called 'Dark Ages' and into the Renaissance. It's good that nowadays the beauties of a building such as the Alhambra in Granada are widely acknowledged, but the truth remains that the Church ruthlessly took over other Moorish buildings in, for instance, Seville and Córdoba for use with their own form of worship.

I don't want here to go in depth into all the history — indeed anyone seriously interested can look it up for themselves — but, putting the Moors aside, I do feel that it's important to elaborate a bit on how those in power in the Church at that time distorted the Cathar beliefs and message to such an extent that there are still very few people with any real understanding of it. Key here is the Greek word *gnosis*, which means that humanity's real nature is divine, and appreciating that (as has been done in India for thousands upon thousands of years) leads to the deliverance of the divine spark from the constraints of earthly existence. Gnosticism has taken various forms and there have been various sects; the Bogomils, who came originally from the Bulgarian Empire, were one of these, but I shall focus on the Cathars both for personal reasons and because our scribe has visited Cathar country several times and has friends in her present life who also know that they have been Cathars in previous lives.

So now it becomes clear why we Gnostics upset the Church: recognising one's own internal divinity eliminates the need for any intermediary between oneself and God and consequently weakens the power of the clergy. Retaliation had therefore to be wrought and the easiest way of doing that was by labelling us as heretics and thus making persecution justifiable. One of the myths that was spread about — and one that sadly endures to this day — was that we believed the world to have been created by the devil. Looking around you at the wonders of nature, can you think of anything so obviously absurd?! We in fact valued the natural world so highly that we devoted our lives to caring both for it and for its people, travelling around looking after the sick and the needy and teaching about Love and Peace.

We were also fully aware that everyone needs to have numerous lives on Earth — another thing that the clergy didn't like, as the notion of having many opportunities for getting things right weakens the power that they have over their people! The above-mentioned Dr Roger Woolger was in his last life a distinguished Jungian psychotherapist and he developed his own unique form of past-life regression therapy, which he named Deep Memory Process. He trained very many people, including Kris, Geoff and Ann, and also led workshops on the Cathars.

His motivation for the latter came from an early regression he'd had done on himself, in which he'd found to his horror that he'd been on the 'wrong side' in the thirteenth century. He probably paid the debt he incurred then several times over and now Kris is doing a marvellous job as his successor, having studied a great deal of the history and leading Cathar tours, alongside performing his own work in Deep Memory Process and for the Quaker movement in France. Like our scribe, he has a deep, intuitive 'knowing' that what the Church perpetrated as 'historical fact' was incorrect and this comes from his personal experience of living at that time.

David Lorimer, in his excellent book on the great Bulgarian prophet Peter Deunov, has a quotation from someone of the time, named Zigabenus, who was actually writing in a denigrating way about the way in which the Cathars lived but which in fact gives a very good summary of what we did. At one point he describes the Cathar ritual for ordaining someone:

> ... they lay the Gospel of St. John on his head, invoke their Holy Spirit [as though the Cathar Holy Spirit was different from anyone else's!] and sing the Lord's Prayer. After this Baptism they again set him a time for more rigorous training ... If both men and women testify in his favour, they lead him to their celebrated consecration. They make the wretch face the East and again lay the Gospel on his head. The men and women of the congregation place their foul hands on him and sing their unholy rite: this is a hymn of thanksgiving for his having preserved the impiety transmitted to him.

Anyway, you might well care to get the book for yourselves.

This, rather than relying upon oppositional forces, can now bring me to tell you more myself about some of the differences between our practices and those of the traditional

Christians, for whom the seven sacraments (Baptism, Eucharist, Confirmation, Reconciliation, Anointing of the Sick, Marriage and Ordination) were so important. It's claimed that these seven were all instigated by Christ, but where, I'd like to ask you, is the evidence for this? Jesus was himself of course baptised by John and the idea of doing this with water is a nice one, since we all use water for cleansing, but where did the notion that the *soul* needed cleansing come from? Yes, we all come in with karma brought through from previous lives, but karma has no effect whatsoever on our true essence and the now very outdated belief that the sexual act is a sin and that each soul was consequently conceived in sin bears no relationship with the teachings of Jesus. The brave Catholic priest Matthew Fox (now also doing good work over here!) challenged this tradition in his seminal book *Original Blessing*, which I'm happy to say is now beginning to become well accepted.

The Eucharist, on the other hand, one could say was in a sense instigated by Jesus, since at his Last Supper he broke bread and shared it with his disciples, encouraging them to continue to do likewise. Well, it is in the very nature of the Cathar way of life to eat together and we never felt any need to confine this to Sundays or indeed stipulate any particular time for practising it.

As for Confirmation, what is it but a reaffirmation of our commitment to living a good life, helping people in need and also encouraging *them* to join in the search for Truth, Love and everything else that's desirable? We felt no need to formalise it when a person reached a specific age.

Now, the sacrament of Reconciliation is the thorny one in my book! It is of course based on the premise that every human being is sinful by nature, rather than loving and good, and that forgiveness of sins has to be obtained through a priest. The effect of this teaching can be truly devastating for a child! Ann herself could tell you something about it from her own personal experience, but I know she won't mind my putting it into my own words. At the tender age of four, while outside in the garden with her father and her sister Alexandra, she committed what she considered to be the gravest of sins. Their father had explained to the children that ladybirds were good insects and that one consequently shouldn't kill them. Alexandra, being exactly two years younger, wasn't yet able to talk very much and so Ann, feeling at that moment some sort of grudge against her, as older siblings often do against their supposed 'inferiors', deliberately trod on a ladybird and then told their father that her sister had done it. This led to Alexandra receiving the ticking off rather than Ann and the latter went on being burdened with this 'terrible sin' on her conscience for another four years.

Then she reached the age of eight and consequently the time for her first Confession. The very thought of being 'shut up in a sort of dark cupboard with an invisible priest on the other side of a grille' was terrifying, but at the same time she looked forward to it being over for the relief she believed she would obtain once this truly grave sin had been officially forgiven. Relief, however, came there none, as, once inside the 'dark cupboard', she simply didn't have the courage to tell the whole truth and compromised by saying: "I quarrelled with my sister and brother and I told a lie." The priest merely dismissed her with a couple of Hail Marys to say as her penance, and so her conscience went on remaining unclear. After that and after making her First Communion, she was expected, like all other children of that age, to carry on going to Confession about every month or six weeks and then, since the penitent was always expected to start off by saying how long it was since their last Confession, the fear of having to admit to an excess of six weeks was too great to be contemplated! So that's a very good example of the sort of thing that we Cathars endeavoured to avoid. We brought our children up in the knowledge that they were precious and pure in the eyes of God, encouraging them always to remember that and never deviate from remaining that way.

Marriage we had no quarrel with, though we didn't believe either that the ceremony should be confined to a church or that the clergy (in our case known as *Parfaits* and *Parfaites*) should be excluded from it. Here it should be noted that priestly celibacy was *certainly* not instigated by Jesus, who had his own consort in the beloved Magdalen; and in any case it was only introduced in the Church in about AD 1120.

'Anointing of the Sick' was part of our one and only sacrament, known as the *Consolamentum*, and is equivalent to the traditional Christian Communion, the difference being that we reserved it as something very special and sacred for the end of life. And since care of the dying was part of our normal agenda, we would give them whatever healing we were able to at the same time.

As our above friend Zigabenus noted, we did go in for Ordination, but, believing in gender equality, we didn't restrict it to men.

So that's the sacraments dealt with and this diatribe comes with my apologies to those devout Christians who might not like it, but I have to be true to myself and to *our*selves. On the subject of reincarnation, I'd like to mention firstly that Jesus himself spoke about it but that all documentation of that got omitted from the Bible, and secondly that it was only abandoned as Church teaching at the Council of Constantinople in AD 553. You might want to ask whether I myself have returned to Earth since that death in 1246. My answer is that I haven't. Many of those who were persecuted at that time have done so — some in order to deal with karmic debts that they still had outstanding, others through choice in order to carry on with their good work 'on the ground' — but some of us have had the good fortune of reaching the point where we have the choice and my choice, so far at least, has been to remain in higher realms. Here I am in the excellent position of being able to observe what's happening on our beautiful planet and also to work for its well-being in an advisory capacity. It's thanks to that that I've been able to see amazing things, such as what took place in Samouillan and the Ariège in May 2022. I may well decide to come back at some point, but right now I see that as being likely only a fairly long time hence, perhaps when the current turmoil of such things as unnecessary war and mindless destruction are over, at least for a while, and I could be of help in establishing the long-promised Golden Age.

Now to conclude, besides urging all interested readers to play their part in getting Catharism as it *really* was reinstituted, I should like to quote in full a wonderful piece entitled 'The Church of Love'. It was intuited in 1981 by the late Colin Bloy, dowser, healer and clearly himself a former Cathar. He was the founder of The Fountain Group in Brighton, UK, and you might well be interested in looking up that group as well, if you don't already know about it. They've done some interesting and useful work. So now I'll bid you farewell, at least for the time being, and leave you to savour and digest these wonderful words, until they've sunk right into the very core of your being. Here we are:

## The Church of Love

It has no fabric, only understanding.

It has no membership, save those who know they belong.

It has no rivals, because it is non-competitive.

It has no ambition, it seeks only to serve.

It knows no boundaries, for nationalisms are unloving.

It is not of itself, because it seeks to enrich all groups and religions.

It acknowledges all great Teachers of all the ages who have shown the truth of Love.

Those who participate, practise the Truth of Love in all their beings.

There is no walk of life or nationality that is a barrier.

Those who are, know.

It seeks not to teach but to be and by being, enrich.

It recognises that the way we are may be the way of those around us because we are that way.

It recognises the whole planet as a Being of which we are a part.

It recognises that the time has come for the supreme transmutation, the ultimate alchemical act of conscious change of the ego into a voluntary return to the whole.

It does not proclaim itself with a loud voice, but in the subtle realms of loving.

It salutes all those in the past who have blazoned the path but have paid the price.

It admits no hierarchy or structure, for no one is greater than another.

Its members shall know each other by their deeds and being and by their eyes and by no other outward sign save the fraternal embrace.

Each one will dedicate their life to the silent loving of their neighbour and environment and the planet, whilst carrying out their task, however exalted or humble.

It recognises the supremacy of the great idea which may only be accomplished if the human race practises the supremacy of Love.

It has no reward to offer either here or in the hereafter, save that of the infallible joy of being and loving.

Each shall seek to advance the cause of understanding, doing good by stealth and teaching only by example.

They shall heal their neighbour, their community and our Planet.

They shall know no fear and feel no shame and their witness shall prevail over all odds.

It has no secret, no arcanum, no initiation save that of true understanding of the power of Love and that, if we want it to be so, the world will change but only if we change ourselves first.

ALL THOSE WHO BELONG, BELONG; THEY BELONG TO THE CHURCH OF LOVE.

# 5

# An Archbishop of Canterbury

*One who faces his own failures is steadily advancing on the pilgrim's way.*

William Temple (1881–1944), Archbishop of Canterbury

Good day. My name is Simon and I was known initially in the lifetime with which I'm concerned here as Simon of Sudbury, that being the Suffolk village in which I'd been born in about 1316. (Records of births in those days were not always scrupulously kept.) My father was a wealthy merchant named Nigel Theobald and I was the oldest of six children, of whom two died in childhood, as of course sadly happened frequently at that time. That left two sisters and my brother John. One sister became a nun in Norwich and the other remained in Sudbury, married into a wealthy merchant family, with whom my father had connections, and had children of her own who continued the tradition of supporting both the community and the Church.

Our childhood was much the same as anyone else's in our sort of milieu in rural England at that time. We wanted for little and were brought up to fear God and live a life that was pleasing to Him. From early on it was clear that I had a good brain and so I was sent off to study in Paris, whose university was then regarded as one of the best centres of learning in Europe. I learnt French well, which isn't normally difficult when one starts at an early age, enjoyed my studies, and then a career in the Church seemed to be the right thing for me. Being more interested in matters of the intellect than of the flesh, remaining celibate didn't appear to me as a problem. I lived in France for some years, but a good century had passed since the persecution and final extermination of the Cathars well south of

Paris, the subject of the previous chapter, so I was pretty much in ignorance of that until after I'd crossed over to the other side. Had I not been, I would most certainly have found it abhorrent. I've always been all for defending the Faith and keeping to the letter of Law, but to burn people to death who were doing nothing other than travelling the countryside teaching Love and Peace and caring for the sick and the dying seems to me to be inexcusable.

I've no doubt that you've heard of the Avignon Papacy. It arose from a conflict between the papacy and the French crown, which culminated in the death of Pope Boniface VIII after his arrest and maltreatment by Philip IV of France. During the period 1309–76 there was a succession of seven Avignon popes, all of whom were French. Well, the fifth of these, Innocent VI, who had been born in the Diocese of Limoges and was Pope between 1352 and 1362, made me one of his chaplains. After teaching law in Toulouse he had held two successive bishoprics and I admired him because he introduced many reforms that were really needed in the administration of Church affairs and he also sought to restore order in Rome. In 1355 the Holy Roman Emperor Charles IV was crowned in Rome with Innocent's permission.

I served for 12 years as an auditor (i.e. judge) of the Rota at the papal Curia and in 1359 Pope Innocent employed me in an attempt to persuade King Edward III of England to open peace negotiations with France. As a reward for my services (whether merited or not, for it was not for me to judge!) Innocent VI then appointed me Bishop of London in October 1361; I was consecrated the following March. London being the third See in importance after Canterbury and York, this was by no means a trivial job and I took my duties very seriously and discharged them to the best of my abilities. Then, in May 1375, I was elevated to the See of Canterbury and just over two years later I had the great privilege of crowning Richard II in Westminster

Abbey. I know that, in my role as Primate, I've gone down in history as having avoided conflict with the state, while dealing firmly with suffragans.

One of the jobs assigned to me while I was at Lambeth Palace was dealing with the trial of John Wycliffe in April 1378. I'm sure all Christians among you will have heard of the Wycliffe Bible. Well, he was a seminary professor at Oxford and an important predecessor to Protestantism, questioning as he did the privileged status of the clergy, who had bolstered their powerful role in England and the luxury and pomp of local parishes. Wasn't the nice-sounding Cathar in the previous chapter raising a significant point when he stressed that it was desire for power that was the root of so much evil? As Archbishop I had a lot of pressure put on me to condemn Wycliffe, but I have to say that I did it somewhat reluctantly, since a big part of me agreed with his arguments. I also thought it made a lot of sense to get the Bible translated into the vernacular! After all, if the Bible really is the 'Word of God', why should access to it be restricted to the Latin-educated clergy?

So, that's what I felt at that time, but none of my fellows agreed with me back then and going against the flow wasn't easy. It's just the way we were brought up, you see, and rebelling against the traditions didn't occur to us. I suppose what John Wycliffe was doing undermined their clerical sense of superiority! Anyway, he fought a noble battle, winning eventually, and I had to admire all the work he put into the biblical translation, even though most of it was probably actually done by a bunch of his minions. I know that, since those early days, multitudinous other translations of both Testaments have been made and into innumerable different languages, but Wycliffe was a true pioneer and one has to admire that. (I also know, incidentally, that many documents of great interest were sadly omitted from the standard Bible. The discovery of the Dead Sea Scrolls, for instance, caused a great deal of excitement!)

Another thing that I'm known for, though it didn't happen until the very last year of my life, was being made Lord Chancellor of England. It may seem strange to you readers living in the twenty-first century that such a post could be held by an archbishop, but there has been much secularisation during the intervening centuries and I'm aware that nowadays the clergy have very limited power compared with what I knew. I do believe that this is all to the good. Not that the rise of atheism is doing the world a lot of good, but it *is* good that a large section of the world's population is now adhering less faithfully to traditional religion and becoming better versed in genuine spirituality.

Besides executing my duties firstly as a bishop and subsequently as an archbishop, I never forgot my beloved Suffolk. Travelling in those days, as you must know, was much more time-consuming, tedious, and challenging than it is now, but I nevertheless went fairly regularly to visit my family in Sudbury and I further took it upon myself to do something about the important church there. The origins of this beautiful church, named St Gregory's, date right back to the end of the eighth century. (A visit to it from Bishop Aelfhun of East Anglia is recorded in the Saxon Chronicle of 797.) Subsequent bequests in 970 and 993 suggest that it was a minster church serving an area much greater than just the little town of Sudbury itself. It stands on an elevated site above the River Stour and has a tree-shaded croft in the northernmost corner of the Iron Age and Saxon settlements.

During the mid-twelfth century Sudbury was owned by the Earls of Gloucester, which probably sounds rather odd to your contemporary ears! At this point the advowson of this church, together with the nearby Chapel of St Peter (later rebuilt as a very large church), was given to the nuns at Eaton in Warwickshire. This seemed somewhat absurd to me and so in 1374 I offered the nuns four shops in Fish Street, London, in exchange for it, and my offer was happily accepted. I also purchased the 200 acres of land that had come with the advowson, plus an additional 570 acres, which represented the manors of Middleton Hall and Ballingdon. These two beautiful mediaeval manors, by the way, are still extant and well worth a visit if you're ever in the area. You could look them up. ('Google' is the word, I understand! You will note that, though not at present incarnate, I do still keep an eye on areas that were important to me during that particular lifetime. I *have* had further lifetimes during the intervening period — a bit more on that anon — but none in which I again made it into the history books.)

Anyway, going back to St Gregory's, another thing that I was keen to do in the area was to found a college for the training of priests and in this, together with my brother John, I was successful. We decided to incorporate into it our late father's house immediately to the west of the church. (Our good mother, Sara, was also long deceased at this point.) We thought it good to raise St Gregory's to collegiate status and to keep St Peter's as a chapel of ease under control of the College. So, in 1375, a deed was drawn up between myself, my brother John and the Bishop of Norwich, in whose diocese the College was to be. (This despite the fact that my own diocese of London came right up to the riverbank nearby.)

I was in the useful position of having had firsthand experience of dealing with masons and master-craftsmen at both St Paul's, London, and Canterbury Cathedral and was thus fully conversant with the then newly fashionable Perpendicular style of architecture. In addition, my own father, Nigel Theobald, had already, in 1365, completed the church's easternmost bay as a chapel in which to house his and my mother's mortal remains. I paid for that myself and I also had the south aisle and clerestory built. There was at one time a series of terracotta gargoyles, but you will see if you go there that, sadly, only one of them has survived. If you do go there and have a particular interest in church architecture, you will be able to purchase for a small price a brochure that gives a lot more details about the church than feels appropriate for me to go into here.

Now, I need to tell you about my rather gruesome and distinctly uncomfortable death. It arose on account of the Peasants' Revolt over the poll tax, of which you have no doubt heard. This revolt, otherwise known as Wat Tyler's Rebellion or the Great Rising, was a major uprising that took place across large parts of England in 1381. It had various causes, which included the socio-economic and political tensions generated by the Black Death in the 1340s, the high taxes resulting from the conflict with France during the Hundred Years' War and instability within the local leadership of London. The final trigger for the revolt, however, was the intervention of a royal official, John Bampton, in Essex on 30 May 1381, when he attempted to collect unpaid poll taxes in Brentwood. This ended in a violent confrontation, which spread rapidly across the south-east of the country. A wide spectrum of rural society, including many local artisans and village officials, rose up in protest, burning court records and opening the local jails. Both words gaol and jail are borrowed from French. The first borrowing, gaol, came with the Norman Conquest, when a lot of Norman French words to do with law and politics and governance were introduced into English. The second borrowing, jail, came about three centuries later from Parisian French. The rebels sought a reduction in taxation, an end to serfdom, and the removal of King Richard II's senior officials and law courts.

The next thing that happened was that a contingent of Kentish rebels, inspired by the sermons of the radical cleric John Ball and led by Wat Tyler, advanced on London. They were met at Blackheath by representatives of the royal government, who attempted unsuccessfully to persuade them to return home. King Richard, then aged 14, retreated to the safety of the Tower of London, but most of the royal forces were either abroad or in northern England. On 13 June (how well I remember it!) the rebels entered London and, joined by many local townsfolk, they attacked the jails, destroyed the Savoy Palace, set fire to law books and buildings in the Temple and killed anyone associated with the royal government. The following day the young king met the rebels at Mile End and agreed to most of their demands, including the abolition of serfdom. But this didn't happen soon enough to prevent the rebels from taking revenge on me, whom, together with Sir Robert Hales, they held responsible for the oppressive poll tax.

I was at the time saying mass in St John's Chapel, but they dragged both of us to Tower Hill and there I was beheaded by eight frenzied sword blows to my neck, one of which also took off the fingers from one of my hands. My body then lay in the open all day, but the severed head had my clerical hood nailed onto it and was fixed to a pole before being placed on London Bridge. My body was later taken to Canterbury Cathedral, where it was entombed very nobly, but my head was taken down after six days by William Walworth, the Lord Mayor of London, and was taken to Sudbury, where it remains to this day in St Gregory's Church. Somewhat gruesome, I'm sure you must think, but people often like to remember things that happened to 'important sons of their area' and it is, after all, merely a physical head, not the real me!

You can imagine that suddenly having one's head chopped off isn't a lot of fun, but one good thing about this sort of death (and I've learnt that the same thing tends to happen when people are martyred by fire, as were so many of those who were subjected to the Inquisition) is that the soul, knowing the end to be unavoidable, leaves the body before the pain becomes unbearable. For me, as a good Christian, the most important things as I was dying were firstly to repent quickly of my sins and secondly to forgive my killers. The latter was probably the easier of the two because deep down I had a lot of sympathy with the peasants, who really were very hard done by. Of course the poll tax was a big imposition on them, but the country needs to have funds with which to run it and I was only doing what I, as Lord Chancellor, believed to be necessary at the time.

My departure from that life was, I'm glad to say, instantly rewarded by meeting Jesus on the other side. That was what I'd always hoped for, though I had wondered whether I would first need to spend a period in Purgatory.

"Purgatory, my dear Simon, what is that?" asked Jesus, laughingly. "It's certainly not anything that I desired, still less instigated! People on Earth often make it for themselves when they fail to meet the challenges that they've been given for their growth. Your work was a challenge that you took on willingly, demanding though it often was, but for some — especially those who have heavy debts to pay from previous lifetimes — the challenges are sometimes too great for them to feel able to overcome and then they feel sorry for themselves and make their lives 'Purgatory' (or even Hell!), from which they're unable to escape even for a while after they've died."

"Previous lifetimes?"

"Yes, Simon, that's something that the Church has unfortunately forgotten about in recent centuries, but I spoke of it when I was on Earth and the Gnostics, such as the Cathars, have never forgotten about it. You don't really think that a single life would be sufficient for all your learning, do you? Shortly, you might like someone over here to take you on a guided tour of the Akashic Library, where you could take a look at all the books in which your own past lives have been recorded."

"That sounds interesting and hopefully I will remember it, but do you know something that's just occurred to me?"

"Yes, I can read your mind and I can see that you're comparing yourself with another son of Suffolk — Edmund of Bury, who was also beheaded! An interesting coincidence?"

"Coincidence, I don't know, but I do know that Edmund, King of England and once its patron saint, is said to have been beheaded by the Vikings in 869 for refusing to renounce his Faith."

"A scholar you are indeed and isn't there an interesting twist to that tale?"

"Yes, it seems hard to believe, but according to the tenth-century account of the saint's life by Abbo of Fleury, who quotes St Dunstan as his source, Edmund was then bound to a tree, shot through by arrows and his decapitated head is said to have been reunited with its body with the help of a talking wolf who protected it and then called out, *"Hic, hic, hic"* (which means 'Here, here, here' in Latin of course) to alert Edmund's followers. A nice story if it's true, but there were no wolves in London to take care of *my* head!"

"You didn't need that, but I'll tell you something that will be happening in your honour in Canterbury in the future. In recognition of your good works for the city, the Mayor of Canterbury, at an annual civic service on Christmas Day, will place a wreath of red roses on your tomb."

"Really! I find that very touching indeed and red roses have always been my favourite."

"So now I'm sure you'd like to enjoy a bit of a holiday in Heaven (if that's what you care to call this realm) and have a tour around. Here come your parents to escort you."

"Greetings, dear son! You must know that we're very proud of you."

"I'm glad to hear that and it's wonderful to see you again!"

\*\*\*

So have a pleasant little holiday in Heaven I did for a while. It was wonderful to be able again to revel in its beauties, to explore new places to which I now had a passport and to meet up with old friends and relatives. One of the people I bumped into was my great hero, King Edmund, after whom the major city in our lovely county is named. We realised that we had been previously acquainted and had an interesting discussion about the strange and, we both felt, rather amusing fact that very often people who have been canonised need later to return to Earth in quite different bodies. Present-day Roman Catholics (who are now becoming fewer and fewer), who sometimes pray to saints of their choosing, should be made to understand this. On the other hand, there is also the fact that no prayer is ever wasted: it goes wherever it needs to.

I also discussed with Edmund the legend about the wolf who had supposedly guarded his head that the Vikings had so brutally cut off. (He was intrigued to learn that I had also been decapitated!) He commented that people on Earth tended to be fond of legends and whether or not it was actually true (we agreed that the notion of a talking wolf was a bit far-fetched) was of no real concern to him. Just like me, he had appreciated as soon as he had crossed over that he had no further need of a physical head.

But after my holiday it was soon agreed with my Higher Self, my guides and my guardian angel that it was time for me to have a new incarnation. A 'resting one', in which I wouldn't need to use my brain so intently, was deemed appropriate and it was also felt that I needed to experience the other side of the coin, meaning that I could come back as a simple peasant and thus experience the poverty that had been so far from the world of Archbishop Simon of Sudbury. That worked out fine; I was born in the far north of England that time, where cold was more of an issue than it is in Suffolk, and, working on someone else's farm, I did a good job of raising a family in not the easiest of circumstances.

Incidentally, I would strongly recommend making a visit to Suffolk if you've never done that. Ann, our scribe, and her good friend Peg thoroughly enjoyed their Martin Randall 'Music in Suffolk Churches' tour when they did it in early July 2022. I myself, as Simon, wasn't particularly musical in that lifetime and so the notion of using those beautiful churches in such a way was slightly alien to me, but I was on the other hand glad to observe that these churches were being made use of at a time when the numbers attending Sunday worship have dropped so dramatically. One thing I found slightly odd was a soprano wearing a dazzlingly sparkling dress, rather than just plain black, inside a church, but no doubt one has to go with the times. (The main thing was that she really did — even to my not particularly musical ear — have a truly amazing voice!) Anyway, Ann, who'd never seen the area at all beforehand, was totally charmed by the beautiful villages and fell particularly for Lavenham (where I understand that Martin Randall Travel also sometimes put on chamber music weekends, as they do at the Castle Hotel in Taunton, Somerset). Lavenham has a guildhall that has been very well converted into an interesting museum.

After that lifetime it was agreed that it was time for me to be a woman again and, at the same time, the decision was made for me to kill two birds with one stone by incarnating into a totally different culture and religion. I became a woman in Saudi Arabia — not a thing I can recommend wholeheartedly, to say the least, but it gave me the opportunity to learn what it feels like to be oppressed and thus be able to feel true compassion for those who undergo any sort of oppression. It also gave me the chance to learn something about Islam and to appreciate and admire the Muslims' rigorous adherence to regular prayer times and the depth of their devotion to the Almighty. Muhammad, after all, was a firm believer in, as well as a teacher of, such vital things as Love and Peace. It's only his followers who have (like the followers of other great Masters) deviated from his legacy.

I have had other intervening lives besides these two, but none of great significance and certainly none other in which I achieved fame. Now I'm resting on the other side again but shall soon have to decide what next. Maybe I'll incarnate in India and learn how to attain Enlightenment. That would probably be very good, I think, and it wouldn't mean that I'd be unable to carry on working to help people on Earth — always a big concern of mine — and I could also do such things as helping souls who get stuck at the time of their passing from this life and consequently pollute the Earth's etheric plane. Right now, however, I'll bid you all farewell and wish you all the very best for your continuing spiritual journeys.

# 6

# Tragedy in Iceland

*There are more things to be thought of by men than money alone.*
The Saga of Grettir, chapter 47

*Góðan dag.* You might well guess that that means 'Good day', though whether you would appreciate that it is actually the ancient Norse way of saying it is another matter. Anyway, I should like to introduce myself to you all as Olssen and tell you that I was one of the early settlers who braved the challenging journey from northern Norway to Iceland in the tenth century. My reasons for doing it were various: the fact that I was a peace-loving soul and there was sometimes warfare in the area of my birth, a spirit of adventure, a desire to forge my own way as a farmer rather than simply follow in my family's footsteps... Perhaps you're wondering how I knew that the island of Iceland even existed to the north-west of where I grew up? Well, the answer is simple; a few of the even earlier emigrants (who had been the bravest of the brave, since they didn't know when they set off whether or not there was any land to be discovered in that direction!) had after a while chosen to return and spend their final days 'back home'. They of course spread the word and words can travel fast in wild winds such as those to which we were accustomed. But I think I should start my tale at the beginning.

I came, as you will already have gathered, from strong farming stock. The oldest of four children and more strongly built than either my younger brother or our two dear sisters, it never occurred to me to work in any way other than on the land. At the age of 20 I fell deeply in love with Greta, the child of another farming family who lived in a village just a few leagues away. When I say "child", that is precisely what I mean, for she was only 10 years of age when I first set eyes on her. Before, however, you have time to express shock at the notion of my having "seduced such a young girl", let me hasten to add that, though I recognised her instantly as the one for me — undoubtedly my 'other half' — in no way was I going to interfere with her childhood. On the contrary, I bided my time patiently, just saying the odd word to her when I occasionally had dealings with her father. She no doubt just saw me then as a kindly older person, perhaps not particularly different from any of her parents' other visitors. We didn't meet frequently, but once she'd reached 'sweet 17' it was impossible not to start dropping hints about my feelings for her. She was very shy at first (as one would no doubt expect in one so inexperienced in the ways of the world) and in any case we were both quite busy — me working on my father's land, she helping her mother with various more womanly chores — but it soon became clear that my sentiments weren't completely unrequited.

We took it fairly slowly to start with, but once she'd reached 20 and I'd turned 30, both families were very happy with the idea of a match. We had a fairly simple ceremony, with an elder asking for our gods' blessings, but many friends and relatives brought delicious culinary delights and after everyone had eaten their fill and sung and danced half the night away, I took Greta home with me and my parents gave us a comfortable small wing of their own abode. We were blissfully happy together, but I took great care not to let her conceive, as something deep inside me made me feel that the time was not yet right. In any case we both always found plenty of work to be done.

In due course the reason for my instinctive desire to delay bringing a child into the world became apparent. As I said initially, there was warfare around that I was keen to avoid and then, suddenly one day, to our immense surprise, a group of men turned up at our farm saying that they were forming a contingent of people to build a large boat to sail north-west to try to locate a large island that they'd heard had plenty of spare land that was ripe for cultivation. While I was instantly intrigued by the idea, Greta was reluctant at first to go so far away from her family with no certainty of ever returning. Her main desire, however, was to spend the rest of her days at my side and fear of the warfare coming ever closer began to fill her mind, too. So I agreed to join in with the boat builders — a thing I felt quite confident about being good at — while she continued to spend her days working on the farm and also making some extra clothes to take with us. My family wasn't too happy with the idea, to put it mildly, but my younger brother stalwartly put his oar in by pointing out that our two brothers-in-law could join forces on our farm. (Both our sisters had married at younger ages than Greta and none of them lived very far away.)

Building the ship was very hard work, but I thoroughly enjoyed it and a great spirit of camaraderie quickly built up among the group. Some of the men were also planning to bring womenfolk — even children, though not any very young ones, who would need a lot of looking after on the journey — as we planned to start new generations in what we hoped would become a land of plenty. The building took well over a year, as we were determined to make the end product extremely sturdy to cope with seas that we well knew could at times be very perilous. Completion finally came quite early in the summer, which felt right because it would obviously be best to make use of as much daylight as possible.

Tears were shed all round when we finally felt ready to set sail, but nobody resented our departure, since those staying behind fully appreciated our need to follow our hearts' desires. We were a group of 50 in all, with a few cattle and sheep to keep us going once we were there, and we felt confident of being able to catch enough fish to supplement the diet of dried beans and so on that our mothers and sisters had prepared.

The ship obviously needed to have several different well-built compartments, so that animals, families and single people could all be sheltered separately; and we also needed big butts for storing rainwater for drinking and cooking. You can imagine the detailed planning involved!

I won't dwell at length on the actual journey, the hazards of which I'm sure I can leave to readers' imaginations, but one thing that we noticed with fascination was the extent to which the daylight hours grew in length the further north we travelled. Nobody starved and the animals, too, survived well on the hay that we'd stocked up for them, but sickness (inevitably of course) did cause us a couple of casualties among the older folk. In each case we all joined forces to pray to our gods to take care of their souls before lovingly dropping the bodies into the ocean, knowing full well that the two friends concerned would remain with us in spirit.

It's difficult to describe the joy we all felt when land was first espied! It happened to be a very clear day with a beautiful blue sky and this was a great help in steering the ship in exactly the best direction for finding a suitable place to land. Not very long after we were safely anchored and had started to disembark, two tall men appeared, seemingly out of nowhere. They greeted us in our own language, saying that a spirit had recently appeared to one of them in his sleep and informed him that a ship of would-be settlers was on its way and that they should welcome us as friends. We felt sure that this spirit must have been that of one of our departed fellow travellers. They then said how happy they would be to have us join their community, that there was plenty of fertile land to spare and that they could start off by helping us to unload our essentials.

The first things that we brought off the ship, besides all the animals, were our remaining foodstuffs, which we told our new friends we could share with them. Some of the men who were already living there hastily erected separate pens for our sheep and cattle and then they got together with their families to work out how we could all be given temporary sleeping quarters to tide us over until such time as we were able to construct abodes for ourselves. Anders and Astrid, a charming young couple with a two-year-old son named Jan, made a nice cosy spot in their house for Greta and me and we brought in the bedding that we'd been using on the ship. Greta immediately offered to help Astrid produce a meal for the five of us, but they insisted that we must all be tired after the long journey and that there would be plenty of other opportunities for Greta to make use of her culinary talents to their advantage. Our gratitude was unbounded and after stories about our origins and travels had been shared over a delicious meal of fish and home-grown vegetables, we fell peacefully asleep, only awaking at dawn, which at that time of the year was round about ten o'clock.

The next months of course involved a huge amount of work, but we newcomers to this amazing island all did it together joyfully, slowly making good friends with our predecessors, who were always ready to give advice as well as helping hands, and we returned the favours as best we could with such things as picking crops, making meals and babysitting. For the building we salvaged driftwood from the coast, as well as cutting down trees, and we never ceased to be fascinated by the country's geysers and the hot springs, which gave us an endless supply of water in which to wash both ourselves and our clothes. As for the cold water, it was the purest that we'd ever encountered!

Gradually enough abodes were constructed for all of us and, since there was no shortage of available land we all had plenty of space. Greta, like most of the other women, had brought a good supply of seeds and so, before too long we were able to be largely self-sufficient. During the long summer months we could work on the land until we dropped, whereas in the winter we had to stay indoors as much as possible, but that gave the womenfolk plenty of time for knitting thick jumpers for their men when they braved the elements to make use of the four hours or so of daylight for working outside. After a couple of years my beloved gave birth to a beautiful daughter, whom we named Ingrid after my mother. (If only she could have come and seen her!)

Little Ingrid was our pride and joy, much admired by our companions and as soon as she was able she played endlessly with other children around the same age. When, however, she reached the age of five the most unbelievable tragedy occurred. One day we all got very excited because a nearby volcano started to erupt. None of us had ever seen anything like it before and many of us remained spellbound for long periods of time simply watching the spectacle. We were very careful of course not to go too close and also to make sure that all the children were aware of the possible danger, but, one evening about a week after the eruption had died down completely, Greta and I tucked Ingrid up safely and told the immediate neighbours that we were going off to find out how safe the lava was to walk on. For lava, we knew, was a wonderful fertiliser.

All was going well and it wasn't yet dark. The lava was perfectly cool to the touch and so Greta, who was just ahead of me, bent down to break a piece off, but suddenly a small chasm opened up under her feet! I rushed to her aid, grabbing one of her arms that was sticking up, but she only sank deeper into the chasm until there was absolutely nothing I could do but let go to ensure that I didn't sink in after her. So I just sat there, shouting down to her not to worry, as I would go and get help, but hardly had I risen to my feet when our neighbours Fredrik and Karl arrived, saying that they had been sent out as a search party since it would soon be dark. When they saw what had happened, they were beside themselves with distress at not having thought to bring a rope with them. All we felt we could do at that moment was to throw my big coat down to Greta for warmth, along with the bread and water bottle that the two of us had brought with us the previous night.

You can well imagine the sleepless night I spent after getting home, waiting seemingly endlessly for the dawn to break. As soon as it did, Fredrik and Karl, accompanied by two other neighbours, arrived at my door armed with a long length of rope, pickaxes and a makeshift stretcher. When we reached the dreaded spot we shouted down, but not a peep came back. Naturally fearing the worst in the bitter cold, Fredrik and Karl started by throwing down a long length of rope, but, with the chasm being so narrow, they quickly set to work with pickaxes. The hard lava came away quite easily and before long we were able to reach the beloved body, now completely cold to the touch. I myself was too numbed with grief to move an inch, but my four friends lovingly got the body out of the chasm and, between them, they carried it back on the stretcher.

Ingrid had been taken into the care of another neighbour, who was giving her a hearty breakfast, but we all agreed that we could not and should not keep the dreadful news from her for very long. It felt important, too, to let her see the body itself, so that she would for the rest of her life be able always to recall her dear mother's face. It still looked as beautiful as ever, but there was also, I was happy to note, a wonderful look of peace in it. We wept long and hard together, initially in a state of incredulity, but then Ingrid and I fell asleep in one another's arms. When we awoke, some hours later, dark had again fallen and Fredrik took us both to his own abode, where his wife had prepared a nourishing hot meal for us all. Eating was of course difficult, but our good friends stressed its importance.

The next few months were truly challenging. A big part of me wanted just to follow Greta into the afterlife, but I knew I had to remain alive and strong, if only for our little daughter's sake. The other villagers were all wonderful, never leaving the two of us completely on our own and constantly checking that we were well fed and warm. Then suddenly one night I had the most amazing dream. In it Greta appeared to me, shining radiantly and, with her indescribably beautiful smile, assuring me that all was well, that everything was as it was meant to have been and that my main task now was to look after our daughter, doing the work that I'd always done and making sure that she grew up in the best way possible in the difficult circumstances. Greta also told me that we could all three regularly meet up at night, when Ingrid and I both left our bodies in sleep, and that it wouldn't matter if we didn't remember anything about it when we awoke, as we could rest assured that she was always with us and that we would be reunited on the other side once our time had also come. The dream was *so* real that it was impossible for me not to believe in its veracity and when I told little Ingrid about it, she replied that she, too, had been seeing her mother in dreams.

The next months and years passed by similarly to those that had come before them and though I could never get quite used to the hole that Greta had left in our physical lives, I was often comforted by the thought that she wasn't really that far away. Ingrid was growing up beautifully and of course, in such a close-knit community, we never needed to be completely alone. Gradually a few of the women were widowed and hints were dropped that I could share my life with one of them, but I knew that I could never contemplate that, as Greta would always be the 'one and only' for me, at least in my present lifetime.

The days were always well filled with farming work, but gradually, after dark — especially during the long hours of winter — groups of us formed the habit of getting together and telling one another stories. These were often elaborated with what we felt to be good words of wisdom and we promised one another that we would keep the tradition alive by passing the sagas on to our children and grandchildren, in the hope that the story of Iceland would be forever engrained in history. Ingrid, who was extremely bright and had an amazing memory, developed the art to a fine degree and everybody particularly loved listening to her.

Another thing that some of us began to do was to explore further afield from the small corner of the island that we had made our own. Some went in certain directions, others in others, and then we would report back on our findings. Those who went a long way north (which Ingrid and I felt no desire to do, as we thought the cold where we were was quite enough for us!) returned saying that the fishing right up there was worth braving the even colder climes for. Interestingly, having believed ourselves to be alone, some of us came across people who had obviously come from other lands. Communication was a problem, but everyone we met was friendly and we all worked on making sign language, sometimes teaching one another words in our own tongue. One discovery that was made was of a group of men who lived together in what was obviously a holy way and who appeared to have a religion that was completely unknown to us, worshipping a man whom they named Jesus who had apparently been nailed to a cross. How barbaric! Now that I'm no longer on Earth I can see that these holy men, known as monks, had sailed over from a country named Ireland.

There was another little group that Ingrid, I, and a few of our friends who happened to be with us at the time came across. These people explained with difficulty and sign language that they had come from somewhere almost equally far north, but from the west rather than the east. As our mutual skills in communication grew, we gathered that the land they had come from was absolutely immense — so big that they could never have begun to travel the full breadth of it. (You readers will no doubt immediately guess that they were talking of what's now known as America.) This group was particularly hospitable and invited us to spend some time with them. Ingrid and I accepted the invitation, while our friends felt that they had better return straight away to their duties at home.

Ingrid was now a beautiful 18-year-old and, among this group whom I can now call 'Americans' was a handsome youth who introduced himself as James and who appeared to be not much older than her and clearly found her attractive. I of course had no objection to her finding a partner, so long as he was a willing worker and would promise fidelity, and anyway the notion of introducing some new blood into our rather closed community seemed to be a good one. So I made a point of leaving them alone together from time to time and gradually I noticed them busily endeavouring to teach one another their own language. We obviously couldn't, however, stay on that side of the island indefinitely, leaving our own crops and animals to be cared for by neighbours, so after about a couple of weeks I suggested to James' parents, Michael and Joan, and his sister, Julia, that they all come and stay with us for a while. They were clearly more recent immigrants than we were, as they were still all busy with building, but the family had a well-constructed cart, with a sturdy horse, and the time of year was a good one for travelling.

So, as this new band of six we made our way together south-eastwards, with Ingrid and James clearly deepening their friendship, and once we were home the newcomers received a very warm welcome in our community. We had a spare room in our abode, which we offered to the parents, and the youngsters were readily given accommodation by some of our immediate neighbours. All four of them quickly made it clear that they were willing to work on the land and our old friend Karl's son, Jørgen, began to take a fancy to Julia. We all worked hard, too, to learn one another's language and, before long, it felt right for the newcomers to be absorbed into our community and they were given plenty of help in building a new house.

I'm sure that by now it won't be a surprise to you to hear that the next big event was a dual wedding! For this our new friends were keen to invite some of their own original companions and so a small delegation was sent over to the other side of the island to give the good news and issue the wedding invitation. Not all of the Americans felt able to make the journey, of course, but a good dozen of them did come, were put up for a few nights and a great time was had by all. We all got together to build two new houses, one for Ingrid and James, the other for Jørgen and Julia. In due course I was gifted with three grandchildren, two boys followed by a girl at more or less two-year intervals. So as I grew older I was always well cared for; James made a splendid farmer and I knew that my descendants would never lack the basics that they needed for survival. The grandchildren naturally grew up bilingual and Ingrid and James both mastered the other's language well.

When it was eventually my time to go, I left my body quite easily, happy to leave the aches and pains of old age behind and well cared for by my family, who organised a beautiful funeral for me. Greta was there waiting for me, as I'd been confident she would be, and before discussing with my guides the lessons that I'd learnt (such as standing on my own) and planning my next steps, we looked back together over that lifetime and had a really good talk about it. She had sometimes listened in on the sagas we had created on those dark winter nights and we agreed that they hadn't been just for ourselves, but would in due course be inscribed permanently by people at a later stage, who would invent a means of writing things down either on parchment or something more manageable that would be created in the future.

I also got a strong sense that *someone*, perhaps many centuries ahead, possibly a sensitive writer who happened to be on holiday in our beautiful land but open to stories of which to make use in a book of hers, would somehow pick up on the energies left by Greta's tragic death. I was given a vision of the area in which she'd died and saw it being converted, thanks to the vast amount of very warm water emanating there, into a huge lagoon in which people could relax and luxuriate at leisure, with the silica in the water doing good to their skin. Maybe it could be named the 'Blue Lagoon' and maybe the holiday-maker I visualised could 'clear the air' by telling our story?

# 7

# Two Very Great Composers

*Music is the one incorporeal entrance into the higher world of knowledge which comprehends mankind but which mankind cannot comprehend.*

Ludwig van Beethoven

*Approval or blame will follow in the world to come.*

Franz Schubert

*Schubert's sonatas express with directness and sincerity some of the most fundamental elements of human experience — longing, consolation, despair, joy, loss, nostalgia, and hope. In our time, his music is as essential and poignant as ever.*

Paul Lewis, pianist

### 19 November 1827

"Welcome Home, Franz! It's great to see you here. I know you've suffered greatly in physical terms in recent months — well, for years really — and now you can have a good long rest and recuperate fully. I mean — cramming all that into your last 13 months: your three, quite incredibly beautiful, last piano sonatas, that amazing string quintet and six of the songs that will later become known as the *Schwannengesang*, not to mention correcting the proofs of the *Winterreise* on your deathbed! How on *earth* did you do it? You must be totally exhausted. When I was on *my* deathbed I did no more than lament the dozen bottles of wine that I was told my publisher had sent "too late"! Of course we were both rather over-keen on the booze, weren't we? Well, we needed it for drowning our sorrows."

"It *can't* be...! It can't really be *you*! My idol... the great..."

"Ludwig. Yes, of course it's me! I've been waiting for you and watching over you for more than 18 months now. And thank you for being one of my pallbearers, by the way. It's just a shame that, though we lived comparatively close by to one another in Vienna, it's taken death finally to bring us together face to face!"

"I just can't believe it! How can it be that you, the almighty Beethoven, have deigned to take the trouble to come and meet me in... is this Heaven? Can it really be Heaven? I seem to be feeling Love all around me and seeing... is it angels? Those wondrous beings over there? I'd always thought that, when I died, I would have to suffer in Purgatory for a long time before I could possibly gain entrance to Heaven!"

"Nonsense, Franz, you wrote countless pages of heavenly music! How could you not deserve to come straight here? In any case so-called Purgatory is entirely of our own making. It's an invention of the Church, just a state of mind, not a *place*."

"I'm not quite clear what you mean really, but am completely bowled over by meeting you at this very moment, just after I've presumably died, when, during the time in which I was alive, such a meeting felt like an impossible dream for someone so unworthy as me!"

"Don't worry, you'll gradually re-remember now that you've returned Home; it'll just be a matter of time. But as for meeting me, how *absurd* to call yourself 'unworthy'! You could easily have just come and knocked on my door in Vienna, for I would always have given you a warm welcome. I might have made the effort myself to go to one of your musical gatherings, or even a concert, had I not been eternally busy with all my own work, my problems with Karl, that nephew of mine, or my thwarted love life..."

"Yes of course, we were both unlucky in love and it's hard to understand why we didn't deserve that kind of happiness. But I could *never* have plucked up the courage to knock on your door!"

"Never mind, we'll have plenty of time to make up for the conversations we didn't have on Earth. As for our ill luck in love, you'll gradually come to appreciate that, if we hadn't made that particular sacrifice (agreed upon, incidentally, in the life plans that we each made before incarnating last time), some of our greatest music could never have been conceived. But right now, you need to go and attend your funeral. People almost always like to do that. Did you know that you were going to be buried close to me, in the Währing Cemetery on the outskirts of Vienna?"

"How could I *possibly* deserve that?"

"Don't worry about deserving or not deserving! Just think the name of that place and you'll find yourself there instantly. I'm sure you'll be interested to watch the proceedings and the two of us can have plenty more interesting discussions after you've returned for your life review and so on, and found out why you only needed 31 short years in order to complete what you'd agreed to. *Auf Wiedersehen*."

## 22 September 1888

"Ah, Franz! What have you been up to since we last met? I trust you *did* enjoy your funeral and have since had a good long rest."

"I've been in total bliss, thanks, Ludwig. Unbelievable really! The funeral certainly was very interesting. It would never have entered my wildest dreams that so many people would come, that so much love and appreciation would be expressed... And afterwards, just as you said, I was taken for my life review. My guardian angel escorted me to that; it took place in a really beautiful temple, in which my guides reminded me how I'd agreed beforehand to have a short life this time, fitting an incredible amount into it. This was to compensate for the lifetime I'd had just before, where I'd lived a long time and had had great talent but wasted it by never completing *anything*."

"Interesting how karma sometimes takes effect instantly! And what happened after that?"

"Oh, Ludwig, it was just wonderful! I met Therese Grob, the soprano with whom I'd been so deeply in love in my youth. She's still on Earth but came to meet me while out of her body one night and she told me straight away that she had really loved me, too, but hadn't dared to get involved with a 'penniless musician', feeling that a baker with a reliable income was a much safer bet."

"That's women for you! But I'm glad to hear that you've been able to revel in all the bliss here after all the great suffering that Franz Schubert endured. Anyway, I have some interesting news to pass on to you. I just had a look back at Vienna, sensing that some changes were being made, and I saw that they were moving both our bodies from the Währing Cemetery to the massive central one, the Zentralfriedhof. It's extremely beautiful, with many trees around, and you're still placed close to me. They're giving us new tombstones of course and guess whose grave is in between ours, but more to the front. Mozart's! I know you admired him greatly, just as I did. Do you know that this is actually my *third* burial?! You see, in 1863, they decided to do some repairs to the Währing and they dug my body up and put it into a better quality metal coffin before reburying it. Why do they go to all this trouble with bodies that aren't needed any more and are only destined to return to the dust whence they came?!"

"I agree! Mine wasn't a very attractive one anyway — certainly not to women — and for one thing it was shorter than I would have liked."

"Well, why not come with me now to have a look at the new site and we can continue our reflections together? Do you know that Vienna now has another up-and-coming composer, who I think will also merit burial in the Zentralfriedhof. His name is Johannes, and for the start of his first symphony he's sort of pinched my 'Ode to Joy' from the fabulous Choral Symphony, but I take that as an honour rather than plagiarism, as it shows how much he admires my work."

"Do you mean Brahms? I've heard of him."

"Yes, that's right."

"That Choral Symphony, by the way, is absolutely unsurpassed! It's one of the many works that made me feel so unworthy of meeting you face to face."

"But your own ninth symphony is one of the greatest that will ever be. You did realise, didn't you, that I was overshadowing you during your composition of it?"

"Really? How fascinating! I certainly did sort of feel your presence in the room while I was writing it."

"Good! I'm glad to have some acknowledgement. Now, here we are. Just take a look at this beautiful site. Does that tombstone and its position finally make you appreciate your greatness? While I was still on Earth I did famously comment: 'Truly a divine spark dwells in Schubert.'"

"I really appreciate your flattery — a thing I'd never have dared to dream of while I was in that body down under the ground just there — but it is true: being back Home now does indeed make me realise how close to God I always was, especially during the periods in which I was actually composing."

"I, too, always had total faith in God, even during my times of greatest depression and when I was behaving the most cantankerously. And even Bach, by the way (that's Johann Sebastian, of course, the greatest of that extraordinary dynasty of composers), who will forever be regarded as the purest of channels from the heavenly realms, did on occasion behave quite badly."

"Genius though he was, Bach was also human! If he hadn't had a body, he wouldn't have been any better than you or I at inscribing notes on paper."

"How true. And that brings us to the interesting question of the precise nature of genius. Is there really any such thing? Or does it simply occur as a result of much practice of one's *métier* in previous lives?"

"An interesting question indeed! Obviously Mozart couldn't possibly have poured out all those wonderful works, as he did in such a short space of time, like milk from a jug, if he hadn't previously had endless practice at it."

"Yes, I myself worked much, much more laboriously on all my music than Mozart did on his. That's why I turned down Diabelli's invitation to write a variation on his piffling theme! I needed the *space* in which to express the most profound of human emotions — that's why I agreed to incarnate as the one and only great Beethoven and undergo such very intense suffering. Mozart did of course achieve greatness (especially, in my opinion, in some of his chamber music), but he lived a short life of luxury and most of what he poured out is on the cheerful side."

"That's interesting, what you're now telling me about turning down Diabelli's request! The 49 contributions that he did obtain, besides mine, weren't published until two years after your amazing masterpiece, were they? And your Variations will prove unbelievably taxing for even the most proficient of pianists, won't they?"

"Yes, some of my greatest works were composed 50 years before their time really. For instance, I actually needed a much bigger and better piano than the fortepiano to which you and I were constrained. I predict that, before too very long, better and better pianos will be constructed and that composers of the future won't be restricted to a mere five octaves. Won't it be wonderful for people on Earth to be able to hear in their full glory not only my Diabelli Variations but also my greatest sonatas such as the *Hammerklavier*? And talking of great piano sonatas, those last three of yours are just out of this world in their beauty!"

"I'm *so* glad you think so, Ludwig. I certainly poured my heart and soul into them, even though I couldn't begin to rival your 32 masterpieces."

"You didn't *need* to when you were clearly going to go down in history as the greatest song writer of all time!"

"But you wrote some truly wonderful songs, too!"

"It's true that my *An die ferne Geliebte* was the first song cycle ever to be written and *Adelaide*, like my other songs, is very beautiful too, but you exceeded me in that field by a long chalk. Comparing people is very silly really, since we're *all* totally different from one another, but, to change the subject slightly, an interesting thought has just occurred to me. In generations to come, when almost everybody in the Western world will have forgotten about karma, life plans and so on, people will firstly feel terribly sorry for me because of my deafness and secondly bemoan your 'untimely' death. Can't you just hear them saying: 'Imagine what other wonderful works Schubert might have written if only he'd lived longer'?!"

"That is indeed a very interesting thought! Maybe I should shout down to them all now: 'Can't you *see* that that's why I had to work so frenetically — even through dreadful illness — because I *knew*, at least subconsciously, that it was "now or never". I was pretty much dried up right at the end.' Of course I did leave my eighth symphony unfinished, but don't you think that those two movements are perfect as they are? Why should a symphony *have* to have four movements? Concerti normally only have three anyway. And I bet you that composers will come along in the future who will write symphonies with varying numbers of movements."

"Great to hear you use that word 'perfect' for one of your own works! Sounds like you are finally beginning to appreciate your own exceptional talent."

"Well yes, during the earthly years that passed so blissfully in between these two 'heavenly' meetings of ours, I did run into numerous people who told me how very much my music had meant to them and how durable it would be."

"So those intervening years certainly weren't wasted on you, if they brought you to a fuller understanding of what Franz Schubert's life purpose had been! That's one of the many differences between us. I knew from the start who I was — that I'd come into the world with the immense task of transforming Western music into something that would have greater power than it had ever had previously — and that's why I needed to get away from my birthplace, Bonn. There I was cruelly overworked by my musical family, who recognised my talents from the start, and so going to Vienna at the age of 21, where there would be much more scope for my development, was much the best thing I could have done. Vienna accepted me instantly for my pianistic abilities and my quite exceptional gift for improvisation — a gift which, as you know, I continued to make use of throughout my life, as the Diabelli Variations of which we spoke earlier bear witness. Although I did start composing at the age of eight, it took longer for me to become fully recognised for that in a city that was blessed with so many composers.

"And the deafness, which began to afflict me later, was a vital ingredient of that whole process. You see, if I hadn't been cut off from the outside world as I was, I simply would never have *heard* the inner world, in which the profundity of something like the *Grosse Fuge*, to give just one example, was contained. OK, the musical world wasn't ready for that final quartet movement at that point and so I had to write a shorter one to keep them happy right then, but I'll bet you anything that future generations *will* become ready for it and sometimes even more eager to hear that great quartet, my Opus 130, end with it rather than with its shorter substitute."

"I thought people were crazy not to accept the *Grosse Fuge*, though I suppose, as you say, it was ahead of its time. But personally the very thought of your deafness upset me terribly. It must have been agony for you to have had to give up conducting your own works!"

"Yes, it was indeed very painful, just as it was tremendously humiliating for the 'great master' to make big blunders with such things as volume, when he was unable to hear well enough to make good judgements. On the other hand, however, it was good for his over-inflated ego to be forced to become aware of his infallibility! (Note that I'm using the third person now that I'm looking back at my lifetime as Beethoven as something complete and never to be repeated.)"

"I see what you mean. We do indeed go to Earth to learn, as well as to give our gifts to the people there and to pay off our karmic debts. Did you, by the way, have a debt to pay to your nephew Karl?"

"Yes, my dear Karl, my poor brother Carl's son; I fought so furiously to gain custody of him after his father's death because I sincerely believed his mother Johanna to be immoral as well as incompetent in her role. No doubt reams will continue to be written on that subject — in fact much already has been — but whether the full truth of the story will ever get into print is another matter. The answer I can give *you*, my now trusted friend, is that I did indeed have a debt to pay from a previous life in which I myself had been Karl's father and neglected him, but my brother Carl was one of the first people I met after crossing over and together with my guides we had a good look at the errors I'd made and apologies were accepted all round. I admitted, above all, firstly to having been wrong to try to keep the boy away from his mother and her love, imperfect though she may have been; and secondly, to have tried to force him into following in my footsteps musically when really his talents lay elsewhere. But don't worry, Franz, that's all been happily sorted out now and I shall never make the same mistakes again. Families can be important, as yours was to you — especially with the love and support given you by your brother Ferdinand — but we always have to remember that biological families are only ever a temporary coming together and that soul groups, with whom we can fully re-establish contact once we're over here, either in between lifetimes or once we've become self-realised, have greater importance."

"I fully appreciate what you're saying and it has indeed been wonderful, while I've been over here, to meet Ferdinand, my parents and other members of the Schubert family, not to mention my many friends who put up with so much during my periods of severe infirmity. But on the subject of relationships: I've met up with Therese Grob, which, as I told you before, was really lovely. Have you met your famous 'Immortal Beloved'?"

"A very interesting question! I'll start, however, by commenting on the fact that you as Franz Schubert were better off with close friendships than I was as Ludwig van Beethoven. (And here I must also point out that it was my then ego that wanted to make my name sound grander by inserting the 'van'!) The reasons for that are twofold: you, as a man lacking in self-confidence, needed the support of friends who really believed in you and your gifts, while I was too intolerant in many ways to really deserve many close friends. I did have some good, faithful friends of course, but they had to put up with a lot! That was as it should be because Beethoven *needed* to assert himself in order to get important things done, but it wasn't the best way to earn love. (And isn't it appropriate that I actually died during a thunderstorm!)

All that no longer matters in the least while I'm on a good long break over here, totally surrounded by Love, but it's one of the reasons why I felt ready to go when I did, even though those closest to me at the time regarded my departure at 56 as still a bit premature. One thing, however, that I never had on Earth was a group of friends to put on the equivalent of your 'Schubertiades'. Those must have been wonderful and I'm quite sure that future generations will organise such things again, even without your physical presence."

"Do you really think so? I'd love to attend some in my present sickness-free state!"

"Why not? Musical talent will develop in quality as time goes on and people will find good venues in which to hold Schubertiades. Similarly, things such as my symphonies will get played by bigger orchestras in ever larger concert halls.

But now for the never-ending question about my 'Immortal Beloved'. Yes, I *have* met her since coming Home, as well as having had my intuition about her being my 'other half' (often described as 'twin soul') confirmed, but if you're hoping that I'll now reveal her identity, I'm afraid that I'm going to disappoint you. The truth is that I thoroughly enjoy listening to the debates of all those learned musicologists (for many of whom I have great admiration) and sometimes their surmises are correct, but I'm not right now going to give *anyone* the satisfaction of being told who she really was. What I *will* tell you is that she is now again incarnate, as a talented musician who's working hard to see that my works are played as they should be. Quite often twin souls make an agreement for one of them to remain in spirit while the other acts as one of their guides."

"So that's what you're doing now, is it, Ludwig? Acting as a guide to her?"

"Yes, that's one of my present tasks. It's lovely because we can meet up at night sometimes (just as you did with Therese), have pleasant times together and discuss her work. I do, however, need to point out that, blissful as such human relationships can be, they pale in comparison to total reunion with the Divine, which will come to us all eventually, once we've learnt all our lessons and become totally God-focused."

"I'll have to remember that. But now, to change the subject a bit: looking back over Beethoven's life as you have been, which works do you feel were his greatest achievements?"

"That's not really a question that can be properly answered. It depends upon what people are wanting at any given moment. If they're looking for excitement or glory, they could listen to the fifth or the ninth symphony. If, on the other hand, they yearn for peace and quiet in the countryside (you and I were both keen walkers!), they should turn to the sixth symphony, known as the *Pastoral*, which paints such a vivid picture of the delights with which Vienna is surrounded, even though it necessitates enduring a storm. For more sophisticated and knowledgeable listeners, however, the chamber music is probably normally better suited. My personal absolute favourites, the works that took me the closest to Heaven, are still the three late quartets: Opus 130, Opus 131 and Opus 132. Again, we mentioned the first of those earlier and that's the one that contains the movement called the Cavatina, which I think for me reigns supreme. I felt when I was putting it down on paper that it was coming straight through from the very highest realms."

"I know exactly what you mean. I felt just the same when some of my best pieces of chamber music were coming through."

"So you are at *last*, Franz, beginning to see yourself as one of the truly greats. That really delights me! We're going to have to part soon — I have work to do giving some advice to the up and coming Brahms, whom I mentioned earlier, and I believe you have an appointment with Mozart, haven't you? [Schubert nods] — but, before we do so, can you tell me what are your plans for the immediate future? You're not in a rush to take on a new body, are you?"

"No, I'm not. I feel sure you will agree that Schubert deserves a long rest! And anyway, aren't there various ways in which we can both be useful over here for a while? What are *your* plans for the next steps?"

"With the idea of Schubert deserving a rest, I'm certainly in full agreement. As for me, I'm not in a rush either. I've been led to believe that our beautiful planet is in for a good couple of hundred years or more of terrible turmoil, with horrendous wars, climate change (caused to a large extent by human error) wreaking enormous havoc, much sickness, increasing selfishness and an ever larger number of serious crimes, for instance murders. I'm really not keen to be a part of any of that. It seems that the Masters say that it's all symptomatic of the end of the *Kali Yuga*, the time in which all the evil is coming to the surface in order to be cleansed, which must be a good thing. But I shall prefer to watch it from afar, offering help where I can. Once it's all over, we shall enter the *Satya Yuga* (*Satya* means 'truth'), when things will be more peaceful, and that will make me more keen to return, but choosing quite a different profession. I feel that as Beethoven I achieved the pinnacle in music, so another time I might go for something such as architecture — in a grandiose style of course."

"I'm sure you'd make a brilliant architect, since the architecture of your music is so astounding! I, on the other hand, would prefer a much more tranquil life, with a family of my own and plenty of time to *listen* to music rather than being in the constant frenzy of writing it."

"That sounds like a good idea. But in the meantime isn't it marvellous to reflect that, even through the forthcoming very difficult times, our music will survive and remain a source of joy and consolation to people who are enduring them?"

"It is indeed! So let us now embrace with that comforting thought in our minds, thank the Lord for having enabled us to achieve what we did and wish future generations much happiness."

"So be it, Franz, and here's wishing you the very best until we meet again."

# 8

# A Suicide That Affected Many People

*The taking of one's own life is not only a crime, but is also an extremely foolish act. You do not solve your difficulties by running away from them, but merely postpone them for a future life ... [A person who takes his life] is merely delaying his own evolution, and until he has faced and overcome these obstacles and thus learned the lessons they were meant to teach him, he cannot advance any further on the journey to perfection...*

> The spirit Acharya, quoted in Pamela Rae Heath and Jon Klimo, *Suicide: What Really Happens in the Afterlife?*

*If soul is essentially involved with the soul in the world, then any suicide must acknowledge this condition, else a decision to take one's life is not truly an act of soul, only an act of independence. The "world" of "others" must be brought into the decision, not deliberatively and literally, but ritually and symbolically. Some representative of the body politic, the so-called "collective", as an emissary of the cosmic invisibles needs to be summoned. The world must bear witness.*

> James Hillman, *Suicide and the Soul*

Following the day when my wife Jean left me, taking our two children, Toby and Rosie, with her, my life became *totally* unbearable. "You're just a good-for-nothing, Craig," she'd said as she slammed the door in my face. "I never want to see you again and you're a thoroughly bad example for our children. You can never hold down a job for more than two seconds, you waste the little money you earn down at the pub and you can never be bothered either to take Toby to his football club or Rosie to her ballet classes."

She'd been quite right of course. I seemed to have failed at everything, starting with having disappointed my parents by failing to get into university. Of course I blamed them to some extent for having pushed me to follow in my older sister's footsteps; it wasn't my fault that I'd been born with a brain that was less good than hers and they shouldn't have expected me to get into Bristol University just because she had. Jo did actually point out to them that I was more practical and less academic than she was and so an apprenticeship somewhere would probably have suited me better, but they would have none of it. On the other hand I could and should have stood up for myself and approached some firms myself rather than just getting a job in the local pub. I might have done quite well in, say, the motor industry, but it was too late by then.

It was actually in that pub that I'd first met Jean. I was rather good looking then. She was in her final year at Shrewsbury College, studying art and design, and she came in with a couple of other female students to celebrate the end of the exams. If it wasn't exactly 'love at first sight', there was certainly an instant mutual attraction and we sort of fell into a relationship which lasted until she went off to Chester to do teacher training. But even after that she always dropped in to the pub whenever she was in Shrewsbury, always encouraging me to better myself by getting an apprenticeship in Chester. So I followed her there and got accepted as an apprentice property administrator. I found it pretty boring, but at least it was better paid than the pub and our relationship picked up again. When, however, she found that she was pregnant and we told our respective families that we were going to get married, there was disapproval on both sides. "Jean had the start of a good teaching career ahead of her and you've messed it up!" said her parents.

"How on earth are you going to support a child on an apprentice's salary? And how are you ever going to manage rent or a mortgage?" asked mine.

We went ahead anyway in our tiny flat, until Toby was born, and I worked three evenings in a pub to supplement my earnings. When the baby was a year old, Jean got a teaching job back in Shrewsbury, where her parents agreed to babysit, and I went back to my original pub, occasionally applying for things that looked more promising and were better paid, but never with much success. Jean did so well at the school that, by the time Rosie came along, we were able to take on a mortgage and I shared the babysitting with Jean's parents. We struggled on for a while, but things gradually went from bad to worse, with me only finding any sort of consolation with my old pals down in the pub. Gradually I fell into a deeper and deeper depression and even before Jean had announced her decision to take the children with her to her parents' house I was already seriously contemplating putting an end to my life.

The last straw came when an enormous bill for mortgage arrears arrived through the post. I didn't even dare to tell Jean about it, since I'd been the one to stop the payments going out. The mortgage was in my name because her parents had brainwashed her into believing the old-fashioned idea that it was always the man who should be the main breadwinner. I was also under the constant illusion that I would one day find my true vocation and start raking it in! I'd been brought up with no religion at all and always assumed that when you were dead you were dead, so, once Jean and the children had gone, the solution seemed simple: "Just put an end to it all and then there will be nothing but oblivion. Problem solved!"

I didn't give myself a lot of time to think. "Put my head into the gas oven? Take an overdose of the anti-depressant the doctor gave me? No, either of those might be too slow or uncomfortable and anyway, what if Jean suddenly came back for something she'd forgotten?" So the answer seemed simple: "Just throw yourself under a train." The next question was "Where? There'll be too many people around at Shrewsbury station, so it would be better just to walk down the line a bit till there's no-one around, by which time the train will have gathered speed anyway." So, putting a timetable into my pocket, I set off. At least it was a nice sunny April day.

***

But oh, what a blunder! Death of that body was certainly instantaneous, but oblivion was there none. I just found myself floating around aimlessly, with only a sort of grey, rather unpleasant mist in sight. I could see other ethereal, lost-looking bodies in the distance, but there seemed to be no way of getting to them. "However long is this going to go on for?" I wondered. "For all eternity? Were those preachers who occasionally came to the door really right when they spoke of 'eternal damnation unless you follow our way'?"

"No, Craig." (I was *stunned* by the gentle, loving sound of the voice!) "There's no such thing as 'eternal damnation' and Hell, when it occurs, is purely of one's own making."

I looked all around me for the source of the voice and suddenly saw right ahead of me a beautiful bright light with the figure of what looked like a handsome, middle-aged man standing inside it.

"Follow me, Craig. I'm your main spirit guide at the moment. We've known one another in previous lifetimes, though of course you don't remember all that right now. We all have lifetimes in which we're cut off temporarily from the spirit world and this time round your family were non-believers, so you had no spiritual back-up, but you *will* remember gradually and fortunately we have eternity on our side. You've already realised that ending your life was a blunder and in due course you'll be taken for a life review, but don't worry about that because the only judgement will be made by you yourself."

"Yes, at the moment I'm feeling rather foolish and ashamed of myself, but it's just wonderful to meet someone as uncritical as you after all the criticism I'd been getting from my wife recently. I'll gladly go wherever you care to take me."

"Well, can you see that beautiful healing temple over there? That's where we'll be heading for first. Gradually you will have to take a serious look at the life you've just curtailed and recognise the damage that your action caused, how it can all be rectified and how you can best pay the debts incurred, but now the most urgent thing is the healing of your etheric body."

"What on earth is that? I thought I'd lost my one and only body under that train!"

"We don't need to go into it all in detail at this very moment, but you'll in due course re-remember that with each new incarnation we take on different bodies, the final one before the physical being the etheric. Well, the shock of being completely squashed by a train had a devastating effect on your etheric body. I expect you feel a bit all over the place at the moment?"

"Yes, I suppose I do, come to think of it."

"Don't worry. We have even more powerful healers over here than any on Earth and some of them specialise in etheric repairs. So right now I'm taking you to that beautiful temple and once they've sorted you out and you've had a good rest I'll come back for you and then we'll deal with everything else that's needed bit by bit."

"Thank you so much. A rest certainly sounds extremely welcome! Oh by the way, can I ask your name?"

"Indeed you can. I was Charles when we last knew one another, so you might as well use that name."

"Thank you, Charles. A good solid name and monarchical, too — if that's a word."

\*\*\*

Goodness knows how long I was cared for in that beautiful temple, filled with loving beings who really empathised with what I'd been through, but time seems to have no meaning here and Charles was indeed true to his word and did reappear as soon as I felt better.

"Hullo, Craig. *Now* you look more like yourself! We're going to take things gradually, but I think it will be best to deal with the worst bit first. So let's head now for that golden temple over there. Your guardian angel is waiting for you, together with two other guides, Amanda, who was once a mother who loved you very much, and Keki, whom you last knew even longer ago and who is one of your soul mates."

"Greetings, Craig! It's good to see you again, even in such painful and difficult circumstances."

"Yes, Keki, it's an incredible surprise to meet you, after I'd been so sure that I was obliterating myself forever, and I'm feeling overwhelmed by all this undeserved Love that I'm being given."

"Love is never undeserved, since — apart from fear — it's the only thing that really exists. And fear is merely something that we're sometimes given the challenge of conquering. As Charles has already told you, you'll gradually be relearning all this, but now I'd like you to begin the process by imagining yourself in the shoes of the driver of that train. I know you were feeling too sorry for yourself to give any thought to him, but you do of course appreciate, don't you, that a train isn't just a machine?"

"Indeed, I didn't give any thought to that at all. Now I can see that it must have been just *terrible* for him! How can I ever be forgiven for that?"

"There's only *you* who can do the forgiving because there's no such thing as judgement over here. Life — our many, many lives — is all about learning and to help you with that I'll tell you now that the train driver's name is Frank and that he is suffering great trauma. His karma is no-one's business but his, but it's easy to imagine what it must have been like for him, isn't it? You're driving along your very familiar route, having just gone past Shrewsbury and heading ultimately for Cardiff, and then you suddenly see this figure and you know you haven't got time to stop. You instinctively slam on the brakes anyway, but you know that by the time the train *has* stopped there will be nothing but a dreadful mess that will somehow have to be cleared up."

"Yes, I see what you mean — ghastly! No wonder that my etheric body got shattered as well, as Charles explained to me, but it must have been almost as bad for everyone else — all the passengers, those who had to clear up the mess..."

"I'm interrupting you, Craig, because, as I said before, we need to look at it all one step at a time and right now we're thinking about Frank, the driver. He was taken straight to hospital in a bad state of shock; his wife was informed immediately so was able to go and visit him there. Fortunately both their children are adults and had already left home, but they, too, are being supportive and he's also getting help from a good psychotherapist."

"It's so awful that I can't bear to think about it! Is there *anything* I can do right now to put *myself* out of this agony of guilt? Will he *ever* be able to work again or is it the end of his useful career?"

"There is one thing you could do right now, if you can face it."

"I'm prepared to face *anything*!"

"Good for you! Then, since it's now night-time on Earth and Frank is therefore out of his body, would you like us to call for him to come and meet you?"

"I suppose that might be the best thing, painful though it would be!"

"Don't worry. We're preparing him for the meeting and telling him how full of remorse you are and that you want to apologise. Who knows? There might even be a way in which you could help him."

"I can't possibly imagine that!"

"Ah, here he comes. Your guardian angel is right behind, supporting you. Just feel her arms gently enveloping you. Frank, this is Craig whom you killed, *totally* not through your own fault. You can see that he's now alive and well and keen to apologise for his thoughtless action." [Craig bursts into tears.]

"Oh Frank, I can't begin to tell you how sorry I am." [Sob, sob.] "It was unbelievably selfish of me not to have stopped to think about what it would have been like for *you*! Now I just can't bear it, but it's too late to go back and start over again in that body that no longer exists."

"Well, all I can say, Craig, is that you must have been incredibly desperate to end your life in *any* way, let alone in such a thoughtless one. I've been shown how I've cleared a bit of my karma by what happened, but I still need to work out what I need to do next — whether I'll ever be able to face getting into a train driver's seat again. I'm only 54, my wife and I still have a mortgage to pay off and my compassionate leave will soon run out. What's going to happen to *you*? I've been told over here that suicides always have to return to Earth and cope better in at least equally difficult circumstances."

"Don't worry about *me*! My future lives will be decided upon later, all in good time. Your decision as to whether to go back to work is much more urgent."

"That's great, Craig," intervened Keki. "Now you really *are* feeling compassion and putting yourself into Frank's shoes. I think you may well be in a position to give him some good advice." [Craig's tears stop flowing.]

"I can't imagine myself ever being able to help *anyone*! But Frank, I'm just thinking what a lucky man you are to have a skill and a useful qualification. So many people need to use trains, even if they have their own transport. I used that line you were working on countless times, particularly when Jean and I were both in Chester, and my parents often went to Hereford by train to visit their parents, as they found it less trouble than going by car. *My* trouble in that last life was that I never had the guts to stick at anything for long enough. I blamed my parents a lot for not encouraging me to find my own personal path rather than looking down on me for not following my sister to university, but now I can see that I could have made more effort to stand up to their criticism. Most little boys go through a phase of thinking 'I'd like to be a train driver when I grow up' (I was certainly one of them), but you went ahead and actually *did* it! I really admire you for that."

"You're undoubtedly right about that, Craig. I never really wanted to do anything else from the time when I was about six."

"So why give it up now then? The railways have been going through a tough time in recent years — especially with this b***** government (forgive my French!) — so people as dedicated as you are must surely be rare treasures."

"Hmm… Thanks! You've certainly given me something to think about… I'm sorry about your parents not having encouraged you. Mine were brilliant in that way."

"Well said, Craig," intervened Amanda, speaking for the first time. "Now just look who's coming to join us!"

"Goodness, it's my *whole* family. I can't believe it… wife, children, both sets of parents, my sister Jo… and they're all weeping. I thought they'd all be relieved to have got rid of me!" [Craig bursts into tears again.]

"Relieved?!" asked Jean. "What a ridiculous idea. We've all been sobbing our hearts out and the children have been so upset about losing their beloved dad (imperfect though he may have been) that they've been refusing to go to school. All I wanted to do was to teach you a lesson; it really never entered my head that you'd go to such extreme lengths."

"Daddy, Daddy!" shouted Toby and Rosie in unison. "We thought you'd died under a train, but here you are looking like your normal self. How can that possibly be?"

"Don't worry, kids," said Amanda. "I'll explain. You see, most people in England don't realise that our physical bodies are just a shell for the more important parts of us. You must have heard of the soul?"

"Yes," replied Toby, "they talk about it in religious education lessons, but I don't know that I've ever really believed in it. I find RE boring anyway and am glad I won't have to do it any more after the end of this year."

"Well, now here's your chance to learn about your soul. Just look back down at your bed in Grandma and Grandad's house and you'll see that your physical body is still lying on it sound asleep. Only when it's time to wake up will this bit of you that's talking to us here, which we might as well call your 'soul', re-enter it, ready to start a new day."

"Good Lord, that's incredible! Now I can't wait to go back to school and tell my friends that my dad isn't really dead at all because I met him in the night."

"Sadly, Toby, it isn't as simple as that," continued Amanda in a comforting tone. "You see, it's very rarely indeed that people remember what they did when they were out of their bodies during the night. If they did, it would be too confusing because souls go to Earth in order to *learn* and for the learning to be thorough they need to concentrate on it fully — just as you do in your maths lessons, don't you, even though you're really good at it?"

"That's true. I think maths is the next best thing to football — and that takes a lot of concentration too!"

"You're right. And Rosie's particularly good at art, just like your mum."

"Yes, I am and I think I'd like to be a teacher like her when I grow up. But that doesn't mean that I'm not good at maths as well, just because I'm a girl. I bet I could teach art *and* maths if I wanted to!"

"Of course you could, Rosie, and it's really good to be ambitious, but now I need to explain to all of you some of the things that your dad's been busy learning over here since he died. You see, even though he looks just the same to you and the rest of your family at the moment, his physical body really did die under that train and there won't be any escaping that sad fact when your own physical body wakes up again tomorrow morning. It will go on being hard because you'll still miss him, but gradually you'll come to understand that we all have lots and lots of lives on Earth and that, with each new one, we decide to learn a different thing. Loss is one of the toughest lessons but also one of the most important, because there's never any escaping it, and personal experience will enable you to be more compassionate and understanding of others who go through it as well. But now morning on your planet is fast approaching, so all of you had better give Craig a big hug, tell him that you'll always love him and then return fast to your physical bodies, remembering that you'll be able to meet him again whenever you want." [All eight of them do as they're told.]

"That's incredible!" exclaimed Craig. "I'd never have believed that they cared so much about me."

"So that's now another lesson and you'll be able to meet them again on future occasions, encourage your children to go on doing well at school, apologise to Jean about the mortgage payments, challenge your parents for not having accepted you as you were and so on. But right now I want us to turn our thoughts to at least some of the other people who were involved at the time of your death. At least, as you said, it was a pleasant day so they didn't have to endure rain, snow, or anything like that, but the next train from Ludlow was delayed by a full hour, which was extremely inconvenient for some of them. As just one example, a woman named Ann, who's in her eighties, missed her connection in Hereford and consequently got back to her husband in Malvern very late for lunch. You won't have any karma to pay her personally, as her only real concern was for you yourself and everyone closely involved, but as for all the passengers on the train, not to mention the railway staff who had to do the clearing up, it was, as you yourself noted, extremely traumatic. Some of them felt true compassion appreciating how desperate you must have been, but..."

"Yes," Craig interrupted, "I really can see now how selfish I was and have an immense desire to make amends to every single one of them. How can I possibly do that?"

"It probably won't be possible to do it all in a single lifetime, but don't worry: you still have eternity on your side and you'll be able to have as many more lives as you feel you want or need in order to pay those debts, but you could maybe, for instance, pay off one big chunk all at once by doing something really worthwhile such as becoming a counsellor or a psychotherapist for people suffering emotional difficulties."

"Perhaps I could specialise in potential suicide cases!"

"Indeed, anything is possible, but I do need to warn you that you will at some point have to face the same sort of challenges as you did as Craig and yet overcome them."

"That makes sense and I'm now feeling really glad that I was quite wrong about the question of total obliteration!"

"Hurray — you're already making excellent progress. And now here's an important point of which you may not be aware at the moment. We've been explaining to you over here that we all have many chances on Earth, but do you appreciate that we often reincarnate together with people we've known before? That can sometimes facilitate paying one's debts."

"So you mean, for instance, that Jean and I could marry again and have Toby and Rosie as our children once more, but with me making a much better job of fatherhood?"

"Precisely. The possibilities are endless, but no need to rush into anything immediately. Your family are still young, Jean might well remarry and the children will be learning an important lesson about loss. (Many children learn a bit about loss when a beloved pet dies, for instance. Losing a father is a much bigger challenge, but one that we all go through at some point.)"

"May I chip in now?" asked Keki, who had just reappeared. "I've been listening to the conversation and was particularly interested when Craig mentioned his idea of possibly one day becoming something like a psychotherapist. Well, with regard to the question of suicide, there's been a truly massive change in comparatively recent years. For centuries suicide was regarded as a 'sin' and people who'd taken their own lives were consequently not permitted burial in sacred ground. But then an eminent and very learned American psychologist named James Hillman had the courage to introduce into his profession the notion of the 'soul' as separate from the body and the mind and in so doing he stressed the importance of both compassion for and understanding of the person who had committed this previously so-called 'crime'. In his work he often treated people who were feeling suicidal and did his best to deter them from taking any final drastic action, but when his efforts failed he was never condemnatory of his patients."

"I suppose I could have gone to see someone like him at an earlier point in my life rather than taking the fateful measure I now so regret, but, to be honest, I got too desperate for it even to occur to me."

"Yes, Craig, and sadly you're by no means alone in failing to appreciate the fact that we're all part of a whole and that any action we take will inevitably affect others too. Now, however, that you've reached this good understanding about what you did, you should be strong enough another time to overcome the challenges you're given rather than being overwhelmed by them. James Hillman, whom I've just mentioned, actually died in 2011, but his influence (along with that of others such as Carl Gustav Jung) remains strong."

"I'm afraid all that is rather beyond my ken at the moment, Keki!"

"Don't worry: you can take as long as you like to digest just as much as you like. You won't be rushed straight into a new incarnation but will have plenty of time to think things over before making any big decisions."

"Talking of 'big decisions', I now have some good news for you…"

"Ah, I see it's Amanda come back!"

"Yes, Craig, and I'm here with Charles as well."

"Hullo, Charles. Good to see you again. So what's the good news?"

"Well, I'm very happy to tell you that, thanks to his psychotherapist and — I sincerely believe thanks also to the advice that you gave him — Frank is now about to resume his job as a train driver."

"That certainly *is* good news and I refuse to take any credit for it, but now I really am beginning to think that I might like to aim to become something like a psychotherapist myself another time."

"Wonderful!" echoed the three of them. "Now you deserve a bit of a holiday, or maybe you'd like to have a bit of time to explore some more around here. Your guardian angel is still right there behind you and will no doubt be more than happy to lead you wherever you fancy within the realms to which you currently have a passport."

"'Passport'?"

"Yes, Craig," replied the angel. "That's just a figure of speech. You see, there are numerous realms above that of Earth and as you're now busy relearning, people evolve at different rates, so the level to which anyone can aspire after they've left their most recent body depends very much upon how they spent the lifetime in which they were in it."

"That certainly makes sense. I don't suppose there'd be any chance of my being permitted to meet this great man James Hillman, or is that too much for someone 'so unworthy' to ask?"

"The word 'unworthy' is one that's banned over here! Although neither Jesus nor any of the other Masters ever used it, the Church (to use a broad term and to which you were probably fortunate, as Craig, not to have belonged) has spent far too long drumming that notion into people without any justification. James Hillman, on the other hand, although quite humble, *is* aware of his own worth and I'm sure that he'd be delighted to meet you."

"How can I thank you all enough?"

"Your future actions will be sufficient thanks," chipped in Charles. "Now we can wish you all the best until we meet again. Farewell for the time being."

"Farewell and let me give you each a hug."

# 9

# Purgatory for a Woman Composer

*From now on, would you be able to regard my music as if it were
your own? ... A husband and wife who are both composers: how
do you envisage that? Such a strange relationship between rivals:
do you have any idea how ridiculous it would appear, can you
imagine the loss of self-respect it would later cause us both ... One
thing is certain: if we are to be happy together, you will have to be
'as I need you', not my colleague, but my wife!*

Gustav Mahler (in a letter to his betrothed)

When Klarmann saw Alma lying in her coffin, 'her face ...
seemed to have the expression of somebody suspiciously
curious, as if she were trying to figure out just where she was'.

Hullo! My name in my last life was Alma. I was born and bred
in Vienna and was best known for my looks (at only 19 I was
renowned as that city's 'greatest beauty'), my high intelligence,
my interest in all the arts and for my three husbands (all of
whom were renowned in their different fields). Alas, I was less
known for my compositions, which were the most important
things to me. Like the majority of my compatriots, I was brought
up Catholic, but the Church let me down in the end, with its
nonsensical teaching about Purgatory, and for that reason I've
only recently emerged from what felt to me like a long spell
'there'. I put that last word in quotes because in fact Purgatory
isn't a place at all — any more than Hell is. They're both states
of mind into which one puts *oneself* while still on Earth. That's
why I'm keen to tell my story: in order to help others to avoid
making the mistakes that I did.

I was born on 31 August 1879. My parents, Emil Jacob Schindler and Anna Sofie Bergen, had had a very difficult start to their married life, as my beloved father, gifted and later renowned artist though he was, took a while to make a name for himself and they were consequently initially truly poverty-stricken. By 1886, however, he'd become so well recognised that Crown Prince Rudolph engaged him to make pen and ink drawings of the Dalmatian coast for a book about the Austrian monarchy that he was working on. Then, thanks to an advance from the banker Herman Herwitz, who commissioned a large picture 'of the south', he took our family, plus his student Carl Moll and a maid, on a wonderful journey of several months while he worked on the paintings.

In addition to that, there were various defining moments that had an immense impact on my entire life. The first of these was when, on 30 January 1889, the said Crown Prince, who was unhappily married, shot both himself and his 17-year-old mistress, Maria Vetsera, in an apparent suicide pact. Even at that tender age of nine I was influenced by the tremors that were sweeping through the Empire and as time went on I witnessed its dying days and final collapse.

Both my parents were musical and it was in fact while singing together in the semi-professional production of a comic opera that they had fallen in love. Yet, gradually picking up on her infidelities, I always believed my father's love to be more genuine than my mother's. For although my younger sister Margarete (Grete or Gretl) and I were always close, I eventually became aware that she'd been conceived while my father was away sick. He nevertheless lovingly accepted this second daughter as his own and always doted on both of us. Later my mother had an affair with Carl Moll, whom I always disliked, and she eventually married him after my father's death at the age of 50, when I was only 13. I was totally unable to recover from that loss. Unlike my mother, my father had understood me. I *adored* him and it was from him that I learnt, simply from watching him work, an enormous amount about the creative process. So from that, too, sprang my quite early desire to encourage anyone whose talent — for whatever it was — I admired.

But music was always my greatest passion and I started composing when I was only nine. In that I was helped while we were in Corfu in January 1888 at the end of Father's wonderful painting trip. We were housed in a stone villa on a hill with views of both the Adriatic and the Ionian seas, and a pianino was sent up from the town especially for me to play on. By the age of 15 I'd become an accomplished pianist, putting in long hours of practice at the same time as producing two or three compositions a week. Later I firstly took lessons from Josef Labor and secondly from Alexander von Zemlinsky, who taught me composition. Labor was amazing: blind, yet he taught me counterpoint, and at one point he told me that he thought my works were better than those of the French composer Cécile Chaminade, who was then beginning to make a name for herself.

From an early age I riled at the fact that girls, unlike boys, were not automatically given an education. Gretl and I had to make do with a series of governesses, some much less satisfactory than others. I never for a moment wished that I'd been born male — I revelled too much in my seductive beauty and femininity to do that — but it really angered me that girls weren't expected to achieve intellectually or to be as good at composition as their male counterparts. I wanted to learn everything about *everything* and was furious with my mother when, after dear Father had introduced the two of us girls to Goethe's *Faust*, she confiscated the book as "unsuitable for girls of our age".

Throughout my teenage years I could never get enough music. I went to the opera a couple of times a week and, like just about everyone else at that time, went absolutely crazy over

Wagner. But I was fanatically interested in art as well, and it was Gustav Klimt who first caused my emotional and sexual awakening. I met him through my stepfather, with whom he was the co-founder of the Viennese Secession, which was so prominent in the cultural scene of the time. Had I not been more wary, since I knew his morals to be of a much lower calibre than his art, he would undoubtedly have succeeded in seducing me. His kisses were tantalisingly delicious, but I was fully aware that he was already in a well-established liaison and consequently determined not to succumb further to his advances.

In actual fact I came closer to losing my virginity with Zemlinsky. We met at a Viennese dinner party in February 1900 and he fell madly in love with me. For me, however, it was far from being instantaneous, as initially I found him extremely unattractive, and what's more (snob that I was!), I despised his lowly background. I admired his intellect and talent, however, and after he'd started coming regularly to my stepfather's house to give me the composition lessons, I gradually began to feel that I'd really love to have children with him. Yet something — I didn't know at the time what it was — always held me back from giving myself fully to him. The somewhat stormy relationship carried on for about a couple of years, with Alexander's frustration growing ever deeper. But then, on 7 November 1901, at a friend's house, I met another well-known conductor and composer, Gustav Mahler. He also fell instantly in love with me and made a proposition of marriage only three weeks later! Hurting Alexander was hard, but I knew that I had to do it, despite my family's opposition to my marrying a man who was 19 years my senior and, to boot, known to be in ill health.

Now that I've so thankfully emerged from Purgatory and the Church's brainwashing against reincarnation and karma, my guides have helped me to see many of the things that lay behind it all. Zemlinsky, to start with, had a karmic debt to me.

Its nature is purely his business and so not for me to tell, but I *can* say that he paid it in full through what he taught me in composition, his faith in my abilities and his encouragement, all of which I still appreciated even after I'd broken his heart. With Gustav, on the other hand, it was quite different: the debt was mine to *him* and I alas failed to pay it. The moment we met he subconsciously recognised me as a daughter he'd once had and who'd neglected him in widowhood, running off to a distant country with a man she'd fallen for. (Don't worry, though! Gustav and I have recently met over here and had a good discussion about how it all might be rectified in a future life.)

Before all this occurred, however, I had to get over losing my father, which, as I mentioned previously, I totally failed to do. At 19 I believed myself to be living among strangers and was convinced that if only the great Emil Schindler had still been there, he would really have understood me, and that to him alone I could have spoken my mind. Sigmund Freud put his finger on it precisely when he diagnosed the main problem between me and my first husband as being for me the loss of my father and in his case the absence of a proper mother. For the poor woman bore 14 children and so obviously never had time or energy to spare, and her husband, Bernhard, was very brutal to all his family. Gustav was the eldest, the first child having died, and only another six survived infancy.

Gustav was 29 when his mother died, very shortly after the deaths of both his father and his sister Leopoldine, and this left him with responsibility for the care of his four surviving younger siblings, whom he installed in a flat in Vienna. Bernhard had, however, supported his eldest son's musical ambitions and agreed to his applying for a place at the Vienna Conservatory. By the time we met, Gustav was already highly reputed, mainly as a conductor, but also for his compositions.

After we'd both met Freud, Gustav did better than I did, as he continued to have sessions with him, and Freud further pointed out to him that a big difficulty in our relationship was caused by Gustav's refusal to permit me to continue with my composing. Anyone reading this in the twenty-first century would wonder (as I indeed do now) at my failure to assert myself in the matter, but that of course was what wives were expected to do in those days. So, rather than seeking more therapy, I just let my frustration and anger simmer deep down, and this was undoubtedly one of the big factors that caused my descent into the purgatory that carried on as Purgatory after the death of my physical body.

Anyway, Freud's injunctions caused Gustav to come home and take a serious look at some of my work and — to his own surprise — he was impressed. (Incidentally, when I first got to know him, while admiring his skills as a conductor and envying his reputation, I didn't actually like his music very much, but it gradually grew on me later!) His being impressed led him to make some efforts to get some of my works published, which did of course please me, but when he tried to encourage me to compose more, this deepened my repressed anger further, as I felt that at that point it was "too late". This in turn did nothing to improve our relationship, and then, I'm very sorry to say, I hurt him deeply by embarking on an affair with the architect Walter Gropius.

Some of my works got lost during the two world wars, and nowadays people who take an interest in me as a composer are disappointed when they discover that all that remains on Earth are 16 of my beautiful songs. Now, however, that I've finally come out of Purgatory, I've been happy to learn that *nothing* is ever really lost; everything remains in the ether and can be found in what are known as the 'Akashic Records'. So I'm now starting to listen to all my compositions one by one. The good thing, too, is that there's no shortage over here of great performers who are delighted to either sing or play any works that one wants to hear. What has yet to be worked out is how to get the lost works back to Earth, but remember that (if this were deemed to be desirable) we have the rest of eternity on our side!

In the meantime, if you happen to be a true music lover, *do* seek out the recording of my 16 surviving songs. You will find — in some of them anyway, I feel — a very deep expression of *Love*. What you won't observe from them, however, is what I've only recently become aware of myself: the fact that my constant need of, as well as dependence upon, love given to me from *others* stemmed from my inability to find the love that I craved inside *myself*. I'm by no means alone in that, since many people find self-love the hardest thing, but I'm now being taught how important it is. (In my case there are past-life reasons for this as well, but I won't trouble you with those details.) Were I to decide to return very soon, I would very likely seek the help of a Jungian (rather than a Freudian!) therapist, but right now I feel a need to spend more time over here discussing with my guides and working out how best to clear some more, if not all, of my karma.

Another thing I'm renowned for is the tragic loss of three of my four children. My first two daughters were Gustav's. When Maria, the eldest, was born, I suffered so intensely with the labour and so on that I found it difficult to bond with her. Gustav, on the other hand, was absolutely devoted to the child right from the start and from when she was quite small he used to take her up into his composing hut with him. Her death from scarlet fever at only four really shattered him. (Anna, our second daughter, caught the disease, too, but survived. She grew up to be a successful sculptor, and I was proud of that of course and loved her dearly, yet our relationship was never an easy one.) So another of the problems was that I imagined that I had, in a way, caused Maria's death, on account of my great neediness and the consequent jealousy I felt over Gustav's intense love for her. But now that I've emerged from Purgatory and have started seriously on the learning that's available here, I'm assured that

Maria's early death was part of both her and her father's life plans. Now, I'm very glad to say, the two of them have naturally been happily reunited.

Gustav, who had never had good health, died in 1911, and my third daughter, Manon, was born after Walter Gropius and I had finally married. This was in 1915, after he'd been drafted into the military for World War I, because his guilt over the affair we'd had during my first marriage initially prevented our coming together again once I was free. Then I had a three-year, tumultuous affair with the renowned artist Oskar Kokoschka. We were mutually obsessed with one another and even after I finally thought that I'd 'got him out of my system' I ran into him occasionally over subsequent years, and each time it yet again caused me certain agonies. He of course famously painted my portrait, though I feel it resembles me very little. If there are women among you who believe that exceptional physical beauty is enviable, forget it! For someone like me, so dependent upon receiving love from others and at the same time always convinced of my ability to seduce *any* man, it was undoubtedly one of my biggest downfalls. The marriage to Walter was ever a difficult one, what with the inevitable periods of separation, and he requested a divorce in 1918 after finding out about my affair with the great writer Franz Werfel.

By now you must be thinking "What a crazy mixed-up kid!" and you're quite right of course, but what I'm learning now (and what you'll learn next time you return Home, if you haven't already) is that we *all* have incarnations which aren't totally successful. The *good* things about it all, though, are firstly that that is how we learn and secondly that, when we return Home in between lives, we find that — contrary to Church teaching — there's no judgement at all on the other side, but just Love and acceptance. It's really wonderful!

Anyway, going back to Manon: after we'd separated, I used to take her regularly to see her father (and in due course his new wife). She was the *sweetest* child. Everybody loved her and she had an extraordinary affinity with animals, which was really touching. Her one aspiration as she was growing up was to be an actress, but that was not to be. She caught poliomyelitis and sadly died at only 18. I was truly heartbroken! But guess what: it was she who was the main person who helped me finally to emerge from Purgatory to one of the lower levels of 'Heaven'. Can you imagine my joy at seeing her again after having given up all hope of it? Of course prayers from Earth sent up for the 'repose' of my soul (that's a laugh!) also helped — they always do — but it was the sight of my darling Manon that really made me take the first step, and now we're having a lot of fun together. She's enjoying listening to my compositions as well as doing some acting. I'm sure she *will* achieve that as a career in her next incarnation, which she's already beginning to plan.

Oh, now you'll never guess who I ran into just the other day. (That's purely figurative, as of course days and nights don't exist here as they do on Earth.) On second thoughts you might guess, because the two of us have an obvious affinity, although she was German rather than Austrian and died when I was only a teenager. Clara Schumann! The big similarity between us is that her husband Robert — now, like my Gustav, recognised as one of the great composers — also forbade her to continue composing as soon as they'd married. The two of us had a lovely long conversation and my admiration for her is *immense*. For one thing she was already a renowned concert pianist when Robert first fell in love with her, and for another, she remained totally faithful to him even during the last two years of his life, which he spent in an asylum on account of his mental health problems, as well as after his death. She bore him *eight* children! Sadly one of them died very young, and he never met little Felix, who was born after he'd been committed to the asylum and who only lived to be 25, but she's told me that, despite his multitudinous difficulties, Robert absolutely doted on his children and was a really wonderful father.

How she coped with all those pregnancies and births at the same time as continuing with her concert tours is to me quite unimaginable! Of course she did latterly receive a lot of help with the children from dear Johannes Brahms, who was madly in love with her and whom she both encouraged and advised with his compositions, but she never agreed to having a sexual relationship with him, which I'm sure *I* would have done if I'd been in her position.

In fact both Robert and Clara (who, it appears, are twin souls) have each returned to Earth once in the interim, but not together. His purpose that time was mainly to work on his mental problems, while hers was to have a well-earned rest with a comparatively cushy life. She married a companion soul mate, who supported her financially, and had just two children and plenty of time to simply listen to music without all the work of making it. Since then they've come together again on this side and she's told me that they're now planning another musical life together, each the same gender again, but this time they'll use birth control and he *will* support her as a composer. In fact she's even suggested that, now that the climate on Earth has become much better for female composers, I might also like to join forces with them somehow and take up composing as a full-time career. I think that's a great idea!

But now I thought I'd change the subject completely and make another confession. Vienna when I lived there as Alma was quite a hotspot of Judaism. Both my first and my third husbands came from Jewish backgrounds, and Gustav had to convert to Catholicism in order to secure his conducting position. (Isn't that *absurd*?) Anyway, anti-Semitism was also quite rife there at the time, and I'm ashamed to say that I, too, quite often succumbed to making remarks that I now regret. My darling Franz Werfel got a bit confused between the Judaism of his birth and Christianity, with which he also got involved, but I now see that as a *good* thing, as it made him a genuinely spiritual person. Because of course I have a better view over here and so can see clearly that all human beings are equal — all one in the Lord — and that where we are on the ladder just depends upon our previous experiences. (If, by the way, you feel like asking whether, in view of my more or less Christian upbringing, I've seen Jesus yet, the answer is "No". That's simply because His light is too strong for me right now, but hopefully I have a good chance of getting 'there' in the not-too-distant future.)

You'll appreciate that I lived through both the world wars. At least, though, I never for one moment supported the Holocaust, but I really don't want to mention any Nazi connections because it's all too horribly close to the bone. What I will say, however, is how thankful I feel to have escaped Hell! Hell, just like Purgatory, does *not* last forever, but I have been told that, for some full-blown Nazis who carried on with their hatred of Jews even after they'd died, escape can take a very long time. And such people *do* need a lot of prayers, so please, please remember that. Thank you!

Maybe you're now wondering: "What about your third husband, Franz Werfel, and the other child you lost?" Well, obviously they're both extremely important, too. When I first met Franz, who, in total contrast to Gustav, was rather younger than me, I didn't find him at all attractive, even though I'd already liked one of his poems so much that I'd set it to music. He, however, quickly fell in love with me, and I gradually got completely potty about both him and his writing and gave him a great deal of encouragement with it. Our son Martin was conceived while I was still married to Walter, so there was guilt again on my part. In fact I didn't know until after he was born, when the resemblance was unmistakable, which of them was the father.

I didn't agree to marriage with Franz for quite a while, and the relationship (typically!) was often stormy despite the real love between us, but it lasted the longest of my marriages — 16 years, until his death from heart failure in 1945. Sadly, poor little Martin was never healthy and only lived for a few months, but dear Manon brought him to see both Franz and me (yes, we two have of course already met up and started exploring the karma between us!) and he's now growing up quite adorably and will return to Earth once he's had the chance to enjoy some more childhood over here. Who knows? He might be either a writer or a musician next time round! It's exciting really to think about the endless possibilities open to all of us.

As for Werfel himself, his writing was so successful that I don't really need to say any more about him. Anyone interested can easily look him up for themselves. (It's 'Google', isn't it, that you down there in the twenty-first century use a great deal?) Plus I've gone on for so long with my story and I know that there are others waiting in the wings to tell theirs. But I do need to say that, because of the Nazis (who burnt his books), we were forced to escape to France in 1938, where we lived at first in a fishing village near Marseille and then, after the German invasion of that country, went to Lourdes, staying for just five weeks before finally reaching safety in the United States. (Hence his famous *Song of Bernadette*.)

I don't want to dwell at length on our time in America either, particularly not my final 19 years, during which I went completely to pieces following Franz's death from heart disease in 1945. That took place before full realisation had dawned about the full dangers of cigarettes, to which poor Franz was addicted. Of course addiction is a very common human failing, whether it be to smoking, drugs, alcohol, chocolate, or work. I was addicted to Benedictine, which is a green-coloured, very strong liqueur made by Benedictine monks in France. A little bit of it just now and again is fine, but I drank enormous quantities of it and frequently. Life on Earth wouldn't be worth living if we didn't have certain pleasures, but everyone needs to learn restraint and find a balance.

Another thing that I was addicted to was *people!* Mine was a very exceptional life, in that I was constantly surrounded by eminent artists of every possible nature — and these huge social circles continued once we'd got to America, both in our homes in Beverly Hills and in New York — but my problem was my dependence upon them, my difficulty in being alone. I lived in such a constant whirl of activity that it's a wonder really that that body survived for 86 years. But I think a big part of my delay in hastening towards death, even during the time when I couldn't believe that I could possibly carry on without Franz, was caused by fear of what might lie ahead. I was desperate to see him again (as well as so many of the most important people who'd gone on before me, such as my father and Gustav), but I couldn't be sure that they *would* be waiting there for me, and the mere thought of death anyway filled me with fear. I know I was far from alone in that, which makes a book like this seem important to me.

I did go back to Vienna, by the way — in 1947, when being there was such a Hell as I don't want to begin to describe — and then I returned to California in 1948 before settling back in my New York apartment in 1951. I did also make a few other trips back to Europe (I haven't even mentioned that I once owned a house in Venice, where Franz and I had some blissful times together), but, though my request to be buried next to Manon in Vienna's Grinzing Cemetery was granted, I couldn't face visiting it again while I was still alive.

I bought Anna and her daughter Marina (my only grandchild) a little house in Beverly Glen, near to the University, where Anna taught sculpture, but since Anna married five times I obviously hadn't given her a perfect example in relationships! Just as my only surviving daughter both adored and hated me, my granddaughter, I think, thought I was jealous of her mother's great love for her.

I finally died in my New York apartment after having had some strokes and much general ill health. You will by now have gathered what a complex character I was and, as Professor Adolf Klarmann, the Pole who worked mainly on Werfel's writings in the University of Pennsylvania, accurately commented when he saw my body in its coffin, "I was trying to figure out just where I was." Yet I wrote a lot as well during my 86 years and though not all of it was successful by any means, I can still stand by these words of mine: "God gave me to know the works of genius in our time before they left the hands of their creators. And if for a while I was able to hold the stirrups of those horsemen of light, my being has been justified and blessed." Now all that remains is for me to return to Earth a few more times, carrying with me what I've learnt over here in the interim.

# 10

# A Pioneering Tennis Player

*The loser is always a part of the problem; the winner is always a part of the answer. The loser always has an excuse; the winner always has a program. The loser says it may be possible, but it's difficult; the winner says it may be difficult, but it's possible.*

Althea Gibson, 1991

My name in my last life was Althea Gibson, and that incarnation was a particularly challenging one but nevertheless successful overall, I feel. I was born on 25 August 1927, in the town of Silver in racist South Carolina. My parents, Daniel and Annie Bell Gibson, worked as sharecroppers on a cotton farm, but the Great Depression hit rural southern farmers sooner than much of the rest of the country and so in 1930 our family moved to Harlem, where my three sisters and a brother were all born. I dropped out of school at only 13 and then, using the boxing skills that my father taught me, engaged in a life of what one can only term as street fighting, girls' basketball and watching movies. In addition to that, my father's behaviour was so violent that I was for some time forced to live in a Catholic protective shelter for abused children. I expect you can at least *imagine* how tough that was for a teenager!

My salvation was the fact that a stretch of 143rd Street, where we lived, had been designated as a Police Athletic League play area. This meant that, during daylight hours, it was barricaded in order to enable the children of the neighbourhood to play organised sports. Even at the age of 12, before I'd left school, I was the New York City women's paddle tennis champion. Then, in 1940, a group of my neighbours took up a collection to finance me for a junior membership and lessons at the

Cosmopolitan Tennis Club in the Sugar Hill section of Harlem. I didn't actually like tennis at first, feeling that it was a game for weak people. Because of my upbringing, I suppose, I kept wanting to fight the other player every time I started to lose a match! But gradually I got the right idea and, in 1941, entered and won my first tournament, the American Tennis Association (ATA) New York State Championship. After that I won the ATA national championship in the girls' division in both 1944 and 1945. I lost in the 1946 women's final but then won my first of ten straight national ATA women's titles in 1947.

I knew that, through the grace of God, I was an unusual, talented girl. I didn't need to prove that to myself. I only wanted to prove it to my opponents, none of whom of course expected a black girl to excel in anything. Now that I've returned Home for a while, I've been shown (among many other things) my life plan as Althea and it's clear that I'd volunteered to be a pioneer for black people in the field of sport. It wasn't until 1968 that Arthur Ashe, the first black *male* tennis champion, made his first win. He was born in Virginia in 1943 and won three grand slams, which was a great achievement, but he sadly died when he was only 50. More recently the amazing Williams sisters have both spoken of their debt to me. And Billie Jean King, who'd previously commented that my road to success was a challenging one and said "I never saw her back down", very kindly once organised a collection to help me out when I was on the verge of bankruptcy.

With Billie Jean the respect was and is mutual, as she suffered discrimination on account of being gay, and I have no doubt that she, too, was an inspiration to the great Martina Navratilova, who has been open about her lesbianism ever since 1981. Prejudice of all sorts is, sadly, a very common failing in the human race. Like sexism, racism has a long history, and in the latter case it dates back at least to the slave trade, my own ancestors having of course been taken from Africa to the 'New

World'. There we blacks owe a debt to, among others, Equiano, whose story I understand will be coming later in this book.

Thank goodness that I can now safely say that there have been some real improvements since I died in 2003. The USA actually getting an African-American president was a massive advance and, in addition to Barack Obama's superb books, his lovely wife Michelle has also written her autobiography, *The Light We Carry*. I love the bit in it about her own mother, who moved into the White House with them in order to help with the care of their two young daughters but who, while agreeing to be interviewed, insisted that neither she herself, nor her daughter Michelle and son Craig was anything special. "We're just", says Michelle, "two kids who had enough love and a good amount of luck to do well as a result." One big tragedy for America was Obama being succeeded by someone very different, but he's neither young nor immortal, and our blessed country now at least has a non-white vice-president.

So you can see that, while enjoying the Love and the learning in which I'm being bathed over here, I can still retain an interested eye on what's going on back on Earth. In fact I'm currently acting as a guide to one of my nieces, but I wouldn't want that to be widely broadcast, as it's nobody's business apart from hers and mine. I'm also beginning to think a bit about my next incarnation, when I might well decide to focus on one of my other talents rather than being mainly in the sporting world again.

Going back for a moment, though, to Billie Jean and Martina with their sexuality, another important pioneer was the renowned Irish poet and playwright Oscar Wilde. After separating from his wife and two sons, that poor man was accused of 'gross indecency with other men' and sentenced to two years of hard labour in prison, so he consequently suffered even more than some of us blacks did. Later, while in exile in France (fortunately he was very highly educated and spoke fluent French), he wrote the celebrated 'Ballad of Reading Gaol'. Initially published under the pseudonym 'C.3.3', standing for 'Cell block C, landing 3, cell 3', it wasn't until the seventh edition was printed that the 'notorious' Wilde was named as its author, and from this poem he drew a small income for the rest of his comparatively short life. He sadly died from meningitis in 1900 and the long, passionate letter written in 1897 from Reading Gaol to his lover, Lord Alfred Douglas, was published posthumously in 1905. So nowadays gay people in America and Europe can read his works and feel thankful for the few improvements that have been made in discrimination. I was, however, appalled to hear recently that the present Archbishop of Canterbury had affirmed the 1998 declaration that same-sex relationships were a sin!

Now you're perhaps wondering whether I'm going to tell you more about my career as Althea. Well, I won a grand total of 11 Grand Slam tournaments, which were made up of five singles, five doubles and one mixed doubles titles, the first being the French in 1956. The following year I won both Wimbledon and the US Nationals (precursor of the US Open), then I won both again in 1958 and was voted Female Athlete of the Year by the Associated Press in both those years. There were other accolades besides, but I'm not really wanting or needing to blow my own trumpet, and anyone who's particularly interested can easily look me up for themselves. Yes, my family were all proud of me, including my somewhat violent father, who, to be fair, had had violence inflicted on him by the white cotton traders.

In 1946 I moved to Wilmington in North Carolina, under the generous sponsorship of the physician and tennis activist Hubert A. Eaton. There I got enrolled at the racially segregated Williston Industrial High School. I riled inwardly of course at the segregation, but at least I acquired some of the education I'd missed out on in Harlem. Despite my great success in tennis, a big problem for me, however, was that, prior to the Open Era, there was no prize money at major tournaments, and direct endorsement deals were prohibited. Players were limited to meagre expense allowances, strictly regulated by the United States Tennis Association (USTA). So the truth, to put it bluntly, is that my finances were ever in heartbreaking shape. Being the Queen of Tennis is all well and good, but you can't eat a crown! Nor can you send the Internal Revenue Service a throne clipped to their tax forms. You see, professional tours for women were then still 15 years away, so my opportunities were largely limited to promotional events. In 1959 I signed a contract to play a series of exhibition matches against Karol Fageros, in which I won the singles and doubles titles at the Pepsi Cola World Pro Tennis Championships in Cleveland, but when the tour ended I received a mere $500 in prize money.

I've already mentioned, though, that I had other talents. Since most sportswomen and men confine themselves to a single field, you might be surprised to learn that I was also fairly successful as a golfer. Well, I was the first African-American woman to join the Ladies Professional Golf Association (LPGA), but I did so a bit late, in 1964, at the age of 37, and my lifetime earnings in that field never exceeded $25,000. Racial discrimination continued to be a problem there, too, since many hotels still excluded people of colour and country club officials throughout the south, and even some in the north, routinely refused to allow me to compete. Besides that, I was often banned from the clubhouse and so was forced to change my clothes in the car. I trust this makes you shudder, as it still does me when I look back upon it!

I said earlier that I didn't want to blow my own trumpet. I did, however, blow a saxophone — and rather well. I was also an accomplished singer and, in 1943, was runner-up in the Apollo Theater's amateur talent contest. Later, in 1957, my aspirations were realised still further when I made my professional singing début at W. C. Handy's eighty-fourth birthday tribute in the Waldorf Hotel. (For those who aren't in the know about such things, he was an American composer and musician who referred to himself as the 'Father of the Blues'.) I found music-making a very enjoyable contrast to the world of sport, although I did also enjoy my time spent working as a sports commentator.

Where I was less successful was in relationships. In 1953 I took a job teaching physical education at Lincoln University in Jefferson City, Missouri, and during those two years I got romantically involved with an army officer and even considered enlisting in the Women's Army Corps. I decided against it, however, when, in 1955, the State Department sent me on a goodwill tour of Asia to play exhibition matches with Ham Richardson, Bob Perry, and Karol Fageros. Many Asians in the countries we visited — Burma (as it then was), Sri Lanka, India, Pakistan, and Thailand — felt an affinity to me as a woman of colour and were delighted to see me as part of an official US delegation. As the United States grappled with the question of race, they turned to me for answers, or at least to get a firsthand perspective and for my own part it strengthened my confidence immeasurably. So that tour saw the end of my love affair and when the six weeks were over I remained abroad for a while and won 16 out of 18 tournaments in Europe and Asia, playing against many of the world's best players.

In 1965 I married the brother of my best friend, Rosemary Darben, and his income helped by supplementing the proceeds of my various sponsorship deals, but we divorced in 1976, and my second marriage in 1983 to the tennis coach Sydney Llewellyn lasted only five years. So it's as well that having children hadn't been part of my life plan and here in the Bardo I've made peace with all three of those former partners.

My final years on Earth as Althea were far from easy health-wise. In the late 1980s I suffered two cerebral haemorrhages and then I had a stroke in 1992. The medical expenses were of course horrendous, but after I'd had no response to the multiple requests I'd sent to tennis organisations, my wonderful former doubles partner, Angela Buxton, made my plight known to the worldwide tennis community and raised almost $1 million! I'm eternally grateful to her and to all the donors. I survived a heart attack in 2003 but died in September of the same year from complications following respiratory and bladder infections. Painful of course, but I know that many people suffer worse, and release from that body was truly blissful. I was buried in the Rosedale Cemetery in Orange, New Jersey, next to my first husband.

Who — interestingly — was one of the first people to greet me here on the other side, after I'd been taken through my life review with a couple of my guides and then escorted by my guardian angel for a spell in a 'heavenly hospital'. Nothing I encountered was totally unexpected, since I'd always been a believer of sorts, even though Catholicism hadn't rubbed off on me very much during the 'life-saving time' in my teenage years, when I was taken off the streets into a Catholic protective centre for abused children. Christianity was anyway pretty much forced onto our ancestors who'd been taken as slaves from West Africa to the plantations, raising crops such as cotton and sugar. (What an irony!) A thing that I've only learnt since returning Home, however, is that those same ancestors took the fact of reincarnation for granted, until the Christian missionaries 'disillusioned' them of their 'ungodly' beliefs.

Looking back on that life now, I feel truly able to rejoice in the fact that my legacy lives on, not only in the stadiums of professional tournaments but also in schools and parks throughout the American nation. It's said that "every time a black, Hispanic, or Islamic child picks up a tennis racket for the first time, Althea touches another life". Now I'm happy to know that whereas, when I began playing, less than 5 per cent of tennis newcomers were from minority backgrounds, today it's some 30 per cent, with two thirds of them being African-American.

I can't say that I envy the Open Era champions their ridiculously large incomes. Yes, for us, their predecessors, the low pay was challenging, but it's always through challenges that we learn and grow. At least the 'mighty Roger' (many still regard Federer as '*the* one-time great') has been tremendously generous with his earnings and now that he's recently retired I wish him the very best should he decide to become a commentator in this most enjoyable sport. So, it remains only for me to urge you readers on Earth to continue with the battle against discrimination of any sort.

# 11

# An Atheistic Philosopher

*Three passions, simple but overwhelmingly strong, have governed my life: the longing for love, the search for knowledge, and unbearable pity for the suffering...*

Bertrand Russell

In the early 1960s, a very left-wing Dominican named Father Matthew Rigby ran a weekly study group for interested members of the Bristol University Catholic Society. At one of these meetings he commented to the small group of students gathered around him: "I think Bertrand Russell is a wonderful man and when he dies I believe he'll go *straight* to Heaven. And by God he'll get a massive shock when he meets the Almighty face to face!"

Well, this good priest was both right and wrong. He was wrong in that, when people die, they each find what they'd expected to find and so I, as a long-time atheist, did indeed initially find *nothing at all*; that is, I was in a total, as it were, void, completely unconscious. Where 'Father Matt', as those Bristol students liked to call him, was right is that, since the only thing that really exists is *Love*, his 'Almighty' doesn't permit any soul who's crossed over to remain unconscious *forever*. I was blessed — I can say this now, though would never have done so in that lifetime! — with friends and relatives who were 'believers'. These good people really cared about me and consequently prayed hard for the "repose" of my "soul". (They'll find out in due course that all the in-between life phases are in fact much more interesting than pure rest would be!)

Since time has no meaning over here, I can't say at all how long it was before I 'woke up'. What I can say, though, is that it was a rather slow process — not the 'immediate encounter with the Almighty' that Matt had imagined to himself. First of all I heard a gentle voice calling my name. It turned out to be that of my father, John Russell (Viscount Amberley), who had been a British politician and writer, and died before I was even four years old. I'd naturally remembered little about him but had gathered later that he'd perished from bronchitis following a long period of depression. (His depression was understandable, since my mother had died of diphtheria when I was two, and my older sister, Rachel, had followed her to the grave not long afterwards.) He took a while to make me register his voice, so reluctant was I to believe that I hadn't ceased to exist, but he persevered with an apology for having "abandoned" me when I'd been so young.

This was hard for even a Taurus like myself to resist! (You probably know that those born under the sign of Taurus often have a tendency to stubbornness.) So eventually I opened my eyes and was totally amazed to see not only the Viscount but also my mother Katharine, both of whom I recognised from the photographs that had adorned my childhood home, Pembroke Lodge in Richmond Park. Then she spoke too.

"Darling Bertrand, I know well how hard it was for you and Frank to have to grow up with grandparents rather than with your dear father and me, but it was the destiny of each one of us and had you had the comfortable and easy early life that we would have endeavoured to give all our children, you doubtless wouldn't have achieved the great things that you did. Now that you're waking up to the reality of there being no such thing as death, let me tell you how proud we've felt as we've watched over you throughout these long years."

"Yes," chipped in my father, "of course it was tough, but occasional very tough lives serve to strengthen us, and so you will probably now deserve an easier one next time round.

Besides, my own parents really did do their level best for you. Don't you agree?"

"Agree! I think I'm a bit too flummoxed at the moment to either agree or disagree with *anything*."

"Of course everything's bound to be a bit confusing right now, but don't worry: you have plenty of time on your hands and you'll gradually meet lots of souls whom you'll remember, not only from the life you've recently completed as the renowned philosopher and mathematician but also from previous lives."

"*Previous* lives! Now Father — is that the right thing to call you? — you surely can't expect me to swallow *that*. It's only Buddhists and Hindus who have that strange notion..."

"I think you called him 'Papa' when you were little," interjected my mother, "but don't worry about reincarnation at the moment either. That's another thing you'll re-remember little by little, and you'll find doing so very interesting as well as helpful for your future."

"Yes, I did like you and Frank (Rachel, too, of course) calling me 'Papa', as it felt less formal than 'Father'. Ah, but here comes your guardian angel, accompanied by a beautiful woman whom I take to be one of your guides..."

"Yes, your father's quite right. I'm Priya, the wife you loved greatly in an Indian life, and I've been your main guide throughout your lifetime as Bertrand. I fully appreciate that you've just had quite a shock — that's a hundred per cent normal for atheists when they first wake up — but, as your good parents have been saying, you have plenty of time to re-remember what our true Home is like, and discovering all that will bring you much joy. Besides, almost 98 was a great age to which to live on Earth, the influenza that finally caused the end of your life took a lot out of you and you must now be tired. So I'd like to suggest that you first allow your guardian angel to escort you to a place of healing and then, once you've rested for a while and fully absorbed the reality of now living in a different sort of body, you'll be ready for a life review."

"'Priya' is certainly a pretty name and I have to admit that it kind of rings a bell for me. But what do you mean by a 'different sort of body'? Now that I've taken a moment to have a look at it, apart from it appearing thankfully a bit younger, I can't see anything very different from the one whose ashes were scattered over my beloved Welsh mountains."

"Let me explain. Each time that a soul is ready to incarnate, it takes on different bodies one at a time, the final one before the physical being known as the 'etheric'. Earth itself has an etheric body, too, which precisely resembles the physical. Now that you've really woken up, just take a look around you and you'll see things that you recognise."

"Goodness me, yes! There's my final home, Penrhyndeudraeth in Merionethshire, which I shared with my dear wife Edith and where, as you say, that nasty bout of influenza put an end to me."

"Great! Now you're getting the idea, but the next thing I have to tell you is that you'll soon be shedding your etheric body as well. That will simply disintegrate; no cremation will be necessary. Then you'll live for a while in your mental body…"

"Phew, what a lot to learn — and I had really considered myself to be quite a learned man!"

"A very learned man you were indeed, but in some lifetimes we focus almost entirely on the physical, ignoring what's most important: the spiritual."

****

Well, I had a very pleasant sojourn in an indescribably beautiful place of healing, but I soon decided that it would be better not to linger there too long, since I'd been told that a life review would have to come next. Before dying I'd always of course pooh-poohed the notion of a 'Last Judgement', but now that I'd had my disbelief in life after death torn away from me, the idea of a life review sounded scary and I therefore felt a desire to get it over with as soon as possible. Then, however, came the next big surprise: the recriminating 'Last Judgement' that religious people always talked of turned out to be yet another myth! Just as in that wonderful healing place I'd been surrounded by beauty, when I got escorted by my guardian angel and *three* charming spirit guides (the other two of whom I also recognised as old friends), I found myself to be totally surrounded by Love! I could hardly believe it when I realised that nobody but I myself was going to be making any judgement.

Anyway, I won't bore you with all the details of my life that I found myself regretting; for anyone who's seriously interested, I had a three-volume autobiography published by Allen and Unwin in 1967. I am nevertheless, however, keen to endeavour here to convey a little bit of what it was like actually *being* the celebrated Bertrand Russell. I shall have to be selective, as it was indeed not only an unusually long life but also an exceedingly active one and, besides packing a lot in, I moved around a great deal.

I was born in 1872 in a Welsh village named Trelleck, 5 miles south of Monmouth and in what's labelled as an 'Area of Outstanding Natural Beauty'. As my parents said, after we'd been orphaned, my brother Frank, seven years my senior, and I were sent to live with our paternal grandparents in their big Surrey house in Richmond, on the outskirts of London. That, however, never took away my 'Welshness', and Edith, my fourth wife, and I were happy to be able to spend my final 15 years close to the mouth of the River Dwyryd. She was younger and outlived me by eight years. Now a brief word to Welsh nationalists: No, I'm afraid I never had the chance to learn the language. That's best done at an early age and even if we two boys hadn't been whisked off to the south-east of England, unlike today, Welsh wasn't taught in schools when we were young.

Our grandfather, the first Earl Russell, had twice served as Prime Minister of the United Kingdom and I'm glad to say that he was a liberally minded Whig, not a Tory. He sadly died when I'd only just turned six, but I retained memories of a kindly old man in a wheelchair, and he had after all lived to be nearly 86. So from then on, while Frank and I were still living in Pembroke Lodge in Richmond, our grandmother, the Countess Russell, who'd been born Lady Frances Elliot and came from a Scottish Presbyterian family, was for us the dominant family figure. The atmosphere at Pembroke Lodge was one of frequent prayer, starting at eight o'clock in the morning and followed by enforced piano practice (which I hated), emotional repression and formality. Yet oddly, my grandmother had successfully petitioned the Court of Chancery to set aside a provision in our father's will requiring us to be raised as agnostics. (That court, by the way, ceased to exist in 1875, but it had had jurisdiction over all matters of equity, including trusts, land law, the guardianship of infants, and even the estates of people who were then called 'lunatics'.)

Frank rebelled openly against the repressive ambience of the Lodge, while I, on the other hand, felt that I had to learn to hide my feelings. He in any case, being older, naturally had more memories of our unconventional parents. Any good therapist nowadays would see this cutting off from feelings as a traumatised child's classic way of coping, but back then therapy would of course not have been given a thought in a household such as ours. Frank was sent to Winchester College for four years, which increased my loneliness still further, and the result was that the depression I suffered during my adolescence went so far as to make me feel genuinely suicidal at times. I only have my 'big brother' to thank for quite literally saving my life! You see, when I was 11 and he was 18 and about to go off to

Balliol College, Oxford, he introduced me to the work of Euclid. This was a revelation to me and much later I described it in my autobiography as "one of the great events of my life, as dazzling as first love".

Before, however, continuing with my own story, I must put in a few good words for my grandmother, the Countess. Despite being distinctly conservative in her religion, she held progressive views in other areas, such as Darwinism, and she supported Irish Home Rule. Her outlook on social justice and standing up for principle also had a big influence on me and her favourite Bible verse, "Thou shalt not follow a multitude to do evil" (Exodus 23:2), became my lifetime motto. Besides being so thrilled by the introduction to Euclid, I became, during my formative years, enthralled by the works of Percy Bysshe Shelley and learnt much of them by heart, often wishing that I had someone with whom I could share my feelings about it all and yearning to meet the poet himself. (Here let me hasten to add that I *have* now met him over here and we've had some wonderful conversations!) By the time I'd reached 15 I was thinking a great deal about the validity of Christian dogma, eventually deciding that I found it unconvincing. It was at this age that I came to the conclusion that there was no such thing as free will and then, at 18, after reading John Stuart Mill's autobiography, I became a firm atheist.

After winning a scholarship to read for the Mathematical Tripos at Trinity College, Cambridge, I began my studies there in 1890. This brought me instant happiness because, while at home mathematics was thought useless and philosophy nonsense, I quickly made lifelong friends among fellow students who shared my interests and outlook. I had, however, a lower opinion of most of the lecturers, who taught mathematics with little emphasis on mathematical rigour. I myself obviously had a good brain, but here I'd like to point out that getting into 'Oxbridge' — particularly if one happened to be an earl! — was much easier in those days than it later became. At least now, though, both Cambridge and Oxford have become much less unisex, and doing degrees in such things as mathematics is more acceptable for women than it used to be.

I won't dwell on my mathematics at any great length, since some of you will have limited knowledge and understanding of the subject, but further information can be found in the three-volume work *Principia Mathematica*, written jointly with my former teacher Alfred North Whitehead, and published between 1910 and 1913. Our scribe's husband, David Pearson, Emeritus Professor of Mathematics at the University of Hull, who has Cambridge degrees in the subject, summarises my main interest as the development of mathematical logic, seeking to base the subject on a firm logical foundation, and in this he comments that my work has an important influence even to this day.

After completing the Mathematical Tripos, I was able to follow my philosophical interests by a further year of study at Cambridge, and later I became better known academically as a philosopher. In 1900 I attended the first International Congress of Philosophy in Paris and in 1910 was appointed to a Lectureship in my own College of Trinity. All this contributed to my finding good reasons for continuing to live in the world and fortunately my improved mental health enabled me to remain active almost to the very end. (Well, look at the inimitable David Attenborough, who is currently rapidly catching me up in years!)

I was considered for a Fellowship at Trinity but was passed over on account of my agnosticism and consequent anti-clerical views. This meant that, when the shock of World War I befell us all, the College was able, in 1916, following my conviction under the Defence of the Realm Act of 1914, to dismiss me on account of my 'pacifist activities'. In February 1918 I was prosecuted for an editorial somebody had written for the weekly paper of the pacifist organization with which I was closely involved. Though my whole nature was engaged in opposing the First World War for more than four years, the offending passage was hardly the most provocative, defiant, or impassioned statement of protest made about it. Yet a London magistrate nevertheless found me guilty of the trumped-up charge and sentenced me to six months in Brixton prison. I used this time usefully for writing 104 letters, each of which I requested to be released 100 years after it had been written. (When, however, it came to World War II, I ceased to regard myself as a total pacifist, since I regarded Hitler's activities as even more serious than the Kaiser's.)

Now it's perhaps to time to say a bit about my somewhat notorious love life. I was only 17 when I met the family of the American-born British Quaker relief organiser Alyssa Pearsall Smyth, generally known as Alys, five years older than I was, and who ultimately became my wife. Being an emotional Taurus and having missed out on parental love at an early age, I soon fell for her despite her puritanical high-mindedness and contrary to my grandmother's wishes we married in December 1894. The marriage began to fall apart, however, in 1901, when I realised that I no longer loved her. We finally divorced in 1921, and during the interim I'd had numerous affairs with other women. It was also in 1901 (February), when I was 29 years of age, that I happened to witness Whitehead's wife suffering an acute angina attack. Interestingly, rather than making me anxious, this caused me to undergo a sort of what I could only call 'mystic illumination'. I found myself filled with feelings about beauty that subsequently led to a desire, which I felt to be very likely almost as profound as that of the Buddha, to find some philosophy which could make human life endurable. Those five minutes transformed me into a completely different person and — as I can see clearly now that I'm back on the other side — they formed the true start of my realising the most important aspects of my life plan, namely caring about humanity and combating any form of injustice.

While I persuaded Dora Black to marry me when she was seven months pregnant with my firstborn and as soon as the divorce had gone through, Alys, perhaps sadly, never remarried. It was, however, thanks to her that, in 1930, I first met Edith Finch, about whom more a little later. Dora, being a well-known figure in her own right, hardly needs any introduction. With her I had John (the Fourth Earl Russell) and Kate, both of whom I'm afraid had a tough time, largely on account of Dora's and my stormy relationship, but now that we're all over here, I've been able to give them my apologies. In fact I've even told Lady Katharine Tait, as she became, that I'm proud of the rather derogatory book that she wrote about me, since she'd exhibited a mind of her own by ignoring my anti-religious 'brainwashing' and becoming a Christian! It was also in 1930 that my third child, Lady Harriet Russell, was born out of wedlock while I was still officially married to Dora. (She also had *two* children by another man while we were married. Libertinism can undoubtedly lead to complications in family life!)

Dora and I were what is known as 'karmic soul mates', and we not only had stuff to clear from a previous life that we'd shared but also work to do as a couple this last time round. Yet campaigning, and even making extended visits to both Russia and China together, failed to make for a harmonious relationship. Anyway, we too have now become reconciled over here and are in agreement that we have nothing that we still need to complete on Earth.

I finally left Dora for Patricia Spence, a 21-year-old Oxford undergraduate whom my wife had taken on as a governess for the children. Our affair started in 1930, we married six years later, and she made a significant contribution to my *History of Western Philosophy*. Her parents having wanted a boy, Patricia's nickname of 'Peter' stuck with her. Any psychologist or therapist would point out that this wasn't a good start to life, yet she nevertheless succeeded in being an extremely seductive young woman. Voltaire, the great mind and libertine whom I've always admired, cared more about his women having good intellects than physical beauty, whereas for me, with my sensual nature, both were important. Since I was 42 years 'Peter's' senior, I suppose our relationship could be considered as the sort of 'final fling' of an older man reluctant to give up his youth and I'm sorry to say that our union ended somewhat cacophonously in 1949.

It's also unfortunate that Conrad, the son she gave me in 1937 and my fourth child, didn't see me again until 1968, and that reunion caused a permanent breach between his mother and me. Despite his difficult childhood, however, Conrad had a highly successful career as both a historian and a left-wing politician. "A son to be proud of," as I told him when he joined me on this side in 2004, and now I appreciate the fact that anyone whose forte hasn't been fatherhood will have further chances to get it right! From my four offspring I also had a total of nine grandchildren and, while still on this side, being on occasion able to act as guide to one or two of them can make any man feel content.

Now to go back to my lifetime as Bertrand Russell: on Earth there's a saying: 'Third time lucky'. Well, in my case it was the fourth time that I was lucky in marriage! As I mentioned earlier, I first met Edith Finch, who was a talented American teacher and writer, through my first wife, Alys; one of her friends, Lucy Donnelly, was in turn a friend and housemate of Edith. It was actually in the same year as when I began my affair with 'Peter', and I no doubt needed to work through my karma with her before I could be ready for life with my soul mate. Edith had studied at Bryn Mawr College and then graduated from St Hilda's, Oxford, before travelling extensively in Europe. She moved from New York to England in 1950 and we soon fell in love and were married in 1952. That brought me 18 years of true happiness, during which, feeling that I'd accomplished all

I needed to, I was able to relax and enjoy life in my beloved Wales.

As you no doubt know, I obtained a Nobel Prize for Literature, and I'm not going to bore you with all my other accolades, especially since anybody interested can google them for themselves. What I will say, though, is that I don't feel that any question of pride comes into it; I was simply doing what I believed I *had* to do in a world that was rushing into the lunacy of making nuclear weapons.

Now you may be feeling a desire to enquire about my next steps and whether I'm inclined to return to Earth in the near future. My reply is that I'm not in any hurry, mainly because there's so much to do over here besides increasing my learning. Also, since on this side we have no physical bodies, which tire so easily, we have more time for useful activity. Right now, with this ghastly war going on in Ukraine, we have the intransigent Putin to deal with. You may want to comment that we're not having a great deal of success, but as Bruce Kent and I were saying to one other recently: "He may be intransigent, but at least we've been preventing him from using nuclear weapons." And please remember to keep praying, as prayers really do help even when you don't see immediate results.

***

Now for an interesting postscript: just the other day (in your earthly parlance) I ran into that left-wing Dominican, Fr Matthew Rigby, who told me that he had long hoped to meet me over here, and we had a fascinating philosophical/theological discussion about the indefinable nature of his 'Almighty'. Matt, after leaving his physical body, had gone to a very good place, completed an eminently satisfactory life review, and then met Jesus. He had, however, been fairly rapidly disillusioned of the massive, all-embracing Father figure of his imagination.

Then, like me, after discarding his etheric body and doing some enjoyable exploration of higher realms, he had begun a study of different Faiths. We agreed that, if the Christian Church had stuck closer to the actual teachings of Jesus of Nazareth, appreciating that He had during those 17 supposedly 'lost years' travelled eastwards for His own learning and if the Church hadn't also dismissed such things as reincarnation and universal equality, someone such as I would have had less difficulty in accepting the 'dogma'.

With regard to the teachings of other Faiths, we were both interested to have found that, while Buddhism doesn't claim to have a 'God' as such, Hinduism and India's various *avatars* (divine incarnations, who were at least as powerful as the Master Jesus) state that we are all God. Sathya Sai Baba (1926–2011, but still very much around in numerous people's minds) would say to his devotees that "the only difference between you and Me is that I know that I'm God whereas most of you have forgotten". We'd also both looked at Judaism and Islam and discovered that each had an esoteric side — expressed in Judaism in the Kabbalah — and that there were people of both these Faiths who recognised such things as the fact of reincarnation. The excitement is that, for any enquiring mind, the scope of research is endless! So, on that happy note, I'd like to wish you all a fond farewell until we meet again either on the Earth's plane or a higher one.

# 12

# Abbess Catherine Gascoigne

*Furthermore He taught that I should behold the glorious*
*Satisfaction: for this Amends-making is more pleasing to God*
*and more worshipful, without comparison, than ever was the sin*
*of Adam harmful. Then signifieth our blessed Lord thus in this*
*teaching, that we should take heed to this:* For since I have made
well the most harm, then it is my will that thou know thereby
that I shall make well all that is less.

Julian of Norwich, *Revelations of Divine Love*

In the lifetime that I'd like to tell you about I was one of a group
of nine young nuns who, when the Reformation in England
was making things difficult for Catholics to carry out their
religious vocations, decided to sail to Flanders and start up a
new Benedictine community there. The year was 1623, I was 23
years old, had been living not far from Beverley in Yorkshire,
where I'd been born into a staunchly Catholic family, and my
parents encouraged my vocation. Leaving them for another
country wasn't a problem — particularly as I had siblings and
some extended family living in the area who were all also good
Catholics — and I'd fancied the religious life for as long as I
could remember. I'd always felt very close to God, especially in
the countryside surrounding our mansion, and had never had
any desire for a family of my own.

My childhood was a happy one. I had an elder brother
named Joseph, whom I adored, a younger sister named Isabel,
with whom I mostly got on well, and a much younger brother
(there had been a miscarriage in between) called Daniel, who
was the apple of everyone's eye, though very mischievous at
times. My father bred horses in addition to earning a good

living from other 'country-type' things, my mother was totally devoted to all of us and very self-sacrificing, and we were never short of a good cook or other servants. Isabel and I always had a governess and my parents chose them well; I was a keen student, with special interests in English, French, and music. One of the governesses we had for a while actually was French and, thanks to starting lessons with her at an early age, I learnt to speak the language fairly fluently and with a good accent. We went to mass faithfully every Sunday, either at the little church in the nearby village or at the beautiful St Mary's Church in Beverley.

Then, when I'd just turned 18, tragedy struck our region in the form of the dreaded disease known as smallpox. Many people around us died within a few weeks and I caught it myself, probably from my best friend Amy when I was invited to tea at her house. As soon as our doctor had given my parents the diagnosis, I got confined to my room, not even being allowed out to go to the bathroom. This was because my parents were (quite rightly!) absolutely determined that my brother Joseph, in particular, should not catch it. For he was the heir to the family home and business, for which he was already being well groomed. I was ill for weeks and weeks on end and of course, at times, very lonely. I won't describe the gory details of this horrid disease to you, not only because I prefer to forget about it but also since there's no need to because, thank the Lord, it's now been more or less completely eradicated and no-one reading this book is in the least danger of catching it. (The world is now of course gripped by another 'plague', but I won't dwell on that, as you have many other people out there who are much better qualified than I am to discuss it.)

Well, I sincerely believe that there is always a reason for everything and unpleasant though it was, the smallpox actually did me a favour. Why? Simply because the suffering that I endured was so intense that it took me closer than ever to God. You see, alone there in my bedroom with the curtains keeping me in perpetual darkness — apart from the occasional meal that was put outside my door, which I, with difficulty, washed down as best I could with water, knowing that my life depended upon it — God was literally all that I had. Quite early on I made a pact with Him: "If you keep me alive *and* keep all the other members of my family free from the disease, I shall dedicate the rest of my life to serving Thee and doing all in my power to help my fellow human beings." Well, the good Lord kept His side of the bargain by eventually healing me completely, leaving nothing but some unsightly scars on various parts of my body, and I was helped to keep my side of it by the appearance in 1621 of an English Benedictine monk named Dom Benet Jones. While on mission duties in England, he'd been in contact with several interested and spiritually minded young women here, and he was introduced to me by the parish priest of the aforementioned St Mary's Church in Beverley. It was he who initiated our project of escaping the shores of England to sail to somewhere where we could set up a community of nuns with no risk of being persecuted for adhering to the one true Faith.

The other eight members of the group all lived further south (a couple of them in the area of Norwich) and they all travelled together straight from England to Cambrai (known to the English at the time as Camerick). It suited me better, however, to go first to Douai, where I was keen to visit a relative, and then proceed from there to join my future companions. Most notable among our group of foundresses was the 17-year-old Helen More, who professed as Dame Gertrude More, and was the great-great-granddaughter of Thomas More, who'd been beheaded for his faith in 1535 and was finally canonised as a saint by the Catholic Church just over three centuries later. (Not that, as I can see now from my higher perspective, canonisation really means very much, since those designated as saints often need to return to Earth in different bodies before they can achieve self-realisation.) Helen was a lovely girl and very mature for her tender years and it was her father, Cresacre More, who provided the original endowment for the foundation of our community. My own father, too, generously gave me quite a handsome 'dowry', knowing, he commented jokingly, that he'd never be obliged to spend the money on my wedding!

I'd never crossed the sea before and was thrilled at the prospect. Dom Benet, who had escorted the others all the way, greeted me warmly upon my arrival in Cambrai, and there we took over the ruined townhouse of the defunct Benedictine abbey of Saint-Étienne-de-Fémy, employed local help to restore it and moved in at the end of 1623. I found it all very exciting. Being still laywomen when we arrived, we had of course to serve a novitiate and it wasn't until we'd all taken our vows that the monastery could be considered to have been formally founded. This was at the beginning of 1625, three nuns from the English monastery at Brussels having been sent to train us. Two of these later joined the nascent community and they included Dame Frances Gawen, who served as our first superior. She was elected Abbess in 1629 and I liked and respected her a great deal. Cambrai was at that time part of Flanders and it wasn't until after my death that it became annexed by France.

I mentioned that two members of our little group had come from the area of Norwich. Well, they had brought with them a truly amazing treasure! In the city of Norwich there had lived during the fourteenth century an anchorite who spent the entire latter part of her life in a little cell attached to the church of St Julian, from which she took her name. Very little was known about her apart from the fact that she'd survived two waves of the dreaded 'Black Death' and had herself very nearly died while in her thirties. Hearing this naturally gave me an immediate feeling of empathy with this long-deceased woman, but, marvel of marvels, it transpired that during her period of illness God had spoken to her personally and she'd written an account of it all in a document entitled *Revelations of Divine Love*. On account of the prevailing attitudes of the time, however, with the clergy being so powerful and controlling, her precious book had had to be kept secret because, since it spoke of a *loving* God rather than a fearsome one, it went right against the official teaching of the Church. What's more, the very fact of Julian of Norwich having been a woman made it 'unforgivable' that she'd actually dared to put pen to paper!

The true miracle was that her book had survived at all. Apparently she'd had a few friends who'd appreciated its great worth and consequently guarded it safely, laboriously making further copies of it and occasionally passing them on to people they felt they could trust. Thus it was that a copy had fallen into the hands of a member of our new community. Not all nine of us had learnt to read before leaving England, but I was from the start determined to rectify that and the moment I set eyes on Julian's book I was deeply moved by it and suggested to my companions that we each systematically copy bits of it into our own prayer books and read them regularly as part of our personal spiritual discipline.

This is no doubt at least part of the reason why, when our first superior resigned, I was elected as the next Abbess of the convent — a position that I continued to hold quite willingly, being repeatedly re-elected for the ensuing 40 years of my life. Excitement occurred when, in 1659, we were visited by one Serenus Cressy, who was chaplain to a branch of the Benedictine nuns in Paris. He was so impressed when I showed him the Norwich book that he got it printed in order that it could reach a wider audience.

Our community grew gradually as other would-be Benedictine nuns came from England to join us. After my own departure from that body and before the *Revelations* could be brutally destroyed by the French Revolution, a further six generations of nuns copied bits of it into their prayer books. Then, by a stroke of immense fortune (or, as I myself prefer to believe, by divine will!), when the remaining nuns succeeded in escaping back to England, at least one copy of the printed book went with them and, at the very beginning of the twentieth century, a Scottish woman named Grace Warrack persuaded Methuen to publish her translation of it into modern English. Since then, as you spiritually minded readers of the twenty-first century will appreciate, this wonderful book has never been out of print and I feel very blessed to have played a small part in its preservation.

I feel that you readers — or anyway those of you with an interest in history — might like me to tell you something about our life as seventeenth-century nuns living in Cambrai. Now, in your twenty-first century, becoming a monk or a nun has gone almost completely out of fashion. As I see it from my perspective over here on the other side, your Western society seems to have two extremes: those (no doubt the majority) who are either agnostic or even atheists and those whose spirituality has gone, as it were, beyond the traditional Church and who are busy studying Eastern philosophy, learning about the afterlife and becoming interested in such things as mediumship and reincarnation. Now that I have a broader vision up here than I did when I was Earthbound, I have a strong feeling of empathy with all those latter interests, but as the Abbess Catherine I was hidebound by my time and my religion — my *Catholicism*! — was very conventional.

The name of our convent was Our Lady of Consolation. Solemnly professed Benedictine nuns of the English tradition use the honorific 'Dame' in the same way that monks of the English Benedictine Congregation (EBC) are called 'Dom'; it isn't at all the same thing as being Dames Commander of the Order of the British Empire. The English Benedictine mystical writer Dom Augustine Baker trained us young nuns in a tradition of contemplative prayer which survives to the present day. It was rigorous, but that suited me well — especially after having made that promise to God to serve both Him and my fellows unswervingly — and I was of course a profound believer in the importance and efficacy of prayer. Seven of us nine foundresses were known as 'choir nuns', but in addition, two members of the original group were called 'claustral' sisters; they weren't bound either to the Divine Office or to keep monastic enclosure, which meant that they could be responsible for shopping as well as for routine contacts with the outside world.

Though not spacious, the situation of our house was healthy and sufficiently commodious, with the buildings being made of brick, very simple and close together. Our church was extremely small but generally regarded as neat and seemly, and there we celebrated the Divine Office in what I regarded as a solemn and edifying manner, being always very closely observant of our Rule. Not being under the authority of the Abbot President of the English Benedictine Congregation or that of the Bishop, we had no right of burial at the local parish church and so we had our own cemetery despite our site being so cramped.

Unusually, we ran a small school for girls inside our enclosure, and the pupils were also subject to the monastic routine. This was particularly important to me, since I valued education highly and I greatly liked the thought of these children being given the same opportunities as I myself had been given, both for education and for getting into the habit of regular prayer. The school fees were of course a valuable source of income for us and in addition, we performed the traditional remunerative work of enclosed nuns, namely fine needlework and embroidery, especially on vestments and liturgical textiles. We had another unusual source of income besides, which was doing fine paperwork; it involved cutting sheets of paper into complicated patterns and making figurative depictions for decorative purposes. We all had active intellectual lives, a lot of it involving translating French spiritual writings into English, and we gradually succeeded in building up a good library, which meant a huge amount to me.

As for my character, I tended to be quiet and self-effacing yet nevertheless resolute, seeking always God alone, and my great privilege was having had Father Augustine Baker, OSB, to teach me how to find Him. I also had a good singing voice, combined with a great love of sacred music, and all these things caused me to be elected repeatedly every four years as Abbess of our community. The first time I was elected I had to obtain a papal dispensation because we'd all been young when we first left England; I was then 28, and the lowest statutory age for an abbess was 30. I also had good organisational powers and for that reason was at one point sent for a short time to assist another community. I was glad not to have to be away from Cambrai for too very long, as it had quickly become home to me and I loved my fellow nuns dearly and missed them sorely while I was gone.

I particularly needed to be firm and resolute at a later date, when Fr Baker's teachings were (for reasons which were to me a mystery) called into question. As part of my defence and in response to a request from my superiors, I wrote a succinct summary of my method of prayer and this helped to vindicate Fr Baker from all charges. The matter didn't end there, however, as in 1655 a further attempt was made to confiscate the Baker manuscripts and intimidate our Cambrai community into surrendering them. Fortunately my position as Abbess enabled me to refuse to allow the documents out of the house. For I knew that they'd all been minutely scrutinised and declared free from error at the 1633 General Chapter. I even threatened to take the community out of the Congregation rather than comply with the order, but mercifully I wasn't in the end obliged to carry out this threat, and (as I mentioned above and as those who are familiar with the Benedictine order will know) Fr Baker's teaching has continued to guide not only the nuns but also many others in the way of prayer right down to your present day.

I did miss my family a bit and regretted being unable to travel back to Yorkshire now and again, but they all came and visited me at various points in my life. I was particularly thrilled when my siblings were able to come over with their spouses, and I did meet each of my nephews and nieces at least once. The times when I would most have liked to return was when my parents were dying — my father went first and my mother a couple of years later — but my family did manage to get word sent over and the whole community prayed for them with me.

Besides the difficulty of making such a lengthy journey was the fact that my health tended to be shaky. The smallpox of my youth had taken its toll on my body, weakening my immune system, and this meant that I tended to succumb all too easily to anything such as influenza when it was going around. This, however, had the advantage of forcing me to increase my willpower and my companions were often amazed by my ability to 'battle on regardless'. Thanks to that, I lived till I was 75 — a good age for those days — but I resigned from being Abbess about three years before I died. This enabled me to have my say in choosing my successor and I was very happy with the choice that was made.

I was fortunate not to have a long, lingering death. Although it was May, we were subjected to an exceptionally cold spell, which was enough to weaken my resilience to a severe bout of influenza. My lungs gave out quite quickly, but I was extremely well cared for and prayers were being said for me unceasingly both at my bedside and in our little church. Once I'd gone, it made me very happy to watch my companions processing past my body one by one to say farewell, and the funeral was beautiful, with some of my very favourite music being played. I'd already chosen my burial spot, right next to one of my closest friends, who'd gone before me by about a year. As soon as it was over, it was absolutely wonderful to be able to speed towards the Light, which was even more blissful and all-embracing than I'd remembered.

We need to appreciate the importance of forgetting our past each time that we return to Earth, because, if it were otherwise, we wouldn't be able to focus our full attention on what we'd come for the next time. Upon reaching the Bardo, I was met straight away not only by my guardian angel but also by my guide Maria, a very old friend, whose job it had been to guide me in the writing that had been important to the whole Benedictine community. My overriding joy at seeing them again was enhanced by their assurance that I'd adhered well to my life plan — namely to compensate for my previous life as one of the Conquistadors who'd gone to South America, been very cruel to the indigenous people there and stolen a lot of their marvellous gold artefacts, taking them back to Spain, melting them down and subsequently living luxuriously on the profits thereof. I then remembered with a shudder that previous life review and how I'd been made to see that I needed to have a subsequent life of poverty dedicated to serving others.

The guides who showed me my life review did say that I could at times have been a little more patient with those less intelligent than myself and also perhaps a bit less intolerant of the Reformers who'd founded new churches rather than concentrating on trying to make reforms *within* the Church. Many of them did have good reasons for what they were doing, since there was indeed a great deal of corruption among the clergy and others, such as the sale of 'indulgences', but on the other hand I had been inevitably caught up in the traditional Catholic ambience of the time. After all, as those of you who are alive on Earth at this moment know full well, it was to be a further good 300 years before members of the different Christian Churches would begin to come together and respect one another as equals.

After this little discussion my parents appeared. They said that they were proud of me and we embraced tenderly. We were joined almost immediately by my beloved 'big brother' Joseph, who'd caught pneumonia just a few months before my death and passed on quite easily with his dear family around him. We then had a good family natter about how the rest of the Gascoignes were doing down there in our beloved Yorkshire, and then — wonder of wonders — Jesus appeared before us! He thanked us all for adhering to the Faith but told us that many people had sadly misinterpreted His teachings, failing to recognise, for instance, that He had *not* in fact been the only divine incarnation ever. India, He told us, had already had several such 'avatars' and would have more in the future. He pointed out that in countries such as India they had, unlike the majority of so-called Christians, conserved the important knowledge of reincarnation as a necessary fact. He reminded me of my worthwhile lifetime as a Cathar, saying that the Gnostics had not forgotten their own inner connection with God and appreciated that they didn't need priests to tell them what to do. They had been wrongly persecuted for serving their fellows in the way that He Himself had taught during the incarnation He'd had at the beginning of the Christian era.

This interesting conversation gave me the idea of sometime returning to Earth as something other than a conventional practising Christian — and I have indeed since done that and finally severed my connection with Catholicism — but that's not what I came through to tell you readers about today. And in the meantime Catherine Gascoigne's weary etheric body (linked, as I quickly relearned, so closely to her physical one) badly needed some time to recuperate and take advantage of the healing that's always so readily given over here. May the Lord bless you all!

# 13

# A Dog's Life

*And on the ninth day God looked down on his wide-eyed children and said "They need a companion." So God made a dog. God said "I need someone to wake up, give kisses, pee on a tree, sleep all day, wake up again, give more kisses, then stay up until midnight basking in the glow of the television set." So God made a dog. Then God said "I need someone willing to sit then stand then roll over... I need someone who can lift spirits with a lick. Someone who, no matter what you did or couldn't do or didn't mean or couldn't take, would love you just the same." So God made a dog. It had to be somebody who would remain patient and loyal even through loneliness...*

Anonymous

*Woof woof!* My name in my last life was Surya (after the Indian sun god), and I spent my nine and a half years in that Cavalier King Charles spaniel's body living with a couple named Ann and David. I'd also been a dog (a terrier) in David's family when he'd been a child and during the period of the Cathars in southern France I'd been Ann's most beloved horse, who was sadly slain by those brutes of the Inquisition not long before Ann herself got martyred for her beliefs. In that lifetime she gave me the name 'Sol', which of course also means 'sun'. So you see we were all old friends already and even though Ann herself no longer recalls it I'd also known her long before that time, when I was a wolf whom she (as a man) befriended.

Now 'friend' is the important word here! Some people — and note here that I'm referring to human beings — claim to own their dogs, while some dogs believe that they own the people they live with. I, however, don't agree with that at all; I firmly believe that nobody has the right to 'own' anybody else. I see us all as companions, friends and/or colleagues. 'Guardians', too, is an appropriate word. When I lived with Ann and David in Ludlow and then Malvern, they guarded me by feeding me my favourite healthy foods, taking me on good walks and making sure that I didn't get run over by crazy drivers on the roads. In return I guarded them by always warning them when someone was approaching our abode, barking when the post arrived or the phone rang (particularly useful for Ann, who is rather deaf) and *invariably* giving them loads of affection, even when they'd had to go out, leaving me on my own for a while. For giving out love to the world was a major part of our joint mission.

I was born on 19 September 2011 in Bromsberrow Heath in Gloucestershire (not far from Malvern, which my companions moved to after falling in love with the new Audley retirement village there). I was what could be known as the 'runt of the litter', being rather smaller than my sister Sparkle, whom my breeders decided to keep. But being small in size did *not* mean that I had a small personality! On the contrary, though people often took me for a girl because they found me "so pretty", I was very masculine in character and very good at asserting my wishes or opinions. For instance, I always had firm views about which side of the road we should be walking on (the reasons for that varied but were often connected with smell) and would never be persuaded to cross unless my walking companion(s) had a *very* good reason for doing so, such as safety.

Ann and David were for a long time very keen travellers and often felt that they had a good reason to go to faraway places where it wasn't possible for me to go with them. I went through a number of carers, who were all fine, but the best arrangement was when they made friends with Muriel, who lived in the same Ludlow street as us and who'd lost her own Cavalier on account of heart trouble (sadly a common feature of our breed). She always *jumped* at any chance of borrowing me and was of course very upset when Ann had to phone her with the news of my crossing over on 30 March 2021.

While we were living in Ludlow, David and I used to go to a dog class in Richards Castle, run by a brilliant woman named Jude. Now I'm going to swallow my modesty and tell you that, from the word 'Go', I was *always* the star of the class. It wasn't just David that said so — Jude did, too! Whenever she was offering prizes I almost invariably won them, and I was always the first to grasp anything new that she taught us. (In fact the honest truth is that I consequently sometimes got a bit bored, but there were always plenty of treats to make up for that.)

In Ludlow there was an ideal dog-walking place, only five minutes' walk from our house, known as Gallows Bank. (Like Ann, I prefer not to reflect too much upon the origin of that name! There is a very large stone at the top of the hill and it's all too easy to imagine what used to happen there in the distant past.) There I could run around safely to my heart's content and there were always plenty of other dogs to chat to. Our own house was in a quiet spot, with a small garden at the back, and there I took upon myself the important task of chasing away the cats who often had the cheek to enter it without asking permission. I had my own bedroom, off the kitchen, which also contained an extra sink and the washing machine, and it had an additional door that opened onto the garden, so it was easy for someone who could reach the handle to let me out first thing in the mornings and whenever I needed it throughout the day.

Now, this chapter is entitled A Dog's Life — a phrase that many of you will have heard used derogatorily. *Why?* I wonder. Well, I suppose there are sad cases of dogs who aren't given the love they deserve and are treated brutally (just as there are children). If that weren't so, there'd be no need for such excellent organisations as the Royal Society for the Prevention of Cruelty to Animals (RSPCA). Fortunately, however — at least in my experience — these are well outnumbered by dogs who

DEATH: Friend or Enemy?

live with people who absolutely dote on them and consequently give one cause to wonder how *any* sort of life could be better! Human beings (although their powers of smell are *incredibly* feeble) are undoubtedly able to do many things that we dogs can't do, but, coupled with that, the adults have great burdens of responsibility: finding work that will pay adequately for all their needs, rearing children and so on. My mother suckled me, along with my siblings, for a few weeks until Ann and David were free to come and collect me, but after we'd parted she wasn't bothered about what became of me and I didn't miss her, as human children tend to do when they first leave home. So no, I wouldn't have swapped my life for *anyone* else's!

And it would be hard to think of a better place to live in than Ludlow. That's certainly what Ann and David had thought when they'd decided to move there from Cottingham, after he'd retired from Hull University, and they didn't imagine ever leaving it. But then one September day, just as I was turning six, a leaflet came through the door about a retirement village that was being built in Malvern. Interestingly, that had been the very first place that they'd taken me to as a small puppy, once I was deemed old enough for excursions further afield. On that occasion we went into Priory Park and though I found the bridge over the little lake there too scary to walk over, I fell instantly in love with it. I got many admirers in that park, too, that day — a thing that never ceased even when I'd grown bigger. That park has a theatre at the top of it and Ann and David were already addicted to going to concerts there. So, since they had to face the fact of being in their late seventies and possibly not being able to go on living in our house forever, they decided to go and take a look at the place 'out of curiosity'. They left me with Muriel and took with them my great friend Alice, their daughter, who happened to be visiting at the time and who almost shares my birthday, treating her to a lunch out in a Malvern restaurant.

It's said that curiosity killed the cat, but that 'birthday excursion' didn't kill them; on the contrary, they fell instantly in love with the retirement village! Ann loves to swim — a thing I could *never* understand, even though I've noticed that many dogs do enjoy it — and, besides proximity to the theatre that I've just mentioned, an added attraction for her was the promise of a swimming pool in the complex. When asked by the salesman who was showing them round the show apartment and explaining how the village would develop, "Do you feel you could live here?", they looked at one another and replied with a simultaneous "*Yes!*" But Ann then added: "Though not for, say, at least five years, as decluttering for such a big downsize would be a very big job. Also, certainly not within the lifetime of our present dog."

Everyone goes to Earth to learn, and one thing that Ann still needed to learn about was the adaptability of us dogs.

As it happened, the move from Ludlow had been very carefully planned on the other side and a number of things transpired to make it take place sooner rather than later. The downsizing was indeed both very hard work and exhausting, but, once it had been done, the reasons for the timing became increasingly clear. Not least of these was the fact that we were all so incredibly well looked after when the Covid pandemic struck. That of course didn't affect me personally very much, since it interfered with neither my walks nor my food, but it was good to feel that I could be a sort of anchor of normality and stability in a world that had suddenly become gripped by fear.

I said that heart trouble tended to be a feature of Cavaliers and I myself was diagnosed with it not very long after the three of us had moved to Malvern. Fortunately we found an excellent veterinary practice, within walking distance, and they put me straight onto heart pills, which didn't bother me in the slightest — especially as the one that had to be consumed half an hour *before* my meals tasted truly delicious. The thing that concerned Ann and David most, however, when they first made the big decision to leave Ludlow, was that the only flat they could afford was on the fourth floor of one of the apartment blocks, which obviously meant that I could no longer be let out easily when I needed the toilet. To start with I found the lift quite scary, but I quickly got used to it and in fact soon decided that I actually preferred it to the stairs. (When the lift broke down, which was a bad habit it had, I couldn't understand why they insisted on using the stairs, and so I sometimes demanded that David carry me. Now, however, that I'm here on the other side, I can get a better perspective of why certain things happen and so would like to apologise to David for the strain sometimes put on him.)

In Malvern the walks were of course different from those in Ludlow, but we were truly spoilt for choice. The immense Common, which is absolutely brilliant for running free on, is only a stone's throw away from Ellerslie (the retirement village) and during our first summer there I made a very good friend called Sparky, who lives with Dorothy in a charming cottage at the beginning of the Common. David and Ann are still good friends with her. She was very sympathetic about my demise, and since Sparky is now 13 years old it's possible that it won't be very long until he crosses over, too. I shall certainly be very ready to welcome him. The Priory Park that I mentioned above is a bit further away, but it's still within easy walking distance and is truly beautiful in all seasons. What's more, I in due course conquered my fear of crossing that bridge and so it henceforth became known in our family as 'Surya's Bridge'.

That tended to be David's preferred destination whenever it was muddy underfoot. I, however, had another particular favourite: Rosebank Gardens, a bit closer to the centre of town, whence it's possible to walk right up to St Ann's Well and beyond, to the very top of the hill. We'd all done that together while we were still living in Ludlow and before Ann's legs had deteriorated. The only snag with that park is that getting there from Ellerslie involves crossing Wells Road, which tends to have a lot of traffic. I knew the exact spot where it was best to cross, but Ann and David tended to be fearful and thought it a bad oversight of the town council not to put a zebra crossing there. So I always had to be *very* insistent about making the crossing! Of course just walking around inside Ellerslie's beautiful grounds is pleasant in itself, but unless I was *really* desperate I naturally preferred to go further afield for doing my poos.

Another adjustment that had to be made with our move was the sleeping arrangements. Since, as I said above, I'd had my own bedroom in Ludlow and since a utility room was one of the many things they'd had to sacrifice, Ann and David had decided that my bed should be in the kitchen. What they'd failed to appreciate was that sometimes the lingering smells from the cooking were a bit too much for me and, also, that in there I was actually closer to the owners of the flat next door than I was to them. So, on the third night, I decided to rebel until, fearful of the disturbance that my barking might cause, they relented and let me join them in the bedroom. Since that room is carpeted and since there was a large beanbag in it anyway, it meant that my bed could go to a charity shop, and they soon got used to me sleeping either under their bed or on the beanbag in front of the window.

Towards the very end of my life, when the vets had seen fit to increase my diuretics, sleeping in the bedroom had the advantage of my being able to let my family know when I needed to go out in the night, though these were rare occasions. Talking of going out in the night, in Ann's partially autobiographical book about womanhood, she wrote about the night of 27–28 December 2020, when she'd failed to get a wink of sleep on account of what was going on with me. She was quite right in surmising that that was the night during which the decision was made about my demise three months later.

It was by no means an easy decision, since the three of us all meant so much to one another and I knew that they would miss me terribly, but my heart had been getting steadily weaker, which of course affected my speed of walking. Then there was also the big question of what to do when they needed to go away. (Human beings *all* like a change of scene now and again and I wasn't allowed on the sort of tours that Ann and David liked to book themselves on.) Muriel in Ludlow was coming up to 85 and they were concerned about her ability to get all my pills right, plus there was always the worry that I might get worse in their absence and incur vet expenses that couldn't be handled by anyone other than Ann and David themselves. In addition, none of us welcomed the thought of night excursions becoming more frequent!

Then, at the start of 2021 a very scary thing happened. I'd already been suffering from itching for quite a while, and three or so trips to the vet had failed to solve the problem. During the first weekend in January, however, it suddenly got much worse; in fact it got so bad that, in addition to scratching myself like mad, I was chewing my fur and tearing out huge chunks of it. Nothing can ever stop David sleeping, but Ann was again kept awake for one entire night, and the trouble was that they of course couldn't phone the vet for an appointment until first thing on the Monday. Covid was at the time preventing the vets from allowing people into the waiting room and since they were very busy that day, all they could do was to tell my companions to bring me down at midday and wait outside until one of them could squeeze me in at lunchtime. This might sound easy, but in fact it was an absolute nightmare, since it was a horrendously cold day and we were kept waiting outside for a full hour and a half. It was well worth it, though, because the charming young vet who eventually came out to take me inside finally made a correct diagnosis: parasites! So she gave me a pill straight away and we all went home feeling immensely relieved. After that

Ann kept on picking up big chunks of my beautiful fur from all over the apartment, but it wasn't too long before I began to feel very much better.

The next step was to improve my appearance, especially as I'd had a very big bald patch on one leg for quite a while. Fortunately Pip, Ann's acupuncturist and a very good friend to both of us, knew that neem oil was a good solution. So Ann looked it up on the internet and ordered two different sorts — one to rub onto the bald patch and the other to take internally — and having the oil mixed into my food didn't bother me. The result was that by the time that had been agreed for me to cross over, my coat was looking as good as it had ever done. Of course at that point I left my physical body behind, as one always does, but it's well known that the etheric body (the next layer up) looks just the same as the physical one, and so I was glad to be able to return Home looking just as good as I ever had during that lifetime on Earth.

Another difficulty that my companions had early on this year was that Tony, David's brother and lifelong best friend, died in a nursing home on 19 January after having been taken into hospital just before Christmas. The worst thing about it was that, what with Covid making all the hospitals extra busy, the two of them had been unable even to speak to one another on the phone. This was extremely sad — for David in particular, there being nobody else still alive whom he'd known all his life. The details weren't of course all clear to me at that point, but I sensed that Ann needed to support him through his grief and that he was glad of my presence, too, for comfort.

The next month was a very stressful one, as there was so much to do, what with organising the funeral and so on. Tony and his wife Shirley, who'd already crossed over a number of years earlier, had never had children and so the brunt of the burden fell on Alice as his executor (another thing that dogs never have to bother about!), but her parents also did all they could with helping from a distance. Anyway, the funeral was fixed for 15 February (exactly a week after David's eighty-second birthday), and Paul, their older son, kindly volunteered to pick him up on his way from Devon, leaving Ann and me to look after one another.

This in fact proved to be vital, as firstly David had to be rushed into hospital when he had a minor stroke during the afternoon of the 13th, and secondly Ann had a nasty fall in the apartment upon returning from a swim the next morning! To our great relief — I'd got *very* concerned when strangers had turned up and carted David away — the 'strangers' actually turned out to be nice ambulance people and they brought him home again by 10 p.m. The next morning David assured us that he felt OK to go off with Paul, but Ann's back went on giving her a lot of pain for a good month or so. Fortunately, however, this didn't render her unable to switch on her computer to watch Tony's funeral, and we both felt very proud when David spoke eloquently about Tony and when Alice read out a poem by Thomas Hardy.

While all this was going on, nobody realised that my end was approaching quite so fast, but my companions were given further warning by the fact that my walking was gradually getting slower than ever. Fortunately I still absolutely *loved* going to the park; the Common was a bit more of a challenge, but the winter weather was a deterrent for that anyway. Occasionally I reluctantly had to bark in the night to be taken out and, in view of my heart condition, the vets couldn't risk reducing my diuretics. So that naturally caused concern in case nightly outings did become the norm.

Easter was now fast approaching, and the plan for that weekend was for Alice to come and drive us all in our car to her Uncle Tony's house in Bracknell. I'd never been there, as Tony was apparently a cat lover rather than a dog lover. (Well, it takes all sorts — a thing that I'm relearning now that I'm back on the other side!) Tony, as I mentioned just now, had crossed over to the other side not long before I did and his house consequently needed sorting out, which was going to be a mammoth task. Anyway, one night prior to that, I had to wake Ann and David up, but I collapsed before they could get me to the door, which was very alarming for them, and I alas had no way of explaining to them that there was nothing to worry about. By the morning I was, to their relief, able to get up, and one of the vets (the same nice young one who'd cured my parasites) gave me what she described as the "last resort" heart pill, whose aim was to make more oxygen go to the brain. At this point the idea of getting me to Bracknell in the car was seeming like more and more of a challenge. So they talked with Alice on the phone and it was agreed that she should be prepared to stay in Malvern for Easter.

The next night passed peacefully, but when it was time for my companions to start making the soup for lunch, I walked out into the hall and collapsed on the floor there. At first they both kept going to and fro from the kitchen to the hall to check on me, but then they noticed that my breathing was slowing down and so Ann sat down beside me, giving me Reiki healing. Partly thanks to that, my last breath didn't take all that long to come and I was so glad to have them both by my side to witness the ease of my departure.

The soup-making had then of course to be abandoned, and Ann had difficulty in holding back the tears when she phoned the vets' office to inform them of my demise. The person on the other end of the phone wasn't very sympathetic, simply asking whether they could bring the body down and then trying to start a discussion about whether they wanted a cremation or what, which Ann felt was a bit premature. On the other hand, when Ann phoned through to the village reception desk, Emily was *very* much more empathetic and helpful. She said she would come in half an hour, which gave the two of them time to eat some bread and cheese.

When dear Emily arrived at our flat, the three of them sat down and talked for a bit, and then she asked whether they had anything such as an old sheet to wrap my body in. The tatty towel that they'd always used to dry me with was the obvious answer, since it wouldn't be needed any more. Ann didn't feel that she was up to driving down to the vet practice, so Emily got her to sit down on the bench outside, with the wrapped body on her lap, while she went to fetch the village minibus. The short journey wasn't a problem, and the vet who received the 'parcel' round the back was very kind and helpful and told us that the ashes wouldn't be ready for collection until after Easter. (I of course at this point hadn't yet strayed far at all and was keeping a watchful eye on my beloved companions to make sure that they were coping all right.)

The next few days were interesting and full of activity, which was no doubt just as well, since it didn't leave time for my family members to wallow in their grief. It was the Tuesday before Easter and Alice's arrival a couple of days later was well timed, she being the person who'd persuaded her parents to buy her a Cavalier for her fifteenth birthday and consequently got them hooked on the breed! Alice had of course been very upset when Ann phoned to give her the news, but it was good for the three of them to have the chance of sitting down together and talking a lot about me. Ann was also helped on the Thursday by her visit to my friend Pip, who really understands about dogs, and she gave her some acupuncture treatment for grief, which was most effective. For Ann well knows the importance of not bottling things up, yet she has never found crying easy. She'd already told Pip, however, about my having previously been her horse during her brief Cathar lifetime and after she'd given Pip her sad news, Pip commented that she'd always been able to see the 'sturdy steed' in me. That evening, when Ann went off for an early night, she found the tears flowing freely about *both* lifetimes simultaneously and that was very healing!

The next few days were quite exciting — at least for me. I knew I'd have to keep a watchful eye on my family just to start with, but once I'd seen that they were accepting the situation — even recognising some of the ways in which it was really for the best — I appreciated that I was now free to cross over to the other side. Leaving my physical body had been painless, and now I found that I no longer had any difficulty whatsoever in moving. In fact I could fly like the birds I'd so often in my youth tried in vain to catch; it was fantastic!

So I travelled on and on, passing places that I recognised and before too long I spied three Cavaliers playing together on a beautiful grassy patch with plenty of trees around. One of them (a black and tan) suddenly noticed me and said: "You're a Pearson, aren't you? Welcome Home! We've been expecting you. My name's Merlin and you must have become used to seeing my photograph in your house."

"Indeed, I know all about you and it's lovely to meet you in the flesh!"

"Not flesh exactly," Merlin replied. "You know that we forget about that encumbrance when we leave our physical bodies behind on Earth."

"Of course I do. I was just speaking figuratively, as it were. Anyway, it's really great to meet you. I know that you were often around keeping an eye on us all, and I know how much love you'd both given and received before your heart finally gave up, as mine just did."

"Correct. A while after I'd crossed over and Ann and David had had a break from dog owning and travelled widely around India, I had a particular task to fulfil as advisor to your immediate predecessor, Apu. Apu only needed a short time on Earth in order to achieve a dual purpose. Firstly he needed to regain a part of his soul that had split off and attached itself to Ann during a very brief foray into the human world; and secondly he'd agreed to give both her and David a big lesson in loss. But when Apu had completed that lifetime, I didn't want to lose touch with the family (whose cat I'd been during an eighteenth-century lifetime in London) and so I popped by from time to time. Now let me introduce you to my friends."

"*Woof woof*, I'm Apu," said a beautiful Cavalier the same colour as me. "We look very alike, don't we, apart from your pretty little white patches, but we're extremely different in character! I'm quite a young soul compared with you and was quite fearful in my last life on account of trauma I'd been through in previous ones, but Merlin's been helping me to gain confidence and trust, so I'll soon be ready for a new, longer incarnation. Now here's Rincewynd, our tricolour friend, who was Alice's first dog."

"Yes, *woof woof*, it's lovely to welcome you here. I had an even shorter life than Apu did last time. That was because part of my mission was to give Alice, who was 17 at the time, quite an early lesson in loss. She coped very well, in spite of her intense grief, and now I'm looking forward to her feeling able at some point to acquire a new doggy companion. (Of all the Pearsons she's by far the most knowledgeable about dogs and could easily have chosen to be a vet this time round.)"

"Well," said Merlin, "now that we've all three greeted you, I think it's time for you to go back and see how those human three are getting on. They're about to set off for Bracknell, where they have an important job to do of starting to sort out Tony's house. I know you don't fancy going there yourself, and anyway they can do without distractions from the mammoth task, but you could perhaps fly along beside the car and guide them through any possible difficulties."

"Yes, you're right. My work down there isn't yet quite complete, so I'll see you anon."

The next few weeks were something of a mixture for all of us. Though the competent, efficient Alice did the bulk of the most urgent work in the house over the Easter weekend (such as making it presentable for the estate agent's photographer), Ann did what she could in spite of her back pain, and David both gave advice and took a lot of stuff out to the bins. Alice then drove them on to her house, where she herself had to get back to her brand new job with the National Health Service (NHS), and the others were able to relax a bit. I of course was used to Alice's house; I'd always enjoyed going there and knew all the nearby walks by heart. Ann, who was waiting for something to be done to her left leg, wasn't able to walk very far, but Alice made sure that her father did enough walking, so I sometimes joined them, and by the end of the week they were ready to return to Malvern.

Needless to say, my physical absence struck my family even more forcefully when they got home. They were still coping well, regularly giving thanks to God for the ease of my passing, but little things naturally kept giving rise to pangs of grief, for instance when Ann finished emptying out my drawer in the kitchen. But the biggest problem was all the tripe in their fairly small freezer that I hadn't had time to eat! War babies are renowned for not being able to stand waste, and Ann was determined to get the tripe to our very close friend, Claire. I'd sometimes stayed with Claire and her family, which, besides two lovely young girls, comprises two dogs, three cats and some chickens. (One of the chickens once chased me, but I was pretty brave!) The problem was that they live right out in the country near Presteigne, which is much further from Malvern than from Ludlow, but eventually our dear Muriel found space in her freezer for it until Claire was coming to Ludlow and could collect it.

Other little things, however, kept bringing tears to human eyes: nobody to eat up the skin when they had such things as salmon for dinner, nobody next to Ann's feet waiting for titbits when she was dismantling the remains of the cooked chicken, nobody to go out for walks with David... But they knew from their previous experience of dogs' crossing over that that was inevitable and that the happy memories would gradually predominate.

Before my time had come, Ann used to say that, since I was so attached to them both, she imagined that I'd still hang around after I'd departed. There was certainly some truth in that initially, but, living in the moment (which dogs tend to be better at than people are), I didn't think ahead at all and simply took each step as it came. However, once I'd found freedom from my somewhat weary body, I gradually began to realise the great potential that one has over here and to start making the most of it, offering my services wherever they might be needed.

Ann consequently soon said herself that she had the feeling that, rather than being near them all the time, I was busy with other important things. I was pleased to see that she appreciated the reality rather than clinging on to me, which is always a hindrance to the departed soul's progress. That doesn't mean to say that, in the early days, I didn't pop by from time to time; in fact David, who has a clairvoyant streak, actually saw me in the apartment a few times, commenting, for instance, "Surya's just jumped onto the sofa." This felt quite natural to him because of a previous experience. When Rincewynd had died, they'd all been in Spain, and that was in the days before mobile phones and internet. Rincewynd consequently decided to call in on them there to say goodbye immediately after crossing over. David, who was sitting reading a book, noticed him briefly on the sofa on the other side of the room. He didn't mention it to the family but made a mental note of the time and that prepared him a bit for the terrible news which the friend who'd been looking after Rincewynd had had to give them when they got back to England.

You've probably gathered from what I've said already that Ann is a writer and by the time of my departure she'd just had the above-mentioned book on womanhood accepted for publication. This continued to entail a lot of work and so was quite a big distraction for her immediately following my demise, but she's also a therapist and here I got called upon to give a bit of help quite soon after I'd begun to settle in to my new life over here.

Therapists — in fact people in general really — are often a lot better at looking after other people than at looking after them*selves*, even though both are equally important. Well, both Ann and her husband had been suffering for several weeks from rather bad eczema (very likely triggered, at least in part, by Tony's illness and death, my ditto, plus all the stress of the various other things that took place during this year of 2021). They both went to see a doctor and tried many different creams and things in vain, in addition to homoeopathic remedies that Mark sent them, but Ann one day reached desperation point with the itching and decided to journey on it to request an answer.

So she put on her drumming CD and the first thing she saw when she'd been up through the clouds was me sitting on Sai Baba's lap. (I'd been delighted, not long after I'd crossed over, to discover that He was real and present, not just someone from history whose photograph she liked having all over the place!) So I jumped straight off and was then guided to take her straight to a scene in the aforementioned twelfth-century Cathar lifetime that we'd shared, in which her healer mother was teaching her how to treat a woman who'd been suffering with eczema for a long time, bandaging her all over with nettle poultices. When the woman, who was finally beginning to feel better, said "I *never* want to have to go through this again!", Ann replied by assuring her that she wouldn't have to as she would take it on for her another time.

This left Ann somewhat puzzled, wondering how her enduring eczema in the twenty-first century could help someone who'd suffered from it way back in the twelfth (not that time has any real meaning, as I can see clearly now I'm over here!). The next afternoon, however, while she was resting on the bed and thinking about it, a voice in her head suddenly said: "You've got to take care of *yourself* in the same way as you took care of that woman." Whose the voice actually was is immaterial; the important point is that Ann knew she had to take the message seriously, and I now see reminding her of that from time to time as one aspect of my current role. (That's best done at night, when Ann is asleep and out of her body and we can chat face to face.)

While I was living with them in my physical body, I was of course aware of how much time Ann spent at her desk bashing away on her computer, but it was difficult for me, with my doggy brain, to understand that what she was doing there bore any relation to printed books that they both sometimes sat reading. Once I'd come Home, however, I was able to appreciate not only that her book on womanhood was now in production but also that she had one final book in mind that she was keen to get written before joining me over here. I also gathered that it was going to be about 'dead' people, so it seemed to me that my story would fit into it very well. So, on one of her nightly forays, I put it to Ann that I'd like to put my paw in. (I wouldn't be able to use an oar, and anyway I don't fancy canoeing.) We discussed the matter thoroughly and she agreed that it was a good idea, adding that she thought that my chapter could come in about the middle of the book. When I asked why I shouldn't be first, since I was ready to start making my contribution straight away, she replied that people would automatically expect the book to be about *people*, adding that she already had one book written by animals. I felt slightly hurt at first but soon came round, knowing that she didn't at all mean to offend me. She further explained that, whereas when people were reading a book they normally started at the beginning and then went through it page by page to the end, when a book such as this, which would contain independent stories, was being *written*, the order in which it was done wouldn't matter.

Now that I'm reaching the end of my story, you might be wanting to ask what I'd like to be in my *next* life, whether I want to be human. Well, my frank reply is that I'm not sure at the moment whether I do really fancy being human. So many people are messing the planet up and there's so much cruelty to animals; I certainly want to keep well away from all that. Merlin's told me that *he* feels ready to be human, and no doubt he'll make a much better job of it than many, but is it actually essential to become human? I understand that Sai Gita, Sai Baba's devoted elephant, was able to bypass humanity and return straight to Him. I certainly wouldn't claim that I'm as evolved as she was, but I don't think I need to make up my mind quite yet about the next stage. I *am* clear that I want to hang around until both David and Ann have crossed over, continuing to be available to them as necessary, but, as I've commented above, we dogs are expert at living in the moment, and wasn't the big lesson of 2020 "*Wait and see*"?!

I'll end by telling you that, once Ann had realised that I'd moved on to higher realms and David (who, I'm glad to say, wasn't hanging on to me either) was no longer seeing me in their apartment, she suggested to him that, each time they were going out for any reason, they could ask whether I wanted to come with them. Sometimes I replied with a 'Yes', but at other times I had a good reason for not accompanying them. When, however, it was a question of realising David's long-held dream of going to Orkney, I was very enthusiastic! For instance, the trip involved not only a sleeper train all the way to the pleasant city of Inverness but also a flight to Kirkwall, and I'd never been on an aeroplane.

Though the so-called 'sleeper' carriage turned out to be appallingly cramped and the train itself impossibly bumpy and noisy, that was all very exciting. David was *really* in his element once they'd reached Orkney — he said that he could easily live there (which Ann of course interpreted as meaning that he *had* lived there in the past) — while they both really liked the little port of Stromness, where their hotel was situated. As for the world-famous site of Skara Brae, they were both extremely impressed and most grateful that the weather was fine for it. I myself couldn't quite see the fascination of ancient ruins that were no longer habitable, but I admired Kevin's (their naturalist guide) immense knowledge about birds, of which there are so many on those islands, and it was thrilling for me to be able to fly with them.

So throughout the week's tour, with its intensely packed programme, I popped back and forth. Ann occasionally felt a bit guilty when it occurred to her at certain moments that she hadn't been thinking about whether I was with them, but I kept assuring her that that was a *good* sign, since I didn't want either of them to be dependent on me. I *did*, however, come into their hotel room on the last morning, when they needed to make an early start for the airport, just to make sure that they didn't forget to pack anything. Ann, the moment she got up, got an immediate strong sense of there being three of us in the room. She was tired and thought it odd at first, but then it quickly dawned on her that I was there. I also went with them on the boat trip over to Hoy — another brand new experience for me! — and that was because I needed to ensure that Ann's next character for this book would make herself known to her. (I knew that Ann had for a long time had her old friend Amos, a human guide, helping with the writing of this book, but sometimes an extra one doesn't come amiss.) So now it's time for me to hand over to dear Betty!

# 14

# The Cruelty of Man

*I wandered lonely as a cloud*
*That floats on high o'er vales and hills,*
*When all at once I saw a crowd,*
*A host of golden...*

William Wordsworth

No, it wasn't daffodils I spied, but bog asphodel, a pretty little yellow, star-shaped flower that was surrounding my grave. My *new* grave, with my name — Betty Corrigal — on it! And I must have wandered lonely for much longer than that well-known English poet did. For about 200 years in fact. So now I feel it right to tell you my story, for it is far from unique. I am but one of countless young (or not-so-young) women who have suffered the cruelty of man. And I'm using the word advisedly, not in the sense of mankind in general, but of the male gender in particular.

I was born and lived all 27 years of my last life on the island of Hoy, not far from the mainland of Orkney, which, though I alas never had the chance to see any of it with my own eyes during that lifetime, is graced with incredibly ancient archaeological sites that arouse interest much further afield than in just our own rather small community. The mainland was also home to the great St Magnus, one of the Orkney Earls, in whose name a great cathedral was later built in Kirkwall. (That's another place I should love to have seen while I was alive, but a little bit more on that subject will come later.)

I spent my life in a cottage named Greengairs, just north of the port of Lyness. I was alas an only child. My parents were simple farmers and good Christians, but they sadly died within a year of one another before I'd turned 20. Although the neighbours were always good to me, their loss made me feel quite lonesome and I also struggled somewhat to keep myself. I had enough land for growing a few vegetables and I was sometimes able to exchange some of my most handsome specimens for a fish or two, or even on occasion a small piece of meat. For the rest I daydreamed a great deal of the time, yearning for a family of my own and to see more of the world. I learnt from passing sailors, as well as from neighbours who *had* been able to travel a bit, that the spot where I lived was but a tiny speck of planet Earth and that there were very different landscapes to be seen, different races living elsewhere, and warmer climates that could be savoured.

Then suddenly one fine day my life changed dramatically! I was outside pulling up carrots when a handsome young man (about my own age I guessed) walked by. "Good morning, pretty lass," he said. "What is your name and are you all on your own here?"

"I'm Betty," I replied, "and I've been living alone ever since my parents passed away a few years ago. Who are you and why have I never seen you before? I thought I knew everybody in these parts."

"I'm known as Jock and I'm not from these parts, but have come from the other side of the island to seek work. My parents wanted me to take over their farm, but I found it boring and wanted to do something quite new and different."

"Such as what?" I asked. "Is there much to be done on Hoy apart from farming or fishing?"

"That's precisely what I'd like to find out! But right now I'm a trifle hungry. Were you by any chance planning to cook those carrots in your fair hand? And have you anything else in your cottage to accompany them?"

"Well, I still have a few potatoes left from last year's crop and a piece of ham that Barney next door gave me only yesterday..."

"That sounds perfectly adequate. Would you care for me to peel your potatoes while you prepare the carrots? I'm quite a dab hand at that, having been taught many such things by my good mother."

Well, that was just the start of the story, and those of you with any knowledge of the ways of the world will be able to guess how it continued. I was completely swept off my feet — as any 26-year-old single girl would be when a handsome young man came into her life for the very first time. Jock wasn't able, as he'd hoped, to find a proper job straight away and so was forced to make do with casual work, such as loading and unloading boats that docked in Lyness. We didn't become lovers instantly; I was much too cautious and God-fearing for that. Anyway I had to be ultra-careful that the neighbours didn't suspect anything, as it would have been impossible to avoid scandal. Jock was often able to get temporary lodging on the boats in which he was working and when he did come to my cottage it was never at night. We had plenty of excuses up our sleeves for when or if questions were asked: he was exchanging fish he had caught for some of my vegetables or fruit, he was the son of a distant cousin of my mother's who'd decided to track me down... and so on.

When we did make love properly for the first time, besides being the greatest bliss I'd ever experienced, it was in a place that nobody would ever have suspected in a million years. We both loved walking the nearby hills, and we'd found a secret place in which to meet inside a very small cave on a beach not far from my home. We always arrived there from different directions, which made it most unlikely that anyone would suspect anything and when we set off together, we always checked carefully that nobody was around. One Sunday, when we met while almost everybody else was at church, Jock told me that he'd made the most exciting discovery and couldn't wait to show it to me. It turned out to be the Dwarfie Stane, of whose existence I'd heard but which I had never actually seen. We climbed up towards it, hand in hand, stumbling initially through low bushes of willow. The last bit of the path was a bit tricky, but we both had sturdy boots on our feet.

I could hardly believe it when Jock showed me the entrance to it, as I'd always imagined it to be no more than a rather large stone. The opening was near the middle of the huge stone — not totally unlike the front door of a house — and when we'd reached the end of a small passageway, Jock lit a candle he'd brought with him specially. Lo and behold, there was a double bed carved out of the stone, and it even had a stone pillow on it! "The kind dwarfies obviously made it for us!" we exclaimed laughingly to one another. "Next time we'd better equip ourselves with something soft to lie on."

We didn't dare stay there very long that first time, but quite long enough for me to lose my virginity and to become acquainted with true bliss despite the initial pain. After that we secretly furnished the place with hay, over which we put a blanket, and we met there as often as we dared. Sometimes I would say to Jock, "So we're now officially labelled 'sinners'! Does that make any sense? Surely 'sin' involves doing harm to others. What harm are we doing to *anyone* by expressing such deeply felt love?"

"Sin", he would reply, "is purely subjective. If either of us was married to somebody else and consequently being unfaithful to them, it would be a totally different matter. As it is, I personally cannot believe that God (if he really exists) is frowning upon us."

Another thing I had to be ultra-careful about was not to get with child. Even if Jock had felt ready for marriage, there was no way he would have been able to support three of us on his meagre casual earnings. So I tried hard to do the opposite of what my mother had done in vain, watching the calendar with my bleedings. My dear mother, who'd lost a couple of babies after having me, had desperately wanted another child, but I feared that I might be more fertile than she had been. We did, naturally, talk frequently of marriage, but were in complete agreement that stable employment would have to come first. Jock sometimes said that he should perhaps go to sea, but I felt sure in my innermost depths that, should he do so, I would never see him again.

Finally one day my deepest fear was realised. Jock told me that he'd been talking with one of the captains of the whaling boats he'd been loading and that the man had agreed to take him on, on trial, as an assistant. Jock promised me faithfully that he'd never be away for very long at a time, saying that he simply couldn't see any other possibility for our future because — especially if we wanted to have a family — a secure job was essential. I saw of course that he had a point, yet my heart was filled with foreboding. I pleaded for a long while, but in vain, and so then we went off at dusk for one last time to our precious 'lovers' nest' in the depths of the Dwarfie Stane, stumbling back through the darkness to my lonesome cottage, where he refused to come in in case we were seen. He forbade me from coming to Lyness the next morning to bid him farewell.

The next days dragged by mournfully; it would soon be the end of October, so the nights were getting longer and not much remained to do in the way of harvesting my vegetables for the winter. I wondered how I would pass the time and how long it would take for Jock to keep his promise — if indeed he did so. I was also keeping note of the number of days since my last bleeding. When six weeks had passed without a drop of blood issuing from me, I began to panic. Now and again I walked down to Lyness and searched the horizon in vain for a boat that could conceivably be Jock's returning to shore. By the time eight weeks had passed and I'd found my appetite to be increasing, I felt completely desperate! I had only myself to blame of course, for I knew that I should have been more cautious on that last evening we'd had together, but what else could a poor, lovesick lass do in such circumstances?

During the next couple of weeks I lay awake at night reflecting on the possible options that lay open to me, yet could see no viable solution. I had nowhere to flee to and if I stayed put, I knew that I would be shunned by everyone around me. Neighbours, who had in the past always been friendly towards my family, would now not only look down upon me as a whore and a sinner but would also spread word about my wickedness throughout the island. So I would never have a chance of employment to help me support myself and my son. (For some reason I felt quite sure that the baby was a boy — and a boy whom I would love with the profoundest passion imaginable.)

I'd been taught that, since all life was considered sacred in the eyes of God and the Church, the punishment for suicide would inevitably be Hellfire. What's more, were I to take my own life, my sin would be a double one, since it would also entail the murder of my son! But what choice did I have? Were I to come to term and give birth to the child, what sort of life would he, a 'bastard', have? It just didn't bear thinking about! So really, I decided, I had no choice but to put an end to both of us. I felt that, whatever 'Hellfire' actually consisted of, it couldn't be any worse than the only alternative, Hell on Earth. I'd never learnt to swim, so the easiest thing, I decided, would simply be to wade out to sea in some forsaken spot. It was certainly scary, but my end would hopefully come quickly...

*\*\**

Wherever was I? Lying on a beach, it seemed, and a man who looked somewhat familiar to my bleary eyes was pummelling my chest and shaking me to get water out of my lungs. "What a foolish thing to do, Betty! Your life can't surely be *that* bad? What on earth would your dear parents have had to say if they'd seen you? Now we'll get you home and dry in your nice clean cottage." Barney and his friend, whose name was now escaping me, were true to their word, and in no time I fell asleep in my own cosy bed. But that was to be the last time!

When I woke up I lay for a while bemoaning my fate and thinking about what to do next. (Those two brave men who'd risked their own lives to pull me out of the sea were obviously doing what they sincerely believed to be the right thing, but how little did they realise that their action had done nothing at all to help me!) No, I'd already made up my mind: no way could I carry on living in my current pregnant state, so I'd have to find a surer way of ending my life. Well, the solution was easy, as I knew I had some good strong rope in the outhouse, as well as a sturdy hook upon which to hang it. Simple! It took me a few days to pluck up the necessary courage, but when Barney and George (how could I have forgotten his name when I remembered how kind he'd been to my father after he'd fallen so sick?) came back the next morning to check on how I was faring, I was floating just beneath the ceiling looking down on that limp corpse with its very slightly bulging abdomen. "Ah," said Barney to George, "so *that's* what was wrong with the lass! I hadn't noticed in the dark the other night that she was with child. I wonder who the scoundrel was?"

"I wouldn't be surprised", replied his friend, "if it was that young Jock who'd come from the other side of the island and recently went aboard with Captain McDonald. I'd heard rumours that they'd been seen together several times."

"You may well be right. So we were really wasting our time going to all that trouble to rescue her — a real tragedy! Well, I suppose we'd better go and tell the village clergyman the sorry tale. I don't know what he'll want done with the body. She had no remaining family."

I followed them to the priest's house and listened in on the conversation. "Well, since it was clearly a suicide, she can't possibly be buried in holy ground. We'd better procure a wooden box to put the body in and then go talk to the Lairds of Melsetter. Perhaps they will be merciful."

But no, the said Lairds refused me a final resting place on their land, so my body was buried in an unmarked grave on the parish boundary of North Walls and Hoy. I watched the whole proceedings, but then I had to find where to go next. There was absolutely no sign of Hellfire anywhere — just a terrible greyness all around me and not a single soul in sight. Even my baby, I realised, my darling son, whom I'd decided to name Jock after his unfaithful father, was no longer with me. I can't even *begin* to tell you how desperately lonely it was! It was as though I was no longer existing, yet I knew that I must be at least partly alive because there was obviously *something* that was conscious of being so lost and so lonely.

Nor would I have known for how long I drifted around in this sorry state had it not been for the fact that one day two men cutting peat came across the corner of the wooden box in which my body had been buried. I overheard them saying that the year was then 1933, that is, over 160 years since I'd left Earth! Thinking that my makeshift coffin might contain treasure, they contacted Isaac Moar, the postmaster, and they then jointly decided to open it. You can imagine their surprise upon discovering my body, and their shock at seeing that the peat (since it contained no oxygen) had preserved it perfectly, so that my long dark hair was still lying in curls around my shoulders. The noose that I'd used to put an end to my life was also in the box, but that promptly turned to dust when exposed to the air. Since my body was so fresh, police were called to come from Kirkwall to investigate, but the Procurator Fiscal simply asked for the coffin and its contents to be reburied in the same spot.

For me to see my body still exactly the same as when I'd left it was very strange indeed, and renewed emotions flooded in, replacing the void that had filled me for so long. I relived my distress at Jock's departure more intensely than ever, wondering how an end to my torture could ever be found. I also thought about my lost baby and would have given anything to find out what had happened to him.

After that I watched my body being re-interred and then returned to my lonesome wanderings. Goodness knows how long after that I noticed it again being disturbed. This time it was by a party of soldiers who were also digging for peat. They commented that the coffin must have been there for a very long time before 1941, when they'd arrived as part of the war effort against Hitler (whoever he was!), and, after investigating their find, they named my body "The Lady of Hoy" before burying it yet again. The curiosity of the soldiers stationed on the island subsequently saw it being dug up several times and so, because of frequent exposure to the air, it then quickly began to decay. This didn't upset me too much, since I had no further use for it, but the matter was brought to the attention of some officers, who then moved the grave 50 yards away and covered it over with a concrete slab to deter the ghouls. It still, however, remained unmarked, which grieved me. I began to yearn for a new body and the chance to return to Earth, which I sort of knew was what ought to happen, but the big question was *how*?

Then, in 1949 (four years, I somehow heard on the etheric grapevine, after that dreadful war had ended), an American minister, the Reverend Kenwood Bryant, visited Hoy and was so moved by my story that he put up a wooden cross at the site, erected a small wooden fence and conducted a service for me. He also asked Mr Harry Berry, a customs officer, to create a proper headstone for the grave. The effect of this was so miraculous that you'd have pains believing it. I found myself suddenly being catapulted towards a dazzlingly beautiful white light, while simultaneously being wrapped in the most wonderful warm feeling of love that was even more powerful than the love I'd felt back on Earth, when I'd lain in Jock's arms!

Then — wonder of wonders — a beautiful little boy appeared before me and I instantly knew him to be my son.

"Mother!" he exclaimed. "How wonderful to see you. We've had to wait for *so* long!"

"Why", I asked him, "did it have to be so long?"

"Well, here comes someone who will be able to explain about it better than I can. You've heard of our great St Magnus, haven't you?"

"Indeed I have! But why should such a saint deign to talk with a miserable sinner such as me?"

"That's precisely the point that you need to grasp: that you're *not* a sinner, but simply a good, totally normal woman."

"Welcome Home, Betty! As your dear son says, you did nothing wrong. The wrong was all on the side of those around you, those so-called Christians who'd misunderstood Jesus' message and believed the sexual act performed outside marriage to be a sin. You had the misfortune of being so brainwashed that, when you left your physical body, you didn't know where to go and so had no choice but to wander aimlessly until someone finally came on the scene to help you. It's thanks to Reverend Kenwood Bryant's understanding, compassion and prayers that you were able to head towards the Light — a light that is always there but can easily become obscured by ignorance and people's lack of faith in their own innate divinity.

I have to confess that, in my lifetime as the Viking Magnus who was one of the Earls of Orkney and ultimately made a saint, I too was ignorant and would very likely also have condemned you for becoming pregnant before marriage. I had the good fortune, however, of being saved by some good deeds that were well known about in Orkney. Unlike King Magnus, who came from Norway some time after I had, and my cousin Hakon, I hated warfare and having been converted to Christianity by the Irish monks who lived on the Brough of Birsay, I took to prayer instead of joining in the fighting. In the end my cousin Hakon, who despised me for refusing to follow the Viking way, had me killed. After my death one or two people saw me in a vision, a bright light was seen over my tomb and many people began to pray beside it. I was so touched by this that I took Jesus' advice and found myself able to cause miracles and healings. As a result I was made a saint, and a beautiful cathedral was built in Kirkwall in my name."

"Yes, I've heard of it and always yearned, while I was on Earth, to see it, but had of course no means of getting there from Hoy."

"Well, let me take you there right now. Travelling is a lot easier once one no longer has a physical body!"

"Thank you. I'd *love* that!"

"Another happy ending to my story is that Hakon later repented of his evil deeds, travelled to the Holy Land, was baptised in the River Jordan and then went on to rule Orkney fairly for the remainder of his life. Being killed didn't bother me in the slightest — especially once I'd come over here and discovered that we all have countless lives in numerous different types of bodies — and I've already returned a couple of times, once as a Muslim and once as a Buddhist. That's how we learn all that we need to learn. You will also have many more chances and it's important that you get your story told. People all need to learn compassion and to understand that nobody should ever be condemned for following their instincts, just so long as nobody else is harmed in the process."

After St Magnus had shown me over his wonderful cathedral, I asked him many more things, such as whether I would ever see my beloved Jock again, whether we might one day have a chance to marry and have a family, and whether I'd known my son before, since he seemed so familiar to me. He helped me to understand a lot more before taking me on a guided tour to meet my parents, other ancestors and also my guides. My parents were delighted to see me after that long time of watching over me and feeling sadly helpless. They explained that, since they'd had no contact on Earth to ask to send me onwards, they'd been really sorry at leaving me wandering aimlessly. They'd also been sorry not only about having died when I was so young but also about my sad fate.

My guides then further explained that I'd only needed a short life that time in order to learn self-sufficiency and also that the pain I'd suffered would help me in the future to be compassionate with others who suffered in similar ways. They suggested that, now that I was no longer trapped, I could spend some time exploring the astral realms and get to know other places well beyond my previous limited horizons. So this I did and found it all wonderfully exciting.

Then, after another longish gap, a really lovely thing happened. The Reverend Kenwood Bryant, as I mentioned above, had asked the customs officer, Mr Harry Berry, to create a proper headstone for my final grave. This caused a bit of a problem because the boggy ground made a stone headstone unsuitable, and it wasn't until after Mr Berry's retirement, a whole 27 years later (in 1976, the year so renowned for its lengthy heatwave followed by serious drought), that a fibreglass headstone was erected instead. The important thing about this is that, as I said at the very beginning, it has my name engraved upon it — a thing that *everyone* deserves, even if their life wasn't perfect.

What's more, when this was done, a second, quiet service was performed, and the result of those prayers, would you believe it, is that Jock suddenly returned to me! We embraced and he assured me that he'd never got over the separation but felt he had no alternative. So I came to appreciate that I hadn't *really* suffered, as so many women do, the 'Cruelty of Man' and that our love for one another had been totally true. This made it easy for me to forgive him for the desertion, and we agreed to come together again at a happier time in the future. Little Jock then appeared, too, and contributed his own views, saying that he'd still like to be our son again (as he had been once before, he recalled, in a different country during the Middle Ages).

The three of us then decided to start straight away on working towards changing people's minds about what really was and was not sinful. We also agreed that we'd prefer to wait a while before returning to Earth. For it was very clear from the perspective we have here that very tough times lay ahead, with yet more wars, climate change causing many natural disasters and grave sickness spreading around the globe. We felt that we really didn't want to be part of all that.

One thing that's giving me great pleasure these days is observing all the tourists who make special efforts to come and look at my grave. I never craved fame during my lifetime but am thoroughly enjoying it now! So God bless you all, and please do what you can to spread my story further afield.

# 15

# A Near-Death Experience

*'Alice, when I say that my father won't be too happy about it,' John says hastily, once the waitress has gone, 'I'm not automatically assuming anything... I mean, I'm not taking it as read that we're going to... get... involved or anything. I mean, it depends on what you think... I don't want to jump the gun...' He grinds to a halt.*

Maggie O'Farrell, *After You'd Gone*

My name is Alice Raikes and I'm a fictional character, but this book was never intended to be fully factual anyway and its main aim is to demonstrate a variety of possible post-death scenarios. Also, when a really good novelist conceives a character, he or she feels totally real to the reader as well as to the author. My original creator was Maggie O'Farrell, whose fame is well deserved, highly gifted as she is at 'painting' people. Those of you who have already read the novel of which I was the heroine will no doubt remember that I had a far from easy life even before I lost my beloved husband John in that terrible London bombing. Before meeting John I'd escaped from two very difficult relationships and, before that, my adolescence had been stormy, with frequent blow-ups with, in particular, my mother Ann. (Interesting, isn't it, that my new author's name is Ann, while *her* daughter's name is Alice?!) I dearly loved my two sisters, Kirsty who was older and Beth who was younger, but after finishing my degree I left my family in Scotland and went to live and work in London.

I can see clearly now that my mother was never happy and that her marriage to my father Ben had been a mistake, deeply though *he* loved *her*. (They had met as students in a physics lab when he came to her rescue following a rather serious accident.)

Her later affair with another man, though carefully concealed from her daughters, was the 'talk of the small town' and though my mother herself was never quite sure about it, I was the fruit of their relationship. I realise now that I'd sort of known that all along — there was the 'mysterious' incident when my mother had taken me as a young child to his salon for a haircut and he'd given me the gift of a necklace of *real* pearls — but I never wanted to acknowledge it either to myself or to anyone else. After all, my father Ben had always loved me as his own, making no distinction between me and my sisters, despite the fact that I looked so obviously different with my jet-black hair, and anyway I adored him and also had until her death a very close bond with my paternal grandmother. So, suddenly seeing them together (that is, my mother and her lover) at Edinburgh railway station long after I'd grown up was too much for me.

My sisters, who'd kindly both come to meet me at the station, after I'd phoned Kirsty to forewarn her of my sudden, impulsive decision to go there, were both baffled and anxious when I told them, without giving a reason, that I couldn't stay. I was, however, much too upset to tell them what I'd seen. Then of course their anxiety, poor dears, was multiplied a thousand times when they heard about my near-fatal accident. Or was it an accident? My family and friends strongly suspected suicide — and after all, what with having lost my beloved husband and then that shocking sighting in Edinburgh, I had enough reasons for feeling suicidal — but the truth is that I was simply unable to think straight and so didn't *really* know what I was doing when I went out into that London traffic.

Isn't it tragic that, throughout history, most wars have been instigated by religion? Idiotic, too, when the whole purpose of *every* religion has always been Peace and Love! The tragedy of John's and my relationship was that his widowed father was absolutely determined that his son should marry a Jewish woman and was so devastated when we'd fallen in love that he refused even to meet me. This affected me profoundly, as I believed parent-child relationships to be very important and I wanted anyway to have the fullest possible picture of my beloved husband. I'd never had even the teeniest drop of anti-Semitic blood inside me and, though not myself at all religiously inclined, hated the fact that all those of different Faiths couldn't recognise their equality and be tolerant of their differences.

Of course all those of us who lost loved ones in that dreadful London bombing of 7 July 2005, which killed 52 people and injured hundreds more, obviously suffered intensely, but I have to admit to having coped exceptionally badly. I now see clearly that such an appalling experience *can* trigger very worthwhile reactions — I myself, for instance, would have been perfectly capable of forming something such as a support group for the bereaved — but instead I simply wallowed in self-pity and believed my life to be 'over'. I did, however, have a burning desire to befriend John's father and later greatly regretted my cowardice in not approaching him, as I could easily have done when I went to his house and watched him leave it to go to the library.

As it was, my going into a lengthy coma was an absolute nightmare for my poor family! My life hung in the balance for a very long time, and I was immensely touched when I realised that John's poor, bereaved father had actually come and sat at my bedside. (Many people don't realise that people who are comatose can be very aware of what's going on around them. This makes much more sense when one appreciates the fact that the soul regularly leaves the body — especially when one is asleep at night.)

Anyway, at one point my Higher Self (as 'the over-soul', the part that one leaves behind on the other side for each new incarnation, is commonly known) decided that the time had come for the choice to be made about whether I was going to live or die. For this decision it seemed useful to bring John in, and you can well imagine my intense joy at seeing him again! Especially as I'd always been an agnostic and open-minded about whether there was any such thing as life after death. My first reaction, no doubt a quite natural one, was simply to want to stay there with him. After we'd embraced, he took me on a guided tour, showing me what he'd been up to since leaving his body and introducing me to relatives who had gone on before. It was intensely interesting and I was overwhelmed by the beauty of the surroundings and the tranquillity, as well as thrilled to meet my beloved grandmother again, but she in particular had strong reservations about whether my time had really yet come.

"You have to appreciate, dearest Alice," she said, "that you're still a young, intelligent woman, who could do a great deal for the world as well as giving your devoted family the joy of finding that they weren't losing you after all!"

"Yes," added my dear John, "you could do a lot for your family, encouraging them finally to bring everything out into the open over your mother's relationship with your birth father — that couldn't increase the pain your poor father Ben has suffered all these years through being aware deep down of his wife's infidelity — and also for my family through making friends with my father. Do you appreciate that time (which doesn't really exist anyway) is a strange thing? It probably feels to you as though you've been over here with me for several hours, but back on Earth it's more like minutes. My father, who has long since come to regret his non-acceptance of our marriage, is still sitting at your hospital bedside waiting hopefully for some sort of sign of life from you. Nothing would please him more than if you were to open your eyes!"

"But what would I *do* with myself if I went back? Quite apart from the fact that I'd still miss you so dreadfully, I'd have an awful lot of explaining to do about why I was so foolish as to virtually commit suicide. And where would I live? I just couldn't bear the thought of returning to *our* home, with that long-lived axolotl of yours still glaring at me in the bathroom, that beloved, neglected cat of mine having no doubt given up on me..."

"No, I certainly wouldn't suggest that you carried on staying put. You could maybe start by going back up to Scotland, at least temporarily, challenge Ann to tell you the whole truth behind your conception and her continuing double life, and perhaps even find work up there for at least a while. And, you know, in connection with your query on suicide, I have an interesting and important point to make. Since being back here, one thing I've observed is that some people — particularly those who weren't really keen to return to Earth in the first place — are born with a sort of 'death wish'. Maggie, your original creator, is very likely one of them because one of her other books, which is autobiographical rather than a novel, is about her own numerous near-misses with death. People could be incredulous as to how one person could possibly have had so many narrow escapes, but it could well be explained by her subconscious desire to clear off. If that's the case, she might have transmitted this to you while composing our story. So now your new challenge, if you returned, could be to embrace life to the full, find new work, new hobbies, very likely a new spouse, and have a child or two. Of course you'd still miss me, but now you would know for sure that I really was still around. We would meet up at night, when you were out of your body, and I could be one of your guides during the day."

"Hmm, that's certainly something to think about!"

"Well, I shouldn't think for *too* long, darling, because there's a limit to the length of time that a physical body can stay alive when the life force has left it. What do *you* think, Elspeth?"

"I certainly think that Alice could do a tremendous amount if she returned to Earth! Just sorting her family out would be one very good thing. My son's grief has bothered me for a very long time. If her parents divorced soon, they could both find greater happiness in more suitable relationships. There's also good reason for Alice to have a family of her own. John is indeed a gem, but there are other male gems around and she is still quite young and undoubtedly very attractive. Now, with the learning that she has behind her, she would exercise greater discrimination in relationships than she did prior to meeting John."

"OK, dearest ones, between the two of you you've convinced me! I'll rush back to the hospital bed now, but promise me faithfully that you'll carry on hanging around."

"We promise," they replied in unison.

As you can imagine, getting back into my body wasn't at all easy. For one thing, I found myself racked with pain. Seeing John's father's face, however, made everything seem a hundred per cent worthwhile.

"Alice!" he exclaimed incredulously. "Are you really still alive — or returned to life?"

"Y-e-e-s... 'returned' is the word." Making my mouth work so as to get the words out was a real struggle, but I knew I had to force myself. "You ma-a-y find this hard, if not imp-p-possible to believe, but I've just been with John."

"John? You mean *our* John? My dear deceased son and your devoted husband?"

"The very one! He's alive and still the same. He showed me wondrous sights on the other side, we talked things through, and he said that I should come back, for all sorts of reasons — not the least of them being to make friends with *you*! I met my beloved grandmother, too, and she insisted that it wasn't yet my time, that I could still do a lot of good things on Earth. What do you think?"

"Well, I *can* believe it. When I'd heard that you were in a coma and that your life was in the balance, a book on NDEs leapt out at me in the library. I read it from cover to cover and found it both fascinating and credible; and in any case my Jewish Faith had already made me sure that John *was* still alive, that it was only his body that had died in the bombing. But now we need to *act*! I must call a nurse, get them to take a look at you, and make sure that you get the care you need. The first thing that will be necessary, I'm quite sure, is a good recovery period. There will be plenty of time for us to talk later."

My father-in-law was true to his word. Once the doctors had examined me thoroughly, my family had been called and a period of bed rest in a comfortable environment had been ordered, he insisted on taking me home with him.

"Scotland is too far for her to travel at the moment," he said to my parents, "and in any case I owe it to her for not having done my duty while John was alive. It was really foolish of me to have been so prejudiced just because your daughter wasn't Jewish! It was hard for him, as we'd always been close, but my son was right to stick to his guns and put love first. Don't worry about the house. It would be too painful for Alice to carry on living there on her own. In due course we can sell it and Alice can use the proceeds to make a fresh start once she's decided what she wants to do next with her life. Don't worry about the axolotl either! I know Alice was never fond of it and I'm sure that my nephew who breeds them will be perfectly happy to take it back."

And so things were for a while. My parents gave their approval to my father-in-law's abode, my sisters came to visit me there as well, and gradually John's father and I opened up to one another, sharing our grief over the loss of John and finding true consolation in talking of our memories of him. Certainly my convalescence was quite slow — my head was very fuzzy at times and John's father insisted on my getting plenty of rest — but none of my wounds was that serious and I was still young enough for them to heal reasonably quickly. My father-in-law was also a rather good cook and I soon got to enjoy the kosher food. He was also an intelligent man and we were never short of topics of conversation. However, he seemed never able to apologise enough for not having welcomed me in the first place. I assured him over and over that his attitude was perfectly understandable, that life was about learning, and that we could perhaps in due course share a mission of improving interfaith relationships.

That was the easy bit compared with the time when I decided that I was finally ready and strong enough to go up to Scotland and deal with my parents! We spoke frequently on the phone of course, and I agreed to their suggestion of finding me a little place nearby to rent on my own. It wasn't that they didn't have room, or wouldn't have welcomed me in their home, but the general agreement among the family was that I could do with time and space to think everything through before deciding upon my next step.

One thing of which I became increasingly aware during my period of convalescence was the pleasure I took in observing such things as nature. Spring was just starting and my father-in-law took great delight in his garden. Sometimes he took me outside to admire the latest buds that were opening, and for me it was almost as though I'd never noticed anything similar before. During my brief visit to the other side I'd seen beauty such as I could never have imagined, with colours more intense than anything we have on Earth, yet I readily accepted that such sights were being kept in store for me for 'later' and that right now my task was to relish to the full everything that we had here and to join in with all efforts to preserve it.

When the time did come for me to head northwards, my father-in-law embraced me tenderly and promised to come up for a visit fairly soon. Fortunately he was still quite physically fit and didn't feel daunted by the prospect of a long train journey. My whole family came to greet me at Edinburgh station and it truly was a thrill to see them all again. Kirsty had prepared a wonderful meal for everyone and once that was over and we'd temporarily paused all our reminiscing, my parents drove me to the little flat that they'd rented on my behalf. It was small but charming, with a really wonderful view, and I assured them that I'd be perfectly happy there for several weeks, if not months, while I made up my mind what my next steps should be. I explained to them that I did believe that my ultimate destiny was to settle back in London. After all, that was where the majority of good jobs in my sort of field were to be found and as I told them besides, I did feel that I should live reasonably close to John's father, since I was now the only person he really had, whereas they all had each other. Before they left that evening, I took the bull by the horns and asked my mother to come back on her own for a coffee at 11 o'clock the next morning.

I was truly dreading confronting her with what I'd seen before hurriedly returning to London a few months previously, but I'd promised John that I would do that and so there was no point in dilly-dallying. Anyway, I knew I'd feel very much better once I'd got it over with. I slept fitfully that first night, going over and over in my head how I would put it to her, but, when the time came and she'd only just arrived on the dot of 11, she made it easier by asking: "Alice, I *have* to find out from you what it was that made you jump onto the next train back to London within minutes of us all coming to the station to greet you."

"Mother," I replied firmly, "have you really no inkling whatsoever of the answer?"

"Did you, er... did you see something that upset you?"

"I did indeed," I said, bursting into tears.

She then burst into tears as well and, putting both her arms around me, she sobbed. "Oh, Alice, if you only knew what I've suffered all these years! Your father really is a very good man, has always been utterly devoted to me, but *you* know yourself, only too well, what *true* love really is compared to mere affection."

As she spoke, I suddenly understood how it was from her point of view. After all, John was really the only man I'd ever loved, or ever felt that I could love, and if it really was the same for her with *him* and her marriage to my dear father had really been a big mistake, I simply must feel compassion for her. So I let her carry on holding me gently like a child, our tears mingling together. After what seemed like a very long time and when we both felt that we didn't have another tear left inside us, we drew apart, heaved a huge mutual sigh, and then I said: "So what do we do now?"

"Well, what do *you* think I should do? I don't think I could *bear* to give him up!"

"The first thing I'd really like to know, Mother, is whether you think that he's actually my real father."

"The honest truth is that I've never been quite sure. Of course your shock of wonderful black hair has always made it look more than possible, but dear Ben has always been such a very good father to you that I simply couldn't face hurting him!"

"Don't you think, though, that the uncertainty, even if only semi-conscious, is even more hurtful for him? What John said to me when I met him on the other side was that we really should get it all cleared up and out into the open. How about starting with a DNA test? That's so easy to get done nowadays and he would surely be willing. You remember that occasion when I was only about seven, you took me there to get my hair cut and he presented me with that string of real pearls?"

"I do indeed, and something deep inside me made me hope that you would always treasure them. What happened? *Did* you keep the necklace?"

"It's still safe in my jewellery box (now stored in John's father's house). I haven't worn it very often — pearls are out of fashion these days — but I've never felt like getting rid of it."

"Well, all that's by-the-by just for the moment. Right now we need to decide what should be our very next step. Would you like me to ask this afternoon how he would feel about a DNA test?"

"Yes please, I would. Now you'd better go home and get some lunch. You've stocked my fridge very well, so now I just need a bit of rest. The journey was tiring and I didn't sleep well last night."

"OK then, darling. You stay put with your thoughts for the time being. Eat and sleep well and I'll drop by again in the morning."

When morning came, my mother appeared with the news not only that her lover was totally agreeable to the idea of being tested but also that she'd made appointments for both of us that very afternoon. I was pleased, as I really didn't want any more time to be lost. The result was crystal clear: Mr Innerdale was undoubtedly my father. After that had been established and he and I had agreed to spend a bit of time getting to know one another, I felt that my mother needed to 'go it alone' in confronting her husband both with the truth and with her desire for a divorce. Mr Innerdale had said immediately that divorce was what he would like and that he didn't think that his wife would object. (We'd better give him a first name, so I'll call him Andrew like his son, who'd had a crush on me at school, thus causing my mother a great deal of anxiety and me to get into trouble for breaking his nose after he'd torn my jumper from me.)

The whole process was of course painful all round (as these things always are), but I felt throughout that John was watching over it all and holding our hands, as it were. One of the first things that I did, once the ball had been set rolling, was to have a really good heart-to-heart with Ben, assuring him that I would always regard him as my real father, and telling him how much I loved him and appreciated the support he'd given me all my life. He confessed to me that he had always deep down suspected the whole truth, but that, loving both of us so very much and not wanting to cause disharmony in the family, he'd made every effort to suppress it and just keep on hoping that Ann would eventually come to love him more.

I won't bore you with all the details of the divorce, the search for new abodes and so on, but I will just say that both Kirsty and Beth were so understanding and supportive of both my parents that, before too long, I felt ready and eager to start sorting out my own life, applying for jobs and so on. Journalism seemed to be the most obvious choice and I knew that my CV would stand me in good stead, so in due course I headed back to the London area, where my father-in-law (who had already got John's house on the market) welcomed me again to his home, saying that I could stay as long as I liked, but that he appreciated that I would naturally be wanting to buy a flat of my own once I'd found something suitable.

We did indeed both join an interfaith group, in which John's father took a special interest in Jewish-Christian relations, made some good friends and ultimately fell in love with a Christian widow and married her. I, however, feeling that I was neither Jewish nor Christian, felt much more drawn to spiritual rather than religious sentiments and activities. In between job interviews, flat hunting and food shopping for the two of us, I read voraciously. I was particularly interested in books about the fascinating American clairvoyant Edgar Cayce (which rapidly convinced me that reincarnation was a *fact*), as well as personal accounts of spiritual experiences; and, though not feeling strongly drawn to Buddhism, I loved the writings of Thich Nhat Hanh and resolved to visit Plum Village at some point. I also joined a meditation group, and there I met someone else who had had an NDE and we agreed to form a group for people with that experience, or who were interested in learning about it.

We were pleasantly surprised to receive half a dozen replies to a little notice we put into a local newspaper and a lovely widower called Martin, who had suffered immensely when his wife Jane had died from stomach cancer, volunteered his pleasant living room for holding the meetings. He hadn't actually experienced an NDE himself, but Jane during her final days had gone in and out of her body and recounted to him wonderful meetings that she'd had with deceased loved ones. This had really sparked his interest and, being already an aspiring novelist (who earned a living as a journalist for a reputable newspaper), he was busy writing up not only his wife's experiences but also those of others. The members of the group all bonded quickly and took to doing such things as eating out together in addition to attending the monthly meetings. With John's father now content in a new relationship, I had no qualms about acquiring a good social life for myself.

As for the job hunting, since I wasn't yet destitute and the sale of John's house was going through anyway, I was determined to be quite picky and not simply accept the first offer I received. Martin, with his experience, was ready to give me good advice and in due course I accepted an offer from the same paper as he worked for. We gradually grew closer and he confided in me that, before her cancer diagnosis, he and Jane had begun to talk seriously about starting a family. After a while he invited me to move in with him, which made a lot of sense as his house was a good size (Jane had had a good job as well), and it was well situated both for our work and for central London. Soon we agreed that we would rather like the idea of having a child or two together. He introduced me to his parents and to his only sister, all of whom lived in the London area, and I fixed a date for going up to Scotland to introduce him to my family.

Once we were there, I found things better than they'd been when I'd left a few months earlier. My mother and my natural father had moved in together and the divorce was in the process of going through. My 'real' father had resigned himself to the situation and had even got in touch with a dating agency; and both my sisters were busy and happy with their own families. Martin and I agreed that marriage should be our next step and a date was fixed for a small wedding in my home town, to which only family and very close friends would be invited.

My longtime friend Rachel, with whom I'd renewed contact and who was gradually coming to terms with the 'new, spiritually inclined Alice', was herself fairly newly wed and pregnant. She said that she was 'too old' to be a maid of honour, but that she would happily be 'best woman'. Martin's old university friend, Bernard, who'd been a great support to him through his bereavement, was also very happy to be best man. Since Scottish weather is even less reliable than England's, June seemed to be a good month to choose, and we were in fact blessed with a truly glorious day.

Not long after we'd settled back in the house and at work, we acquired a kitten (but *not* an axolotl!), and then I found myself to be pregnant, which was a cause for great joy all round. We named our son John Benjamin, and Martin and I agreed that we were sure that both John senior and Jane were watching over us with approval. I was granted six months' maternity leave and when that had come to an end, Martin and I were able to take it in turns to work from home. John was a bright child, very high-spirited and independent, and more than ready to start nursery school as soon as he was three. By that time I was pregnant again and John got very excited at the thought of acquiring a younger sister. Her birth, like the first one, went smoothly and we named our daughter Mary (after Martin's mother) Jane.

We carried on with our regular spiritual meetings and reading and made new friends as gradually some of the founder members of the NDE group were replaced by others. Our two children were brought up to take such things for granted and at one point a spin-off group was formed for people who had children who spoke of past-life memories. It was all immensely interesting and once John had completed his first degree in psychology he decided to do a PhD in past-life regression studies, before himself training as a therapist. Mary was more scientifically inclined, and she read physics at Cambridge and then became a university lecturer. And Martin did eventually get out a couple of novels on spiritual themes.

Both our children made good partnerships and we were in due course blessed with four grandchildren. When our time came — I went first at the age of 88 and Martin survived me by only a few months — all the family gathered at our bedsides. John and Jane were of course both there to greet us and once we had all four gathered, each recognising the other three as old friends, we agreed to work as a team, offering help to people on Earth who suffered 'premature' bereavement.

# 16

# The Wife of One of the World's
# Greatest Writers

*Joy can only be real if people look upon their life as a service and
have a definite object in life outside themselves and their personal
happiness.*

Leo Tolstoy

My name in one of the most difficult lifetimes that I've ever had
on Earth was Sofia Tolstoya and though it brought me much
joy periodically, my marriage to the great Lev Nikolayevich has
been described as "one of the unhappiest in literary history".
Since returning Home, however, I've been helped to see that that
life had had a very important purpose — well, a dual purpose
really — to which I had agreed prior to incarnating. The first
thing, which I feel no need to go into here, is that I had a karmic
debt to pay on account of having in a previous marriage been
unfaithful to the man you in the West now know as Leo Tolstoy;
the second is that, with the high intelligence and gifts that I had,
I was ideally suited to supporting him in the important tasks
that he was taking on.

I was born on 22 August 1844 as Sofia Behrs (known to
family and friends as Sonya, which is the Russian diminutive
of the name) and was one of three daughters of the German
physician Andrey Evstafievich Behrs and his Russian wife
Liubov Alexandrovna Islavina. One of my claims to fame is that
my maternal great-grandfather, Count Pyotr Zavadovsky, was
the first Minister of Education in Russia's history. We were a
happy family, with a lot of love in the house, and it was only in
1862, when I was 18 and first introduced to Lev Nikolayevich,
that things changed radically for me. At 34, he was obviously

16 years my senior, but I was deemed to be what was then regarded as of marriageable age, and the impact of the death of his brother Nikolay in 1860 had given him a desire to marry.

Count Tolstoy was by then already well known as a novelist, having first achieved literary acclaim in his twenties with his semi-autobiographical trilogy *Childhood*, *Boyhood*, and *Youth*, followed by *Sevastopol Sketches*. The latter was based upon his experiences in the Crimean War, but his horror at the number of deaths involved in it had caused him to leave the army as soon as that war was over. My parents had ensured that my sisters and I were well educated (at home of course — the custom in those days!) and I'd also read *The Cossacks*. So I naturally felt flattered by Lev's interest in me and also found him irresistibly attractive.

We became formally engaged on 17 September 1862, after he'd given me a written proposal, and we were wed in my birthplace of Moscow merely a week later. What I only found out on the eve of the wedding, when he gave me his diaries to read, was that he had led a dissolute youth and even fathered a son by one of the serfs who lived on his family estate of Yasnaya Polyana. You can, I'm sure, well imagine the impact of this information on a young virgin excited by the thought of her imminent marriage! Yet I knew that I had no choice but to go through with it. (I now see clearly that I knew subconsciously then that our partnership was firmly in my life plan.) I myself was at the time already a serious diarist, too, and so he also looked at my diary and we made an agreement between us never to hold any secrets one from the other.

Yasnaya Polyana is well over a hundred miles south of Moscow and I hadn't had the chance even to see it before we were wed, so the move was quite a big culture shock for me. Not that I didn't appreciate the peace and quiet compared with the hustle and bustle of a big city, but I missed my family badly initially and adapting to such a new way of life naturally wasn't easy. In addition to that, I was immediately thrust into a total of 16 pregnancies. This was of course the lot of all women before birth control became a norm, so I trust that you, my twenty-first-century readers, fully appreciate your good fortune in this matter! Thirteen of my pregnancies reached full term and eight of the children I bore survived. Child death was again one of the great hardships so common at that time and I'm sure that *anyone* who has lost a child will fully appreciate the terrible grief that it brings.

For me the very worst of these losses was that of our youngest child, Vanechka, who died of scarlet fever when he was only seven. He was a truly exceptional boy, who used to surprise us grown-ups by speaking with depth on abstract and spiritual matters. Not only was he admired by all who met him, but his father also visualised him becoming his 'spiritual heir', someone who could be moulded to embody the highest principles of Christian love and virtue, and he once wrote: "I somehow dreamed that Vanechka would continue after me the work of God." My grief at the loss was absolutely uncontainable and, much later, following Lev's own death, Ilya, one of Vanechka's older brothers, said that he believed that, if the child had lived, their father's life might have been very different and that there was "unquestionably an intrinsic relationship between the two events".

If, however, you are already knowledgeable about spiritual matters and/or have learnt something from your reading of earlier chapters in this book, you will appreciate both that death is only a temporary separation and that there is invariably a good reason for it, whenever it occurs. So, with that assumption in mind, I think you won't be surprised to hear that darling Vanechka was waiting to greet me when I crossed over, and you can well imagine my intense delight upon seeing him. My death, in November 1919, had been extremely welcome anyway. At 75, totally worn out by so many years of hard work and, despite the moments of real joy, so much stress and distress, I was more than ready to go and leaving that weary body felt very easy.

Lev soon appeared as well, and the three of us gave each other big, emotional hugs, with my beloved husband (for there had never really been a time when I hadn't loved him, even at moments when the predominant feeling had been hatred!) apologising for mistreating me and so often failing to express his appreciation of me. Then our 'little one', who now appeared to have grown into a mature adult, explained the reasons for his early departure. "I had come, you see," he began, "partly to help you both to learn the lesson of agonising loss — a lesson that often needs to be repeated, human memories being short — and partly as an example for my older siblings, who were less spiritually inclined than I was. But I was called back at an early age to give help to people over here who were feeling a bit lost for varying reasons." "And aren't we proud of him, dearest Sonya?" intervened Lev. "He's a highly evolved soul, you see, and we were privileged to have been his parents for seven years."

Then our other deceased children all joined us one by one. Foremost among them was Masha, our fifth-born, who had died of inflammation of the lungs in November 1906. Of her, Ilya wrote: "That death shook him [their father] more noticeably than even the loss of Vanechka." For Masha had always been the person who could give him warmth, who could caress his hand and say affectionate things, and her father had responded to her very differently. "It was as if he became a different person with her," Ilya had said. "And so her death deprived my father of the one source of warmth which, with advancing years, had become more and more necessary to him." So I'll now leave the picture of our celestial happy family reunion to your imaginations and return to our lifetime together on Earth.

Lev Nikolayevich had been the fourth of five children in the old Tolstoy family (who traced their ancestry back to the fourteenth century with the arrival of the nobleman Indris "from Nemec, in the lands of Caesar"), but his mother died when he was only two years old and his father seven years later. So he and his siblings were brought up by relatives, which, as I've been able to see ever more clearly since returning Home, must have had a devastating effect on him. Now I regret my failure to appreciate his early suffering and the fact that learning to *give* love can be quite a difficult thing for someone who hasn't received nurturing parental love as a child. It also explains his scepticism about Church teaching. When, however, we'd started producing our large family, I resented his lack of attention to, as well as caring for, me and the children.

At the age of 16 Lev started studying law and oriental languages at the University of Kazan, but the teachers there described him as "both unwilling and unable to learn"! So he gave up his studies and returned to the family estate before embarking on a lax and leisurely lifestyle, moving between Moscow, Tula and St Petersburg, and starting on his career as a writer. It was after running up heavy gambling debts that he joined the army and went with his brother to the Caucasus. All this of course repelled this 'innocent virgin' when given his diaries to read, thus adding to the difficulties of starting out on a life with a 'genius'.

Here, as a sort of aside, I'd like to make a few comments on the somewhat thorny subject of genius. A dictionary definition of this word is a person with an exceptional ability, especially of a highly original kind, and spiritually knowledgeable people can appreciate the fact that the person concerned will have honed their particular original gift or gifts over many previous lifetimes. How else could Mozart, for instance, have started both playing and composing so brilliantly at such an incredibly early age?

But none of this touches on the immense difficulties of *living* with a genius! Beethoven (who shares an earlier chapter with the equally unmarriageable Schubert), much though he wanted love and partnership, was totally unable to find it and, as I assume you will have read, saw clearly in the Bardo that his intense suffering had been a vital spur to much of his very greatest music. Lev, however, couldn't possibly have lived his life without either passionate sexual expression or a woman such as myself to help him by, for instance, spending long hours copying out his manuscripts, making necessary corrections as I did so, and producing end products that were more legible than the originals. (Infinitely more difficult by hand than on a computer!) I must add here, though, that, despite our many quarrels, he *did* appreciate all the work I did, admiring my boundless energy, and modelling some of the major characters in his novels on me.

From my mention of three of the world's greatest composers you will appreciate that I was myself passionately keen on music. Music being one of the things that girls in my day *were* taught, I was a gifted pianist and would have loved to have had more time in which to study the piano, encouraging at least some of the children to do so, too. Yasnaya Polyana had two pianos in the house — one upstairs and one downstairs — and playing was important to my husband as well. We also frequently welcomed well-known musicians to our home, for Russia at that time had an abundance of them. (The horrendous persecution of such geniuses as Shostakovich came a bit later. I've met him over here and we've had some excellent tête-à-têtes about both persecution and music. He said that he had a great admiration for me, which was very gratifying, and we could of course each empathise with the trials that the other had endured.) Another cause of the dissension between my husband and me was my friendship with Sergei Ivanovich Taneyev. He was a brilliant pianist and composer, and also the teacher of several gifted musicians, for instance Alexander Scriabin, with whom we were also on good terms. Taneyev stayed with us during the summers of both 1895 and 1896, and although he was 12 years my junior, I, alas, developed quite an attachment to him, which both embarrassed the children and made Lev jealous. It wasn't that I was madly in love with Sergei or anything like that, but he seemed at times to understand me better than Lev did. And after all, while Lev had sown his wild oats before we met, I as a teenage girl had never previously had a relationship with any man. Fortunately I think that Sergei himself was unaware of my sentiments, but I did at times feel depressed about the way things were going between us.

Something else that I often found annoying was my husband's lack of trust in me, but now that I'm here and am aware of the previous life in which I'd been unfaithful to him, his attitude in that regard seems understandable. Also, after meeting up since our respective crossings over, we've been able to talk very thoroughly about all the misunderstandings, hurts and disagreements that we had on Earth, appreciate that they were part of our learning, and see how we can do things differently another time round.

But now it's more than time that I told you something about my dear husband's spiritual conversion and the rather mixed reactions that it caused me. His experience in the army, combined with two trips around Europe in 1857 and 1860–1 (not long before we first met), had already converted him from the dissolute and privileged society author, whose early diaries had so shocked me, to a non-violent and spiritual anarchist. Witnessing a public execution in Paris had been a traumatic experience that marked the rest of his life and in a letter to his friend Vasily Botkin he'd written: "The truth is that the State is a conspiracy designed not only to exploit, but above all to corrupt its citizens … Henceforth, I shall never serve any government anywhere." And I'm sure you'd be interested to know, if you didn't already, that, following some correspondence with the young Gandhi, who had sought his advice, Lev instilled in him the concept of *ahimsa* (non-violence). My husband's *A Letter to a Hindu*, addressed to the man who later became the Mahatma, had been bolstered by his reading of a German translation of the Tirukkural. This ancient Tamil text, which dates back to at least 300 BC, is considered to be one of the greatest works ever written on ethics and morality and is known for its universality and secular nature.

Lev's political philosophy had also been influenced by a visit, in March 1861, to the French anarchist Pierre-Joseph Proudhon, who was at the time living in exile in Brussels under an assumed name. They discussed education and Lev regarded him as "the only man who understood the significance both of that and of the printing press in our time". Fired with enthusiasm from this encounter and following the emancipation of the serfs in 1861, he then returned to Yasnaya Polyana and founded 13 schools for children of the local Russian peasants. He described these schools' principles in his essay 'The School at Yasnaya Polyana', written in the year we met, but sadly these educational experiments were short-lived, partly due to harassment by the Tsarist secret police.

None of this caused me any problem — in fact it accorded a hundred per cent with my own instincts — but a profound moral crisis in the 1870s, followed by what he regarded as an equally profound spiritual awakening, caused Lev to become, as I just said, a fervent anarchist and pacifist. He outlined all this in his non-fiction work *A Confession*, of 1882, and his ideas on non-violent resistance had a profound impact on Martin Luther King Jr, as well as on the Mahatma.

His literal interpretation of the ethical teachings of Jesus, centring on the Sermon on the Mount, *did*, however, cause me a lot of heartache. Not because I myself had any objections at all to Christianity but on account of his falling under the influence of a hateful, so-called Christian named Vladimir Chertkov. The two of them first met in Moscow in 1883 — a meeting that completely changed Chertkov's life — and it's even said that he became more Tolstoy than Tolstoy himself. Born into a wealthy aristocratic family, Chertkov grew up assured of his own innate advantage over other people and with an entourage of servants, who would rise from their seats when he passed. I thought him a hypocrite, since he decried wealth yet had his own fancy estate. What drew my husband to him was that, under the guise of 'moral self-improvement', he gave all his heart and soul to educational activity.

Following Lev's initiative, this Chertkov both founded and funded, in 1885, a publishing house that he named 'Intermediary', and he ultimately became Lev's editor, publisher, secretary and chief confidant. Despite pressure from the imperial censorship and the hostile attitude of the Eastern Orthodox Church, Intermediary was also supported by other important writers, such as Chekhov, and it succeeded in publishing works aimed at educating the Russian people. In fact, in 1897, when members of the autocracy were regarding 'Tolstoyism' as an enemy while Chertkov admired the tradition of free speech in England, he even visited that country. Thanks to some correspondence he was already having with a collective in Purleigh, Essex, who were looking at putting my husband's ideas into practice, a publishing company named the Free Word Press was set up, and it produced Russian-language versions of Tolstoy's works and kindred literature, much of which was smuggled back into Russia. Then, in 1900, a separate branch of the business, the Free Age Press, was set up to produce English-language texts and when the original group began to split up, Chertkov's mother bought him a house in Bournemouth and he moved there with his family. Anna, his wife, being a Trustee of the Free Age Press, produced several texts for both arms of the business.

That, too, was all well and good, but, for totally unjustified reasons, Chertkov took against me and actively endeavoured to destroy my relationship with my husband. Just to jump ahead briefly, I know for a fact that he also played a big part in Lev's final flight and death. You've probably already read about that — maybe even seen the film on the subject — and my distress is so well known that I probably need to say very little. It arose as a result of Lev's finding me in his study searching for his will because of my suspicions that Chertkov had persuaded him to make various changes to it. I really prefer now to gloss over all that pain, especially since '*over*' is the key word and I've now, I'm very glad to say, moved right on from it all. For anyone wanting to know more, however, there is an enormous amount of material available — my own diaries for a start — and of course you who are at present on Earth have things like Google ever at your fingertips.

Another thing I prefer to gloss over are my own quite substantial achievements, particularly in the field of literature. Not because I don't recognise them — soon after I'd crossed over and was taken for my life review, I was encouraged to give myself plenty of pats on the back for my publications — but because I know that I'm only one of countless people who've made at least equally good literary contributions. More of a challenge (since writing came naturally to me) was the massive amount of work involved in running the Tolstoy Estate after Lev's death. Readers will appreciate the agonies that we both suffered after his hasty departure and his demise at a railway station. I was left quite literally suicidal, but it's through big challenges that we all learn and grow and now that he's over here, Chertkov has made me a big apology. One thing I've omitted to mention, simply because the story is so well known that elaboration of it seems to me to be unnecessary, is my husband's decision to give away his wealth and take on the attire of a simple peasant. I was very upset by this at first, but now I fully appreciate all the good that he did, for instance by founding soup kitchens.

So now what next? Does such a towering figure as Lev Nikolayevich Tolstoy actually *need* to return to Earth again?

And if he does, or chooses to do so, should I accompany him? Well, the two of us have talked it all over between us, as well as with our guides over here, and we've come to the conclusion that a return could well be beneficial to the world. Now that we've resolved the karma between us, we've agreed that we have no particular reason for living as a married couple again but that we could do worthwhile things working as colleagues in some way or another.

And where do we think might be the best place for us to reincarnate? We both feel that the blood of Russia runs very strongly in our veins and that, despite all that has gone so horribly wrong there, it is still, potentially at least, a truly great country. I would expect readers of this book to be spiritually knowledgeable, and so you may consequently be wondering about the well-known prophecy of Edgar Cayce: that Russia was "the hope of the world". This statement very likely seems even harder to believe right now, but one has to remember that time has no real meaning and obviously Vladimir Putin and his colleagues aren't immortal! Lev and I therefore at present feel inclined to return after this horrible war is over and when the time has come to rebuild Ukraine jointly with spiritually minded Russians, of whom there are very many in the younger generation. Our scribe has been well aware of this on her stays at Sai Baba's ashram in India, to which young Russians have been flocking in recent years. You may also know about, or even have read, writings of the entrepreneur Vladimir Megre, whose series of 'Anastasia' books, *The Ringing Cedars of Russia*, has given rise to a whole movement of people concerned with the best possible approach towards child-rearing on self-sufficient plots of land, surrounded by woods and meadows with a water source.

That said, since I haven't as yet spoken of my own spiritual inclinations, it seems appropriate for me to end with a quotation from my own diaries:

Lev Nikolayevich was explaining something about St. John's Gospel to them, and I heard a discussion about religion going on.

I don't understand religious discussions: they destroy my own lofty relations with God, which cannot be put into words. There is no precise definition of eternity, infinity and the afterlife — there are no words for these things, just as there are no words to express my attitudes and feelings about the abstract, indefinable, infinite deity and my eternal life in God. But I have no objection to the Church, with its ceremonies and icons; I have lived among these things since I was a child, when my soul was first drawn to God. I love attending mass and fasting, and I love the little icon of the Iversk Mother of God hanging over my bed, with which Aunt Tatyana blessed Lev Nikolayevich when he went to the war.

And now that I'm here, in close proximity to the great Masters, for instance Jesus, I feel no differently from how I felt when I wrote those words. May the Lord bless all of you.

# 17

# A Former Slave

*People generally think those memoirs only worthy to be read or remembered which abound in great or striking events, those, in short, which in a high degree excite either admiration or pity: all others they consign to contempt and oblivion. It is therefore, I confess, not a little hazardous in a private and obscure individual, and a stranger too, thus to solicit the indulgent attention of the public; especially when I own I offer here the history of neither a saint, a hero, nor a tyrant...*

Olaudah Equiano

Yes, my *real* name, that is, the one given me by my parents, was indeed Olaudah Equiano. A perfectly good West African name — one to be proud of — and it was only after my sister and I had been captured as slaves, stolen from our beloved homeland, that I was given a succession of other names. To those, however, I'll come gradually, as my tale progresses; right now I'll begin by giving you a few statistics. Did you know, for instance, that during the period 1500–1866 about 12.5 million Africans (at least twice as many people as were killed by the Nazis in the Holocaust) were transported across the Atlantic to the Americas, with a large percentage of them perishing at sea? Not only the deceased but also the sick were thrown overboard during these crossings, while others threw themselves over in preference to enduring the appalling conditions to which they were subjected. Since they're white, was the massacre of the Jews the worst thing to have happened in the history of humankind, or was the cruelty to 'mere blacks' (as many *still* regard us) equally abhorrent? My constant prayer has for long been that lessons from it all have been learnt and that no atrocities on such a gigantic scale will *ever* be repeated.

The African coastland from which the slaves were captured and taken extends for 3400 miles, from Senegal to Angola, and it included a variety of kingdoms. I was born the son of an elder or chief, in around 1745, in the village of Essaka, Eboe, in the Kingdom of Benin, which now lies in the south-eastern part of Nigeria. It was a charming, fruitful vale and I'd never even *heard* of either white people or the sea before I got captured, so you can easily imagine the shock! My father was styled 'Embrenche', a term importing the highest distinction and signifying grandeur. The physical mark made on such people may well sound unpleasant to white Europeans or Americans, but it was then the traditional custom, anyway in that part of Africa. It was made by cutting the skin across at the top of the forehead and drawing it down to the eyebrows, applying a warm hand to rub it until it shrank into a thick 'weal' across the lower part of the forehead. Most of the judges and senators were thus marked, my father had long borne it, I'd seen it being conferred on one of my brothers and, had I remained in the place of my birth, I would also have been destined to receive it.

It was the task of the 'Embrenche', when they assembled, to decide upon the outcome of disputes and punish crimes. Proceedings were generally short and a law of retaliation normally prevailed; for instance, an adulterous woman would be handed over to her husband, who might even condemn her to death. This no doubt sounds unfair to you, since fidelity wasn't demanded of the men, who would often have two wives, but when one reflects that women tend to live longer than men this perhaps makes it seem more reasonable.

My father, like his equals, did have slaves, but they were only either prisoners of war or people who'd been convicted of crimes deemed to be heinous. He had a large family and seven of his children survived, of whom I was the youngest.

One day, when I was about 11, my sister and I had been left alone to look after our family premises while the adults were out working when we were suddenly kidnapped, separated and then transported to the coast. I tried in vain to escape, but was eventually, after at least six months, sold to traders, who took me off, along with 244 other captives, in their European slave ship.

My sister and I got separated during that long journey, on which we had a series of different owners. We met again at one point but weren't allowed to stay together and then had no way of keeping in touch with one another. I was never able to find out what became of her, but since crossing over I've found her again and we've had plenty of opportunity to talk about the horrendous things we were made to endure. For her, these included being raped several times by her master and bearing him a daughter, who also spent her whole life in slavery. Both of them died young, mainly on account of the amount of work put upon them, but both are glad to have thereby paid off a good deal of karma and have since had happier lifetimes on Earth. I'm sure you can easily imagine the feelings of a young boy kidnapped in such circumstances, and I prefer not to dwell on the terrible conditions to which we were all subjected. On the ship, not bothering to find out what my name actually was, they called me Michael, but after that my first American owner named me Jacob.

We docked in Barbados initially, where many slaves were employed in working on the sugar plantations, but then some of us, including me, were sent on to the British colony of Virginia. There I was sold to a lieutenant in the Royal Navy, whose name was Michael Henry Pascal, and he renamed me Gustavus Vassa after the King of Sweden who had started the Reformation in that country. I refused the name at first, having by then become accustomed to being called Jacob, but after suffering many a cuff for my objections I eventually succumbed and that name was thenceforth my official one. I don't know what you think, but to my mind failure to acknowledge a person's given name — an important part of their identity since birth — is one of the most horrendous insults to their humanity. But that of course is an integral part of what white slave traders and owners did to black men and women: regarding us as animals rather than human beings.

Following that aside, it's time I told you a bit about my life as a slave. Well, when my owner Pascal was called upon to serve in the Seven Years' War with France, which lasted from 1756 until 1763, he took me back to England with him as a valet. I was trained in seamanship, expected to assist the ship's crew in times of battle (hauling gunpowder to the gun decks), and I witnessed both the Siege of Louisbourg and the Battle of Lagos, which is a small port in Portugal. None of this endeared me to war, but fortunately my master favoured me and decided to send me to his sister-in-law in Britain so that I could attend school and learn English. This was a privilege not granted to many lads who'd been captured and taken from their beloved homeland, and I also had the good fortune of learning about Christianity. I was baptised at St Margaret's Church in the parish of Westminster on 9 February 1759.

After that, however, I was sold again in Gravesend, to one Captain James Doran, who took me back to the Caribbean. He in turn sold me to an American Quaker named Robert King, who set me to work on his shipping routes and in his stores. Here again I was among the more fortunate, as this master taught me to read and write better than I'd done before and he also guided me along the path of religion. I was ever grateful to have the Master Jesus as my leading light.

Further good fortune came in that I was permitted to engage in business on my own behalf as well as on my master's. I sold fruits, glass tumblers, and other items, on the route between

Georgia and the Islands of the Caribbean, and thus it was that I was enabled to save the sum of £40, which was the price in 1766 for a slave to purchase his freedom. The Captain then tried to persuade me to stay on as his business partner, but I refused, knowing that it would entail quite a chance of being kidnapped back into enslavement, and I did in fact have a narrow escape from that while loading a ship in Georgia.

Robert King was, I feel, basically a good man. Any twenty-first-century Quaker would no doubt shudder at the thought of one of their predecessors having owned slaves, but times were different back then. One night recently, when I met Ann, our scribe, while she was asleep and therefore out of her physical body, she told me that, of the numerous previous lives that she has remembered, the one that appalled her the most was when she'd been a slave master. She'd paid for it, of course, by having another life as a slave herself, but we discussed it all and agreed that, had she not had all that experience, she wouldn't have been given the incentive to campaign against racism in her present life. We all learn through our mistakes!

Anyway, following my narrow escape, I was able to go to Britain, where I continued to work at sea before settling in London. After the United States had gained its independence in 1783, I got involved with helping the Black Poor of London, who were mostly those African-American slaves whom the British had freed during and after the American Revolution. The black community by then numbered about 20,000 in London, as it also included some freed slaves from the Caribbean, plus some who'd been brought to England by their owners and freed after the decision had thankfully been made that slavery had no basis in common law.

Following the American Revolution, some 3000 former slaves were transported from New York to Nova Scotia, where, along with other Loyalists who were also resettled there, they became known as Black Loyalists. Making new lives in London or Canada was difficult for many of the freed men and women, so I was glad to be able to be of help in some small ways.

I made friends with abolitionists in Britain, who supported me financially and since I'd become highly literate they also urged me to write my autobiography. I was very happy to do this and although I was still generally known as 'Gustavus Vassa, the African', I at last felt free to assert my *real* name of Olaudah Equiano. Not so difficult, is it? Olaudah only has three syllables and isn't hard to pronounce! I think that it's particularly the English — and perhaps even more the Americans — who are generally rather bad at bothering much to speak other languages and simply expect others to learn theirs.

The book was published in 1789, to great acclaim, and I'm happy to tell you that there is now a commemorative green plaque on what is now 73 Riding House Street in central London, where I lived when I was writing it. It was placed there as part of Black History Month in October 2000 and, for the unveiling, some students from Trinity College of Music played a fanfare composed by Professor Ian Hall. (It's not so much that I feel proud of being probably the first African in Europe to have achieved such a thing, but more the fact that I believe it important for people to know that an abhorrence such as the slave trade was able to carry on for such a long time.) Eight editions of the book were printed during my lifetime alone and it was translated into both Dutch and German. It's said that its structure and rhetorical strategies were influential and that they created a model for subsequent slave narratives. In fact it's proven to be so influential in the study of African and African-American literature that it is nowadays frequently taught in university classrooms in both English literature and history departments. I'm also very glad to tell you that the work has been republished in the influential Heinemann African Writers Series.

After its publication, I toured all over Britain promoting the book and in May 1791 my appearance in Belfast was celebrated by abolitionists who five years previously had defeated plans to commission vessels in the port for the Middle Passage. There I was hosted by Samuel Neilson, the leading United Irishman and publisher of their Painite newspaper the *Northern Star*. Sadly this society was suppressed in 1799, following evidence of communication between its leading members and the insurrectionary United Irishmen. This was after the onset of war with revolutionary France, when leading members of the radical political group known as the London Corresponding Society (LCS), including Thomas Hardy (not the later-born poet and novelist), with whom I had the privilege of lodging in 1792, were charged with treason.

Before that, however, I was appointed in November 1786 to the position of 'Commissary of Provisions and Stores for the Black Poor going to Sierra Leone'. Here I have some *very* important points to make, because, since human beings often want the worst truths to be suppressed, there are various facts that aren't widely known, yet should be. The city of Freetown was officially founded by Lieutenant John Clarkson (younger brother of the abolitionist Thomas Clarkson) on 11 March 1792, but the reality is that, rather than it being a subject to rejoice about, after the slaves had finally been emancipated, the British didn't want us in their country any more and so these freed slaves were forcibly deported. Since very many of them hadn't even been taken from Sierra Leone in the first place but (like myself) from other areas of West Africa, it's not as though they were now being sent 'happily home'! And what's more, very large numbers of them quickly succumbed to diseases in their new 'home' and fatalities were numerous. I myself was sent to work in Freetown for a while but returned to London after being dismissed for protesting against financial mismanagement.

Talking of Sierra Leone in particular, I imagine that some readers are enamoured of the television presenter Romesh Ranganath. (You may be wondering how it is that I, who am now on the other side, happen to know about such things as British television. Well, the answer is simple! One of the great joys of not being limited by a physical body is that one can travel wherever one wants, both instantaneously and for free, and isn't it natural that, as a one-time campaigner against slavery, I should still have a great interest in *anything* on Earth that's being done to combat the great evil of racism?)

Anyway, I already mentioned having talked to our scribe, who incidentally has a particular interest in Sierra Leone since her adopted son's late birth father was a native of that country who went to England for his studies. Well, Romesh, when he was planning a recent visit to the country in order to do a programme on it, also wanted to talk to me while out of his body one night and so I was able to encourage him to do some real digging for the truth about exactly what had happened during those dreadful times. For the benefit of anyone who didn't see the programme, I can tell you that Romesh was taken to see the ruins on the tiny island, 20 miles upriver from Freetown, where that particular slave port had been situated. He was told that no fewer than 30,000 black people had been temporarily housed there prior to being put onto the slave ships that transported them to the Americas. His guide showed him the remains of both the front of the building, where the British who were in charge had been housed and entertained in luxury, and those of the windows at the back through which they could keep a careful eye on the captives. These latter were lodged in small premises, two to three hundred at a time.

This was of particular interest to Ann because she and her whole family went to Sierra Leone for the Christmas of 1989 (shortly after their younger son's tenth birthday and fortunately before the country's horrendous civil war). Although their hosts looked after them extraordinarily well and took them to see, among other things, the Freedom Tree — a cotton tree, where people still go to pray (and which is heavily populated by bats) — they didn't see the slave port. Romesh, however, was shown the old cannons marking the spot where the British flag had flown for 130 years. Something that shocked him deeply (and which was also news to Ann) was that the people descended from the deported ex-slaves, known as Creoles, are, to this day, not permitted to buy land outside the peninsula upon which Freetown is situated!

All this leads me naturally to another less well-known point. The city of Hull in northern England is twinned with Freetown (not the reason why the late Drissa Yilla, the birth father of Ann and David's son Christopher Pearson, went to university there), and Hull was also the birthplace of the politician William Wilberforce. Hence that city's Wilberforce Museum, erected mainly to honour the man who was supposedly the 'leading light' in the abolition of the Slave Trade. Well, while Ann and David were bringing up their three children in the area, they formed, together with a fellow university wife who is Trinidadian, plus some other families who had adopted black children, a branch of the anti-racist organisation named 'Harmony'. This was invaluable for mutual support, but in addition they did a good deal of historical research and learnt not only that Wilberforce had actually (initially anyway) *opposed* the emancipation of those who were still being employed as slaves, but also that most of the abolitionist work had actually been done by black people. The group consequently launched a campaign to improve the Wilberforce Museum, though not, I'm sorry to say, with any success. I am, however, very happy to tell you that when they were forced to disband the group, owing to almost all of its members moving away from the area, they still had a small sum of money in their kitty and this they decided to donate to the first-class Slavery Museum in Liverpool.

Having got all that off my chest, it's time to return to my personal life as Olaudah Equiano (whom you *can* find duly honoured, along with others, in the Liverpool museum). After my book had first been published, I fell in love with a beautiful English woman named Susannah Cullen. We were married in April 1792 at St Andrew's Church in Soham, Cambridgeshire, and had two lovely daughters, Anna Maria and Joanna. Sadly, however, Susannah fell ill and died, at only 34, in February 1796, and Anna Maria followed her, at the age of four, just a few months later, on 21 July 1797. Anna Maria is commemorated on a gravestone at the church where we were married. Since I myself had already departed from my mortal coil on 31 March that same year, the orphaned Joanna was left to inherit my estate once she reached the age of 21. When I crossed over I was living in Paddington Street, Westminster, and the death was reported in American as well as British newspapers. My body was buried on 6 April, in a small ground that lay on either side of Whitefield's Tabernacle, Tottenham Court Road (now Whitfield Gardens and the site of the American International Church). The actual grave has since been lost, but that is of no importance.

It was hard for Joanna being orphaned so young, but she did fine, first being cared for by relatives in her mother's family and then, once she'd come of age, being awarded her inheritance. Thanks to the proceeds from the book, the estate was substantial and, five years later, she married a Congregational minister and lived to the age of 50. Needless to say, we've all been happily reunited over here.

That, I think, is about all I need to say about my slave life on Earth because anyone who's seriously interested can always find more information on the internet and/or read my autobiography. I feel very happy that it's still in print after all this time! I will, however, say a few more words about my Christianity: I mentioned before that Jesus had been my guiding light after I'd first been introduced to Him at the age of 14 and that I was baptised into the Church of England in 1759. A few upsets caused me to question my Faith, one of which was my failure to rescue my black cook friend, John Annis, after he'd been kidnapped by one William Kirkpatrick, who transported him to St Kitts. But I'd done all I could, and now I fully appreciate that the good Lord always favours effort and never imposes blame. I further now appreciate that Jesus is but one of many great Masters/avatars, but it was He, as I'd trusted, who first welcomed me into the higher realm, to which I passed quite easily.

Although the world still has a long way to go in combating racism, many good things have happened as a result of my, often very challenging, time on Earth as Olaudah Equiano. Still not wanting to boast about my personal achievements but nevertheless desirous of the whole world finally coming to recognise the equality of all races, I'll mention just a few of these:

- In 1976 a crater on Mercury was named 'Equiano'.
- In November 1996 an Equiano Society was formed in London with the aim of publicising and celebrating my work.
- In 2007, the year in which the UK celebrated the bicentenary of the abolition of the Slave Trade, it was agreed to include my life and achievements (along with those of Wilberforce, with whom, by the way, I've made good friends over here!) in the National Curriculum.
- In 2008 a statue of Equiano, made by pupils of Edmund Waller School, was erected in Telegraph Hill Lower Park, New Cross, London.
- In 2022 the city of Cambridge, England, renamed Riverside Bridge 'Equiano Bridge'.

Now you may feel like asking: "What else do you need to achieve?" Well, my answer is that, although there is much work that can be done on this higher plane, I still want to see a great deal more action on Earth to end racism permanently. To quote the distinguished geneticist Sir Adam Rutherford in his fairly recent book *How to Argue with a Racist*:

> elite sprinters in the Olympics are not a dataset on which a statistician could draw any satisfactory conclusion. Yet it is precisely the data on which an extremely popular stereotype is based. The idea of Black athleticism in sprinting is drawn from a hugely skewed and fatally flawed sample, one which due to the relative absence of West African sprinters doesn't even support its own hypothesis. If people of West African ancestry have a genetic advantage, why are there few West African sprinters when slavery does not account for the difference?

With this purpose in mind I could of course return in a white body, but the truth is that I feel more comfortable being black — especially when living in the warm continent of Africa — and there is, besides, obviously an overwhelming need to put an end to poverty and starvation there. I also feel that, compared to when Equiano was alive, this is now a good time to incarnate as a woman. I've been chatting with my dear lost older sister (whom our parents were happy to welcome Home before me) and we might well consult with our guides about returning together to work on some joint project. Though neither of us was particularly scientifically inclined during the eighteenth century, we both have a tremendous admiration for Anne-Marie Amafidon, a British-Nigerian mathematician and computer scientist, born as recently as 1990, who completed a Master's degree in the two subjects from Oxford University at the age of 20. She made it into the New Internationalist 2020 'Women of the World' calendar as a result of founding 'Stemettes', a social enterprise promoting women into scientific, technological, engineering and mathematical careers.

Now to conclude I'd just like to return, with a reflection, to my first paragraph, where I compared the Slave Trade with the Holocaust. Which is more illogical: to persecute people because they originated in a hot country, where darker skin colour is an advantage, or because their distant ancestors had been responsible for putting our beloved Lord Jesus to death?

# 18

# Klever Kaff

*My work is done,*
*My task is o'er,*
*And so I come,*
*Taking it home,*
*For the crown is won.*
*Alleluia,*
*For evermore.*

The Angel in 'The Dream of Gerontius' by Cardinal John Henry Newman, set to music by Sir Edward Elgar

Hullo! It's lovely to talk to you about my last life, which was certainly one of the best ones that I've ever had. It embarrasses me somewhat to say this, but it seems that, a whole 70 years on from my supposedly 'premature' departure from Earth, I'm *still* regarded as the world's greatest contralto singer. Well, on second thoughts, maybe I don't need to be embarrassed about it, since after all my voice was nothing but a gift of God and being able to make people happy by using it was the greatest pleasure that I could have, and indeed still *do* have. You see, my death from breast cancer at the age of only 41 was generally regarded as an immense tragedy, but what many people — especially in the West — need to learn (and it is one of the reasons for our scribe's decision to write this book) is that nothing happens without reason. Hence my use of the word 'supposedly' above: I didn't in fact depart prematurely, but (like our 'Covid doctor' in an earlier chapter) was called back because I was needed even more on this side.

But I mustn't jump the gun, so I'll start with a bit of autobiographical information. I was born, the youngest of three children, on 22 April 1912, when my mother Alice was 40. My father, William Ferrier, was headmaster of the village school in the Lancashire village of Higher Walton, and that's where we lived until I was two. We then moved to Blackburn because my father got appointed as Head of St Paul's School in that town. He hadn't been trained musically but was nevertheless an enthusiastic member of both the local operatic society and of several choirs, one of which I also joined, at an early age. My dear mother was a competent singer, too, with a strong contralto voice, and she spotted my musicality early on. She was keen for her children to be well educated anyway. I learnt to read before starting school and, since I showed promise as a pianist at an early age, I was given the privilege of receiving lessons from the noted north of England teacher, Frances Walker. I absolutely *loved* it from the start and soon did well in a number of competitions.

Our family had some financial difficulties, however, as my brother George, my senior by five years, went off to Canada, got into trouble and looked likely to continue being a drain on my parents. (I don't care to go into that, as it's his business, not ours, and anyway has no relevance to my own story.) So I had to be taken out of school when I was only 14, and in addition, my father's impending retirement prevented me from realising my ambition to go to a music college. Instead, the General Post Office (GPO) telephone exchange in Blackburn took me on as a trainee. Although I didn't take to it with alacrity, people there were friendly towards me and I was good at the work. I was good at sport as well, impressed my colleagues with my cartwheels and joined their tennis team.

All my spare time, however, was taken up by music, and at 16 I was the regional winner in a national contest for young pianists organised by the *Daily Express*. Despite being unsuccessful in the London Finals, I was given a Cramer upright piano as a prize and this stood me in good stead for a number of years. In 1929 I made a well-received appearance as an accompanist in Blackburn's King George's Hall, and this was followed by further piano competition successes and a short recital at the BBC's Manchester studios. This was around the time of my completing my training and becoming a fully fledged telephonist.

When I was 19, I was very happy to pass my Licentiate at the Royal Academy of Music and in that same year I also started having occasional singing lessons. In December 1931 I was given a small solo part in a church performance of Mendelssohn's *Elijah*. Little did I know then that it was going to be singing that would ultimately make me about as famous worldwide as Elizabeth, who was crowned Queen just a few months before I died! In fact, if people had told me when I was 20 that at 32 I'd be dashing around the world giving concerts, I just would have laughed at them.

Everyone seemed to find me both beautiful and good fun to be with and through a mutual love of dancing I met a bank clerk named Albert Wilson and consequently, early in 1934, transferred to the Blackpool telephone exchange and took lodgings close to where he was living. My decision to marry Bert put paid to my telephonist job, as in those days the GPO wouldn't employ married women. (I can hear cries of "Scandalous!" from my twenty-first-century readers!) Even before going into it, however, I sensed that the marriage wasn't going to lead to great bliss. My older sister Winifred had never thought us well suited, but I now appreciate that I had a little bit of karma to complete with Bert because, soon after I'd crossed over, I was shown my relevant Akashic Records and so was then glad to have been able to achieve that.

Anyway, his being called up to serve in the War in 1940 brought a natural end to our relationship and we divorced in 1947 but remained on good terms. He later married my friend Wyn Hetherington and I was extremely happy for both of them. As for me, I did have quite a long-standing friendship with Rick Davies, a Liverpool antiques dealer, but, much though I sometimes felt that I would have loved to have had a family, it simply wouldn't have been compatible with my career, and music was always my first love. The marriage to Bert did also serve another purpose because he once bet me a shilling that I wouldn't enter as a competitor at the important Carlisle Festival. Unable to resist the challenge, not only did I go to Carlisle and was successful in the singing as well as piano competitions, but also my voice got noticed there by the great teacher Dr Hutchinson and he offered to give me lessons. I used to call him 'Hutchie', and my voice really blossomed under his tuition.

It was this success, at age 25, that gave me the confidence that I'd previously lacked. After the outbreak of World War II, the Council for the Encouragement of Music and the Arts (CEMA) sponsored concerts throughout Britain to entertain the troops and bring music to the lives of people who had little opportunity to hear it. In 1941 this council gave me the privilege of a contract and for the next four years I travelled all over the country singing in church halls, basements and barns — wherever it was possible to put a piano. I can't begin to tell you how rewarding it was giving pleasure in this way, and it was thus that I established an extensive repertoire of English folk songs, along with works by Purcell and Schubert, in addition to being involved in singing numerous performances of Handel's *Messiah*.

At this juncture I'd like to give you a quotation from the distinguished musicologist, the late Humphrey Burton, who worked for many years with the BBC. He wrote:

> For more than a decade, when she should have been studying music with the best teachers, learning English literature and foreign languages, acquiring stage craft

and movement skills, and travelling to London regularly to see opera, Miss Ferrier was actually answering the telephone, getting married to a bank manager and winning tinpot competitions for her piano-playing.

What Humphrey didn't appreciate *then*, but does now that he's back 'up here', is that we all have life plans before coming in each time and that — along with our previous lives — we have to forget them in order to be able to start again with a clean slate rather than getting confused with what's passed. I needed the challenges I had for many reasons, one of them being to serve as a model for what can be achieved even without sailing into a music college at 18 and being surrounded by fellow students and having good teachers right on the spot.

In contrast to me, another well-known musician who is deemed to have died 'prematurely' is the very great French horn player Dennis Brain. Born in Hammersmith in 1921, he had the 'advantage' of incarnating into a family of professional musicians, his mother being a singer at Covent Garden and his grandfather, father *and* uncle all being horn players. In addition to that, his older brother, Leonard, was a leading player of oboe and cor anglais. I have a vivid memory of hearing both Leonard and Dennis as soloists in a concert featuring a Mozart horn quintet and an oboe quintet. At the age of only 15, Dennis was admitted to the Royal Academy of Music to study under his professor father, Aubrey, and later, while serving with the Royal Air Force (RAF) in World War II, he played in both its band and its orchestra. Among others who wrote for Dennis, Benjamin Britten composed his wonderful *Serenade for Tenor, Horn and Strings* with him in mind (as well as his partner Peter Pears of course).

Dennis' 'downfall', however, was his passion (one shared, incidentally, with the great conductor Herbert von Karajan) for fast cars. His brother named him "the finest driver I have ever driven with", but his end came instantly on 1 September 1947, when, driving down the A1 back to London after playing in the Edinburgh Festival, his Triumph Herald sports car came off the road and crashed into a tree. This death at the age of 36 shook the musical world beyond belief. Our scribe Ann's younger brother John, who was 10 at the time and completely potty about Mozart, spent a whole day in bed feeling sick, and he told her recently that he *still* hadn't got over it! I, however, had already been over here for nearly four years, and so I was there to greet Dennis and was among those who helped him to understand that he'd died.

It was a big shock for him at first, as it always is in cases of instantaneous death, but gradually he was shown his life plan and told that he'd been called back to play in orchestras and chamber groups over here. He's been having a whale of a time doing that but says that he's now thinking of returning to Earth fairly soon. He reckons that, having reached the pinnacle with the French horn, and greatly admiring two Young Musicians of the Year, the cellists Laura van der Heijden and Sheku Kanneh-Mason, he might well decide to have a go at the cello next time round.

Now to return to my own life on Earth: under the guidance of my singing teacher, 'Hutchie', I extended my repertoire to include Bach, Handel, Brahms and Elgar. The last, alas, died the year before I got married and I never had the chance to meet him before following him over here, but gosh, how I *adored* 'The Dream of Gerontius'! Edward told me when we met soon after I'd died how much he'd enjoyed my singing of the Angel in that work. He then reincarnated in Portugal in 1968 and later, thanks to discovering her book *Life Without Elgar*, became a good friend of our scribe. Ann, however, who wants that bit of 'Gerontius' sung at her funeral, has found that my version isn't available, but she will be very happy with the Janet Baker recording, which Elgar himself also loves.

DEATH: Friend or Enemy?

Edward and I joked, too, about the fact that the above-mentioned conductor Herbert von Karajan regarded his music as "second-rate Brahms". We agreed that Herbert had no doubt been prejudiced by Brahms having been German, whereas Edward (now 'Eduardo' with a three-year-old daughter named Alice after Elgar's wife!) had been the epitome of Englishness. (Not that either of us doesn't love Brahms' music, too, and Ann, when she visited the main cemetery in Vienna in order to have a look at Beethoven's and Schubert's graves prior to writing Chapter 7, had also been very happy to find Brahms' grave close by.)

Speaking of Elgar, though he lost his Faith somewhat towards the end of his life, he was of course brought up Catholic. I, on the other hand, was born into a nominally Anglican family. We only went to church on special occasions, yet I always had a firm belief in God and the spirit world, and my relatives were all so naturally loving that things like kindness, joy and generosity were a strong part of my make-up.

Isn't synchronicity a fascinating thing?! Just as I was thinking about religion, our scribe received a WhatsApp message on her mobile phone from her friend Ruby Kempaiah in Chicago, whose acquaintance she'd made on her last visit to Sai Baba's ashram in India. (Yes, you see, I do *try* to keep up with these technological developments on Earth, which of course all originate here anyway.) It was extraordinary because I really felt as though the words were being taken from my mouth! So Ann promptly got Ruby's permission to quote her and here is part of the little piece she sent out:

Religion is intellectual. It has its use for a time ... To go beyond religion takes courage. Experientially, the sense of oneness has no religion. It's a way of BE-ing with or without the use of words. Our true nature is much like the sun that shines upon all without effort. A purity that knows no "other". A love that is ineffable. A seeing that is non-dual. And without a past or future...

Well, while I was on Earth as 'Klever Kaff' (I can't remember precisely when I gave myself that nickname, but it somehow stuck), I always wanted to be like a sun shining upon all those around me. My darling 'big sister', Winifred, who was eight years older than me, used to say that I'd inherited all the best characteristics of each of our parents. I always enjoyed being the life and soul of any party or gathering and was, I have to admit, notorious for my naughty limericks and "dirty big beers"! All that was more important to me than any rigorous religious observance. After all, what's the point of going to that beautiful Earth if we don't savour it to the full?

We did indeed all have Hitler's horrid war to contend with, but that was one of the instances where music had such huge importance and why my four-year CEMA contract was so valuable to all concerned. While my friend Dennis, with his RAF wartime experiences, was called Home to play in celestial environments, I was told after I'd arrived here that I was required specifically to give consolation to Holocaust victims. Many of them had done such a magnificent job of forming choirs and orchestras in the concentration camps, but what they'd gone through there couldn't possibly be wiped out instantly and so more healing music was a great consolation to them. I'm still doing that sort of thing over here now. You can imagine how much it's needed, what with all the poor people who are perishing in this ghastly war of Putin's!

Returning again, however, to my worthwhile life on Earth: for a short time following my marriage I sang under the name of Mrs Wilson, but that *never* really felt quite right for me and as I became better and better known, it just *had* to be 'Kathleen Ferrier', with no title. The first time I appeared under my own name was in *The Messiah* with 'Hutchie' directing it. I don't want to go on and on boring you with dates, so I'll just say now that my first trip abroad was to Holland and the beginning of a love affair with that country. The Dutch, who were very troubled by the German occupation, welcomed me with open arms, and sombre music (such as the wonderful *Art thou troubled? Music will calm thee...*, one of the songs for which I'm best known) struck a strong chord with them. I'd been tremendously flattered, too, when Benjamin Britten, at the time England's leading young composer, decided to have me star in his chamber opera *The Rape of Lucretia*, which was premiered at Glyndebourne, and I also sang in a performance of that work in Holland.

It was the celebrated Malcolm Sargent (whom some of you will still remember conducting the Promenade Concerts) who first told me I'd have to go to London if I was to get anywhere with my singing. So my first performance in the capital was in 1942, at one of the famous lunchtime concerts organised by the great Dame Myra Hess. It was through Sargent that I secured an audition with John Tillett from one of the world's most important concert agencies. Fortunately he accepted me immediately and on Christmas Eve 1942 I moved with my sister and our by then widowed father to a small rented flat in Hampstead. Oddly enough, on that very same day I'd been on the train with the well-known tenor Roy Henderson, after we'd performed in the same concert. We were both employed by the Tillett agency and he told them that he'd been unimpressed with the new contralto. His precise words were: "It was a good voice, but too dark. And she kept her nose in the score the whole time, terrified to look up. I told her she should learn the words and throw away the book." I took Henderson's words to heart and sought him out at the Royal Academy of Music, where he was teaching, and he then kindly gave me regular, invaluable lessons for the following four years.

After Sargent, who had had me learn Brahms' *Four Serious Songs*, which he'd recently orchestrated, the next great conductor to take me under his wing was Bruno Walter. The Brahms songs were so moving that they sometimes brought both me and my accompanist to tears, and then I had to switch hastily to one of the many bawdy rhymes that I knew. Walter taught me to sing in German and got me properly on to *Lieder*, which, needless to say, was total bliss. Even in the year before I died I was able to sing Mahler's *Das Lied von der Erde* under Bruno in Vienna.

He believed that in me he'd found the perfect voice for Mahler (who, being Jewish by birth, had been previously banned by the Nazis) and it was he, too, who first got me across the Atlantic. I wasn't well received in New York initially, but after a rave review I was travelling extensively all over both the USA and Canada. The only bad thing about it was that I had to pay all my own expenses and found myself running into debt. So the next time I was invited over there, I stood my ground and told them all firmly that, as the best paid soloist in Britain, I wasn't going to let them get away with any such nonsense again!

Back at home, Sir John Barbirolli — another great Elgar conductor — was my next mentor. He, to Walter's surprise, extended my voice upwards. The lovely Dame Evelyne befriended me too, and I always stayed with them when I had engagements in Manchester. They also once invited me for a visit to their holiday home in Sussex. *How* privileged I was! Janet Baker, whose recording of 'Gerontius' with Barbirolli is still a classic, commented that my singing of *Blow the Wind Southerly* (the song for which I'm probably the best known) was the one that typified the quality of my voice more than any other.

Another thing said about my voice was that it was enhanced by a touch of melancholy, stemming at least partly from the awareness of cancer that had come to me quite early on when I'd known someone who had it. My dear mother's death naturally also saddened me, especially since she, who'd encouraged me so much, didn't live to see me at the height of my fame. (Not that I wasn't sure that she was watching over me — and she did indeed confirm this when we met over here — but there's always something special about physical contact.) I was in Italy when I heard about my father's death, in January 1951, and that was inevitably another cause for sadness.

It was soon afterwards that I first noticed a lump in my breast, but I really don't want to dwell on the mastectomy, radiotherapy and everything else that ensued. So I'll just say now that I couldn't bear letting people down and consequently battled on, keeping all the engagements I had for as long as I could, continuing with tending to my beloved garden to the best of my weakening abilities, and entertaining the friends who came to visit me in hospital with an ever-ready supply of drinks. Despite the radiation I developed secondaries, and, as many of you must know, these tend to get into the bones and weaken them. As you can imagine, I wasn't too happy when one of my legs gave way on stage and I had to be helped off, but everyone was full of understanding and compassion when my final engagements had to be cancelled.

I died peacefully in my sleep in University College Hospital, London, where I'd received my Commander of the British Empire (CBE) ribbon, on 8 October 1953, and the body was cremated a few days later in Golders Green Crematorium. Obviously I had at times been contemplating my death for a while and when it came, it was exactly what I'd dreamed of, with my guardian angel carrying me gently off to the strains of that marvellous passage in 'Gerontius' that I'd always so loved singing. I was taken straight to a heavenly hospital for a good rest and a great deal of healing. My life review, which took place not long after that, was, I have to say, pretty much faultless.

Ann was only 13 when I died, so my name naturally didn't mean a great deal to her at the time, but she has a vivid memory of her mother being incredibly upset about it. Then, as she grew older and her passion for music was developing at speed, she, too, got to know and fall in love with my very distinctive voice. As for her mother Norah (who has incidentally recently reincarnated in Australia), she was of course able to hear me again after she'd crossed over in 1987 and also learnt the reason for my early departure and consequently felt better about it, as have so many other music lovers who were on Earth then.

Should you be wondering whether *all* of my time is now being taken up by singing to people in need, my reply is that groups of us here take on other projects when the need arises. One major example is the promotion of women — especially female composers who were unjustly neglected during their lifetimes purely on account of their gender — and a number of us got together to inspire the BBC in their comparatively recent project in that field. An interesting person is the British composer Ruth Gipps, who said during her lifetime that her music was being written "for the future". And another one of many featured by Donald Macleod in his *Composer of the Week* radio series is the Russian Leokadiya Kashperova, who, as Donald said, was "very undeservedly" new to many people, as she was to me, even though she'd been on Earth during a lot of my lifetime. It's great getting to know some of these marvellous people and learning from them as well as entertaining them. Assuming that I do return to Earth in due course (and I'm told that, as a highly evolved soul, I now have the choice — lucky me!), I can't imagine wanting to make a life in anything other than music.

Now I'd like to close by telling you about another interesting instance of synchronicity. On the very same day as Ann and her husband had been to the annual lunch held by the West Midlands Branch of the Elgar Society, the friend she'd been sitting next to emailed her a link to the recent episodes in the popular British TV series *Flog It*. Well, one would think that a programme designed for people wanting to sell their antiques would be an unlikely environment for something about me to come up in! However, Paul Martin, the show's presenter, was in Blackburn on that occasion and so they showed the plaque put up on what had been our family home there and also St George's Hall, where I first used to sing in public. So I joined in with watching the television and was truly delighted to see that Mr Martin, rather than talking about the 'tragedy' of my 'premature death', stressed the fact that I'd done more in a mere ten years than most musicians achieved in a long lifetime.

He further spoke with my biographer Paul Campion and, in addition, showed extracts from the delightful one-woman show with which with the actress and singer Lucy Stevens had toured the UK. Although not tall and elegant as I'd been, she did a delightful job of mimicking me, giving extracts from the many letters I wrote, while travelling, to my relatives and friends. In these I was truly the "girl next door", as the locals had often affectionately referred to me, since I frequently mentioned such down-to-earth things as the difficulty in finding the time "for washing me smalls". So it's really good to know that, along with the quite reasonable recordings made of some of my performances, my legacy is still treasured 'down there'! Now I look forward to meeting some of you when it's your turn to cross over.

19

# A Great Children's Author

*Appley Dapply, a little brown mouse,*
*Goes to the cupboard in somebody's house.*
*In somebody's cupboard there's everything nice,*
*Cake, cheese, jam, biscuits —*
*All charming for mice!*

Beatrix Potter

It's lovely to meet you! Like the wonderful writer of the previous chapter, I would never during the first part of my life have dreamt of achieving lasting fame, but now I feel extremely happy about it. While Kathleen's great passion, however, was music (particularly singing and playing the piano), mine was drawing, painting and natural history. I died nearly ten years before she did, but at 77, which was a perfectly respectable age to reach in those days. Unlike her, too, I was born into a rather well-to-do family. My date of birth was 28 July 1866, and we lived comfortably in number 2 Bolton Gardens, West Brompton, in London. Sadly the house got bombed in the Blitz (quite a while after we'd all crossed over), and Bousfield Primary School now stands in its place, but a blue plaque on the school wall marks the site of the former Potter home.

I had a younger brother, Bertram, born on 14 March 1872, and we were always close despite the age gap. Our family were originally from the Manchester area, and (like the great Charles Darwin, one of whose daughters I gather you'll be hearing from later) we were Unitarians. Unitarianism is a non-Trinitarian branch of Christianity, its adherents believing that, though His teachings were inspired by God, Jesus is not equal to God. Unitarians tend to be more open-minded towards other Faiths than are the majority of Christians, and I feel that this helped me when I crossed over, because I wasn't hidebound by what I expected to find here. But now I'll tell you a bit more about my family and the interesting life that I had on Earth as Helen Beatrix.

My father, Rupert Potter, who died in the year in which the First World War started, had been educated at Manchester College, where he was taught by the Unitarian philosopher James Martineau, and he then trained as a barrister in London. He married my mother, Helen Leech, in 1863 at the Hyde Unitarian Chapel. Her father was a wealthy cotton merchant and ship builder, so money was never a problem; in addition to that, my father invested very successfully in the stock market and so, by the early 1890s he, too, was a very wealthy man.

While the Ferrier parents were both musical, mine were talented artistically, and my father was also an adept amateur photographer. They were both great lovers of the countryside and nature, hence our holidays in Scotland for the first 15 years of my life. There we stayed at an estate named Dalguise, on the River Tay in Perthshire, but when that had ceased to be available, we changed the holiday venue to the Lake District, where we sometimes stayed in Wray Castle, close to Lake Windermere. It was in these areas that my brother and I, who were allowed great freedom to roam as we willed, developed an immense love of landscape, flora and fauna, and we both became keen students of natural history. We not only observed it all very closely but also made numerous sketches and paintings of the things that we so enjoyed looking at.

When I was only eight, I made my first sketchbook from those holidays, and I'm delighted to say that this is now held at the Victoria and Albert Museum in London and has also been digitised (a possibility I'd never have dreamt of back then!). Then, when I was round about 14, I began to keep an illustrated diary of all those wonderful holidays. I wrote it in quite a simple code that I devised myself, in tiny handwriting and some 15 years after my death it was deciphered and transcribed by one Leslie Linder. Though I didn't fully appreciate it myself at the time, this journal was clearly invaluable for the development of my creativity, since it served as both a sketchbook and a literary experiment. Rather than giving an intimate record of my personal life, however, I wrote in it such things as my impressions of art and artists and my own maturing and intellectual interests. I also recounted stories from the life that I observed around me.

This early work of mine is consequently now seen as a useful source for providing an understanding of a vibrant part of British society in the late nineteenth century. People also apparently enjoy what they regard as amusing insights into the places that I visited and my unusual ability to observe and describe nature. Having started it in 1881, I ended the journal in 1897 because, by that time, my artistic and intellectual energies were totally absorbed with scientific study and efforts to publish my drawings.

Bertram and I grew up almost completely isolated from other children, but we always had numerous small pets, such as rabbits, mice, a hedgehog and a few bats, some of which we would take on holiday with us. In addition to that, we made collections of butterflies and other insects and besides observing them all very closely we produced endless drawings of them. Since we did these things purely for our own pleasure, it never consciously occurred to either of us at that time that they would one day be useful to others or bring us fame. Bertram in fact grew up to be a professional artist as well as a farmer.

Formal schooling was then more or less unheard of for girls of my social standing, and I had a succession of three governesses, of whom the last, Annie Carter, who became Annie Moore when she married, was only three years my senior and we remained lifelong friends. Although I never found a great deal of use for any foreign languages, she taught me German, besides acting as my 'lady's companion'. It was actually thanks to Annie that the children's tales for which I ultimately became so very well known originated. This was because she ended up having a total of eight children, I enjoyed sending them illustrated letters, and one day she suggested that these letters might make good children's books. So I then wrote and illustrated the first of these, which I entitled *The Tale of Peter Rabbit*.

This I self-published in 1902, when I was in my thirties, and it rapidly became so popular that, happily, my subsequent children's 'Tales' were taken up by the publisher Frederick Warne and Company. I then became, in 1903, a pioneer of merchandising by having Peter Rabbit made into a children's stuffed toy. This toy, and those that followed it, were also very successful and they led on to the equally popular 'Beatrix Potter pottery' — plates, bowls, mugs and so on — which are still, as you're no doubt aware, often given to young children today. All of this made a great deal of money for both myself and my publisher.

Norman Warne, who served as my editor, and I fell in love, but my parents didn't approve of the match on account of the fact that he was "in trade" and therefore not "socially suitable". By that time, however, I felt sufficiently 'my own woman' not to need their approval and so we went ahead and became unofficially engaged. Norman loved the Lake District as much as I did and we had our eyes on Hill Top Farm in Near Sawrey, not far from Windermere, which we felt would make a wonderful holiday home. Sadly, however, he died suddenly of pernicious anaemia when he was only 37. You can well imagine how heartbroken I was, but I resolved not to let the tragedy ruin the rest of my life and so, thanks to a small inheritance from an aunt, supplemented by some of my own income, I went ahead and bought the farm anyway. It was a place I'd always yearned to own, and the idea of living in that charming village delighted me. I wrote over 60 books in all, but the best known are undoubtedly *Peter Rabbit* and the other 22 Tales that followed on after his. You can see that I would never have imagined such a thing when I first started drawing and writing purely for my own pleasure!

Another important thing that I did was to make watercolours of fungi, and these led to my being widely respected in the field of mycology. In case you didn't know, mycology is the branch of biology that studies fungi's genetic and biochemical properties, which include their taxonomy and their use for human beings, as well as the dangers they pose from toxicity or infection. Many Victorians, you see, had a passion for botany and nature study in general, and I was in fact interested in entomology as well. I collected fossils and also studied archaeological artefacts from excavations in London. I found it all quite fascinating. Meeting the revered naturalist and amateur mycologist Charles McIntosh, while on holiday in Perthshire in 1892, had also been invaluable to me. Besides teaching me taxonomy and helping me to improve the accuracy of my drawings, he supplied me with live specimens to paint during the winter months. I suppose we were fortunate that our parents had never objected to our having such things in the house!

Bertram and I, as you will have gathered, hadn't always seen eye to eye with our mother and father, but they did approve of higher education. Had I been born, like you readers, in more 'enlightened' times, I could no doubt have studied for a degree, for instance in botany. Yet we girls in those days, who were on our way towards womanhood, generally accepted our lot without protest. You probably remember of course that back in our day (as in our scribe's for that matter) adulthood was deemed to start not at 18 but at 21. Undoubtedly, youngsters nowadays grow up more quickly than we did! Is that a good thing? Personally I'm not at all sure, because after all isn't childhood something to be treasured? I certainly felt that when I wrote my books for children!

Anyway, for me, nature was my university and I really didn't need anything else. I did at one point — no doubt inevitably — suffer discrimination on account of my gender. Thanks to connections of my uncle, Sir Henry Enfield Roscoe, who was a chemist and Vice Chancellor of the University of London, I was able to meet botanists at Kew Gardens and consult with them about my ability to germinate spores. In fact I managed to convince George Massee there of my theory of hybridisation, but (surprise, surprise!) the then Director of Kew, William Thiselton-Dyer, refused to accept it, not only because I wasn't a man but also on account of my being a 'mere amateur'.

Undeterred, however, I wrote up my conclusions for the Linnean Society, in a paper entitled 'On the Germination of Spores of the Agariciniae'. Since, as a woman in 1897, I wasn't permitted to attend the Society's proceedings or to read my paper myself, Massee kindly did it for me. Although I subsequently withdrew it because I realised that some of my samples had been contaminated, I continued with my microscopic studies for several more years. Now I'm pleased to be able to tell you that, following this paper's recent rediscovery, my work, along with the artistic illustrations and drawings that accompanied it, is at last being properly evaluated. Later I gave my other mycological and scientific drawings to the Armitt Museum and Library in Ambleside, and mycologists can refer to them there when they want to identify fungi. Also, Charles McIntosh, to whom I referred above as having been an invaluable teacher for me, donated a collection of my fungus paintings to the Perth Museum and Art Gallery.

Then, in 1967, I learnt over here that another mycologist, named W. P. K. Findlay, had finally fulfilled my dream of getting many of my fungus drawings published in a book! (He came and talked to me about it one night when he was out of his body. His lovely book is entitled *Wayside and Woodland Fungi*, and it delights me that my drawings are admired for their 'beautiful accuracy'.) Another thing of interest, which might amuse you as much as it does me, is that in 1997, that is, 54 years after my death, the Linnean Society issued me a posthumous apology for the sexism displayed in the handling of my research.

For my brother, getting formal higher education was of course easier and he read Classics at Magdalen College, Oxford. I was happy for him and he did enjoy his life there, but, like me, he felt the call of the North and so, after graduating, he moved northwards and concentrated fully on both art and farming. Dear Bertram's falling in love, however, caused as much trouble from our parents as it had for me! The name of the young woman he married (in 1902 in Edinburgh) was Mary Welsh Scott, and she came from the nearby town of Hawick. Since she had previously been a mill worker, Bertram knew that her social standing couldn't possibly gain our parents' approval, so he kept his marriage a secret from them for a whole ten years. To my horror, his ultimate disclosure resulted in Father writing his poor son out of his will.

About a year after they were wed, Bertram and Mary bought Ashyburn Farm, near the village of Ancrum in the Scottish Borders. He did very well with his art, exhibiting at both the Royal Academy and the Royal Scottish Academy, and some of his work can now be seen in my former home near Ambleside and Windermere. Many of his paintings and etchings depict the countryside near his farm, and we're both delighted at their being preserved in my home. My dear brother was ever a popular figure in the village and surrounding area, and the couple hosted an annual New Year's Day football match in Ancrum as well as occasional musical evenings.

In 1914 Bertram attempted to enlist in the armed forces, but it was felt that farmers couldn't really be spared for the war effort. On 22 June 1918, however, when he was only 45, he sadly died suddenly from a stroke after working in his garden. He was buried in the parish cemetery outside Ancrum, but Mary continued living at the farm for many years and I used to enjoy visiting her there occasionally well into the 1930s. So, whereas my brother only saw the first of the world wars, I lived through a good half of the second one as well. Those were indeed hard times, but, what with Putin's horrible war that's going on now, it seems that humanity has yet quite a long way to go before learning the lessons necessary for living in peace and harmony. I am, however, assured by wise beings whom I have the privilege of meeting over here that such a time can and *must* come, even if you on Earth who are at present reading this book don't live to see it.

Going back to my own life as the renowned Beatrix Potter: once I'd become an established author, with the profits from my books and the many things I'd patented providing a good income, I saw no reason for staying on in London and I consequently settled permanently in the Lake District. Soon after acquiring Hill Top Farm I'd become interested in the preservation of the indigenous fell sheep, known as Herdwick. This breed was probably introduced to the area by the Vikings (*herdvyck* meaning 'sheep pasture' in Old Norse) and it was important here by the end of the twelfth century. Ideally built for the climate of the Lakes, with an exceptionally thick coat whose wool has bristle-type fibres, these wonderful creatures have been known to survive under a blanket of snow for as much as three solid days, even at times consuming some of their own wool to help them survive!

I was always enchanted, too, by their unusual appearance; their heads are white and the lambs are born with the wool on the rest of their bodies being black, but that changes initially to brown and then becomes a pleasant shade of darkish grey after the first shearing. They are prized for their robust health, their ability to live entirely on forage and their territorial tendencies, which prevent them from straying far over the difficult upland terrain. Being coarse and not easily dyed, their wool is best used for carpets and can also make good loft insulation. When these sheep are slain for consumption, their meat has a particularly distinctive, strong flavour and is popular for banquets. (Here I must apologise to the vegetarians among you, but I hope you appreciate that vegetarianism wasn't at all common in my day!)

Fortunately, when I'd decided to make a permanent move to the area, my tenant farmer, John Cannon, agreed to stay on with his family to manage the farm while I was making improvements to the house and learning the techniques of fell farming. These included the art of raising livestock such as pigs, chickens and cows and before long I was able to add sheep to the brew, breeding and raising them myself. All sheep farmers of course need to own sheep dogs, but, great animal lover though I was, I never kept highly domesticated dogs in the house. You see, the trouble with dogs, who generally believe that they *own* the people they live with and very often become human in their next incarnations, is that they have the habit of worming their way into those people's hearts to such an extent that the said people tend to have serious trouble getting over their loss.

Sheep, on the other hand, though their normal life span of 10 to 12 years isn't dissimilar to that of dogs, are generally somewhat less 'personal'. I did actually over the years have a few particularly 'special' ones — for instance those who'd had difficulties when they were lambing — and these were there to greet me when I crossed over. It was lovely having these dear animals come to nuzzle me, which was their way of showing appreciation for the extra attention I'd given them through their distress, but I think that the majority of them had moved on to 'pastures new'.

Again returning to my life on Earth, I realised in due course that I needed to protect my boundaries, and so I sought advice from W. H. Heelis and Son, a local firm of solicitors with offices in nearby Hawkshead. With William Heelis acting for me, I then bought more pastureland contiguous to my own and in 1909 I added to it with the purchase of the 20-acre Castle Farm across the road from Hill Top and moved there. I still visited Hill Top, however, at every opportunity and some of the books that I wrote at this time (for instance *The Tale of Ginger and Pickles*, which is about the little shop in Near Sawrey, and *The Tale of Mrs. Tittlemouse*, who was a wood mouse) reflect my increasing participation in village life and my joy in country living.

By the summer of 1912, William Heelis had proposed marriage to me and I had joyfully accepted. I refrained from telling my parents about it straight away, as I knew that a mere 'country solicitor' wouldn't meet with their approval, but at 47 I didn't need their blessing! We were wed on 13 October 1913 at St Mary Abbots in Kensington. Bertram and Mary were among those who came down for the ceremony, and we went on to have a very happy 30-year marriage. We moved immediately to Near Sawrey, choosing to reside in the renovated cottage at Castle Farm, but Hill Top remained a working farm and we remodelled it to allow for my workshop and studio as well as the tenant family. At my age there was of course no question of having children, but that didn't bother me, as I felt that my books and my animals were my children and besides, William's large family were very welcoming to me; I helped with the education of some of his nieces, as well as sometimes giving comfort to his siblings.

My father died on 8 May 1914 and so then, as a wealthy woman feeling responsible for my mother, I persuaded her to move to the Lake District. Initially I found her a property to rent in Sawrey, but she found that dull and so moved to Lindeth Howe, a large house in Bowness that our family had previously rented for holidaying in the summer. (I understand that this house is now a 34-bedroom hotel, but then my mother was accustomed to luxury!) Had Bertram and Mary had children, maybe she would have come round to accepting their match and enjoyed grandmotherhood, but Bowness was at least a friendly place in which to end her days.

In 1923, with my dear husband's support, I purchased Troutbeck Park Farm, formerly a deer park, and I restored its land with thousands of Herdwick sheep, thus establishing myself as one of the major farmers of these sheep in the county. I was fortunately able to employ some of the very best sheep breeders, shepherds and farm managers, and I was also generally admired for my willingness to experiment with the latest biological remedies for diseases in sheep. By the late 1920s, together with Tom Storey, my Hill Top Farm manager, we'd made a name for my prize-winning Herdwick flock and I was often asked to serve as a judge at local agricultural shows. In fact I later became the first woman to be elected President of the Herdwick Sheep Breeders' Association, but I didn't live to enjoy that position.

It was partly my acquisition of so much land that instigated my association with the National Trust (of which I'm sure many of you are paid-up members!). I had for long been a disciple of Canon Hardwicke Rawnsley's land conservation and preservation ideals. I'd first made friends with him way back, thanks to our family holidaying at Wray Castle, when he'd been the Vicar of Wray. His interest in the countryside and country life had not only inspired me but also had a lasting impact on my life, for he later became a founding member and the first Secretary of the 'National Trust for Places of Historic or Natural Beauty', which originated in January 1895. I supported their efforts to preserve not just the places of extraordinary beauty but also those heads of valleys and low grazing lands that would be irreparably ruined by development.

In 1930 William and I became partners with the National Trust in buying and managing the fell farms included in the large Monk Coniston Estate. This was composed of many farms spread over a wide area of north-western Lancashire, including the Tarn Hows. In addition to that, I was the Trust's de facto estate manager for seven years, until they could afford to repurchase most of the property. Though I was subject to some criticism for using my wealth and my husband's position in order to acquire properties in advance of their being made public, I gained full regard for observing the problems of afforestation, preserving the intact grazing lands, husbanding the quarries and timber on these farms and my stewardship of them.

If all this sounds like boasting, I feel I have no need to apologise, as most of you will appreciate that I'd agreed before coming into that lifetime to pay off quite a big chunk of karma. Though it's only since coming back Home that I've remembered any of them, it's obvious that my great love of the area dated back to previous lives I'd spent there. In one that I've been shown in the Akashic Records I was a very skilled craftsman, much sought after for both woodwork and stonework, but the man that I was then often tricked his customers into paying more than they needed to. So, as Beatrix Potter, I retained what I'd learnt then by becoming an authority on traditional Lakeland crafts, period furniture and local stonework, but I used the knowledge much more honestly. So, when I restored and preserved the farms that I bought or managed, it gave me great pleasure to make sure that each farmhouse had a piece of antique Lakeland furniture in it.

When I died, I left nearly all my property to the National Trust. Since this included over 4000 acres of land and 16 farms, with cottages and herds of cattle and Herdwick sheep, this was the largest gift made at that time to the National Trust, and it enabled the land now included in the Lake District National Park to be preserved and fell farming to be continued. In 2005, when the central office of the National Trust was opened in Swindon, it was named 'Heelis' in memory of me and William continued with his stewardship of our properties and my literary and artistic work during the 20 months in which he survived me.

Then, when he died in August 1945, he left all of the remainder to the National Trust.

My death was caused by complications from pneumonia and heart disease. My body was cremated at Carleton Crematorium, Blackpool, and later dear William scattered the ashes over the beloved hills that had meant so much to me for so long. Pneumonia is a horrid disease, as you may know, and it's hardly surprising that my heart had begun to fail after a lifetime of pretty hard (though of course enjoyable!) work. The winter of 1943 was a hard one and I caught the pneumonia early in December. I suffered a great deal, but William and his family did a very good job of nursing me through it. I died peacefully in Castle Cottage just three days before Christmas, with my dear husband right by my side, and his family all came to pay their respects while doing their best to give him the most joyous possible festive season.

I can't even *begin* to tell you how blissful it was going to the Light — even more wonderful than anything I could have imagined. Some of my most special sheep, as I said earlier, were there to greet me and together with them were both Bertram and Norman. My brother, who thanked me quite unnecessarily for caring about Mary, explained that he'd planned on having a fairly short life, partly because she needed another lesson in loss but also because he'd more or less completed his work anyway. Norman and he had been watching over me, and my one-time fiancé said how sorry he was not to have shared his life with me but that he'd been delighted to see me getting together with William and that, being companion soul mates, he and I had been together many times previously.

My life review, I have to admit, was pretty much impeccable and then, after a comparatively brief time spent in a heavenly (in both senses!) hospital, my guides took both Bertram and me to find our parents. We four agreed that the two of us had needed their artistic genes, and they said how very proud they were of both of us and apologised for their disapproval of our matches, explaining that they'd been hidebound by the climate of the times. They then added that they'd been looking forward to our joining their little team of souls who were working hard on the other side to redeem the Lake District from the problems with which it's been beset. So that's what I'm still doing at the moment and would prefer not to give a distressing elaboration of these difficulties, preferring instead to urge you to go and visit, unless you've done that very recently, hopefully inspiring you to give some sort of help with them. And if you've never seen the Lakes, I can assure you that you will still be gobsmacked by their beauty at whatever time of year you choose.

# 20

# Two Women Who Get Stuck,
# for Differing Reasons

*As we live now and as we are now, so shall we be on the other side
of death, and our life shall be conditioned by the thoughts with
which we have surrounded ourselves down here.*

Peter Richelieu, *A Soul's Journey*

Hullo! My name is Beryl and I've lived in Ludlow all my life.
I've heard it said, however, that I'm commonly known in the
town as "Mrs Misery". Sounds unfair, doesn't it? But then
what's ever happened to make me anything but miserable? I
was born in the Sandpits Road area and my parents never
gave a damn about me. They were always too busy trying to
make ends meet and getting enough food onto the table for my
younger sister Eunice and me, as well as for themselves, to have
any time for play. My mother worked nights as a cleaner in the
community hospital and my father worked all day sweeping the
roads, so we never had a spare moment to do anything together
as a family. Except on a Sunday, when we usually got on a train
down to Hereford to visit my grandma. She was a right bore
if ever there was one! Always moaning at my mother for not
doing her duty as a daughter, never taking her out to nice places
or even accompanying her to the doctor on the many occasions
when she had something wrong with her. "I had to get the bus
all on my own," she would say, "and then I had to sit forever in
the waiting room while everyone else was called in before me.
It was *terrible*, and then the medicine he gave me never did an
ounce of good anyway."

When Grandma finally died it was a relief to all of us! The
only trouble was that we were expected to provide a wreath

to put on the coffin and the cost of that was *horrendous*! My parents made us go without sweets for weeks on end to pay for it, and we couldn't have jam on our bread either. At least Grandad had left enough money in his piggy bank to pay for the tombstone. Apart from the woman next door, who said she'd miss having Grandma to chat to over the wall, there were only the four of us there at the funeral. It didn't take long and when the clergyman had said his little piece and we'd sung a couple of hymns, we just went back to Grandma's council flat for a cuppa before getting the train back to Ludlow. We had to bin most of what she'd left behind — even burn some of it because it was so revolting — and all she'd left in the piggy bank was five shillings and sixpence, which didn't nearly cover the cost of the undertaker. So my mum and dad went into debt, and Eunice and I had to keep on wearing the clothes and shoes that we'd outgrown.

Neither of us did very well at school. We hated it, we hated Miss Brown, who always ticked us off for looking scruffy, and none of the other children were ever nice to us. We just about learnt to read before leaving at 15 (me two years before Eunice of course), and I got a job in the corner shop, where they worked me endlessly stacking shelves. It was dead boring, but sometimes, at the end of the day, I was given a packet of biscuits or a bar of chocolate. At home I was now expected to make meals for my dad when he got home and my mum was just clearing off to work in the hospital. I did beans on toast usually and occasionally sausages, and Eunice and I usually ate with him in front of the telly. Not that we enjoyed the telly very much; we found the sport that my dad liked very boring, and none of the comedy shows were very funny either.

One day Eunice brought a boyfriend home. My parents weren't at all pleased because they thought she was too young to be mixing with boys, but I was dead jealous. But then after a while I started dating Ed, who looked after the wines in the corner shop, and we soon decided to get married so that we could get our own council flat rather than having to go on living with our parents. The ceremony was a simple one at the Registry Office, with just our parents, Eunice and Ed's brother Dave there as witnesses, and we got offered a council flat close to Gallows Bank, which was still within easy reach of the corner shop. Then we both had to start working longer hours to pay the rent and once I'd fallen pregnant with Ethel, things got harder still. Luckily Ed got a bit of a promotion, to working on the till and when Ethel got to six months my mother said she was very ready to give up working nights in the hospital and would look after the baby so long as we paid her eight shillings a week. This seemed a fair deal, but I vowed not to have another child. "All that hard work and what do you get for it?" I asked Ed. "Sleepless nights, dirty nappies, and food thrown onto the floor. No, babies really aren't my cup of tea at all!" So I got myself sterilised and never regretted it for a second.

Ethel was a naughty child as well, as she got older. Always running off with friends from school and we never had a clue where to look for her. So there was constant worry on top of all the work and we both got very weary. Eunice, on the other hand, got married four years after we had, having worked her way through quite a string of boyfriends that our parents disapproved of. Why I never understood — they all seemed much of a muchness to me — and when she finally married Darren from Shrewsbury we hardly saw her at all because she wanted to move there. "More exciting than Ludlow," she said, "and did you know that the great Charles Darwin had been to school there?"

"Charles Darwin?" I replied. "Who the heck is he? Some boring old churchman, I suppose, who told people that they'd go to Hell if they didn't do as he told them!"

"Actually no, he was a real revolutionary and brought up Unitarian. The Unitarians are much more open-minded than most other church people. But there's no point in explaining it all to you, Beryl, 'cos you'd never understand."

"I'm sure I wouldn't. Nor do I care to. I have more than enough on my mind trying to cope with Ethel!"

Anyway, Eunice and Darren had three children in the end — two boys, then a girl — and she absolutely doted on them. Luckily they didn't come to visit very often. "Too busy," they said, "and anyway trains are expensive." She was quite right of course, which is why we virtually never went to Shrewsbury, although, when we did, I really did like browsing in all the shops there. Once, when it was my birthday, Ed treated me to a beautiful hat, but I very rarely had occasions to wear it. It's still in the cupboard, so Ethel will be able to inherit it, which is just as well since I haven't got anything else of value to leave her. I did wear it for both of my parents' funerals and it was much admired.

We both carried on working in the shop while Ethel went through school. She did a bit better than I'd done (which wasn't saying much of course) and she finished up at 16 with three GCSEs under her belt, which made us quite proud. After school she decided she wanted to go to Hereford, where there were a few more job opportunities, and there she worked for a bit as a cashier at the Leisure Centre before marrying Danny, who already had a fairly decent council flat as well as a reasonable job. They had two boys a couple of years apart and brought them to visit now and again, but she was *never* available when I really needed her for my many doctor or hospital appointments. Ed, annoyingly, died of cancer at only 58, which meant that then I never had the help I needed for such things as carrying heavy shopping or fixing doors that broke in the wind. So life got tougher than ever.

After a while I got a white terrier for companionship, and I took him to Gallows Bank regularly for walks. I called him Terry, but all he ever said to me was '*Woof woof. I want some* more to eat'. So that cost money, too, and I often wondered if it was worth it. At least on Gallows Bank there were benches and tables where I could sit while Terry ran around with other dogs. There were always people as well, most of them there exercising their own dogs, but they never seemed to want to talk to me! I always tried to make conversation, telling them about things like the last time I'd been to the doctor's and how he'd kept me waiting for over an hour before prescribing me some cough medicine, which was useless anyway, or how I'd missed the train to Hereford the last time I went to see Ethel and then the next one got cancelled so I'd got fed up and just didn't bother to go. But nobody ever seemed to want to listen. What a life — winter was bad enough, when I had to hang around in the cold while Terry was chasing the other dogs, or being chased (which happened more often as he got older), but summer heat was sometimes even worse.

As time went on, Terry got so old that his walking got terribly slow. I found a thing in a charity shop that I could push him around in as well as put my shopping in, but that got too heavy for me sometimes. Then the vet put him on heart tablets and a diuretic, but they were ever so expensive, so in the end it was quite a relief to be told that I'd best put him to sleep. No, I wouldn't have another dog — much too much trouble!

One day it was really icy, but I had to go out to get some milk and some cornflakes. I slipped on the ice and came crashing down on the pavement, bashing my head really hard on the kerb, I think, so I suppose I ended up in hospital. At one point it was really weird because I was floating around just under the ceiling and I could actually see what looked to me exactly like my body, only with the head all bandaged up. I just didn't know what to do, or where to go, and some time later I saw the body being carted away. So then I thought I'd better go looking for it, but it seemed to have disappeared completely. Another thing that was a bit weird was that my head wasn't aching or *anything*! That was a big relief and although there was still a lot of ice on the ground and I was only wearing a hospital nightie, I didn't feel cold at all. There were a few people walking around in the streets and I recognised one or two of them. So I tried to ask them what on earth was going on, but they completely ignored me. It was just as though they were looking straight through me!

Well, I had to do *something*, so I decided to get a train down to Ethel's. First of all I went home to get some clothes on, so at least I'd look decent even though I wasn't feeling the cold. The door was locked and I didn't have a clue where my handbag had got to with the key in it, but I found to my astonishment that I could walk straight through the door. The house looked just the same and my dirty dinner plates were still in the sink, but, not wanting to bother with any of that, I just went straight down to the railway station. The man in the ticket office wouldn't sell me a ticket, even though he must have known me very well by sight, so I just got on the next train anyway. Ethel and Danny lived quite near the station and they were all in, but not one of them acknowledged my arrival. I found that very hurtful because, although Ethel was lousy as a daughter and Danny not much of a son-in-law, the grandchildren were normally eager to show me their latest iPhones or whatever.

So I just went straight back to Ludlow and there I wandered around aimlessly. But after what could have been only a day or two, or could have been a hundred years for all I knew, I suddenly felt myself being pushed inside a foetus, which was again very strange because of course I had to shrink to fit into it. Then a nice gentle voice whispered into my ear: 'Don't worry, Beryl, your physical body didn't survive that nasty fall, and now your ashes are buried in the cemetery. It's all fine, since you didn't have anything else you needed to do in that lifetime. Often when people die very suddenly it's hard for them to realise that they're dead because the etheric body, which is the next layer up from the physical one, looks exactly the same. That's true for the whole planet actually, so it's all too easy for souls who've got lost to imagine that they're still in the place that they're used to, rather than its etheric counterpart. All this is probably hard for you to understand right now, but you'll have plenty more lifetimes in which to learn about it. Some good Christians in Ludlow, Hereford and Shrewsbury have all been praying for you and here on the other side we've had a discussion and are agreed that you've had more than enough suffering for the time being and that it's time now for you to learn about Love. So a young woman called Angela, who's been dying for a baby for quite some time, has finally succeeded in getting pregnant, and she and her husband Jimmy have just found out that they're expecting a baby boy. They're thrilled to bits and are thinking of calling you Brian. They'll give you lots of love, and Jimmy's got quite a well-paid job, so that will give you a much better start than Beryl had. I'll be watching over you, as I always do, and some spirit guides will in due course be appointed to help Brian make the best choices right from the very start. God bless you!'

So now I'm feeling very comfortable in here and it will all be 'wait and see and fingers crossed'. And I hope you're all pleased to hear the happy ending to my tale.

***

*A Bodhisattva knows his own worth and has no need to shout to make himself heard.*

*He is always a good listener.*

*A Bodhisattva knows that everyone is equal, but that all are on their own unique path and on different stages of the Journey.*

*He will therefore respect the other, even when he believes her to be in the wrong, and not to try to force his own views on anyone who is not ready to understand or accept them.*

> *He is always ready and willing to offer help and advice, but only when asked for it.*
>
> Anonymous

Hullo. My name is Fiona and since crossing over I've undergone a massive change, as you will see as my story progresses. Since, however, this change only came gradually after my death I'd prefer, if you don't mind, to start at the beginning, writing from the perspective that I had during my last life on Earth. So here goes!

As you might have guessed from my name, I'm Scottish, but I'm very glad to say that I was brought up Catholic, *not* Presbyterian! I left Glasgow at 18 because I wanted to be a nurse and my parents thought I'd do best to go to London, where my older brother was already studying medicine, so they thought he could keep an eye on me. I got on reasonably well with Duncan, though it did trouble me that he no longer bothered to go to mass every Sunday. He said it was because there wasn't a Catholic church nearby, like we'd always had in Glasgow, but I thought that that was a pretty feeble excuse. I, on the other hand, not only *never* missed a Sunday but also made it to early mass as often as I could. That depended on my timetable of course. They worked us student nurses very hard at Guy's Hospital, with many early morning starts. That was just as it should be, because there was a great deal to learn, for which a lot of hands-on nursing was essential.

I worked hard and didn't have time for much social life, but occasionally Duncan invited me out with a group of his friends. That was all right, but they sometimes went in for dirty jokes and none of them was religious. In fact some of them even laughed at me for going to church 'so often'. I told them that they were risking Hellfire and that they'd make much better doctors anyway if they prayed for their patients and helped them spiritually rather than just studying their illnesses and their anatomy. But I might as well have been talking to a brick wall.

Once I'd qualified, I applied for a few jobs, had a couple of offers, and settled for a post as a junior nurse at Hull Royal Infirmary. I didn't really fancy going back up to Scotland, where my parents would have expected me to live with them, and this was sort of halfway, which seemed a good compromise. To start with, Amanda, another Guy's nurse, and I found a flat to share that was quite close to the hospital. We'd got on quite well in London, but after a bit she started dating young men on her free evenings and sometimes got back so late that I was already in bed. This annoyed me because I found it difficult to get to sleep until I knew she'd come in, and that made early starts (of which there were many) a problem. The crunch came one night when she didn't get back at all! So I accused her of fornication, which made her absolutely furious. "It's none of your bloody business!" she yelled. To which I replied that I didn't fancy sharing a flat with a whore and asked her what on earth would happen if she got pregnant.

"Haven't you heard of birth control?" Amanda asked, and so I had to inform her that women who had sex before marriage would probably go to Hell. This made her so cross that I decided there and then to move out of the flat and look for a room on my own. She didn't give a damn, saying that her boyfriend would be only too happy to move in in my place. And that was the end of that friendship.

Fortunately I found a reasonable bedsit with a small kitchen, which served me well for a couple of years, but then I met Graham, a solicitor, and we started going out. He told me he'd always fancied marrying a nurse, because it would give him a sense of security when he fell ill, and also that her knowledge would be useful for rearing children. I wasn't totally convinced that that was a good reason for matrimony and anyway he wasn't a Catholic, but on the other hand being married to a solicitor sounded safe to me and I could always go full out to convert him. So I took him up to Glasgow to meet my family and he took me across the River Humber in a ferry to meet his parents in Lincoln, and then the wedding was fixed for a Saturday in September, six months later. We thought that would give us plenty of time to make all the arrangements and to find a little house to buy, for which Graham had already managed to save up a deposit.

We settled on Cottingham, said to be England's largest village, which seemed quite pleasant and wasn't too far for either of us to get to work. I took driving lessons so that we could each get to work independently, as our hours were of course different from one another's. One of the best things about Cottingham was its Catholic church, and fortunately we found a little house to buy quite close to it. Before we'd married I'd made Graham promise to come to mass with me. The parish priest was of the old school — not one of those who were madly into ecumenism — and on the first Sunday that we went there he preached about it being vital to send one's children to Catholic schools. I of course intended to do that anyway, but Graham fumed at me afterwards, saying that the education of his children (assuming that we had some in due course) was none of the priest's business. We had quite a row over that and he got even more cross when I gave him a catechism to learn by heart.

Graham's parents were vaguely Anglican and hadn't forced any religion onto him, but I was quite determined to save him from Hell and so went through a bit of the catechism with him each evening. He gave up resisting in order to keep the peace (he told me he had an aunt and uncle who were always arguing and didn't want to have a marriage like theirs), but after a few months he refused to come to church with me any more. I was very upset, but nothing would persuade him. "It's dead boring," he protested. "I don't like the hymns, the sermons are always more or less the same, and I always have much more useful things to do on a Sunday morning, such as redecorate the bedroom in the colour that *you* said *you* wanted it to be."

"Of course I do really appreciate your doing the decorating, but I'm concerned for the welfare of your *soul*."

"Well," he replied, "if your God really did give me a soul (about which I can't feel completely sure), then surely it's up to *him* to take care of it." I was almost in despair, but, as my friend Brenda at church kept reminding me, I could still go on praying for him.

After we'd been married for a year I got pregnant with Dominic. I didn't give up work straight away because we wanted to save for a bigger house, but when the time came I felt very ready for some maternity leave. Dominic was a pretty good baby and the breastfeeding went well, but when Elspeth came along a couple of years later, she turned out to be a nightmare. Always screaming, getting herself into tricky predicaments as soon as she was mobile, and breaking her brother's toys, which made him furious! So I prayed hard that we wouldn't have another child and at least that prayer was answered.

The children grew, as they always do, and when they reached 11 we sent them to the Catholic comprehensive school, which was renowned anyway as the best school in Hull, so Graham was all right about that. He was always kept very busy by his work and I too went back to work part-time, which of course helped pay the mortgage when we did move to a bigger house. The new house still wasn't that far from the Catholic church and I became increasingly involved in events there. A new priest came who was more forward looking than his predecessor, and he made big efforts to increase the social activities, as well as laying on catechism classes for the children and teenagers. I helped with the organisation of all that but had a terrible job getting Dominic and Elspeth to come along. For some unknown reason they were very rebellious — just the opposite of how I had been at their ages!

A group of us mums were able to band together during school hours and occasionally went off on outings to places in the area. (I remember one particular trip when we went birdwatching in Bempton on the Yorkshire coast, which was very enjoyable and interesting.) But one member of this group, while still claiming to be a good Catholic Christian, got corrupted by falling under the spell of a supposed holy man in India. She was influenced in this, I think, by her good friend who was our church organist, who had read a couple of books that convinced her that this man was as great as Jesus! The two of them even went off with a group to see him at his ashram in India and what's more, they got involved in healing. How could they not appreciate that Jesus Christ was the only ever healer?! Worse still, the one who wasn't the organist got herself trained in something called 'past-life regression therapy' and then started working at a therapy clinic in the centre of Hull. This was the worst possible heresy because, as all Christians should know, everybody has only *one* life; it's only strange people like Buddhists and Hindus who believe in reincarnation.

Anyway, when this woman (I'll call her Judith) reached the age of 60, she invited me to her birthday party. She also invited my good friend Brenda, but Brenda had the guts to refuse the invitation on the grounds that Judith claimed to perform healing. I myself decided on a different strategy: I took with me to the party my friend Andrea from a parish in Hull, not Cottingham, who happened to have heard of this Hindu heretic who was corrupting both the organist and Judith. Andrea, who took Judith a nice present of a cuddly toy to make up for not having been invited, didn't actually say anything at the party, but Judith had a big picture of the Indian 'holy man' in her hall and so Andrea wrote her a strong letter afterwards, pointing out the disastrous error in which she'd got trapped. Alas, it didn't do any good. Judith just wrote a letter back, in which she said ridiculous things such as "There are as many paths up the spiritual mountain as there are people to climb it" and also recounting some so-called miracles that her guru in India had performed.

I happened to share with Judith a cleaner named Kathleen, who was theoretically a Catholic but didn't go to church very often and so I feared for her soul, too, just as I did for those of my own family. Kathleen was very hard up, little educated, widowed and struggling with two children, so I did a great deal for her besides paying her well to work for me. Once, near Christmastime, I even treated her to a performance of *The Messiah*, but that proved to be a waste of money, as she didn't appreciate it. Some years later, however, we fell out, which was a nuisance because *I* was then the one left struggling.

This was when I'd just had a hip replacement, some time after Graham had died from a heart attack. The children had both already left home (not that either of them would have been much use anyway). Being alone in the house, I did really need help and since Kathleen was also alone I thought she might be glad of the company if she came and looked after me until I was a bit more mobile. She agreed to this suggestion and became my 'carer'. One day, however, I couldn't find my favourite brooch anywhere, so I was sure she must have pinched it. When, however, I mentioned it to Kathleen, she got really upset, then cleared off in a huff and I haven't seen her since. So that's another soul to fear for! Ah well, so long as I can save *myself*, I suppose that's the main thing, and I do say my prayers faithfully each day, even when I'm unable to get to the church.

Judith, whom I mentioned earlier, eventually moved away from the area when her husband retired, and I've heard on the grapevine that she took the opportunity to leave the Church as well and joined a group of people who all worshipped her

Indian guru instead of being faithful to Jesus. A few years before she left, however, she had a fall and broke her hip, so I kindly went to visit her in Hull Royal hospital, saying she should let me know if there was anything I could do to help her. Her husband was sometimes invited to work abroad and that summer she was keen to join him in Geneva, abandoning her rather badly behaved, black adopted son, who was in his last year at school. She was told that, before flying off, she could exchange her crutches for a walking stick, but that she should get these NHS crutches back to the hospital. So, since I worked there myself, she phoned and asked if I could kindly take them back for her. I agreed, but somewhat reluctantly, as it involved going all the way to her house and collecting them from her son before setting off to work. Seeing him made me really wonder afresh how anyone could bear having someone of a different race in their own family!

A few weeks ago — at least I think it was a few weeks ago, but it's odd because I seem to have completely lost track of time recently — I'm sure that I suddenly had a fatal heart attack. Being a nurse by profession, I obviously know enough about such things to be able to recognise them, and I reckon that I ought now to be dead. The weird thing is, though, that I haven't yet seen any sign of my beloved Jesus! Since I've been such a good Catholic Christian all my life, He surely ought to have been there waiting for me? I know for sure that I left my body because, when I looked down and saw it there lying on the bed, it looked no different from the many bodies I've seen in hospitals after people have had fatal attacks.

Anyway, not having found Jesus waiting there as I'd expected, the first thing I did was to head for a church from which I could hear familiar hymns being sung. After going inside to check that it was indeed a Catholic church, I sat down amidst the congregation and joined in the hymn singing. Before too very long there was a rather good sermon and I listened to it quite intently because, just as the first priest I knew in Cottingham had often done, this priest was explaining what one should do to avoid going to Hell for all eternity. When the mass had ended and people started going out, I asked one of them where Jesus was, since I hadn't met Him yet. She simply looked at me as though I was mad and replied: "What on earth do you mean? Nobody can meet Jesus until they've died!"

The conversation then continued thus:

"But I *am* dead and you must be, too. Otherwise you couldn't be in the same place as I am."

"*Me* dead — don't be ridiculous! If I were dead I wouldn't now want to go home for breakfast. Anyway you don't look any more dead than I do, so I'm afraid you must be either dreaming or have a very vivid imagination."

"Imagination?! I was a nurse by profession and I *certainly* didn't imagine the sight of my dead body lying on my bed. So where do you think *your* home is?"

"I don't *think*; I know perfectly well that my home is here in Scunthorpe, and I don't want to be held up for any longer because I really am getting hungry."

Well, I certainly didn't want to follow this woman to her home in what she imagined to be Scunthorpe, so I wandered around for a bit. I quickly felt sure that I wasn't any longer in Cottingham because I found that there was quite a long line of churches all in a row and then, adjacent to them, was a mosque, a Buddhist temple, a Hindu temple and even a synagogue! Each of them had a notice outside saying that they had the one true Faith and that anyone who wanted to be saved should join their congregation. Even more puzzled, I went back towards the Catholic church, where I knew I could at least feel safe, but then I got accosted by a couple of women who told me that they were Jehovah's Witnesses and that I should join *them* if I wanted to be saved. At that point I could take no more, so I just went inside the church and burst into tears.

Then, to my astonishment, I suddenly felt a loving presence and an arm put around my shoulders. Not even daring to open my eyes, I asked tentatively: "Who are you?" A gentle voice then replied: "I'm your guardian angel, Fiona, who, as you were taught in your good Catholic childhood, is always with you. Don't worry: everything will gradually be explained, but right now it's time to take you for your life review."

"Life review? Am I now to be judged before I can meet up with Jesus?"

"Well, you were brainwashed into fear of the 'Last Judgement', but let me reassure you that that notion is really a total myth. The only judgement made is by the soul itself, and there are always caring guides around to offer help. On Earth there are no mistakes, only learning, and here on the other side nothing except Love exists. So please forget what you were taught about Hell and Purgatory; now it's time to look at what Fiona needed to learn in that lifetime which ended with a fatal heart attack. Just follow me and you'll be amazed at what you'll see."

So follow the angel I did, and amazed I indeed was, but I'm not going to even attempt to describe the beauty of what I saw. Instead let me just say to all those of you who are still on Earth and perhaps fearing death: "Please take my word for it that there really is *nothing* to fear. Of course there may well be physical pain — as I had with my heart attack — but nothing lasts indefinitely and it can be instantly forgotten in the wonderment of what lies in store for you."

When my guardian angel mentioned guides to me, at first I had no idea what he meant, but, once he'd left me with the three of them and they'd introduced themselves as 'old friends', I remembered them as people I'd known in previous lives. (For yes, I've now recognised my error in believing that Buddhists, Hindus, Cathars and so on are wrong about reincarnation!) Anyway, I won't linger on my life review, as it would be both boring and irrelevant to anyone else, but my guide friends did tell me firstly that I'd been unfair to Kathleen, as it had in fact been my daughter Elspeth who had borrowed the brooch without asking permission. So I now have a karmic debt to pay to Kathleen. (I'd forgotten about karma, but they lovingly explained it, helping me to remember.) They also explained to me that I'd got trapped, as very many people do, in a repeated pattern of lives of bigotry; for instance, I'd once been a Muslim who'd believed that everyone should be converted to Islam, and another time even a Jehovah's Witness. (Once we'd discussed that one, I agreed with my guides that the Jehovah's Witnesses' courage and intentions had to be admired, however little one likes their teaching!)

After that we discussed what should be the next step and agreed that the first thing I could be granted was the sight of Jesus for which I'd been yearning for so long. He then appeared instantly, gave me a loving embrace, thanking me for the service I'd given him as Fiona, and then gently went on to explain that I'd been just one of millions upon millions of good, well-intentioned and genuinely caring Christians who'd misunderstood some of His message when they took on the belief that His was the only divine incarnation ever. He explained that Rama and Krishna, for instance, who had come to Earth *long* before Him and were known as *avatars* (divine incarnations similar to Him as Jesus), were among the best-known names throughout the world. Then he added: "Sathya Sai Baba, whom your two fellow parishioners followed, went to Earth much more recently, partly to remind people that they were *all* divine — that the problem was simply that most of them had forgotten it."

Needless to say, this was all a bit hard for me to swallow straight away, but, after Jesus had said goodbye to me and promised to see me again soon, my guides returned and took me on a little tour of what's known as the Akashic Records. I can't begin to tell you how amazing this is! It's a vast library in which is stored records of absolutely everything that has ever happened. Being very familiar with it, my guides were able instantly to pull out my own records and then thumb through to pick out some of the other past-lifetime stories most relevant to me right now. They showed me a Buddhist monk, who (untypically of Buddhists!) had tried to convert Christians, and then a Hindu who had persecuted Muslims. After that they explained that it *was* possible to deal with the karma incurred by such actions while still on Earth, mentioning among other things that something like Deep Memory Process/regression (a comparatively new therapy) could often be tremendously effective in helping to understand the reasons for one's problems. Since, however, I wouldn't as Fiona have been open to anything like that, they suggested that I could come back next time as a Jewish person, either male or female, and thus learn that it had in fact been only a tiny group of Jews who had persecuted Jesus.

I said that it was all very interesting but that I now felt quite tired, to which the reply was: "That's perfectly natural following a heart attack such as the one you had. Now your etheric body can have a good rest in one of the hospitals we have over here and then, when the time has come for you to shed *that* body, do you fancy using your nursing skills on this side for a while before returning to Earth in a new physical body? Oh and by the way, don't worry at the moment about the names and nature of the different levels of body. That's something you might well like to study next time round, by getting into the esoteric side of Judaism, known as the Kabbalah."

I then thanked them for everything they'd told me, commenting that it was good to have been given so much to think about, but then I suddenly remembered another thing that had been puzzling me greatly, so I asked: "Can you just, please, explain to me how it was that the woman I spoke to when I came out of the Catholic church was convinced that she was still alive and well and living in Scunthorpe?"

"Ah," came the reply, "that's actually quite a simple question to answer. You see, as I hinted at a moment ago, *everything* has different levels, and just as you are at present in your etheric body, which you will soon be shedding and then continuing for a little while in your mental body, so Earth itself has an etheric body that looks exactly the same as the physical. It's consequently only too easy for someone less aware than you are not to appreciate the fact that they've died and consequently endeavour to carry on living in just the same way. But don't worry about such souls! They'll all be helped in due course — another reason for prayer being so beneficial; none of the prayers that you yourself made as Fiona was wasted. Now it really *is* time for you to rest, and remember that you have the rest of eternity to continue with your learning."

"That's a nice thought, but yes indeed, a rest will be most welcome!"

After saying that, escorted again by my guardian angel, I went off with pleasure to relax in what turned out to be by far the most wonderful, best-equipped hospital that I'd ever seen. So now I'll conclude by saying: "Farewell and see you anon, back on that beautiful green planet that we all need to work so hard to preserve."

# 21

# Enhancer and Protector of an Island

*Hay un fenómeno que tenemos la obligación de difundir, que es, sencillamente, enseñar a VER.*

*(There is a phenomenon that we are obliged to communicate and that is, quite simply, to teach people how to SEE.)*

César Manrique

*Hola! Buenos días! Yo me llamo César Manrique y nací en Arrecife, capital de Lanzarote, en el año 1919. Ah, perdón...* I forgot for a moment that you wouldn't all speak Spanish. You see, it's so much easier over here, as we all communicate by telepathy. You'll remember that again when you've crossed over, too, but right now I can use the (American — sorry!) English that I learned when I lived for a while in New York. Anyway, my name is pronounced Thaysar (with the stress on the first syllable, just like Julius, after whom I *wasn't* named!) Manrikay, rolling the 'r' nicely, and 'my' island in the fascinating Canaries is pronounced Lantharotay. (Our scribe was told many years ago, by one of her Spanish lecturers at Bristol University, that there was a theory that Philip II had had a lisp and his courtiers had consequently imitated him to make him feel less embarrassed about it! Whether that's true or not I don't know, though I suppose I could look for him to ask, but I've been so busy following my fatal car crash in 1992 that I've never thought to get round to it. It's odd, too, isn't it, that the 'th' sound has never penetrated the part of Spain known as Andalusía?)

*So*, I was born, as I said in the 'wrong language', in the capital of my island in 1919 — in its Puerto Nao district, on 24 April to be precise — and I had a twin sister (Amparo) and was later gifted with both another sister (Juana) and a brother (Carlos).

My father was a food merchant and my grandfather a public notary, which made us a typical middle-class family with no financial burdens. We were an extremely happy family, too, and some of my best times as a child were spent in Caleta de Famara on the north coast of Lanzarote. My father (whose architectural gifts I obviously inherited) had built a house there and I just *loved* both the taste of the sea and the intense sun. I felt the Atlantic to be my true master, a constant source of enthusiasm, passion and freedom. For I was *born* a free spirit, and fortunately my parents did nothing to change that by imposing religious beliefs, or anything similar, on me.

Talking of family, I must just say something about my dear little brother Carlos, of whom I'm *so* proud! He lived to be 96 and only died on 23 January 2022, thus outliving me by over 29 years. He'd been having treatment for heart problems for some time, yet, on 12 March 2020 (just two days before the Spanish Covid-19 lockdown), he received on my behalf the Gold Medal of Honour awarded posthumously by the town of Teguise. His death followed a heart operation in which two stents were inserted, but then there were complications. The funeral took place the very next day in Arrecife and I was there of course, waiting to greet him and escort him with his spirit guides to his next port of call. Since his recovery from the physical problems he suffered latterly, we've been able to have some lovely chats about all sorts of things, some of which we'd regretted never having had time for while on Earth.

Anyway, back to my own life on the planet. Our family moved to Caleta de Famara completely when I was 15, and only the Spanish Civil War (17 July 1936 – 1 April 1939) did anything to mar my innate, overwhelming joy in life. I prefer to gloss over that war, however, as it was all such a traumatic experience, and I regret to say that I joined up in support of Franco, simply because it was the 'done thing' in my section of society and I was a bit young to have formed any strong political opinions.

(Later of course I read your great George Orwell on the subject and would love to have met him while still on Earth.) So, after my return home in 1939, I coped by just refusing ever to talk about any of it. Later still, in my more mature years, I wrote these words: "I see the creation of national flags, borders, anthems and political organisations as having contributed to the progressive paralysis of any sane, peaceful effort towards human coexistence." And I've felt no different about any of it since crossing over, because I believe that all the world needs is common sense rather than separatist ideas, and so I will forever fight against labels, cultural models and uniformity.

Of course the Canaries (like so many other countries worldwide) did very likely suffer from conflict in the past, when they were conquered by Spain in the late fifteenth century. Although nobody can be quite sure where their early inhabitants, known collectively as the 'Guanches', originally came from, there was already a flourishing culture here long before the arrival of the Spanish. The islands' original dwellers were an agricultural people, living mostly in caves, and their society had a hierarchical structure, with kings known as *guanartemes* and priests named *faycans*. Lanzarote was a single kingdom and it was named after the Genoese Lanzarotto Malocello, who discovered it when he led an expedition there in 1339. I'd like to think that there wasn't too much bloodshed and cruelty when they arrived, but, knowing the Spaniards' reputation in Latin America...!

Anyway, from my very earliest days I never wanted to be anything other than an artist, yet — partly because my own father's building of our house had impressed me so much, I suppose — I went initially to La Laguna University in Tenerife to study technical architecture. I found, however, that the subject wasn't really for me and so gave it up after two years. Then, in 1945, I moved to Madrid and studied art on a scholarship at the Real Academia de Bellas Artes de San Fernando, where (despite the horrid, cold winters!) I had a very productive time, and it led to my graduating as an art teacher and painter. Following those studies, I'm happy to say that I fairly quickly became an internationally acclaimed artist, prospering in Madrid, Paris and New York, and my paintings were exhibited in both Japan and the USA, as well as across Europe. I loved all the travel, and the world became my next teacher. I was fascinated by China and also especially loved Japan, whose art, with its emphasis on the spaces between objects, known as *Ma*, is so very different from that of the Western hemisphere.

During these years, too, I made friends with many well-known twentieth-century artists, such as Andy Warhol, to name but one, and I fell madly in love with Pepi Gomez (less well known than Warhol but very talented nevertheless). We had, until her death from cancer, a marvellous 18 years together, and — to put right any speculation to the contrary — we did actually marry, but we didn't want to make a fuss about it and only had a quiet, informal ceremony. So discreet were we in fact that, when Ann, our scribe, did the César Manrique Tour with her friend Peg, in March 2023, she asked the guide whether I'd had a family and the reply was that I'd had plenty of relationships with both women and men, but never married or had a family of my own.

I suppose people would call me 'bisexual', and I was criticised (particularly in Franco's Spain!) for the period in which I embraced homosexuality, but the truth is that for me life and love were such marvellous gifts that it would have been foolish not to find pleasure in every aspect of it. Though certain countries are, alas, still lagging behind in the recognition that same-sex partnerships are no less commendable than heterosexual ones, I'm pleased to have noticed a sea change in that field in recent years and trust that improvement in the eradication of *all* prejudices will soon speed up. I once wrote that "the only important reality is the great mystery of life and of man with his inexhaustible imagination and his infinite ways of acting". I was, myself, never short of companionship and always revelled in friendships of every nature. Dogs, too, were something I never liked to be without, for dogs are so often wiser and more reliable than human beings, don't you think?

But Pepi's and my commitment to, and support of, one another was unique in my life, and her falling ill was truly devastating for me. After her early death in 1963, friends wisely advised a change of scene and so, appreciating that life had to go on regardless, I flew to New York, where I really enjoyed the city's exciting cultural and social scene for a good two years. Needless to say, Pepi was eagerly awaiting my arrival over here and though I'd never doubted that I would at some time see her again, I was absolutely thrilled when our meeting happened immediately after my fatal car accident, once it had dawned on me fully that I was no longer in my physical body. Pepi later pointed out to me that, despite the harrowing time that I'd had during the Civil War, I'd still needed to experience a more *personal* loss and when the time came for my life review, my guides added that I'd recently had a few rather cushy lives, with little responsibility. This one had consequently been more to do with getting to grips with real work, and intense relationships could therefore have got in the way of what I'd planned in advance to do for Lanzarote.

By 1966, however, I felt a strong call from my native land, and my return was naturally welcomed by my family as well as the multitudinous friends I'd left behind. My twin sister and I were always good companions, but we were very different from one another and she was now happily married with her own family. I found it very pleasant having children around sometimes, but feel that having my own wouldn't have been compatible with my travelling so much for my work, as I would have wanted to give them a lot of my time. In any case, when I was shown some of my Akashic records, I saw that I'd already done plenty of parenting in the aforementioned cushy lives (at least one or two of which had been shared with Pepi, a companion soul mate).

Before, however, concentrating on my legacy to Lanzarote, I'd like to mention to you another, completely different sort of thing for which I made myself a big name. It was the design of a BMW car! If you'd like to see a picture of it, you can easily find it on the internet and you may be surprised to see that it wasn't by any means all painted in a single colour. For this project (realised in 1990) I collaborated with the German designer and artist Walter Maurer, who had already designed some of the legendary BMW Art Cars jointly with other artists such as Andy Warhol. Maurer was an interesting man, with many interests, who had initially studied graphic design and colour theory in Munich, and he later lectured on the latter at Munich's Academy of Fine Arts. He was born in 1942 and the pain caused by his father's early death in World War II served partly as a catalyst for the artistic commitment he made to advocating peaceful coexistence without hatred, exclusion or discrimination. His extensive work, which is closely linked to the aviation world as well as to that of the automobile, is committed both to ethical issues and to complex philosophical questions about humanity and contemporary problems. (So, obviously very much a man after my own heart!)

I personally regarded the automobile as an indispensable feature of daily life, which shaped the picture of our towns and greatly influenced the way we see the world around us. My idea in painting the BMW car was to make it appear as if it were gliding through space without encountering any form of resistance and in its design I was inspired by differing concepts of movement. I was trying to unite the notions of speed and aerodynamics with the concept of aesthetic appeal in one and the same object. Hence my glowing colours and broad sweeping strokes, which blend into the car's outlines and are suggestive of effortless gliding and lithe movement. You see, I was ever an advocate of harmony between humanity and nature, as of harmony between culture and nature, always fully aware that, with the invention of the wheel, human civilisation had taken a quantum leap forward. Mobility was certainly a key theme of the BMW Art Car's international exhibition tour.

Now — especially if you've never been there — you might like to hear a bit about my fascinating island, so different from anywhere else that our well-travelled scribe had ever seen in her 83 years. The whole volcanic archipelago of the Canary Islands is barren and often very windy, but, along with closely neighbouring Fuerteventura, Lanzarote is the most barren of them all. Between 1700 and 1730, the Timanfaya volcano on its east side was active almost non-stop, which forced its inhabitants to move away (some to Gran Canaria, others even further, to Latin America). The volcanic ash, however, formed what we call *picón*, that is, dark cinders that collect and retain the dew, thus making a natural irrigation system. This enabled the inhabitants upon their return to grow a good variety of vegetables, as well as cultivating vines. Rather than growing up canes side by side, as one observes in, say, France, each vine stump is planted separately, a low semicircular wall being built around it with lava rocks to protect it from the wind. Though I myself was neither a smoker nor a drinker, I know that Lanzarote wine is considered to be excellent, and it's been quite a good money spinner for the island.

The year 1824 saw another series of smaller eruptions and although there haven't been any more since, the interesting thing is that the heat is still very close to the surface, and nowadays tourists can be regaled by the sight of someone pouring water down a pipe and causing an instantaneous 'geyser'! Hence also my 1970 design for a local restaurant named *El Diablo* (The Devil), where tourists can enjoy meals with chicken cooked in the volcanic oven. But the island's other main attraction is of course its wonderful sandy beaches, the best of these being

Puerto del Carmen, on the south side towards the east, and easily accessible from the airport.

The first thing I did, however, upon my return from America was to instigate the creation of Jameos del Agua, for which I rapidly became internationally renowned as a designer/ architect as well as a painter. The word *jameo* means a 'collapsed lava tunnel', and I found myself irresistibly intrigued by what could be done with them. Just two years later I'd created the home in which I was to live for the next 20 years. It had started when I discovered a cave in the huge lava flow that spills down from Timanfaya, passing Tahiche to touch the sea near Arrecife. I climbed down to rest under one of the fig trees that farmers often planted in these hollows and was amazed to discover a series of volcanic bubbles and a tunnel. That original cave is now the centrepiece of the main room into which you first enter the building, and it's a space surrounded by artworks, photos and other mementoes of my life. The spiral staircase leading to the underground level is no longer in use, but if you go there, you'll find that you can still descend outdoors and relish the spectacular view of the pool and garden below.

The first stop is the White Bubble, which celebrates my renowned love of parties, and it contains several photos of me relaxing, laughing and holding court in my headquarters, which people, I'm delighted to say, never cease to find truly amazing. Several articles from magazines of the time made clear my huge appetite for life, also stressing the 'space-age setting' and the relaxed atmosphere, where nudity and hedonism (in its *positive* sense!) seemed to be everywhere. A small tunnel then leads to the Red Bubble, the cave where the original fig tree that first inspired me, though now long dead, still stands. The swimming pool area is where I first developed my artistic ideas in that direction, and the really beautiful turquoise pool is highlighted in brilliant white, surrounded by black lava walls and tumbling greenery. And there's even a small dance floor!

After that, passing through the Black and Yellow Bubbles, you eventually go back upstairs to reach the room where I built a window over a tongue of lava. This enters the room beneath a beautiful view of the volcanic landscape beyond, and you can see solitary palms nodding in the breeze.

Another aspect of the Jameos is the Green Caves, to which the entrance is an alternative option for tourists doing the Manrique day tour. Interesting though they are, however, they sadly cannot be recommended to anyone without good balance and an ability to get through some smaller spaces, or to anyone who minds about twisty stairways or being bent double at some points. (One comment by a visitor has been: "It's fine if you take your time and listen to the guide when he tells you to watch your head", but the writer of that one was no doubt fairly young and physically fit.) You see, the descent here is into a labyrinth of passageways and caves, which really have to be seen to be believed. They were left by the passage of molten volcanic lava flowing through its vast chambers. Never mind, though, if you don't feel up to the Green Caves, as both entrances lead eventually to the impressive Auditorium on which I started work in 1976 and where concerts of various sorts are still regularly held.

In 1968, following my definitive return to Lanzarote, I created the massive, glaringly white statue named *Fecundidad* ('fecundity' or 'fertility'), a monument which I conceived as a tribute to the island's peasant farmers who work so hard to produce crops from the volcanic land. Standing 15 metres tall, it marks the precise centre of the island, on the connection between the roads from the capital and Teguise, and was constructed from disused water tanks. I gave to a man named Jesús Soto the challenging task of creating a base suitable for withstanding Lanzarote's somewhat notorious winds. The monument, which requires no entrance fee, has a staircase for tourists to climb if they wish and also a very pleasant visitor centre. (If you can figure out which bit of the sculpture denotes what, then you're cleverer than was our scribe, but I fully understand her difficulties!)

You can easily find any of the other things I was responsible for conceiving and building on the internet, and you can always, if you care to as well, google the 'Lanzarote legend of the bride and the devil' and find a picture of the pitchfork that I designed. (You can make up your own minds about the legend's history. As you'll probably have gathered by now, I was always something of a joker and a tease!) I must, however, just mention the abode that I gave to the admirable César Manrique Foundation and which certainly shouldn't be missed. If you don't want, or don't have time for, a full tour it's only a short drive from, say, Teguise and since it's a small island, you could also comfortably fit in a quick trip to the 'Mirador del Río', which is situated on the northernmost corner of the island at 474 metres above sea level. From it, when the conditions are clear, you can see over to the little island of La Graciosa, and it contains a pleasant, circular cafeteria with windows all the way round. One nice comment about it is: "It is camouflaged on the rock in a way in which only a genius of Manrique's magnitude could conceive."

So that's enough said about the 'Enhancer'; now for the 'Protector' bit of my chapter title. I once wrote: "The hour has inevitably come to launch a fierce attack on the devastation of the natural environment in the Canary Islands, a destruction which is yet another example of the atrocities committed against Mother Nature all over the world." Fortunately my reputation enabled me to have a very big influence on the regional council and they actually gave me a free hand to do whatever I wanted. One thing I insisted upon was that, apart from church steeples, no building should be taller than a palm tree. This rule was adhered to, with the unfortunate exception of a 'skyscraper' hotel being built in Arrecife during a period when I was away. I encouraged people to renovate their homes, maintaining a character that was in keeping with the local environment, and I recommended that — apart from coastal areas, where the odd bit of blue was permissible — villages should be painted only in white or green. I further banned roadside hoardings and rubbish tipping, and also decreed that electric cables should be laid underground. Being seen as largely responsible for preserving the island's natural state, I received the World Ecology Award in 1968 and, in 1976, the Europa Nostra Award for Conservation. I don't really like boasting, but neither do I see any reason for modesty, for the simple truth is that I incarnated as a passionate man with strong views and a strong character, and nothing and nobody was going to deter me from my mission.

I mentioned earlier that I'd had a fatal car accident. Well, here are two things I said about death at some point in the past:

> Death seems a marvel to me; to know that I am going to die enables me to create the moment. It's like a pastime since it permits me to abandon the responsibility of carrying on with existence because I know that, at some given moment, I shall vanish!

> Death is the great escape which allows us, during our brief period of life, to do the most daring and fun things.

Often some tragedy has to occur in order for a dangerous situation to be rectified, and the big irony about my accident is that, loathing the amount of traffic on the roads, I'd been campaigning for roundabouts to be created at busy junctions in Lanzarote. The crash was partly my own fault, as I'd recently had a cataract operation and wasn't supposed to be driving, but the chauffeur I'd been given was off sick and didn't turn up, so I took the rash decision to drive myself to my final home in Haría from the Foundation, where I'd been working to finalise the events for World Tourism Day on 25 September 1992. There was in fact by then a roundabout at the junction coming from the Foundation, but it was heavily overgrown by bushes, which made it difficult to see clearly, and a Toyota went into the side of my Jaguar when I was only moments into my journey. I got trapped inside with very serious injuries and a passing ambulance was diverted to rush me to Arrecife hospital, but nothing could be done and I was pronounced dead within an hour, at 3 p.m. in the afternoon.

So what were my feelings? Well, excruciating pain all over my body of course, but I just *knew* instantly that all that wasn't going to last impossibly long, that it *must* be my time, even though I hadn't been consciously prepared for it. Then, when I did just float gently away from Earth, it was nothing but total bliss. I was a bit bewildered at first, since the whole thing had been so sudden, but, as I mentioned earlier, Pepi was there to greet me and she explained precisely what had happened. Needless to say, my family and friends were all very upset and the press gave the accident immediate coverage as a 'terrible tragedy', but I myself didn't see it that way *at all*. For one thing, I'd completed my work — my legacy is so visible all over the island — and for another, I know for sure that I just couldn't have coped with old age and all the aches and pains, not to mention serious illness, which it seems inevitably to bring. I'd always been extremely fit and active, both physically and mentally, and the thought of having to endure losing any of that had filled me with horror. (Maybe I'll have to come back another time to go through a lot of it — or, hopefully, I've done it enough times in the past — but right now I'm really busy over here.)

Why am I so busy? Well, for one thing, the noble people who work so hard keeping the Foundation and all the other Manrique tourist attractions going need good support all round. For another, the Lanzarote Council members, when out of their bodies at night, still seek my advice on how best to preserve the island. And last but by no means least, you'll appreciate that the Canaries really depend upon tourism for the population's living, and Covid-19 naturally caused a good two-year disruption of that and consequent hardship. So may I urge you, if you haven't been there already, seriously to consider doing so? I promise that you won't be disappointed! In addition to the sights I've described (besides those I haven't, including my beloved Cactus Garden — such odd-looking plants, yet I always saw in their very oddness a strange kind of beauty!), you'll find all sorts of nice things to take home with you. Aloe Vera products of numerous varieties abound, and the lovely art and craft souvenirs made locally include coconut shell bowls. Well, the coconuts themselves are imported from nearby Africa, but Lanzarote artists decorate them absolutely beautifully in every possible design and colour imaginable. If, on the other hand, you *have* paid a visit there already and have good reasons for not repeating the experience, you might care to give friends or relatives a nudge in our direction.

Now I'll conclude with another couple of our scribe's favourite quotes of mine:

The difference between good and evil is really simple: doing one creates happiness while the other only pain.

Beauty raises us to higher states and draws our attention to such simple things as the fluttering of birds' wings or the concise structure of the veins in a dry leaf, thus enabling us to concentrate on the development of life energy.

# 22

# Someone Who Finally Worked
# Through Her Anger

*Anger, pride, and other passions reduce man to the level of a lunatic and sometimes degrade him to the level of an animal ... The cause for all the troubles, confusion and turmoil is the fact that we have lost mastery over our senses. By leaving the senses unfettered and unregulated, we will not be able to discriminate properly, or think coolly, calmly and rationally. Thus, many times we are misled into wrong actions. Anger is like an intoxicant. Internally, it induces us to do wrong things ... In our daily lives, we know that when we become angry, our nerves become weak and feeble and we lose grip over ourselves. Even a moment of anger takes away our strength that we gather by eating good food for three months. Anger not only debilitates us and takes away the merit of our good deeds, but also enfeebles our condition.*

Sathya Sai Baba

How do you do, everyone! I need to tell you about the last *two* of my lives because it's how I behaved in the first of these that forced me to come back into the following one. In the first one my name was Agatha and I was born in 1892 into a reasonably well-to-do middle-class family in Liverpool. My father had a senior management position on the Docks and my mother was a full-time housewife (as of course were most mothers in those days). I had a sister, Jacqueline, who was a couple of years older than me, and our brother Edward was three years younger. We had quite a big house in some pleasant outskirts of the city and a pretty normal sort of family life with a couple of servants, a cook and a series of nannies to help look after us three children, some of whom we liked more than others. While Edward was educated at the Blue Coat School in Waverley, which had a very good reputation, Jacqueline and I had governesses come to our home, which again was the norm for girls back then.

We were all three quite intelligent and Edward was expected to follow in our father's footsteps and go to Cambridge. Although younger than us, he sometimes lorded it over his sisters simply because of being a boy, which annoyed both of us, since we didn't believe that boys or men had any good reason for being regarded as superior. On the other hand, I was always a bit jealous of Jacqueline because our parents thought her prettier than me, and also the governesses generally considered her to be a better student. Well, she did learn to read more quickly than I did and was better at arithmetic, but that was partly because I was a bit of a dreamer and my mind would often wander off when I was supposed to be concentrating a hundred per cent on the lesson. I enjoyed writing stories — mostly love stories — but my spelling was bad and I couldn't understand why it mattered, just so long as people could read what I'd written.

Every Sunday the whole family went faithfully to the local Anglican church, which was an easy walk from our house, and we were taught to say our prayers each night, as well as to be obedient to our seniors so as not to run the risk of eternal damnation. It never occurred to me in those days not to believe in God. We both learnt to play the piano, which I actually enjoyed more than Jacqueline did, and the governess who taught us that often got us to sing little songs to her accompaniment. Since we didn't go to school as Edward did, it was less easy for us to make friends, but my mother sometimes organised tea parties to which she invited the daughters of her friends who were more or less in our age group. In the summer, too, we sometimes joined up with other families to go to the nearby park. Once we'd reached 18 (which Jacqueline obviously did before me), the governesses stopped coming to the house and we were encouraged to occupy ourselves with things such as embroidery, but I found that quite boring.

When my sister reached the age of 20, our parents decided that it was high time for her to be found a suitor. They discussed the matter with friends who had sons aged between, say, 22 and 25, and then some of them got introduced, but they didn't want to involve me in any of it because the older daughter should naturally be married first. Having spent some of my tender years writing love stories, I yearned for my 'Prince Charming' to appear on the scene and was extremely envious when Jacqueline's engagement to Nicholas was announced. The next step was a celebratory ball, fixed for a date about a year before the wedding, and lo and behold, my 'Prince Charming' *did* attend it! His name was Paul, I thought him much more handsome than my sister's betrothed, and in due course I found out that he was five years my senior. When he invited me to be his partner for the next waltz, I trembled with shyness and kept treading on his toes, but he just laughed and asked whether I liked the music. I replied in the affirmative and told him that I enjoyed playing the piano and singing, which seemed to impress him, but then for the next dance he commented that he'd better follow the etiquette and invite another young woman to join him. As we parted, however, he gave me the most beautiful smile imaginable and whispered in my ear: "I'll be back." I sat out for the next couple of dances, feeling sure that I must be very red in the face, but my eyes were constantly on Paul, noticing with trepidation exactly how he was reacting to his next two partners.

You can imagine my joy when the final dance was about to start and he came over and took my hand, raising me gently from my seat and putting his arm around my waist. We exchanged not a single word throughout, but he held me so tightly as we waltzed that I could feel his warm breath upon my neck. Once it was all over, he asked: "How can we meet again?", to which

I replied: "I suppose you'd better ask my parents", and he said "I will", squeezing my hand tightly. Both on that night and the next I hardly slept, but on the third day I was summoned to my father's study.

"Well, Agatha," he said sternly, "a certain Mr Paul Roberts has come to see me, saying that you'd danced together at Jacqueline's ball and that he'd like permission to meet you again. You will of course appreciate that we can't consider permitting you to have a suitor until after Jacqueline's wedding is over and done with and our finances have recovered. That will take a good two years and so I suggest that in the meantime you go down to London and attend a finishing school. Your Aunt Rosemary went to a very good one when she was your age and thoroughly enjoyed it, so I'd be happy to finance that and you could live with your cousins."

"But Father," I protested, "you can't regard Paul as a suitor when all we did was have a couple of dances with no opportunity to get to know one another. He would merely like us to meet again to see whether we'd like to be friends. I have very few friends."

"All the more reason for you to go to London, where your cousins could introduce you to many people of around your age. My mind is made up, so please go back to your needlework now and I'll look into making all the necessary arrangements."

Needless to say, I was absolutely devastated. I had no friends around to talk to and I couldn't confide in Jacqueline since she was so wrapped up in her own engagement and thinking ahead to her wedding. Later, however, Edward, with whom I was by now quite close and who was also fairly mature for his tender years, caught me sobbing my heart out and insisted that I confide in him. As soon as he heard the name, he exclaimed: "Oh, he's my good friend Martin's big brother! I still remember him from when he was a prefect at our school and I thought he was *really* nice. Tell you what, just write him a note and I'll give it to Martin and ask him to give it to Paul secretly."

So that's what I did and it worked a treat, as Paul immediately sent a reply via his younger brother. The two lads thought it great fun being part of a conspiracy and after a few letters had been exchanged in this way, we even managed to have a few secret meetings in the park. Then, once everything had been fixed for my going to London, Paul said that he'd be able to meet me there, as his firm had agreed to give him a transfer to the City. It seemed too good to be true, though there was still the hurdle of Aunt Rosemary, my father's sister, and her husband Michael to be got over, since I was going to be living in their house in Kensington. Yet there another 'miracle' occurred! Before Paul had even had a chance to make any attempt at working out how we could meet, my lovely aunt told me the story of how she and Michael had defied their parents and got together when she was considered 'too young'. That gave me the courage to tell her my secret, and she obligingly offered to invite him to tea so that she could decide whether or not he could earn her approval.

Gaining Aunt Rosemary's approval was a doddle, thanks both to Paul's standing with his City position and his natural charm. So she told me after the little party that she'd be perfectly happy to let him visit once or twice a week and take me for the occasional stroll in Kensington Park, just so long as I gave her my word that I would never do anything 'unseemly' for a virgin from a good family. I kept my word to my aunt. Paul's and my love grew steadily deeper and I always had his visits and our occasional walks to look forward to when I wasn't busy at the finishing school or with homework I'd been given. Sometimes we even managed a passionate embrace under a big tree in the park. My studies were pretty boring, but I made friends with a few of my fellow students, my cousins were quite good companions and once Jacqueline and Nicholas' wedding was over and they were happily settled in their own home, my kind aunt tackled my father very tactfully about my friendship with Paul. Following my return home to Liverpool and negotiations with the Roberts parents, our engagement was officially announced.

Paul's working in London wasn't too much of a problem, as he didn't mind travelling back to Liverpool at weekends, and you can imagine my joy when, on one of his visits, he took me to a jeweller's to choose a really beautiful diamond ring! He even started looking at houses in Kensington, but then, in 1914, just as our wedding date was being fixed, *World War I broke out*. When Nicholas was called up, I knew it couldn't be long until Paul's turn came. Edward's going up to Cambridge to read for a degree in natural sciences fortunately gave him a bit of leeway, but we knew that that could only last for three years, and nobody had the slightest idea of how long the wretched war would last.

Nicholas' first spell of leave did in fact coincide with the departure of my betrothed, and I was glad that he wasn't there to hear his future brother-in-law's horror stories. Once Nicholas had returned to the Western Front, I consoled myself with the thought of having Paul's first leave to look forward to, but did that occur? *No*, it didn't! I received a couple of loving letters from him, with promises of a never-ending stream of them, but then I waited in vain until suddenly one day the Roberts parents called round with the heartbreaking news of their beloved son's death in action. The official letter included high praise for his bravery as well as sympathy, but could that bring me any consolation? We all five wept together initially, but then Paul's parents went home and I was left fuming with rage. My rage was addressed not only at the Kaiser but also at God, and I just went up to my room screaming: "How can you expect me to carry on believing in you and your supposed Love if this is what you do to me?! What have I done to deserve it?"

My parents did their level best to comfort me and a few days later Aunt Rosemary even took the trouble to come up especially all the way from London, but I was absolutely inconsolable. Jacqueline did her best to be sympathetic, but she was of course preoccupied with fears for her husband. When Edward took his Cambridge MA he was persuaded to stay on to do a PhD, natural sciences being regarded as particularly important, and he thus escaped the war altogether.

So I really had no-one to turn to and I ignored all the suggestions put to me, such as: "Other 'war widows' are getting together to give help where it's needed." (In reply to that one I screamed: "I'm not even a widow! Paul and I never had so much as a single night together...")

Or: "Why don't you look for a job, or do some sewing? Many of the severely wounded are in need of new garments and you have quite a talent for that." One thing that the people around me *did* appreciate was that there was no point in saying "You'll find another man one day", since everyone knew that there would be a great shortage of single men once the war had ended. Then of course the war did finally end. Nicholas came home permanently to Jacqueline, and the two of them lost no time in making babies — five in all and each time that another one appeared on the scene, my jealousy and anger were given further fuel — and then Edward finished his PhD, was given a Lectureship and married the girl he'd been courting for a while. So he could no longer ever be really there for me either.

I won't bore you with the details of how I spent the rest of that life, trying the occasional job just for a bit of money but never finding anything to do that gave me either pleasure or a sense of fulfilment. I'll simply tell you that I died very suddenly at 50 from a heart attack, and what happened next was what I've now learnt may be typical for somebody who dies in anger. Rather than spending at least a little bit of time in the Bardo, my soul got drawn straight into the womb of a woman in Manchester who was equally angry.

***

My new mother's name was Margaret and she was angry with the lover who had dumped her the moment she told him that she was pregnant. She had trained as a nurse and since it was now 1942 and there was another war on, she met Geoffrey in the hospital to which he was taken after being wounded. She'd nursed him back to health, but the wound was too serious for him to be able to return to the Front, so he simply went back to his normal job in business. He had a wife and two small children, but since their home was on the outskirts of the City and she was pregnant with their third child, visiting him in the hospital was too difficult for her to manage. Geoffrey, however, didn't mention having a family until after he'd made a few dates with my mother *and* gone back to her hospital flat to make love to her. She was naturally terribly upset but was by that time so hooked into the relationship that all she could do was plead with him to leave his family for her. He agreed to think about it seriously, but the news of the pregnancy was the last straw and he fled without disclosing his address or telephone number.

Single mothers in those days weren't permitted to carry on with their work in the hospital and my grandparents, being 'good Christians' and very shocked by their only child's 'grave misdemeanour', refused to let her go home to them. Fortunately she had an aunt who was single, reasonably well off, and loved the thought of helping to look after a baby. So she moved into my Great-Aunt Mary's little cottage in the nearby countryside, where a midwife came in due course to deliver me. After a brief recovery period (my mother was young, so the birth was quite easy), she was allowed to return to her hospital post, since nurses were of course vital throughout the rest of World

War II as well as for quite a while afterwards. I was born on 15 September 1942 and therefore a Virgo, while my mother was an archetypal stubborn Aquarian.

She named me Amanda after her grandmother, without appreciating how appropriate it was since that name is all to do with Love — a thing that I did eventually discover later on in my life. Not having cause to mix with other families, it wasn't until I was five and started at the village school that I queried the fact that I had a mummy and an auntie but no daddy. At that point my mother told me bitterly that my daddy didn't want me, which of course made me wonder what was wrong with me. Since I was all she had apart from her job, my mother was very possessive of me, but she flatly refused to answer any more questions about my father, not even giving me his name. My great aunt was always good to me, which was something, but even she claimed to know nothing about him. From talk among my fellow primary school pupils, I gathered that babies came out of their mothers' tummies, but how they'd been put there in the first place remained a mystery.

At school, too, I felt horribly different; a couple of my classmates whose fathers had been killed in the war bragged about their bravery, but I of course had *nothing* to brag about, which increased my feelings of inferiority. When I went up into the secondary school, which involved going into Manchester on the school bus from our village, a kind teacher finally gave us the 'facts of life', explaining that the sexual act should only be performed between two people who were married and who loved each other very much. When I got home that afternoon and said: "Well, Mummy, you must have been married to my daddy and he must have really loved you...", she simply exploded with rage and sent me up to bed until the evening meal was ready.

I did make friends at school and also did quite well in most subjects, but only the exceptionally intelligent among us were expected to stay on after 16 and try for university. My mother was undoubtedly good at her nursing and so Great-Aunt Mary suggested that I might care to follow in her footsteps. This sat well with my natural Virgoan characteristics such as gentleness with those who were helpless, dedication and being well-organised, and my mother, knowing that she wouldn't be either able or willing to support me indefinitely, supported the idea. She insisted, however, that I train at the same hospital as she had, so that I could still live at home. I greatly resented her domination but didn't have the self-confidence to try to go elsewhere. Great-Aunt Mary, by the way, had at one point put in a good word for me to her sister, my maternal grandmother, who replied that she and my grandfather might be willing to meet me one day, once I'd 'proven myself' by obtaining a good qualification in something useful. (Having no grandparents in the background had been another thing that had singled me out as different.) So a course of nursing training at my mother's hospital was agreed upon and I was granted an interview, which was successful. My joy at the insistence upon my living in for the first couple of years was, however, not shared by my mother!

I got on well, nevertheless, and the friends that I made among my fellow students were empathetic about Mother's frequent bargings in to check on my practice. A few of them had dreams of falling in love reciprocally with one of the unmarried junior doctors, but I knew for sure that no such luck could possibly come to *me*! When one particular friend, Jenny, invited me to her home on one of our days off, my mother showed huge resentment, but Jenny encouraged me to talk more about my difficulties and we remained lifelong friends. I was even, much later, invited to be bridesmaid at her wedding to one of the attractive junior doctors!

Once we were fully qualified, Jenny and I were both offered posts in the same Manchester hospital. I was tempted to look further afield, but firstly I was afraid of my mother's wrath at the idea, as well as nervous anyway about leaving for somewhere new, and secondly Jenny had just started courting, so naturally didn't want to move, and I didn't want to leave her. What we did do was find a flat to share rather closer to the hospital, and my mother even complained about that. My great aunt was firmly on my side, however, and she also insisted that my grandparents agree to meet their 'bastard granddaughter'. I was always on my best behaviour when I went to their house (well, I'd never learnt to be anything else really!). I never found making conversation with my grandparents easy, but fortunately I was never expected to stay very long. My poor mother was still never invited, however, and when they eventually died she was bypassed in their will and so every penny went to me. Great-Aunt Mary insisted that I had no reason for guilt about it, saying that she would leave her house to my mother and that in the meantime her own earnings were sufficient for her needs anyway. She also urged me to put the money away carefully, since there was no knowing when it might come in handy.

This I did, without having the least idea of how handy it would be once my life had taken a totally new direction. I was never unhappy with the actual nursing work but was nevertheless quite prone to occasional bouts of depression, which intensified when Jenny married Malcolm and moved out of our flat to a new home with him. However, a mutual friend, Rose, whom we'd got to know on the wards, had already agreed to take her place, Jenny still kept very much in touch and the three of us often had little get-togethers when we had time off and Malcolm was working.

Then some major things happened. My great aunt died (leaving me some money, and her cottage to my mother) and after a very few more years and when Jenny had completed her family of three lovely children, my mother developed cancer of the liver. This was, as I was to learn later, no big surprise, since anger is stored in the liver. Initially I nursed her as best I could in my spare time, but always dreaded going to the cottage, as she never did anything but complain about the way I did everything and shout and scream both at me and at God, who had never done her any good in spite of her having always been a reasonably faithful churchgoer. (I, incidentally, had given up churchgoing in adulthood, since I never felt it did anything for me either.)

It was a huge relief when my mother was taken into a hospice for her final weeks. She still never did anything but complain at me, though I did feel quite a lot of sympathy, fully appreciating how intense her pain must be. I was at her side when she took her last breath and trying hard to send her love and compassion, though it wasn't at all easy. Nor could it be said that she died peacefully and easily: her face was contorted, not so much with physical pain because the morphine was easing that, but more with expressions of bitterness and anger. After the probate and so on had all gone through, I was torn between moving to the cottage that was now mine, selling it or letting it. I wasn't very keen either to commute into the city centre or to be further away from my friends, so I decided to let it out, at least for a while anyway.

Rose, at 35 like me, was also still single and our flat sharing worked well in every respect. My depression was still an issue (though I was determined not to get onto drugs for it), and in addition I started suffering from back pain caused by having sometimes to lift patients. Then an acupuncturist named Gordon started working in our hospital one day a week. Malcolm, no longer a junior doctor but training in surgery, was very open-minded and he suggested that I try having some acupuncture to help with my back pain. I liked Gordon a lot and his treatment did help, but he also recommended that I see an osteopath named Lyn. These two therapies in harmony worked wonders for me physically, but I soon found myself confiding in Lyn about my depression and about not feeling good enough for my father to have wanted to know me. She was immensely sympathetic, since her own background had been not dissimilar from mine, and she then in turn recommended Maisie, a psychotherapist who had helped her immensely. I clicked with Maisie as much as I had with Lyn and when I had my third session with her, she talked about the value of doing 'inner child' work and recommended John Bradshaw's classic book on the subject. She warned me at the same time that working through all his chapters would be painful, but stressed that if I had the determination to give it an hour each day, I'd never regret it.

And how right Maisie was! Shut up in my bedroom, with a supportive flatmate either out for the evening or keeping sympathetically quiet in her own room, I cried buckets (a thing I'd never previously been any good at) as I worked steadily backwards through each year of my life, writing down my feelings of anger with my mother and giving that unappreciated child the love that she had never been able to. The result was completely life transforming and although I realised that I still had anger against my unknown father to deal with, I began to think about sometime moving from nursing to psychotherapy as a career, especially since it wouldn't induce further back injuries!

When I talked with Maisie about my progress, she was not only delighted but also had another idea: Deep Memory Process (past-life regression) therapy. She herself had always been open to the notion of reincarnation — especially since she'd often felt moments of déjà vu — and had once been greatly helped by some sessions with a Woolger graduate named Isobel, who worked in a clinic not too far away from Manchester. Maisie also stressed that it wasn't necessary to believe in previous lives for the therapy to be useful and I, who had, as I mentioned earlier, long since given up churchgoing and was by now quite open to

Buddhism and Hinduism, was fully prepared to try anything that was recommended by someone I trusted.

Isobel instantly put me at ease when I took a day off to go for my first session. I talked to her at some length about my life history, my feelings of unworthiness (now greatly alleviated thanks to the 'inner child' work I'd recently done), my periods of depression and my new ambition to train in psychotherapy. She took notes as I was talking and then asked what I felt to be my biggest issue at that very moment. I thought hard and deeply before replying that it was anger with my father, whose name and whereabouts I didn't even know. She then got me to lie down on a mattress on the floor, with her sitting on a cushion beside me, and asked me to scan my body and tell her of any aches, pains, or anything else that I was experiencing. Almost immediately I felt an ache in my heart. She then put her hand on my heart and asked me to describe the nature of the pain as precisely as I could and then exaggerate it.

Once I'd done that, Isobel told me that on a count of three she would clap her hands and I would then plunge straight into the lifetime that was most relevant to my problem. Instantly I found myself as the dying Agatha whose tale I recounted above. I was fully conscious and found myself amazed at the clarity with which I saw first the death scene and then the rest of the wasted life, as Isobel took me back to its beginning and then steadily through it until I once more reached the painful but speedy death from a heart attack, followed by the instantaneous trajectory into Margaret's womb.

Isobel then explained that the normal procedure in Deep Memory Process was for the soul to meet his or her guides in the Bardo, go through a life review with them, decide what the learning had been, and then detach from it, appreciating that what had happened was in the previous life, not the present one. Since, however, Agatha had not spent any time in the Bardo, it was now up to me, as Amanda, to work out what the lessons had been. I had no difficulty in finding the answer: Agatha had refused to let go of her anger and do something worthwhile with the rest of her life, but I now had plenty of opportunity to reverse the previous actions.

I went home feeling tired but so, so much lighter! After that I booked just a few more sessions with Isobel, thanks to which I discovered that I'd become trapped in a repeated pattern of anger and now finally had the chance to break it permanently. This wonderful realisation not only increased my desire to become a therapist myself but also cured my depression *completely* — magic! In one of the subsequent sessions, Isobel guided me into a lifetime in which I'd worked as a healer (without having been burnt at the stake, which she said was unusual!), and this proved to be a trigger for my embarking upon a path that was truly spiritual rather than religious. Talking enthusiastically to Rose and Jenny about it all, together with their observing the radical change in me, caused the three of us to agree to form a group for people who fancied reading spiritual books and sharing ideas and information. So we put out a few advertisements locally and were delighted at the response we received. Jenny and Malcolm's house being inhabited also by three young children, we decided to hold our first meeting in Rose's and my flat, but we quickly realised that it wasn't going to be big enough.

Fortunately my cottage had just been vacated and I hadn't yet found another tenant, so, money not being an issue for me, I decided to hold our group meetings there, intending ultimately to move back into it and then work there once I'd become a full-time psychotherapist. That would also give Rose, who was still happily single and content in her nursing profession, plenty of time to find another flatmate if she wanted to. I then got the hospital to agree to permit me to work part-time and used my free periods for psychotherapy training and further reading. In this our newly formed group (which we named 'The Seekers') was very supportive, and I also made more very good friends among them.

My new training went well, and before too long I'd gained enough clients to be able to work full-time in that field. One of our new friends from the Seekers group was more than happy to take over my place in the Manchester flat and, since I found the psychotherapy work both interesting and rewarding, living on my own proved to be no problem for me. I had no plans for retirement, but then, as you'll all no doubt remember only too well, the Covid pandemic struck. I kept on seeing people for as long as I could, but eventually, what with the lockdowns and so on in 2020, I had to resign myself to remaining at home and taking solitary walks in the nearby countryside. I was never lonely, however, as my friends and I made frequent telephone calls to one another, formed a WhatsApp Seekers group and shopped for each other whenever necessary. I also did phone consultations with several of my clients.

Then, shortly before my seventy-ninth birthday, I myself caught a very bad dose of Covid. I got rushed to the hospital, still so very familiar to me, and there friends kindly braved all the rules and regulations to come and visit, but I only survived for a very few days. I'm sure I don't need to tell you how unpleasant the disease was, but the care was fantastic despite all the horrendous pressures on the NHS and when the end came, I floated gently out of my body feeling nothing but relief and gratitude. I had long since appointed executors from among my closest friends, made a will distributing everything I'd left among my favourite charities, and given instructions for my ashes to be scattered in my favourite bit of woodland.

Once I'd crossed over, who should be there to meet me but Paul Roberts, Agatha's one-time betrothed! My joy was unbounded and once we'd embraced he explained to me that we were twin souls, hence the very short time we'd needed to fall in love for the umpteenth time and feel that we knew one another inside out. He further said that, unlike me, he hadn't yet reincarnated but had been serving as one of my spirit guides, something that twin souls tended to do for one another from time to time. Having watched over me right from conception, he'd rejoiced at seeing the progress I'd made and assured me that I'd only need a short time in a 'heavenly hospital' before recovering sufficiently to return to work.

Paul proved to be perfectly right and after the 'heavenly' nurses had done their work on my somewhat battered etheric body and I'd been able to shed it, I was summoned to a meeting with my other guides in the most beautiful place imaginable. They told me that I'd been called Home in order to work with people who'd needed just the same sort of help as I had myself but who hadn't had the chance to complete it all before crossing over. They said that it wouldn't be a problem for me, since I'd already worked out a good healing system for those needing to do 'inner child' work and learn how to forgive their parents, or anyone else who'd harmed their development, adding that my system could even be conveyed to people on Earth who also needed it, through a book that was at present being written.

I replied that what they were telling me all sounded great but that I first had just one request: to find out who my father had been and meet both him and my mother Margaret. Then the two of them appeared instantly, smiling and holding hands! Geoffrey explained that he knew he'd been cowardly in not owning up to his adultery and in fleeing from Margaret, whom he had genuinely loved, but that the forgiveness work that I'd done on Earth had helped them both, as well as giving him the courage to apologise to his wife. The three of us then talked a bit more and I was interested to learn something about my father's characteristics and tastes, some of which undoubtedly coincided with my own!

So now I think all that remains to be done for the time being is to list for the benefit of any interested readers the bare bones of my therapeutic system, for which, I hasten to add, I claim no originality.

- Step One: Articulate *all* the deep-seated anger justifiably felt against the person or persons concerned. (When it's two parents, it's best to deal with one at a time.) A good ploy at this juncture can be to put all your feelings into a letter and then burn it.
- Step Two: Invite him or her to give their side of the story and listen carefully to what they have to say. If you're working with a therapist rather than on your own, the 'Gestalt method', which involves asking the person concerned to speak through the client, can be very useful.
- Step Three: Once you've acquired a full understanding of the other person's perspective, *total forgiveness* becomes possible.
- Step Four: This then leads to *gratitude* for all the pain suffered on account of the *learning* that it's brought you.
- Step Five: Realisation then comes that we often get trapped in repeated patterns and that, once recognised, the cycle can be broken forever. Hurray!

# 23

# A Child

*A child is so much nearer to the soul-life. Even this child's few short years on earth … had scarcely separated him from his before-birth contact with Divine Love … For me it has been a precious and wonderful experience to have witnessed the re-birth here of such innocence; the soul of this child, unpolluted, untainted by the materialism and separation of earth beliefs, was so ready for the heaven world.*

Frances Banks, speaking from the other side to
Helen Greaves in *Testimony of Light*

*Every adult carries some sense of the 'inner child' as a means of expressing the emotional and imaginative part of the psyche. At a deep, psychological level, then, the death of any child violates that precious and vulnerable part of us.*

Celia Hindmarch, *On the Death of a Child*

In 2021, our scribe, who had already completed a plan for this book, knew that, since her aim was to cover in it a wide variety of death and afterlife scenarios, a childhood one was a vital ingredient, but she didn't yet have a particular character for the chapter concerned. So, on one lovely day when she and her husband were having their customary walk, they chose to return home via the cemetery of Malvern Priory. At one point they sat down briefly on a bench at the edge of the cemetery and I then saw my chance of diverting them from their habitual route. This caused them to notice for the first time a small gravestone upon which was inscribed the following in clear black letters:

# IHS

## ANNE ELIZABETH DARWIN

BORN MARCH 2.1841
DIED APRIL 23.1851

A DEAR AND GOOD CHILD

And just a few yards below it, at the edge of the path, is a slab explaining how I'd died in Malvern and with a photograph of me on it. This, needless to say, caused Ann to exclaim: "Ah, here's who I'm supposed to have for my 'child' chapter!" and then to rush home to her computer for the story. So here it is.

You will all of course have heard of my dear papa, whose first name was Charles, but I'll nevertheless start with a few facts about his life. He was born in a huge house, named The Mount, in Shrewsbury, Shropshire, on 12 February 1809. The house is still standing and in 1897 a big statue of him, seated in an armchair, was erected outside that charming town's public library. (What a proud moment that was for *me* and if you're already wondering how I could have known about it, I'll explain all that later.) My grandpapa, Robert Darwin, who died when I was only seven, had his own medical practice in Shrewsbury and my grandmama's name before she married had been Susannah (though she was affectionately known as 'Sukey') Wedgwood. *Her* father, Josiah Wedgwood, had founded the famous Wedgwood pottery firm in Stoke-on-Trent, so you can well imagine that there was no shortage of money in the family. He was also an active Unitarian, his mother Mary having been the daughter of a Unitarian minister, and was interested in science and political and social reform. He was close friends with the scientist and Unitarian

316

minister Joseph Priestley, the social reformer Thomas Day, the inventor Erasmus Darwin (my papa's grandfather), and the prominent abolitionist Thomas Clarkson. In fact he made a major contribution to the anti-slavery movement by designing, producing and distributing at his own expense a cameo based on the seal of the Society for the Abolition of the Slave Trade. It featured a kneeling black man in chains, bore the motto "Am I not a man and a brother?", and was a precursor to the modern campaign button, being among the first fashion accessories to show the wearer's support for a political cause. These cameos were worn as jewellery, cufflinks, and hatpins and the design was also printed on dishes and tea caddies. Josiah's factory was progressive for its time, offering decent working conditions and an early form of sick-benefit plan.

Papa was the fifth of his parents' six children, but Grandmama Darwin sadly died when he was only eight, from some sort of stomach problem, and he was then cared for by three older sisters. He was educated initially at the traditional Anglican School in Shrewsbury, where he hated the forced learning of Classical Greek and Roman literature by rote and where (as in other English public schools at the time) science was considered to be 'dehumanising'. He consequently got condemned by his headmaster for dabbling in chemistry and his classmates nicknamed him 'Gas'! He did, however, stand in awe of his overbearing father, whose astute medical observations taught him a good deal about human psychology, and that proved to be very useful to him later on.

Papa's greatest interests had from a very early age been such things as natural history and geology, yet my Grandpapa was determined that he should follow in his footsteps and become a medical doctor. So he was initially sent up to the University of Edinburgh to study medicine, but at the end of his first two years there he succeeded in persuading his father to allow him to transfer to Christ's College, Cambridge, with a view to going into Holy Orders. Hence the lovely statue in the grounds of that College of him, as a young student, sitting on the arm of a bench. Yet his two years at Edinburgh had in fact been a formative experience, since there was at the time no better science education in any other British university, and there he was taught to understand the chemistry of cooling rocks on the primitive Earth and how to classify plants by the modern natural system. Also, in the Edinburgh Museum, he was taught to stuff birds by John Edmonstone, a freed South American slave, and to identify rock strata and colonial flora and fauna.

The Holy Orders, however, quickly got forgotten once the things really closest to his heart had taken over! Instead, thanks to his professor and mentor H. S. Henslow, he was invited to go straight from Cambridge to work as a naturalist aboard the HMS *Beagle* on its second (and even more groundbreaking) voyage of discovery. The ship's captain, Robert Fitzroy, had had to convince my grandfather that his son's services were really needed for the expedition, but eventually he'd agreed to fund Papa's part in it. His adventures on that journey were both innumerable and astonishing — how I loved it when I was very young indeed, sitting on his knee while he recounted tales about it all to me! — and his copious notes, along with lots and lots of fascinating specimens, were all sent back to Cambridge.

Since poor Papa suffered greatly from seasickness, he was always much happier during the periods he spent on land, which were fortunately rather longer than the times at sea, yet he nevertheless managed to write many of his notes while on board. It was thanks to these that, at the end of what ultimately turned out to be a journey of almost five years, he was able to expound his, initially very controversial, Theory of Evolution. He had formulated this bold theory in private during 1837–9 and finally gave it full public expression a couple of decades later when he published *On the Origin of Species*, the book that has influenced modern Western society and thought so very deeply.

Here I feel it is worthwhile noting that, when Papa wrote about 'the survival of the fittest', he meant by that not the strongest or the cleverest but rather those that were the best equipped to adapt to changing circumstances. 'Darwin's finches' in the Galápagos Islands are of course renowned, but another excellent example of adaptation can be witnessed among the celebrated giant tortoises of those same 'Enchanted Islands'. Those tortoises born on the drier and more arid islands have what's known as a 'saddleback' shell, which means that they have a raised rim right above the head, thus allowing the creature to extend its neck much further in order to eat from bushes and low-hanging branches. Some of you may well have heard of Lonesome George, a saddleback born on Pinta Island in 1910 who had become the very last member of his sub-species. The locals did their level best to find him a mate, but all efforts to produce offspring failed and he sadly died in 2012 (just a year before our scribe and her husband visited Ecuador and the Galápagos).

Papa and I watched over all the above proceedings with interest from this side, and he was undoubtedly influential when, after the tortoise's body had been frozen and shipped to the Museum of Natural History in New York, their taxidermist carried out the necessary preservation work, with a certain amount of input from some scientists. Then, however, a dispute arose about dear George's final 'resting place'. He was eventually returned to the Galápagos and is now on display in a building especially dedicated to him at the Galápagos National Park headquarters on the island of Santa Cruz.

While we're talking about the fascinating Galápagos, I find it truly delightful to know how those 'Islas Encantadas' acquired that nickname. You see, it's because they tend at times to become so shrouded in mist that they disappear from sight and so the very early explorers, who were more mystical than the nineteenth-century ones, believed that, at those times, they had *really* disappeared and were thus clearly 'enchanted'!

And now for another interesting aside: did you know that Robert Fitzroy, the captain of HMS *Beagle*, had founded, in 1854, what later became known in the UK as the Met Office? He was an able surveyor and hydrographer and a pioneering meteorologist who made accurate daily weather predictions, and it was he who coined the word 'forecast'. Born in 1805, he'd entered the Royal Navy in 1819 and received command of the 240-ton brig *Beagle* in 1828. During that first voyage he surveyed the South American coast around Patagonia and Tierra del Fuego, returning to England a couple of years later. He was, however, a somewhat paradoxical figure and came to a sad end when he committed suicide on 30 April 1865. The paradox is that whereas, during a stopover in Brazil early on in the voyage, he had famously argued with Papa (with his Unitarian, abolitionist background) about the question of slavery, he later, as Governor of New Zealand, made himself wildly unpopular with the British settlers because of his enlightened insistence that the native Maori should be treated fairly.

Fitzroy was also a strongly religious man and during their 1831–6 voyage he continually resisted Papa's growing doubts about special creation and the fixity of species. Interactions with him, however, helped my father to clarify his views about evolution and anticipate many objections to his theory prior to its publication. Fitzroy was actually present at the famous meeting of the British Association for the Advancement of Science in 1860, at which T. H. Huxley successfully defended Darwin's *Origin of Species* from attack by Samuel Wilberforce, the Bishop of Oxford, and his attempt at that meeting to support Wilberforce against Huxley led to ridicule. His death, as I said, was by suicide, during a period of mental turmoil, probably induced at least partly by the growing success of the idea of evolution.

Isn't it curious that Jesus (who *didn't* found the Christian Churches!) was a left-wing revolutionary, who had a mission of spreading such things as Peace, Justice, Truth, and Love, as well as encouraging people to heal others and to remember their *own* innate divinity, yet those who now claim to be His followers so often ignore His actual teachings? It took 300 years for the Roman Church finally to pardon poor Galileo, and they still haven't done any more than *talk about* erecting a statue of him in the grounds of the Vatican! At least Papa was never put under house arrest, but, in view of the way in which the Churches condemned his revolutionary work, can one blame him for being something of an agnostic?

The simple truth is that my father, like Galileo, was a genius of the highest order. Definitions of that word may well abound, but one that I understand has already been propounded in this highly original book is that it's the result of nothing other than the person concerned making use of a talent that he or she has already honed during numerous previous lifetimes. Certainly that's what Papa and I discovered together when he joined me on this side on 19 April 1882 and no doubt Galileo, too, has spent many lives performing work of a scientific nature.

But now to return to Papa's lifetime as Charles Darwin. After disembarking from the *Beagle*, with a £400 annual allowance from his father, he settled down among the urban gentry as a geologist, joining the Geological Society in January 1837 and becoming its secretary by 1838. It wasn't until a little over two years following his return that, though he'd known her virtually all his life, he fell deeply in love with and then proposed matrimony to my darling mother Emma, his first cousin. An intelligent, level-headed young woman, she was also, among many other things, an accomplished pianist. How I always loved hearing her play that wonderful instrument! They were married in 1839, the year of the publication of Papa's diary under the title of *Journal of Researches into the Geology and Natural History of the Various Countries by H.M.S. Beagle* — and this both made his name and secured him a £1000 Treasury grant, obtained through the Cambridge network. This enabled him to employ the best experts and publish their descriptions of his specimens in another book, *Zoology of the Voyage of H.M.S. Beagle*.

My parents' first home was a rented house in Gower Street, London, but, the year after I was born they moved to Down House, a Georgian manor in the Kent countryside, 15 miles south of London. After Mama's death, which was 14 years after Papa's, the house was rented out initially, but fortunately, in 1996, English Heritage managed to acquire and restore it, and it's now open to visitors all year round. If you're able to visit, I'm sure it will give you a good idea of what a lovely, happy family we were.

I was the second of us ten children, the first one having been William Erasmus, who was educated first at Rugby, then at Christ's College, Cambridge, and who later became a banker (as well as a keen amateur photographer). His main claim to fame, however, is that he was the chief subject of Papa's study of infant psychology. Papa was very different from most nineteenth-century fathers — and indeed many twentieth-century ones — whose motto tended to be that "children should be seen but not heard", in that he doted on all his children. In the case of William in particular, whom he described at birth as "a prodigy of beauty and intellect", he kept during the infant's first three years a detailed diary of his gestures and facial expressions. He made many notes besides about all of us, as did Mama (though hers were mainly written later on). Here's just one example: "Annie [that's what they always called me] at two months & four days had a very broad sweet smile and a little noise of pleasure very like a laugh."

All these studies formed part of Papa's comparison between animal and human development, and he also noticed the development of more profound personality traits, such as reason and, at the age of two and a half, conscience. In due course he published his findings in the journal *Mind* in 1877 and his work also inspired other psychologists, such as the German William Preyer and the American James Mark Baldwin.

I was alas not the only one of the ten to die young. Mary Eleanor, born the year after me, lived for less than a month, and the youngest one, Charles Waring, died of scarlet fever before reaching the age of two. So I of course only saw him from the other side while he was on Earth, but I knew already that he was a very special soul. This was because, although the condition hadn't been officially recognised or given a name at that time, it's pretty clear from the photograph which my brother William took of him that he had Down's syndrome (also known as Trisomy 21), which is caused by the person concerned having 47 chromosomes instead of the more usual 46. It occurs more commonly in the babies of older women, and our dear mother was in fact 48 when little Charles was born. The symptoms vary greatly in degree and people who have it tend on the whole not to live very long, but a thing they all seem to have in common is that they both emanate and induce love to and from those around them. This indicates that their 'soul purpose' in entering a particular family is a teaching one and, consequently, when this darling youngest brother and I met again over here, we both appreciated that each of us had completed a particular mission.

Ah, so I think that this is now the point at which I need to explain, as I promised above, how it is that I know things normally beyond the capacities of the 10-year-old that I was when I departed our beloved Earth. Well, you see, there are plenty of mothers or would-be mothers over here only too keen to care for those who die young and in my case it was my paternal grandmother, Susannah ('Sukey'), who very happily took on the task. As you will appreciate from what's gone before, she'd died before I was born and she explained upon my arrival over here that she'd been one of my guides ever since my birth, that my early death had been agreed upon beforehand, and that her task now would be helping me to go on growing up nicely towards adulthood. So you see, when Papa himself crossed over 31 years later almost to the day, he was mildly surprised to encounter not the beloved 10-year-old Annie whom he'd missed so dearly, but a fairly sophisticated 41-year-old woman. It made no difference to him, however, since we were old friends anyway and besides, you can be sure that I'd been keeping a close eye on my family ever since I'd left them physically!

Having observed problems in animals who were closely related, Papa had worried a bit that marrying his first cousin might have been partly responsible for the three of us dying young. Yet, in those days, rearing seven out of ten children to adulthood was a pretty good record and, of those seven, three became Fellows of the Royal Academy *and* gained knighthoods! George (nearly four years my junior) became an astronomer, Francis (seven years my junior) was a botanist and Horace (born barely three weeks after my death) was a civil engineer. Then, as though that wasn't already enough distinction in a single family, Leonard (who was about 16 months older than Horace and the last of my siblings to die) initially joined the Royal Engineers in 1871. Between 1877 and 1882 he worked for the Intelligence Division of the Ministry of War, going on several scientific expeditions, including those to observe the Transit of Venus in both 1874 and 1882, and after being promoted to the rank of major he left the army and became a Liberal Unionist Member of Parliament for Lichfield constituency in Staffordshire.

Leonard wrote vigorously on economic issues of the day, such as bimetallism, Indian currency reform and municipal trade, and was President of the Royal Geographical Society from 1908 to 1911 and Chairman of the British Eugenics Society from 1911 to 1928, becoming that society's Honorary President in 1928. In 1912 the University of Cambridge conferred on him an Honorary Doctorate of Science, and he also played an important part in the life of Ronald Fisher, the distinguished geneticist and statistician, supporting him intellectually, morally, and sometimes even financially.

So you can well imagine how interesting and rewarding it's been for both me and Papa (Mama, too, of course, after she'd crossed over in October 1896) to watch our family's development. But now it's more than time to tell you about my own passing. I was, as you will have noticed, 10 years old at the time and when I fell seriously ill with what was then called 'consumption' (tuberculosis or TB) my parents were naturally truly distraught, especially since I'd always been "the apple of my proud father's eye" and (as Papa later confessed to his friend and cousin William Darwin Fox) his "favourite child". He wrote *so* many lovely things about me, of which I'll quote just a very few:

> Her figure & appearance were clearly influenced by her character: her eyes sparkled brightly; she often smiled; her step was elastic & firm; she held herself upright, & often threw her head a little backwards, as if she defied the world in her joyousness.

> She was very handy, doing everything neatly with her hands: she learnt music readily, & I am sure from watching her countenance, when listening to others playing, that she had a strong taste for it. She had some turn for drawing, & could copy faces very nicely. She danced well, & was extremely fond of it. She liked reading...

Her health failed in a slight degree for about nine months before her last illness; but it only occasionally gave her a day of discomfort: at such times, she was never in the least degree cross, peevish or impatient; & it was wonderful to see, as the discomfort passed, how quickly her elastic spirits brought back her joyousness & happiness.

It is indeed true that I never wanted to upset any of those around me — especially as I knew full well at a certain level that I didn't have much time left in the world — and so I was keen for them to have only happy memories of me. My dear younger sister, Henrietta, by the way, also recorded her own reactions in a poignant set of notes, which Mama kept, along with a box of my treasures that she'd collected.

Once the doctors in Kent had found that they could do no more for my health, my parents decided as a last resort to risk taking me on the long journey to the spa town of Malvern, renowned for the success of its water treatments. Mama would have loved to accompany us there, leaving the other children with the servants, but she obviously couldn't do that, being so heavily pregnant with Horace at the time. Papa and I therefore set off with only one of our servants in addition to the horse and carriage driver. While I slept fitfully, well bundled up in blankets, poor Papa couldn't sleep at all, but the warm welcome we received soon after our arrival from Dr Gully, who was well known for his hydrotherapy treatment, did much to comfort him. We both saw just enough of both the town itself, and the hills under which it nestles so neatly, to appreciate its attractiveness. (No wonder that our scribe and her husband jumped at the chance of moving to a retirement village there!)

I can't in all honesty say that I didn't suffer from the illness — sometimes the coughing and so on were *really* painful — but all the people caring for us (and Papa would be the first to admit that he needed at least as much care as I did!) couldn't have been more pleasant. Dr Gully himself was so very sad when he realised that I wasn't destined to be one of his successes and did his utmost to comfort Papa while he was still at my bedside. As for me, however, when the end came, I just floated so gently and easily out of my body that it's difficult not to call it 'blissful'. Now I'll quote Papa again:

> In the last short illness, her conduct in simple truth was angelic; she never once complained; never became fretful; was ever considerate of others; & was thankful in the most gentle, pathetic manner for everything done for her. When so exhausted that she could hardly speak, she praised everything that was given her, & said some tea "was beautifully good." When I gave her some water, she said "I quite thank you"; & these, I believe were the last precious words ever addressed by her dear lips to me.

It was wonderful, too, as I mentioned before, to find Grandmama Sukey waiting for me. Between us we did our very best to console Papa — not to mention Mama as well, once the sad news had reached her — and that was of course easier at night when they were out of their bodies. How I wished at times that they'd be able to remember our nightly meetings during the day, but on the other hand I knew full well both that everyone, through their countless incarnations, has to have lifetimes of varying length and that loss is also one of the important lessons that we all need to learn.

Papa, on account of his agnosticism, wasn't by any means totally sure about the existence of the afterlife, yet he was sufficiently openminded not to get stuck in the Bardo for a while after he'd died, as complete atheists tend to do. Also, strong character as he'd needed to be for the lifetime of Charles Darwin, it was marvellous how he was able to dwell on the good aspects of having had me as his oldest daughter rather than constantly bemoaning the loss. Now I'll just give you a couple more final quotes from his writing about me:

> ... looking back, always the spirit of joyousness rises before me as her emblem and characteristic: she seemed formed to live a life of happiness: her spirits were always held in check by her sensitiveness lest she should displease those she loved, & her tender love was never weary of displaying itself by fondling & all the other little acts of affection.

> We have lost the joy of the Household, and the solace of our old age: she must have known how we loved her; oh that she could now know how deeply, how tenderly we do still & shall ever love her dear joyous face. Blessings on her.

All this was dated 30 April 1851 — merely one week after my departure — and, needless to say, I *did* know and he knows too, now that he's joined me over here, that the love between us can *never* die! Many parental relationships fail to survive the death of a child, each one of them finding that dealing with their own grief drains their capacity to support their spouse, but my parents' love for one another was even stronger than their grief and also, baby Horace's arrival so soon after my death brought them both some consolation.

Papa's final years were hard both for him and for my mother. He'd suffered from various complaints from an early age — scarlet fever at the age of nine, excessive fatigue at only 20, stomach pains, mouth ulcers, skin problems and heart palpitations — yet, as he grew older and his physical problems inevitably increased, he never let anything get in the way of his writing. Mama did a noble job of looking after him (trying, though unsuccessfully, not to let him overwork!) and she was of course heartbroken when he departed at the age of 73. At least she had my siblings, and grandchildren besides, to support her in her own final years, and now there's a big group of us Darwins over here, enjoying one another's company and watching proudly as Papa's legacy develops and spreads. You can well imagine our delight at seeing his body being interred in Westminster Abbey and, since his death, both a city in Australia's Northern Territory and the Charles Darwin Scientific Research Buildings in the Galápagos Islands, Ecuador, have been named after him. How many people could achieve all that without becoming obnoxiously big-headed? Yet my papa, a highly evolved soul, remains the beloved, thoughtful and loving being that he always was. What a great privilege it was for me to have been one of his daughters!

**24**

# A Renowned Poet

*Oh as I was young and easy in the mercy of his means*
*Time held me green and dying,*
*Though I swam in my chains like the sea...*

*Do not go gentle into that good night,*
*Old age should burn and rave at close of day;*
*Rage, rage against the dying of the light.*

Dylan Thomas

Gentle, indeed, did I *not* go! Especially since I was still far, far away from old age with its burning and raving. In fact, at 39, I was just entering what most people regard as the 'prime of life'. But of course I hadn't *ever* been even remotely like 'most people'. How could a great poet be like *anyone* but *himself*? That is, if he were able to both know and *understand* himself. I certainly couldn't — at least not then! Now, a good 20 years on (nearing the close of 1973, or so my 'rescuers' have told me; time never has any real meaning), I'm beginning to work on understanding at least a little bit about myself: why and for what I chose that short, not particularly attractive body, with its brilliant, avaricious brain, ever needing to shine, ever desirous of beaming forth entertainment? To what extent had I realised Dylan Marlais Thomas' purpose? In how many things had I failed? And so on and so on!

But I fear I'm jumping the gun. First I'd better tell you what actually happened in late October and early November 1953. You will just have to wait patiently for a few relevant details about the years before that. So, I was on my fourth visit to America. Why? Why on earth should a Welsh poet, who spoke only English *well*, who not only wrote both prose and poetry in English but also *sounded* more English than any Englishman, yet lived by choice in a fairly remote part of Wales, nurtured by its so-often-wet beauty and nourished by its irresistible beer, want to accept invitations to give readings of his poetry to appreciative Americans in the land of their not-so-ancient nation? The answer is pure and simple: *money*! (Well, money *and* sex. That maybe goes without saying.)

For yes (just as our scribe's younger son discovered when he'd won a basketball scholarship to do a whole four-year degree course in that goddamn country), the Americans just *loved* my English accent and could never get enough of my powerful voice booming out that endless stream of extraordinary, often incongruous and invariably unexpected *words*. And, for this, they were prepared to pay good money — a thing of which the traditionally impoverished poet is forever in need — as well as (in the case of certain of the women) loan their bodies for the occasional night. For fame is, for such women, as you may well be aware, every bit as attractive as physical perfection.

So there I was in New York, where they'd thrown a party for my thirty-ninth birthday, sick as usual — I'd struggled with both bronchitis and asthma since childhood — and, on top of that, the air pollution in that city, which always exacerbated conditions such as mine, had risen dramatically, yet nevertheless determined not to let down John Brinnin, my American agent, over my readings of *Under Milk Wood*. I'd got through the first rehearsal, then gone with Liz Reitell (Brinnin's assistant) for a good booze-up at the delightful White Horse Tavern in Greenwich Village, before returning to the Chelsea Hotel. The next day I'd refused Liz's kind invitation to her apartment and we'd been sightseeing instead, but, still feeling very unwell, I'd rested during the remainder of the afternoon. Liz had given me some drug or other to help me sleep and then spent the night with me at the hotel. However, when it was time for the third rehearsal, on 23 October (four days before my birthday), I told them I wasn't fit for it. But, *still* not wanting to admit defeat, I struggled through it nevertheless, shivering and burning with fever before collapsing on the stage. So the next day Liz took me to see her own doctor, who gave me some cortisone injections, and these enabled me to give the first actual performance, but I again collapsed immediately it was over and have a memory of saying to a friend who'd come backstage: "That circus out there has taken the life out of me for now." I'm stressing the 'for *now*' because at that point it hadn't entered my head that I wasn't 'immortal'.

So you see, I did remember pretty much everything right up till then, but not afterwards, though I do know that the very day after my birthday party I attended a recorded symposium on 'Poetry and Film' and that over the next few days I received friends into my hotel room for drinks and even went out one evening to keep a couple of other drink appointments. The rest is a blur, but at one point I overheard it being said that I'd wildly exaggerated the number of whiskies that I'd downed. Then I realised that I'd been put into an ambulance, so presumed that I'd ended up in hospital. Suddenly my wife Caitlin appeared at my bedside, which seemed strange as I was so sure that I'd left her at home in the Boathouse in Laugharne, and — typically of her! — she was ranting and raving and threatening to kill John Brinnin. I think they took her away and I was then left musing about our darling 'baby', Colm, who was only four, and yearning to see him. After that I seemed to be near the ceiling, looking down at a body lying apparently lifelessly on a bed, but that didn't really surprise me, since I knew full well that many people died in hospitals.

After that the amazing thing was that, still yearning to embrace our youngest child, I suddenly found myself in the Boathouse, although I had no recollection of having got on an aeroplane or anything! (Why on earth do those semi-literate

Americans call them 'airplanes'?) But the really dreadful thing was that our home was completely *empty*! How could that be, since it seemed to be evening, when Caitlin should have been preparing a meal for us all? Then it occurred to me that I'd seen her in New York, so assumed that they'd called for her because I was ill. Well, I was often ill; this last sickness had only been a bit worse than usual on account of that dreadful fog, but now I was feeling a lot better anyway. Why the heck hadn't she come back here with me once I'd recovered? I suppose the traitress must have seduced some handsome guy over there. (Yet another awful American word! Though, come to think of it, the word 'bloke' isn't really any less ugly.) Of course she, too, always complained wildly about *my* little infidelities, but weren't women *supposed* always to be faithful to their husbands?! And what the heck had she done with the children before going off carousing in New York? Dumped them on some aunt or other no doubt, as usual. So I headed straight for the most likely nearby home and, sure enough, Colm was there, playing happily while being dotingly encouraged to come and eat. Yet, to my horror, rather than running up joyfully, shouting "Hurray, you're back!", he completely ignored me. I couldn't believe it, but decided reluctantly to go home to bed and then phone New York the next day to find out what had happened to that dratted wife of mine.

The next morning, however, for some strange reason, I couldn't get the phone to work. I resolved to get it fixed later, but in the meantime, finding no food in the house and not feeling hungry anyway, I went straight up the hill to my safe little writing shed and endeavoured, as usual, to write down a list of possible rhyming words with the aim of converting them into what I believed might well be my best piece of poetry ever. Yet, after what felt like a good couple of hours, I seemed to be getting nowhere with it. This was frustrating, to put it mildly, but then it dawned on me that it must be well time for a beer or three anyway, so I headed straight for Brown's in the centre of town. At least one good thing I noted was that the walk was much easier than it had been of late. "Well," I said to myself, "looks as though those American medics must have done me *some* good after all. Thank the Lord, whether he exists or not!"

When I entered Brown's, however, my pals were all there as I'd expected, yet, rather than arguing over which of them should buy me my first drink, they *all* ignored me. As did my good friend the barman when I tried to order it for myself on credit. I then went over and sat in Caitlin's and my usual place in the bay window, but *still* nobody paid any attention to me. If I said that I felt unjustly hurt, that would be the understatement of the year, but, what with my enormous ego, I wasn't going to give up that easily, and anyway there were other pubs in the neighbourhood. So I trailed to each one in succession, invariably seeing a few people who knew me well, yet never getting any response whatsoever. Before long, my patience (never, I have to admit, my strongest virtue) ran out completely and craving a drink more than ever, I simply flew into a rage and tried to seize hold of the glass of one of my so-called friends. Yet nothing seemed to happen! I just couldn't understand it. I could smell the beer all right, even sort of feel some of it going down my throat, but it simply didn't give me the normal satisfaction.

Apparently — so my splendid 'rescuers' eventually told me — I'd carried on in this sort of way for 20-odd years in Earth time. Who were these 'rescuers'? Well, they were a group of half a dozen friends who all enjoyed reading my stuff and had trained together in shamanic work. They'd learnt on their courses that alcoholics, when they died, very frequently didn't realise that they'd left their bodies and would consequently hang around in pubs, endeavouring to get a trifle of satisfaction from inhaling the alcoholic vapours. They naturally felt it likely that that was what I was still doing and so decided to make a trip to Laugharne together to see whether they could track me down. Amazingly (though I speak as someone totally ignorant of such abilities as clairvoyance or clair*sentience*), they were successful in their mission. Working in conjunction with, in my case, the spirit guides who were watching over me at the time, they managed — though I assure you with considerable difficulty — to convince me that Dylan Thomas was as dead as a dodo and that a much better life was awaiting me on the other side if I could brace myself to cross my beloved estuary. The total irony here was that, though Caitlin was furiously angry and a bit later (as I know *now*) wrote as part of her rantings and ravings: *Dylan and dying, Dylan and dying, they don't go together*, she immediately added: *or is it that they were bound to go together; he said so often enough, but I did not heed him.*

Anyway, crossing my beloved estuary turned out to be less challenging than I'd imagined. The reason? It was because, very quickly, an indescribably beautiful figure (an angel perhaps?) came and 'gently' took my hand and guided me across as though we were flying together. I can't *begin* to describe the feelings of total bliss that swept over me, but here, please note, that in the previous sentence I deliberately used the adverb rather than the adjective 'gentle'. Once a wordsmith, ever a wordsmith, and no reason for it needs to be supplied! He/she then explained (again *gently*!) that, at one level of my frequently blurred consciousness, I'd always been aware that I'd planned a short life. That was why I'd started writing seriously at such an early age; a bit like Schubert in a way — and he too, after all, also abused his body grossly and died even younger than I did. Consciously, I'd simultaneously feared and courted death. Consciously *and* constantly, both Caitlin and I had suppressed this awareness with alcohol.

So, now that you've heard about the end (which is, as you'll hear later, in reality a new beginning), it's high time to recount some of the earlier bits, and I thank you for waiting so patiently. Well, as you quite likely know, I was born and brought up in

Swansea, where my father, David John Thomas (known as Jack), taught English literature at the Grammar School and my mother, Florence (née Williams), had worked as a seamstress in a local draper's. They were married at the end of 1903 and sadly lost their first child the following year. In 1906, however, my sister Nancy was born and then, a bit over eight years later (on 27 October 1914, if you like precision), my dear mother gave birth to *me* in the front room of the newly built number 5 Cwmdonkin Drive, for which my parents had succeeded in obtaining a joint mortgage (unusual at the time) the previous February. If you're *really* interested and happen to go to *that lovely, ugly town*, as I described it, you can visit 'The Dylan Thomas Birthplace' on either a Wednesday or a Sunday.

From my disciplinary and erudite father, who had gained a First Class Honours degree in English from the University of Aberystwyth, I inherited a good capacity for whisky (though I undoubtedly improved on it considerably!) and a massive capacity for literature. In every imaginable corner of the house there were piles and piles of books and yet more books, which he encouraged me to read as soon as I was able, and so, with these two passions combined — not to mention of course the mortgage payments — it's no wonder that there was never a penny to spare. From my mother I inherited the gift of the gab and a great love for people; she had farming family dotted all over Carmarthenshire, was a great storyteller and honoured as the 'Family Historian'. Ever protective and indulgent, she, along with both Nancy and the nurse, doted on me unboundedly, as did the innumerable aunts and (less numerous) uncles, many of whom are commemorated in my writings. For that reason — of which my wife Caitlin, who always 'babied' me too, was very conscious — I never needed to grow up. Nancy was garrulous as well and often in trouble for her socialite tendencies, but I of course always empathised totally with that.

My grandparents had all departed this precious Earth by the time I was three, and the branches of family that we visited regularly — or to whom I was farmed out, or (later) to whom I went of my own accord to escape my father's discipline and rages — were all greying. Hence my teenage obsession with decay and the above-mentioned unmentionable *thing* that I feared as well as courted, and hence the poem quoted second underneath the title of this chapter, which I wrote much later for my father during his final illness. I suppose my relationship with him was somewhat ambivalent really, since, while resenting the rules imposed on me, I revered his knowledge of literature and lapped up the material he introduced me to. While he was living in Laugharne in the early 1950s, despite his deteriorating health — he died less than a year before I did — we were still able to enjoy our mutual love of words and would often spend the morning together completing the *Times'* cryptic crossword. Obviously I'm jumping about now, but then didn't the great Jean-Luc Godard say that a film had to have a beginning, middle and end, though not necessarily in that order?

Carl Gustav Jung apparently said pretty much the same thing regarding the *four* stages of life (childhood, adolescence, maturity and old age). Of course, that particular time round, with apologies for being repetitive, I myself only did the first of those. Ann, our scribe, on the other hand, after hearing this statement of Jung's from her therapy teacher, and since her father had barred her from childhood, resolved one summer vacation when she was in her early sixties and her husband had taken her back to their beloved Geneva for his work, to 'do childhood' by taking advantage of the long evenings and enjoy going on swings and roundabouts in the deserted playgrounds.

I'm all for that — my playground, when I was a child at the 'normal' time, was the park in the Mumbles, which I made entirely into my own world — but what I'm less keen on is

Ann's constant desire to find out and *understand* people's behaviour. It must be the wretched therapist in her! I know I said earlier that, now I'd properly crossed over to the other side, I was starting to work on understanding Dylan Thomas, but there are limits! Ann, you see, though never teetotal, was totally ignorant about alcoholism and had assumed that it was generally caused by some such thing as depression. But one useful thing about writing books, or anyway the sort of books that she writes, is that it's a huge learning process for the author *herself*. So now, thanks to the research she's been doing into *me* and despite Caitlin having written (I have to admit, from my new perspective, wisely): *For ironically, the more depressed drink makes a victim, the more desperately she needs it. It is a depression that has become her natural habitat, she clutches onto it, as a drowning man clutches onto a rotten branch of a tree*, our scribe has now learnt that excessive drinking doesn't *have* to have a cause; sometimes it just *is* what one does, and that was certainly the case with me. No apologies either for that too-long sentence — too-long paragraph in fact — or for jumping the gun again.

Ann is now wondering whether this is the worst chapter in this, her 'swan song' (at least she knows it's her 'swan song', which I didn't when I was ill in New York but still thinking poetry), or the best, but my reply is that there is no possible reply to that question. Because people's opinions, tastes and interests differ, which is partly what makes each one of us unique. And Ann's comment on that point (deliberately misquoting Orwell) is that "everybody is unique, but some people are more unique than others". But now I should perhaps stop denigrating our scribe completely* because, for one thing, she's dead right there — Caitlin and I were both among the most unique people in history — and, for another, despite the fact that I always disliked psychologists, philosophers and others of that ilk, now that I've thankfully been rescued by some well-trained shamanic practitioners, I have to admit to being able to see that a therapy such as Deep Memory Process can, at least for some, be damned useful.

Now at this point I'd like to mention another thing that always used to irritate me: those (often serious literary scholars) who tried to work out the precise *meanings* of certain bits of my work. These people would sometimes come up at the end of one of my reading sessions and present me with some learned analysis that they'd written of a poem and ask what I thought of it. Well, often I didn't even remember what I'd meant at the time, but, never liking to offend, I would take their comments away, promising to let them know in due course, but the 'due course' never materialised. Here's a typical question: "Why, in the phrase *Though I swam in my chains like the sea*, did I use the word 'like' rather than 'in'?" Your guess is probably at least as good as mine or theirs, if not better.

I've been meandering again, but now I'll go back to where I left off before those important red herrings. (Hey, there's a thought! Does anyone ever think to query the origin of *that* phrase?) Although my parents were pretty much bilingual in English and Welsh and living where we did, it was impossible not to pick up a good smattering of the latter, they wanted their offspring to speak the former perfectly and almost entirely. While at primary school I was even given elocution lessons by one Gwen James, who had studied drama in London and won several major prizes in the subject. In fact all my immediate family were interested in theatre and had dramatic talents, I was involved in various ways and in numerous performances throughout my life, and later, in 1979, our Little Theatre in the Mumbles was relocated to Swansea's Maritime Quarter and renamed the Dylan Thomas Theatre.

Once I'd progressed to the Grammar School, the only lessons I actually enjoyed were those of my father and so, having done very poorly at school, I left at 16 and got a job as a reporter for the *South Wales Daily Post*, which I stuck for 18 months — quite a feat for someone of my ilk! (Oh and by the way, most of the Grammar School got destroyed in the Swansea blitz of 1941 and in 1988 its one surviving building, at that point part of the Swansea Metropolitan University, was also renamed after me. I fortunately avoided going off to fight in the war thanks to my poor health and after the blitz my parents moved to Laugharne.)

My lack of desire to go to university was naturally a disappointment to my father, but my achievement of fame at the age of 20, through the publication in London of *Eighteen Poems*, must have made up for it. For yes, from a very young age indeed, I just *knew* that I had to be a poet. *Words* were for me the be-all and end-all of everything; their meaning was immaterial. My first attempts were published in the school magazine, of which I ended up becoming editor, and three quarters of my poetry was written by the time I'd reached 20.

The combination of my father's agnosticism and my mother's puritanical Congregationalist background caused some tension inside me, but not even the church services, to which I was reluctantly taken by Williams relatives as a child, did anything to dampen the development of my innate radical left-wing tendencies.

In early 1934 I started to think seriously about moving to London — an obvious place to live for anyone involved in the arts — and was settled there by the end of that year. Radical change occurred before I was 22, in a West End pub, where Augustus John introduced me to Caitlin Macnamara, his lover at the time. (John had a reputation for seducing the young women whose portraits he painted, and in this case they'd met through his son, whom she'd initially been dating.) Unlike me, Caitlin had come from an unstable, though very literary, background. The youngest of four children, with a mainly absent Irish father (described as a 'professional eccentric'!) and an inadequate mother of French Quaker descent, she'd run away from home at the age of 15, intent upon becoming a professional dancer — the next Isadora Duncan to be more precise — and at 18 had joined the chorus line at the London Palladium. You can read her story in her very own words in the books for which our scribe has expressed gratitude in the 'Acknowledgements' at the front of *this* book. (After the immense task, which Ann was given with her penultimate book, of putting all the footnotes right at the end, I really don't blame her for wanting to avoid them altogether in this book. Had *I* lived to 83, as a technological moron, with various physical handicaps to boot, I'm sure I would have rebelled similarly. In fact I never even had a typewriter!)

Anyway, returning to that wife of mine: I liked to joke that we were in bed together ten minutes after we'd first met. It's certainly true that an immediate 'compulsion' drew us together and although she didn't ditch John straight away, we began a correspondence, were courting by the second half of 1936 and got married in the Penzance Registry Office in July 1937. It was the craziest and stormiest of marriages, with constant rows as well as infidelities, and with neither of us being naturally cut out for parenthood. Despite all that, we had three children (a girl sandwich), and, as I see things now, I marvel at how well they each turned out, against all odds. (With each birth Caitlin wondered whether the new arrival was actually mine, but the physical resemblance was always instantly irrefutable!)

I won't bore you with details of the various different places in which we lived, but I was always at my most productive when living close to the sea (that *long and splendid curving shore*) and Laugharne, for numerous reasons, drew me particularly strongly. We didn't move into the Boathouse straight away — there's a plaque outside Seaview, the house that we rented for a while, saying 'Former Home of the Poet Dylan Thomas' — but, having had, as I already mentioned, the gift of the gab and being an 'eternal entertainer', I was never short of friends and would-be patrons. One such was the wife of the great historian A. J. P.

Taylor, who in due course kindly bought the Boathouse for us. Close to this house is a shed, which proved to be very useful as my Writing Shed. (You can actually go inside it if you're prepared to pay £30 for the privilege! Our scribe did so and took photographs not only of my lists of words but also of my wastepaper basket, left exactly as they were before I left Earth.) And here I have an important point to make: if you imagine that much of my work was written when I was in a drunken stupor, you're mistaken. I tried doing that once or twice, to no avail. I always had to sleep off the effects of over-drinking before setting to work, and *all* my published writings are the result of very meticulous craftsmanship.

* Nor should I have been making anti-American remarks either! In reality I loved the Americans; they are in general a wonderful, hospitable people.

***

Now I'm fast-forwarding to 31 July 1994, when my wife joined me over here. Since being rescued from my lengthy and futile pub crawl (which, incidentally, caused me to miss witnessing Caitlin going completely potty while accompanying my coffin on the ship back home and, before fleeing to Italy with Colm, wanting to dig into my grave in the cemetery of St Martin's Church, Laugharne), I'd spent the intervening years both interestingly and usefully. Besides keeping an eye on all my family and watching with admiration Caitlin's total transformation to 20 years of sobriety, I'd been attending all sorts of classes laid on over here in numerous aspects of spirituality, including karma of course. There are *so* many things one forgets about while on Earth, and one of these is that, in a case such as mine, one can be useful to, say, writers or would-be writers down there by making oneself available for giving advice. It's tremendously rewarding and, for someone like me, can help to make up for some of the things one regrets about one's last life.

Anyway, my wife Caitlin — the central force in my life and art, the bohemian who recognised the necessity of my writing, lighting the stove in my shed in the early mornings to enable it to take place — shed her mortal coil in Catania, at the age of 81 and following a lengthy illness. Her *earthly* 'rescuer' had been a man named Giuseppe Fazio, a Sicilian whom she'd met in a Rome restaurant towards the end of 1957. Thanks to him, she eventually, at the age of 60, joined Alcoholics Anonymous, having given birth to their son Francesco at the age of 49! But one thing I haven't already mentioned about Caitlin is that, besides being the most amazing dancer, she had absolutely phenomenal physical strength, which she attributed to all the goat's milk her mother had fed her on. No body, however, whether strong or weak (and mine was the latter), can possibly withstand the abuse that we each inflicted on ours through years and years of excessive drinking. So, when Caitlin did *go gentle into that good night*, first of all, having, like me, never been at all religious, she was a bit bewildered and uncertain as to where she was. I, however, having been informed by one of my guides that she was on her way, was there waiting to greet her. She was astounded, initially, on account of the fact that I looked so *well* — so different from the Dylan she'd last seen in New York, not to mention the corpse that she'd escorted to the grave and for which she'd chosen the simplest of white wooden crosses — and so I had to work quite hard to convince her that it really was me! Then, after the joyful truth had dawned and we'd embraced tenderly, her guides came and explained that she needed a spell in a 'heavenly hospital' but that, after she'd recuperated, we could talk together to our hearts' desire and *without* any acrimony.

And so it was and *had* to be because, when we'd been together in that last life on Earth, despite being aware of her own literary inclinations, I'd expected her to be just a housewife and do *all* the childminding. (I really did nothing to help with that, apart from reading to the children at bedtime, and we were both hopelessly impractical anyway, so the house was always in chaos.) So, once she'd had her period of recuperation and was ready to start on some of the spiritual education in which I was now temporarily ahead of her, it was important for me to say how proud of her I was for the books she'd written after my departure! I pointed out that, although strictly speaking, as a Scorpio (me) and a Sagittarian (she),* our relationship should have been harmonious, in actual fact each of our over-inflated egos had got in the way of that harmony. She responded by agreeing that she'd never *not* wanted me to be a writer, but the fact that she herself had for a long time had aspirations in that direction as well was at least partly the reason for her never having been very keen to listen when I offered to read her my latest poem. Once all that had been aired and I'd apologised for never having given her the encouragement she deserved, we embraced again and agreed that it was then time to turn to other matters.

Well, when I'd been relearning about karma and discussing with my guides about Caitlin's and my relationship, it had become clear to me that the reason for the intensity of the bond between us was that we were 'karmic soul mates', that is, that one of us had a debt to pay to the other. My guides had suggested, however, that it would be better for us to explore that bit of karma together, once her life had also come to an end. Caitlin immediately agreed to that idea and so we were both taken to the vast, indescribably beautiful hall in which the Akashic Records are stored. It took only a moment for one of Caitlin's guides to locate the relevant lifetime in her personal book and we read it together lovingly. It was a seventeenth-century life in England, in which I'd been the eldest son in a wealthy family and she (surprise, surprise!) had been a professional and seductive dancer. Finding it hard to earn a reasonable living, she'd turned on all her charms while performing in our mansion and then persuaded me — without much difficulty, I hasten to add — to run away with her to Italy, taking a large portion of the family fortune with me. My parents, needless to say, had been furious and so, once my funds had been extravagantly spent (much of it on wine of course) while we'd toured around looking, mostly in vain, for work and I'd sent them an urgent appeal that had been refused, we'd both died in penury.

Not an easy one to swallow, but it rang big bells in both our memories and though the debt had been more on Caitlin's side we agreed that it made a lot of sense and undoubtedly explained the instantaneous mutual attraction between us. We further agreed that we'd both had a great deal to learn from that lifetime and that she, while in her final, stable relationship in Italy, and having many more years in which to do it, had got further along the road than I had on Earth. I, on the other hand, had made a more substantial start on this side. Our guides then assured us that the debt had been paid and that we consequently wouldn't need to return *together* again but could remain good friends. We then spent some happy time reminiscing, talking about our families — particularly our three children, a great source of mutual pride — and then we met up with our parents and other relatives who'd gone on before us, and Caitlin's parents apologised to her for their inadequacies. Oh, and I haven't mentioned that my dear mother, Florence, lost both my father and Nancy, who'd died from cancer, in the same year as losing me and had then taken over the Boathouse after Caitlin and the children's move to Italy.

* Ann also has an interest in numerology, a form of astrology elaborated by Pythagoras, and so, when reading the dates of my birth and death (27 October and 9 November), she saw significance in the fact that both were nines, the divine

number. (NB: this book has 27 chapters for that same reason.) This, combined with the fact that my overall numerological number was seven, which is all to do with spirituality and unconditional love, indicates to her that, without myself recognising it at the time, I was basically a very spiritual person.

***

Now some further years have passed, and Llewellyn, Aeronwy and Colm have all joined us over here. Since I've already taken up more space than I perhaps deserve in this book, I suggest that, if you want to learn more, you do as our scribe did and google them. They all died in their sixties, were all highly intelligent and had all received more formal education than I did. Aeronwy, our daughter, not only wrote poetry herself but also worked as a translator of Italian poetry and when the five of us met up again and they'd accepted our apologies for our failures in parenting, I told my two sons that I didn't blame them in the least for having wanted to keep out of the limelight regarding their famous father.

Hannah Ellis, on the other hand, Aeronwy's daughter and a teacher, wrote beautifully thus in the book she'd nobly agreed to edit for the centenary of my birth:

> With an element of embarrassment I had to admit that I had not read my grandfather's work. What if I didn't like it? What if it was too difficult? So, it was with amazement I found myself reading beautiful and descriptive poetry, surreal and dark short stories, memories of Dylan's childhood in Wales … I suddenly became aware that I was incredibly lucky to be the granddaughter of not only a talented wordsmith, but also a sensational actor. Dylan

could move audiences with powerful and thoughtful readings, and then, in an instant, cause the same group of people to roll about with laughter, with a quick and witty comment.

So, that's a nice way to be remembered, despite my imperfections, and it also pleases me that my wife, rather than leaving her mortal remains to be dealt with in Italy, chose to have her name added to the white cross in the Laugharne cemetery.

Now, in conclusion, all I'd really like to add is that, if you feel that you are approaching death and want to *rage against the dying of the light*, please take it from me that there is in fact no such thing as dying. On the contrary, you will find that the light in fact becomes, amazingly, wonderfully clearer and brighter. And you will then see that death *shall*, indeed, *have no dominion*!

# 25

# A Very Great Artist

*You think that he is something more than an ordinary human being, but I think that it would be much better if he thought himself just an ordinary being.*

From a letter to Theo van Gogh written by one of his sisters

*His religion makes him absolutely dull and unsociable.*

From a letter to Theo sent by another sister

*... it's my constant hope that I am not working for myself alone. I believe in the absolute necessity of a new art of colour, of design and of the artistic life. And if we work in that faith, it seems to me there is a chance that we do not hope in vain.*

From a letter sent by Vincent van Gogh to his younger brother Theo

*Bonjour!* Hello! What language would you like? Not Dutch, I take it, since that's far from being a universal tongue and it seems that our scribe (despite the fact that French has always been her favourite language and it's also one that's very familiar to me) prefers to write in her mother tongue, which *is* pretty much a universal one. I would really prefer to convey my story and thoughts to you purely in the language of the spirit, but, since those who will be reading this book on Earth will be doing so in print, I, too, shall endeavour to use the 'language of the Bard', if an updated version of it. (Though, having left the world about ten years before the dawn of the nineteenth century, I would be even less able than is our scribe to keep abreast with modern parlance.)

Anyway, I dare say that most of you think of me as the mad artist who cut off his ear and gave it to a prostitute, never got any money to speak of for his works (unwisely spending some of the little he did receive on such things as absinthe or whores), spent some time in a mental hospital near Arles, ultimately shot himself at the age of 37, and only achieved great fame posthumously. All correct of course, but it barely sums up a zillionth of who or what I was and am.

So who or what *was* I really? A genius no doubt — that goes without saying — and how many true geniuses have had pleasant, cushy lives? I'll take just one example each from two other forms of art, both of whom figure in earlier chapters of this somewhat curious piece of literature: Franz Schubert (whom I outlived by six years), as well as drinking too much, had no proper love life at all; Dylan Thomas (who outlived me by a couple of years) drank *much, much* too much and in addition had *too much* love life. And we're not by any means the only 'greats' to have had short lives and done an incredible amount during them. There must be reasons for it, so here let me posit a simple one: we'd each agreed before coming in to endure immense suffering for the sake of our art and consequently decided to pack everything in as fast as possible so that we could then move on speedily to better things, leaving future generations to bask in the glories of our legacies.

But I suppose I'd better begin at the beginning, thus hopefully giving you a better understanding of my nature and character. Well, like the hero of the previous chapter, I was born (on 30 March 1853) into a 'good', well-recognised and loving family; in my case, my place of birth was Groot-Zundert in the North Brabant province of the Netherlands. My father, Theodorus van Gogh, was a minister of the Dutch Reformed Church, which supplied him and our family with a house, a maid, two cooks, a gardener and a horse and carriage. My mother, Anna Cornelia, had come from a prosperous family in The Hague and, though exceedingly tender-hearted, was rigidly religious and instilled in all her children a duty to uphold the family's high position. I was named after both my grandfather and the son who'd been stillborn a year to the day before I was born, and so my arrival was naturally especially welcomed. The next one to arrive, on 1 May 1857, was my dear brother Theo (whom I now understand to be a 'companion soulmate' of mine). I also had three sisters, Anna, Elisabeth (Lies) and Willemina (Wil), and another younger brother, Cornelis (Cor), who was born in 1867 and died in 1900.

My paternal grandfather was a prominent art dealer and, of his six sons, three followed him into that profession. I was a serious, thoughtful child, with a great love of animals and flowers (of which I made numerous collections), but often troublesome and strong-willed. Once, when my paternal grandmother gave me a box on the ears, my doting mother expressed great anger with her. I inherited that kind heart and was also very religious — at least to start with — and I had a constant desire to help others but was at the same time always very self-effacing. Initially I was taught at home by my mother and a governess, but I got sent to the village school in 1860 and then, in 1864, to a boarding school in Zevenbergen. There I was very unhappy and nagged to return home, but instead my parents sent me a couple of years later to the middle school in Tilburg, where I was again deeply unhappy.

When our scribe read some details of my early life and saw how caring my family had been, she felt that some of my problems must have had roots in a previous life. She consequently decided to lie down, go into meditation and ask me whether I'd discovered anything about those roots. I replied that, some time after I'd crossed over into the Bardo, I had indeed been shown *two* previous lives that were relevant to the one as Vincent van Gogh. I'd found some of it hard to swallow, but soon saw that it all made sense, which now makes me feel quite happy for the information to be shared with you readers, who are no doubt true spiritual seekers with a good understanding of the laws of 'Cause and Effect' (otherwise known as 'karma').

The first thing that happened while Ann was lying comfortably on the bed was that she suddenly felt very hot. Then she saw a bonfire and the big bulk of a man, who was obviously rather a bully, getting into an argument with another man, who was physically weaker than he was. The scene ended with the weaker man falling into the fire and being severely, though not fatally, burnt. So I then told her what I'd been shown in the Akashic Records: that that bully had been a wealthy merchant in Provence who'd wanted to lord it over everybody else, using his money and power to show himself to be superior to all those around him. He hadn't actually *wanted* the person with whom he'd had that particular argument to be seriously hurt and he had been a bit repentant, but his anger had prevented him from being *sufficiently* repentant, even on his deathbed.

In my next life, therefore — it's time for me to use the first person now! — I'd had to make up for that arrogance by incarnating into a much poorer family, in which I had a bullying father, who undervalued me, and a mother with too many troubles of her own to be able to defend me. That lifetime was in the Netherlands, and my mother was the same one as I had this last time. These two past lives explain not only why my mother Anna cared about me so very deeply and gave me so much encouragement in every possible way, but also the reasons for both my constant desire to help others and my asceticism. (I never, for instance, cared about my clothing, always ate frugally and when working as a missionary in January 1879 in the coal-mining district of the Borinage in Belgium, I gave my comfortable lodgings to a homeless person and slept on straw in a small hut. For this the church authorities dismissed me for "undermining the dignity of the priesthood". What do you think Jesus would have had to say about that?)

Needless to say, I'd honed my artistic gifts in numerous previous lifetimes but never in those attained anything like the pinnacle that I did as Van Gogh. Unlike the extraordinary Dylan Thomas, however, I didn't start on my true calling incredibly early but only began to draw seriously after moving to London at the age of 20. I have already mentioned that art dealing was very much *the* family profession, and it was my uncle (who was known as Cent — there were several 'Vincents' in the family) who'd secured a position for me with the company Goupil & Cie in The Hague. After completing my training, I got transferred to the firm's London branch, where I was both successful and happy to start with, and from there I began sending home drawings that I'd done of my surroundings. Another thing that happened, however, was that I fell for the daughter of my landlady in Stockwell. My love life being forever ill-fated, in this case it turned out that she was already secretly engaged to their previous lodger. From then on I spiralled steadily downwards, ultimately becoming probably what is now labelled 'bipolar' (previously, in our scribe's lifetime, but not in mine, the label would have been 'manic depressive'). I rapidly became increasingly isolated and my only refuge was in religious fervour.

I won't bore you with all the details of my subsequent efforts to enter the ministry in one form or another, but prior to all that my father and uncle arranged an unsuccessful transfer for me to Paris, where Theo kindly invited me to share his flat in Montmartre. I mentioned above my having learnt over here that he and I were 'companion soul mates' and these are normally the most comfortable of soul-mate relationships, but in that particular life (I've been shown others in which we were happily married) my being such a difficult character was distinctly challenging for my dear brother and he was incredibly long suffering. For instance, after I'd got dismissed from my post in the Paris gallery on account of certain complaints I made against the management, he still stood by me through thick and thin, and it was he who first suggested that I become a professional artist and later encouraged me to make use of oil paints. Our parents never gave up their concern, either, and my father told Theo that he thought I should leave Goupil altogether, commenting that I wanted to do good in the world, but "not in an art gallery". At least the time that I spent in that area gave rise to some of my most celebrated paintings, for instance those done in Asnières and Montmartre.

Of course another thing that Theo always did was to give me financial support, and it may be worth noting that this was not on account of a karmic debt but simply one of the products of the strong bond between us. He was the person who understood me the best and it was to him that I wrote the majority of my very numerous letters. Thanks to his having carefully preserved them, the world can now see that my writing was as prolific as my art. (Sadly I didn't do the same with his replies; this was caused partly by my rather nomadic existence and partly by my disorganised nature.) When Theo was getting engaged to Johanna, he told her about the importance of our relationship, and I was deeply touched when they named my nephew after me.

Other important steps towards my becoming an artist rather than an art *dealer* were firstly the year I spent from 1879–80 as a lay preacher, living in the village of Cuesmes (near Mons in the Borinage), in the annexe of a house occupied by a miner and his family. There I became very concerned about the lives of the miners, actually went down a mine myself, and all this gave rise to many drawings. (This house has subsequently been made into a museum — a mark of the fame that I'd never have dreamt of while on Earth!) Secondly, moving from drawing to colour, I had the following year the great privilege of studying under the artist Anton Mauve in The Hague, who was married to my cousin Ariette and whom I revered greatly. He did much to encourage me in my use first of oils, then watercolour and unlike the mighty Beethoven (who claimed to have learnt nothing from his lessons with Haydn), I acknowledged the debt I owed him even after we'd fallen out. Nor did our disagreement prevent me from sending one of my favourite paintings (of peach trees in bloom) as a gift to his widow after he'd died.

Mauve had complained that I had a "vicious character", but our falling out was also caused at least partly by his disapproval of the relationship I had with a pregnant prostitute, Clasina ('Sien') Hornik. At the time that I met her, I was madly in love with my cousin Kee and it took a long time for me to come to terms with her rejection of my advances, but I felt compassion for Sien and the child she already had, as well as the one in her womb. On this subject I wrote: "The clergymen call us sinners, conceived and born in sin, bah! What dreadful nonsense that is. Is it a *sin* to need love, not to be able to live without love? I think a life without love a sinful and immoral condition." You could perhaps see me as a precursor of the great twentieth-century American theologian Matthew Fox, the founder of what he named 'Creation Spirituality', and one of whose seminal books is entitled *Original Blessing* (in contrast to the Churches' out-of-date doctrine of 'Original Sin').

Going back to the mighty Beethoven for a moment, I feel that, though he didn't, with good reason, have the humility I had, there are parallels that can be drawn in our work. I once wrote: "In a picture I want to say something comforting, as music is comforting." Yet, like the ever-struggling musical master (whose struggle I didn't *deliberately* mimic!), so many of our most famous pieces reflect the moods and emotions we were experiencing at the time of their composition. Take his Pastoral Symphony (No. 6), for example: the beginning of it reflects the joy of walking in the countryside, which is surely akin to the glowing colours of my Provençal paintings with their sunflowers and so on that I loved so much. Yet even within that wonderful symphony there comes a storm! That's how life always is, is it not? Periods of happiness are interspersed with unhappy ones; times of challenge are compensated for by those in which things go smoothly. (Thence the lessons for which we return repeatedly to Earth.) Then, look at the darkness in my powerful painting *The Prisoners' Round*, a late one created in 1890 during my spell at the mental asylum of St Rémy. As all truly great artists know deep inside them (even if not consciously), if their work is to touch people — or even go as far as changing lives — it must cover the full gamut of human emotions and feelings. Is there anything in music more profound than, say, the Cavatina movement in Beethoven's late string quartet, Opus 130?

For sure, just like him, I had my own, utterly unique, inimitable style, crafted even more by my own efforts than by the teachings of any other master. (Oh, and here I'd love to give you a quote I heard recently from the twentieth-century composer Stravinsky. He said that, whereas good composers(/artists) borrowed, the great ones *stole*! Well, didn't Brahms, in his First Symphony, steal from the 'Ode to Joy' in Beethoven's Ninth? And I will readily admit to having stolen from Mauve, among others.) Often, however, I really didn't know exactly what I was doing — especially of course when I was confined to the mental hospital — but I just knew that I *had* to do it; it came from something deep down inside the very marrow of my bones, and what anyone else would think of it was completely immaterial. As I once wrote to Theo:

> I shall work on till I am absolute master of my hand, so that I can work even more quickly than now and, for instance, bring home about thirty studies within a month. I do not know if we shall earn money, but if it is only enough to let me work terribly hard, I shall be satisfied; the main thing is to do what one wants to do.

'Confined' to the mental hospital is actually the wrong word there. I wasn't locked up in that tiny room with the iron bed in it but was able to go for walks under supervision, and I also had a small studio in which I could do paintings of what I'd observed. The hospital is still in existence, and nowadays part of it is a museum dedicated to me; after walking up the path lined with prints of my paintings, visitors can see inside and imagine the nature of my life there for themselves. It wasn't quite the same as the endless wandering that I'd been free to do in other neighbourhoods that I'd lived in, but I nevertheless painted and painted like fury during that time.

Maybe I was completely 'out of my mind', as the saying goes, yet it could also be said that in some odd way I was in fact totally *in* it. For always, walking around whichever area I was living in, my eyes would become fixated with, and a hundred per cent focused on, whatever they were beholding, be it the vibrant colours of the Provençal sunflowers and lavender, the apricot trees in bloom, or the drabness of the world of the potato eaters.

There is much, much more I could say about my life, but I think it's now time to tell you about my death and what happened afterwards, because neither your beloved Google nor my own writings, nor the numerous books written about me will tell you anything at all about the latter. I haven't elaborated on the start of my total mental breakdown, at the end of 1888, and the famous episode in which, following an argument with Paul Gaugin, with whom I'd hoped to form an artists' colony, I cut off part of one of my ears and had to be rushed to hospital for treatment. I never recovered fully from that, and it was in April 1889 that I checked myself into the St Rémy asylum. After my year there, it was poor Theo who searched for a new home for me and, on the artist Camille Pissarro's recommendation, arranged for me to receive treatment from the homoeopathic doctor Paul Gachet, who was also trained in psychiatry, at his home in Auvers-sur-Oise. Well, I spent the final 70 days of my life lodging in a nearby inn there, the Auberge Ravoux, and completing as many pictures during the time, including portraits, plus my only etching, of the good doctor. For, being himself an accomplished engraver and an aspiring painter, he had a particular interest in working with artists. I actually did my one and only engraving under his guidance. He cared for me, too, to the best of his abilities, and his understanding of my difficulties was equalled only by Theo's, but I failed to heed his advice to give up smoking and drinking. In any case, it wasn't in his life path to interfere with my destiny.

Somehow or other — I don't remember how — I managed to get hold of a Lefaucheux pinfire revolver. The whole thing was a complete blur, with no physical witnesses, but I was told some time after I'd crossed over that I'd shot myself in my chest in a field near Auvers, that the bullet had been deflected by a rib, and that I'd managed to walk back to the Auberge Ravoux. There I was attended to by two doctors, but, with no surgeon present, it was impossible to remove the bullet and I died in the early hours of 29 July from an infection in the wound that hadn't been treated. This, however, was not before my dearest brother had rushed to my side. According to his account, my last words were: "The sadness will last forever."

But, to my own intense surprise, I was wrong there! When the blur did finally end, I found myself completely dazzled by the most wondrous, unimaginable light and cradled in what felt like angels' wings. As soon as I was able to open my mouth, I remember exclaiming: "Where on *earth* am I?" The gentle reply that instantly came was: "You're no longer on Earth, Vincent dear, but in Heaven." The dialogue (with I knew not whom) then continued thus:

"How can that possibly be? I thought I was in an auberge in Auvers."

"You were indeed, but that was before the result of the bullet wound had caused your soul to leave your physical body."

"Who for goodness' sake was responsible for wounding me? I never wanted to cause harm to *anyone*!"

"Of course you didn't and that's precisely the reason why you've come straight here. It was you yourself who, unknowingly, used the gun."

"Good Lord! So are you telling me that I've committed suicide? It's true that I often thought of it, but now I recall that suicide is a mortal sin according to church doctrine, so why am I not in Hell yet?"

"Dear Vincent, I'm your guardian angel and I have much to tell you. First of all, we don't care to use the word 'sin' over here; 'error' is more apt. And besides, anyone who isn't fully aware of what they're doing — as you weren't while you were so beset with troubles — cannot have any wrongdoing attributed to them. What you need straight away is a long, long rest, and so now I together with Gustav, who was your main guide in that life which has just ended and an artist friend in one of your previous lifetimes, are going to escort you to one of our heavenly hospitals, where you will be given all the loving care and attention that you're needing. Your etheric body has suffered a lot of damage, not only from your recent wounds but also from the lifetime of neglect that you inflicted on your physical body."

"Hullo, Vincent. I'm sure you'll remember me in due course, even if you don't recognise me immediately in your present state of bewilderment. We are very old friends and it's lovely to have you back here with us after that lifetime of incredible achievements."

"Incredible achievements?! I'm not at all sure about that. But yes, Gustav, you do certainly look familiar to me."

"Undue modesty and excessive lack of self-esteem were ever your gravest faults, if we are to use such an unnecessary word. But another important thing I have to tell you is that the Churches have all got it quite wrong about 'eternal damnation'. The only Hell that has ever existed is that of our own making and it never lasts forever, as you'll relearn while you remain in this inter-life state. Now let's hasten to the hospital and then, when you've made a good recovery, we'll help you with your life review, and please remember that the only 'judgement' will be your own. Our all-loving Almighty never condemns any of His children."

***

I can't *begin* to tell you how wonderful everything's been since I arrived here! The spell in hospital did me the world of good, with everyone being so gentle and understanding, and one of the best things that happened while I was still there was that my father came to see me. That was really good because we hadn't always seen eye to eye while we were on Earth and had argued a lot, but the first thing he said was how very proud of me he was. That was immensely gratifying because I'd always admired him, despite our agreements, and of course I'd always been grateful for the financial support he gave me from time to time in addition to what I received from Theo.

And talking of that very dear brother, he sadly only outlived me by six months. He'd been unwell for a while and found the trauma of my death too much for him. He was buried in Utrecht, while my grave was in Auvers-sur-Oise, but, 15 years or so later his wife Jo, who'd always acknowledged the very strong bond between us, had his body exhumed and reburied next to mine. *So* touching, and at that point we were able to watch it all from this side *together*. In the meantime we'd of course had endless opportunities to discuss an infinity of matters; and another splendid thing that happened was that our dear mother lived until 1907, which enabled her to see my name grow throughout the world. It had been hard for her losing both of us, but when she joined us over here she told us how much seeing my work widely recognised had compensated for the difficulties she'd had to endure during my lifetime.

Once I'd finished my long and welcome spell in the heavenly hospital and been confronted with making my life review, it turned out to be much less scary than I'd imagined. In fact the truth is that it wasn't scary at all because my guides, rather than focusing on my faults, chided me for my frequent lack of self-appreciation (which, as I mentioned earlier on, stemmed to a large extent from the lifetime when my mother Anna had been unable to defend me from a bullying father). My guides challenged me to analyse some of the characteristics of my work that made it so unboundedly popular. After reflecting long and hard, one of the points I made was that, while I'd greatly admired the skill of, say, Velázquez, unlike him I would never have had the least desire to paint pictures of royalty. My interests were rather in down-to-earth people, such as miners and peasants, and I felt that my pictures covered pretty much the broadest possible spectrum, not only of humanity itself but also of the natural world in all its aspects. I can tell you that I got given a good pat on the back for that analysis!

So, there is so much that has taken place in the more than 130 years since I've been here that I haven't felt any urgency to reincarnate. I realise that I'll need to do so at some point — partly to lead a more balanced sort of life with less intense distress — but for the time being I'm well employed over here. As well as overseeing some of the efforts that have been made on Earth to look after my work and promote it wherever it can be useful and fully appreciated, I've done quite a lot of teaching and counselling of other artists or would-be artists. As you must know, a great deal has been written about me, and one of the things that my biographers have found immensely useful is the vast numbers of letters that I wrote, the majority of them to

Theo. The intense labour of love that my sister-in-law made in compiling them, endeavouring, often with difficulty, to arrange them in chronological order, is really unimaginable. And then, when I saw her getting them out to the public in three large volumes, translating many of them herself into English, my admiration for her became unbounded.

Since that time innumerable other things have happened, some of them totally crazy. What lunatic, for instance, could want to pay $182,000 for the rusty old gun with which it is believed that I possibly shot myself?! (Since there were no witnesses, there isn't even any certainty about what really happened. A possibility has even been propounded that it was actually someone else that was in the field at the time who committed the crime, but I, who have long since put the whole episode behind me, now quite honestly couldn't care less.) Anyway, that's what the weapon was sold for at a Paris auction on 19 June 2019! I can only suppose that the buyer hoped one day to sell it on at an even more absurd price. What good will the money do him?

Much more importantly, Dr Paul Gachet, who shed bitter tears at my funeral, had in his safe keeping at the time of my departure the work that I'd completed during the period I spent in his village and thanks to his lack of desire to use any of it for his personal gain, most of it has been preserved in museums around the world. When he died, in 1909, we greeted one another with alacrity and later, in 1973, we watched together the opening of the Van Gogh Museum in Amsterdam. (Nowadays a portrait that I did of him is said to be worth around $149 million. Had I been told that during my lifetime, no way would I have been able to believe it. It's just as well, however, that I myself was never paid even a minute fraction of that sum, as I would surely have just squandered it!)

Incidentally, when our scribe and her husband were living in the north-east of England, they once took an overnight ferry and went to Amsterdam for the weekend. Having booked a hotel conveniently placed in between the Rijks Museum and the Van Gogh Museum, they were able to visit both at leisure and they brought back a couple of prints, one depicting some of my much-loved apricot blossom trees and the other of a bridge at Asnières. These they got framed and were fortunately able to take both with them when they moved south. Their second move, from a house in Ludlow to a small apartment in a retirement village in Malvern, obviously entailed a massive downsize, but they were determined to find space for these prints on their brand new walls. This is a typical example of people's love for my paintings and is a thing that, no doubt needless to say, affords me great pleasure now that I'm so happy over here.

On the other hand, a thing which I find very distressing is when criminals get 'in on the act'. Having themselves neither knowledge nor appreciation of art, such people become aware of the immense monetary value of works such as mine and they acquire great skill in breaking into art galleries and getting away with treasures in virtually no time at all. There is probably no other famous artist to have had as many of their pictures stolen as I have and sadly some of these have never been recovered. But the distinguished British art historian Andrew Graham Dixon put on a very interesting television programme entitled *Stealing Van Gogh*, which recounted the theft from the Amsterdam Museum of two of my small early works, both of which had a particularly personal value to my family. One was my very first oil painting, created on a sombre evening on a beach at Scheveningen. I found it very difficult to do, as the wind kept blowing sand onto it, but later I added some boats to it and have to say that I was pleased with the finished product. The other painting, of particular sentimental value to my family, was of the little church of which my father was pastor and I'd given it as a gift to my mother when he'd died.

Happily, these two paintings, which were whisked from the Museum in December 2002 in the space of just three minutes, were eventually retrieved (from under the false floor of a kitchen in Naples!) a whole 14 years later. The thieves had made the blunder of dropping their hats on the floor inside the Museum, and these enabled the experts to trace their owners' DNA, which in turn eventually led to a criminal by the name of Raffaele Imperiale, who was very well known to the police. The search, however, cost an absolute fortune, involving as it did numerous professional investigators in several countries. What a horrible way to spend so much time and money, and how much distress it caused Theo's great-grandson when it seemed that the paintings might have been lost forever! I myself, having a better vantage point over here of the future as well as of the present and past, didn't have to suffer over the incident as those on Earth did, but I sincerely hope that one day an even more secure system of guarding these treasures will be invented. Or — better still of course — that humanity will eventually come to its senses and come to realise that money has no lasting value.

Well, I think I've kept you quite long enough now with my story. So I'll just say in conclusion that I hope it's helped you to see that there's basically no such thing as a 'tragic life'. Yes, we often make mistakes while we're on Earth and do foolish or even evil things that we later come to regret, but it's all just a part of our long process of learning. We make a plan before we come in each time, sometimes too hastily, but nothing is ever set in stone. I knew beforehand that I *had* to be an artist — it was even suggested by my guides that I might well become famous — but had I concentrated on achieving fame and money rather than being totally focused on doing what I really *wanted* to do, both for others and for myself (with a greater emphasis on the former), I wouldn't ultimately have attained the great joy that I now have over here. Of course I suffered intensely and in numerous ways, thereby also causing distress to those around me, but I believe that if I'd had a happy and easy life, my work wouldn't speak to people in the very personal way that it now seems to. Ah, here comes Ludwig van Beethoven (with whom I was having a good chat the other 'day', as you would call it) and I can see him nodding his head in agreement!

# 26

# The Man Who Knew Infinity

*An equation for me has no meaning unless it expresses a thought of God.*

Ramanujan

*Sai Ram!* That form of greeting, which can be roughly translated as "The God in me salutes the God in you", is commonly used in, for instance, Sathya Sai Baba's ashram in southern India. Ann, our scribe, went there 16 times, in between 1998 and 2019, and is overwhelmingly grateful for the help He gave her (partly through therapists, first in Geneva and then in England) in her transformation from 'stupid and useless child, who'd been rejected at birth on account of her gender' to 'contented older woman with a wonderful family of her own and a clear purpose in life'. (Sai Baba actually left His physical body in 2011, but His vast numbers of devotees all over the globe still believe Him to be present and Ann herself, who's returned to the ashram a few times since His departure, points out that there 'Sai Ram' can also denote anything from 'Please' or 'Thank you' to 'Excuse me, but you're treading on my sari'!)

As previously mentioned in this book, one of the big differences between religion/spirituality in India and that in much of the West is that, whereas Christians think Jesus was the only divine incarnation ever, we Indians believe that there have been many of them, over a period of *thousands* and *thousands* of years. We call them 'avatars' and one of the earliest and most celebrated was named Rama — hence the first part of my name, the whole of which means 'younger brother of Rama'. The day of my birth, 22 December 1887, was a Thursday, as was that of my namesake, the Vaishnavite saint Ramanuja, who lived around AD 1100 and whose theological doctrines injected new spiritual vitality into a withered Hinduism. The two of us also shared various astrological features.

You will have gathered from this that I was a devout Hindu and more on that later, but now I'll just mention that you in the West probably think of me as "the mathematician who died tragically young". That is, *if* you've already heard of me, and I wouldn't blame you at all if you hadn't; it's just that a film was made from the book with the above title, and often films do more to bring fame than do biographies, however good they are. Well, let me tell you straight away that I agree wholeheartedly with the great artist of the previous chapter who stated that there was basically no such thing as a 'tragic life'. Right now, however, I'd better start by giving you some facts about myself in that particular lifetime.

I was born into a South Indian Brahmin family, whose caste name was Iyengar, in the Tanjore District of Tamil Nadu, close to the great River Cauvery, which is regarded locally as sacred to the same extent as the Ganga ('Ganges' to you), a thousand miles north of it, is considered to be sacred. The custom there was for a pregnant wife to return to her parents' house to give birth and I was consequently born in Erode, 150 miles upriver from Kumbakonam, where my mother (Komalatammal) had set up home with my father (Kuppuswamy Srinivasa Iyengar). A year later my mother returned with me to my father, who worked for a pittance as a clerk in a sari shop. She, as a traditional Indian housewife, didn't have a formal job as such, but she was paid a few rupees for singing in a local temple. So, as for many Indian families to this day, covering our needs was a constant struggle and my parents sometimes took in lodgers as an additional source of income. In view of the fame that I ultimately achieved, it probably won't surprise you to hear that our small traditional house in Sarangapani Sannidhi Street is now a museum.

When I was very young, there was a smallpox epidemic in the area, and the brother who was born 18 months after I was contracted it and lived for less than three months. I caught the disease, too, but survived (obviously — a word now much misused in Britain, but in this case clearly used correctly!). I was left, however, with enduring 'pockmarks', which I found unsightly, but was encouraged not to worry about them, especially since neither of two other younger siblings that I had lived for even a year. Later, two other brothers did survive, one born when I was 10 and the other when I was 17. I consequently grew up with (in the words of my excellent biographer, Robert Kanigel) "the solicitous regard and central position of an only child".

I was a difficult — one could even say 'recalcitrant'! — child. While still a small infant in Erode, I wanted to be fed only in the temple, which is surely a clear indication of my having been a priest in several previous lifetimes. Then later, if I wasn't given what I wanted to eat, I would sometimes roll in the mud in frustration. In addition to that, I scarcely spoke a word during the first three years of my life, which initially caused some anxiety, though it could have been that, as an immensely self-willed little boy, I simply chose not to bother to speak. I don't believe the cause to have any significance, but in any case the problem was later solved by my mother taking me to visit her parents, who had by then moved to Kanchipuram near Madras (now Chennai). There a friend of my grandfather's suggested adopting a ritual practice, known as *Akshara Abikesham*, whereby my hand was held and guided in tracing out each of the Tamil characters in a thick bed of rice spread across the floor, while its sound was simultaneously spoken aloud. I also had a tendency to exhibit certain eccentricities, such as taking all the brass and copper vessels in the house and lining them up from one wall to the other.

When I was five and the traditional day of opening the *pial* school on 1 October had been reached, I quickly took a dislike to the teacher and consequently made a big fuss about attending, even though, with my 'priestly' background, the ancient Vedic chants that had accompanied the enrolment were pleasing to me. (*Pial* is the name of the porch at the front of most of the houses in the area, and it was in one of those that a teacher would gather with no more than, say, half a dozen pupils.) In fact, from a very early age indeed, I was so self-directed that (again quoting Robert Kanigel) "unless he was ready to do something on his own, in his own time, he was scarcely able to do it at all; school for him often meant not keys to knowledge but shackles to throw off". The reason for this is now totally clear to me: I'd gone to Earth with unbounded mathematical knowledge and interests that I subconsciously knew it was my destiny to share, and I consequently needed scarcely any formal teaching.

At the age of seven, after my paternal grandfather had died from leprosy, I broke out in a bad case of itching and boils, and this was taken as an indication of a temperament inclined to extreme and unexpected reactions to stress. One of the most important aspects of my childhood, however, is that I literally breathed spirituality and Hinduism into the very marrow of my bones. Or perhaps it would be more accurate to say that I'd been born with it all inside me and so the upbringing I received — mainly from my mother — merely reinforced what was there already. For yes, my father's work left him little time for paying attention to me, whereas my mother, who was an extremely forceful character, very pious and scrupulous about preserving the religious and spiritual traditions of our section of this great country, held prayer meetings in our home, and the name of our family deity, Goddess Namagiri of Namakkal, was ever on her lips. She was also credited with having psychic powers, as well as a great imagination, and she often told me tales from the great

Indian legends, such as the Mahabharata and the Ramayana. With her, too, I regularly attended *pujas* at the temple, and she taught me to sing the religious songs. The population in our part of India at that time was about 90 per cent Hindu, and Hinduism is in any case generally more tolerant of other faiths than are most other religions.

In October 1892 I was enrolled in the Kangayan Primary School, but then I was again sent to my maternal grandparents' home near Madras. There, however, I disliked the school so much that the family felt obliged to enlist the help of the local constable to make sure that I attended! So within six months I was back in Kumbakonam, and at Kangayan I performed well and, shortly before my tenth birthday, passed the primary examinations in English, Tamil, geography and arithmetic with the best scores in the district. By the age of 11, having exhausted the mathematical knowledge of two college students who were lodging in our home at the time, I was seen as a child prodigy.

Later I was lent a book on advanced trigonometry by S. L. Loney, and I'd mastered this by the age of 13, while at the same time discovering sophisticated theorems on my own. Throughout the rest of my school career I received merit certificates and academic awards, and I also assisted the school in the logistics of assigning its 1200 students (each with differing needs) to its approximately 35 teachers. I always completed mathematical exams in half the allotted time, showing a familiarity with geometry and infinite series. In 1902 I was shown how to solve cubic equations, but later developed my own method for solving the quartic. At 16 I obtained a library copy of *A Synopsis of Elementary Results in Pure and Applied Mathematics*, a collection by G. S. Carr of 5000 theorems, and found the study of it quite fascinating and totally absorbing. The next year I investigated the Bernoulli numbers independently and developed and calculated the Euler-Mascheroni constant up to 15 decimal places, thus causing my peers, who said that they could rarely understand me, simply to stand in respectful awe of my abilities. Yet, rather than feeling proud and big-headed, I tended merely to be grateful for the discovery of my true purpose in life, which, probably more often than not, doesn't come to people quite so early on.

In 1904, having been awarded the K. Ranganatha Rao prize for mathematics by the headmaster of the Town Higher Secondary School, I was awarded a scholarship to study at the Government Arts College. Here, however, a problem arose simply because of my single-pointed devotion to mathematics and consequent failure to be interested in anything else. This meant that, not doing sufficiently well in subjects such as English, my scholarship was rapidly withdrawn, which was of course disastrous for my family. My forceful mother was so incensed that she stormed in to confront the college principal, but even she couldn't persuade him to bend the rules. So I hung on for a few months, at least managing to obtain a certificate attesting to my attendance. This, however, caused me great distress, as I found laying mathematics aside in order to give satisfaction in other subjects unbearably painful. So eventually, in August 1905, I endeavoured to resolve the problem by running away from home. You can imagine the pain thereby caused to my family!

Being a mathematical child prodigy — or no doubt any sort of child prodigy — is invariably a huge challenge, as both Ruth Lawrence and Alan Turing would also testify. Being sent to do a degree at Oxford at the age of 10, obtaining one's first degree at 13, and then being awarded a doctorate at 17 is patently absurd! Ruth nevertheless survived the deprivation of so much of her childhood remarkably well and now, married to an Israeli, with a professorship at the Einstein Institute of Mathematics at the Hebrew University, she is determined that her own four children should have a normal childhood. For Turing, however, who lived in between the two of us, things were much more difficult.

Being persecuted by his peers at his British public school for being 'different and something of a weirdo' was only the *start* of the suffering that he was made to endure, and thank goodness that most people nowadays cringe with horror at the thought of the way in which homosexuals used to be treated. His code-breaking work cut the Second World War short by probably two years, thereby saving millions of lives, but it wasn't enough to save him from a prison sentence for homosexual acts, with only a very unpleasant alternative ('chemical castration'), and what good did a posthumous pardon do him?

A Cambridge person himself, Turing of course knew about my work, and he and I were having a good chat about it all recently; we were in total agreement about the incredible sacrifices people sometimes agree to take on before incarnating, simply for the sake of the work that they know to be invaluable! (Turing also shares with me the experience of having had a film made about his life. In *The Imitation Game*, Benedict Cumberbatch did a quite incredibly good job of acting its hero, while in *The Man Who Knew Infinity*, not only did Dev Patel get 'right inside me' when portraying the suffering I went through at Cambridge, but also Jeremy Irons was pretty much the spitting image of my mentor, Harold Hardy.)

I, on the other hand, had in childhood the advantage of being a lovable character with "sparkly eyes and a wonderful sense of humour", which always endeared me to my peers as well as elders, but my genius didn't give my family an easy life at all. My forceful mother, determined to bring some form of normality to her beloved 'school dropout' son, and without even consulting my father on the matter, espied while visiting relatives a child named Janaki who she thought could well be a suitable wife for me. Janaki's family, like our own, was a poor Brahmin one, but they had five daughters, and so my mother, thinking that they might consequently be grateful to secure a husband for any one of these girls (even though I had at the time neither job nor prospects!), selected Janaki after finding us to be well matched astrologically. Now that belief in astrology in the West has declined a great deal since, say, the Elizabethan era, some of you Westerners may well be shocked when I tell you that my mother had followed this Indian tradition. In addition, when we got married on 14 July 1909, while I was 21, my wife was only 10 years of age.

On the first point, I'd like to mention, to those who pooh-pooh the use of this branch of science for the selection of life partners, that the fact remains that the great majority of marriages arranged in this way do work extremely well. (Falling in love *after* marriage is certainly no less reliable than doing so beforehand and when you look at the present divorce rates in Europe and America...!) Anyway, my father was so angry about not having been consulted on the matter that he refused to attend the ceremony. He also felt that we deserved a better match financially, namely a family that was able to afford a decently sized dowry. The wedding was a double one, carried out together with her sister Vijayalakshmi and her groom and after it had taken place, as was also the custom then, Janaki remained in her parents' home for another three years until she'd reached puberty, whereupon she joined my mother and me in Madras.

Now that we're here together again on the other side, Janaki and I have seen clearly that we're companion soul mates who'd jointly made life plans in the full knowledge that my life was destined to be a brief one and that part of her task would be to support me fully against all odds. After my death, she moved to Bombay (now Mumbai) for a while, where various distinguished mathematicians made a point of visiting her, but in 1931 she returned to Madras and settled in Triplicane. Right up until she died in 1994, she went on doing a really noble job of ensuring continued recognition of my work and was awarded various well-deserved pensions. We still love one another dearly and should we decide to come back together another time (which I'm told that, as a highly evolved soul, I won't *need* to do) she might possibly be the mathematician rather than me, since the opportunities for women in that field have now at last improved considerably!

Now to go backwards again: sadly, soon after we'd started living together, I developed a condition known as hydrocele testis, which required surgery that my family couldn't afford. Six months later, however, a kind doctor volunteered to do the operation for free, and after that I began a serious hunt for work. I went looking all over the place, staying with a series of good friends who were willing to support me. Clerical positions were very hard to obtain, but I did manage to make a bit of money from tutoring students at Presidency College who were preparing for the Fellow of Arts Examination. Later in the year, however, I fell ill again, which was worrying, and so I asked my friend Radakrishna Iyer to hand over my notebooks to either Professor Singaravelu Mudaliar at Pachaiyappa's College (which I'd previously attended myself) or to the British mathematician Professor Edward B. Ross of the Madras Christian College.

These precious notebooks were a bit of a hotchpotch of stuff that I'd been doing over quite a few years and not easy to decipher even for people who understood *something* of my highly advanced field. Part of the problem was that, paper being expensive, I'd often had to write on slate initially and then transfer my results to a more permanent form. The biggest problem in finding my niche, however, was my lack of a BA degree in mathematics. I won't bother you with all the details of my attempts to obtain education elsewhere, but I will tell you how happy my friends made me by giving the support I needed in order to have the freedom to pursue my work. So, once I'd again recovered physically, I retrieved my notebooks and took them to show to V. Ramaswami Iyer, who had founded the Indian Mathematical Society in 1906.

As you very likely know, while the West was still using awkward Roman numerals, in India, where the zero symbol had originally been invented, we had for long been using the number system that's so widely used today. Yet, in several hundred of the more recent years, our country's contribution in the field had dwindled dramatically and our mathematicians had become overly dependent upon connections with the West. So it seemed that one part of the task for which I'd reincarnated was to redress this imbalance.

Anyway, to cut a long story short, 1911 was a very important year for me, as it was the one in which my first paper appeared in the *Journal of the Indian Mathematical Society*. (Incidentally, it was also the year in which Madras acquired a new sewer system and also in which its oil-lit streets began to give way to electricity.) V. Ramaswami Iyer had sent me, together with letters of introduction, to his mathematician friends in Madras, but debate then arose as to whether what I'd done was genuine or whether I was a fraud. I therefore mentioned to Ramachandra Rao, the Secretary of the Indian Mathematical Society, some correspondence I'd previously had with the notable Bombay mathematician Professor Saldhana, who, while failing to understand my work, had nevertheless concluded that it was genuine.

The eventual outcome of much correspondence was contact with some Cambridge University mathematicians, as a result of which I was finally offered a two-year research post at the University of Madras with an allowance of Rs 75 per month. Godfrey Harold Hardy, who also showed my work to his colleague John Littlewood and eventually became my mentor at Trinity College, Cambridge, said that he'd never met my equal. Littlewood was instantly impressed, too, and the two of them collaborated in getting recognition of my capabilities. It was then Hardy who, after several other British mathematicians had refused to trust my work, finally said "Yes" to my request for help. Upon receiving my letter dated 16 January 1913, he found some of my formulae "scarcely possible to believe", describing me as "a man who could work out modular equations and theorems ... to orders unheard of, whose mastery of continued fractions was ... beyond that of any mathematician in the world".

Already famous at 35, Hardy wanted this 'unknown Indian 24-year-old' to come and work *with* him at Trinity College in his world-renowned university, but the problem was that a Brahmin wasn't permitted to leave his native land. Besides, in addition to that, although the British had invaded this very special country in a desire to dominate it completely, I myself had had very little contact with them and therefore, while fully believing them to be no less important to God than anyone else, I couldn't help seeing them as a trifle alien. (In the words of Rudyard Kipling, born in 'British India' in 1865: "East is East and West is West and never the twain shall meet.")

So only divine intervention could resolve this apparently insuperable twofold problem! My mother then had a vivid dream in which our family goddess, the deity of Namagiri, commanded her "to stand no longer between her son and the fulfilment of his life's purpose". Consequently, on 17 March 1914 and still somewhat reluctantly — especially since the separation from my dear young wife was very painful — I embarked upon a ship to England, leaving Janaka with my parents in India. The fact that World War I broke out just over four months later naturally didn't make things any easier for *anybody*, and my difficulty in obtaining foods appropriate to my strictly vegetarian diet was obviously deleterious to my already precarious health.

In addition to all that, I, used to dressing in a simple cotton dhoti tied around my waist and with my hair bunched into a knot on the top of my head, had to get it cut short and clothe myself in Western dress, that is to say, underclothes underneath a formal shirt and suit and, on top of all that, a thick coat and a big woollen scarf. Yet even all those were insufficient to protect me from rain or snow. (Not that Madras doesn't see rain, but it never makes one cold. Snow was more exciting — and pretty to boot — but the heating in college rooms was inadequate, to put it mildly.) As for the racism in this eminent British city, I prefer not to even mention it in a book that has already dwelt fairly thoroughly on this unpleasant subject, but I can leave what I suffered to your imaginations. When, however, something is in one's life plan, the challenges will invariably be overcome one way or another.

Yet the biggest problem of all, which Hardy and I had to work through *together*, was that of our diametrically opposed methods of approach to mathematics, Hardy of course working in harmony with the traditional British — nay, *European* — system. His comment about the method I employed to reach my solutions was that it was "a process of mingled argument, intuition and induction, of which he was entirely unable to give any coherent account", but the simple truth is that I had the exceptional gift (there's no other way in which to describe it) of being able to *see* in my head what was the result of a problem without going through all the steps that others regarded as necessary in order to *prove* it. Hardy, however, inspiring champion and friend though he ultimately became, was an atheist and therefore ever unable to appreciate the help that came to me from the world of spirit.

He, like myself, had been a mathematical child prodigy (his only other great interest that came anywhere near to approaching it being cricket!). Despite not coming from a wealthy background, he'd had the perhaps somewhat dubious privilege of having won a scholarship to one of the top English public schools, Winchester. Though things have no doubt improved a bit in more recent years, the honest truth is that back then these renowned schools gave their pupils a pretty tough time. Hardy had actually survived his days there remarkably well and everybody who knew him liked him immensely, but one thing that those schools didn't encourage doing was having *feelings*, and this caused an inevitable barrier to any real intimacy in our relationship. However, of all the distinguished mathematicians who had looked at my work, he, along with Littlewood, finally came to believe in my results as confidently as I did myself. Thanks to this, I was at last able to work exclusively on what I most wanted to do, which brought me real happiness.

In addition to that, while Hardy was considered to be extremely good-looking, he had no love life, and his friends and colleagues were never quite sure whether he was a non-practising homosexual or quite simply asexual. However, since his overriding characteristic was *kindness*, this question was completely immaterial. And despite that dreadful war impinging increasingly on our lives, with, for instance, some of the wounded being brought right into the college premises, both Hardy and Littlewood (when he was there) gave me every possible encouragement.

The big problem was, however, that in order to convince any of his fellows (the other Trinity College 'Fellows'!) of my abilities, Hardy had to nag me unceasingly to write down clearly on paper all the steps I'd taken towards arriving at each result. This was an incredibly difficult task for me, since I hadn't ever needed to go through those steps thanks to my God-given abilities. So Hardy's first attempt at obtaining for this 'unknown young man from *India*' a College Fellowship was — to my bitter disappointment — unsuccessful. Then, however, he got the bright idea of introducing my novel work to the Royal Society and once its worth had been recognised by that honourable institution and I'd been made one of *their* Fellows, the Trinity Fellows had no choice other than inviting me to join them. (One must understand that, in Britain, being able to put 'FRS' (Fellow of the Royal Society) after one's name brings incomparable distinction!)

This honour truly delighted me, simply because I knew that my task on Earth was to introduce new concepts into mathematics, but, alas, my poor health then became even worse and I was forced to spend some time in a sanatorium. There I was diagnosed with both tuberculosis and vitamin deficiency, but Hardy, who came to visit me, couldn't bear the thought of my work suffering on account of the sickness, and I was also determined not to let him down. There is a famous occasion of him coming to see me in Putney when I was ill and remarking that the number of the taxi cab he'd ridden in, 1729, seemed to him to be a "rather dull one" and that he therefore hoped it wasn't an unfavourable omen. To that I replied: "No, it is a very interesting number; it is the smallest number expressible as the sum of two cubes in two different ways." Immediately before that visit, Hardy had quoted Littlewood as saying that every positive integer was one of my personal friends!

I spent a total of nearly five years at Cambridge, and, in addition to the physical sickness, I suffered quite badly from homesickness. So, in 1919, Hardy finally had no choice but to let me return to India, extracting as he did so a promise from me to come back to Cambridge one year later. By that time at least the dreadful war was over, but back in Madras I discovered that poor Janaki's letters to me had been intercepted by my mother. Dear though mine was to me, with the powerful support she'd always given, Indian mothers-in-law have a reputation for insisting on ruling the roost, and my beloved young wife had consequently suffered considerably in my absence, so I felt I had to do my level best to make it up to her.

I was nevertheless able to continue working fairly comfortably for a while — until, that is, the sickness got the better of my *body* (though not of course my spirit!) and I died, at the age of 32, on 26 April 1920. Thirty-two years may seem "much too short" to you, but what else did anyone really need to do in a single lifetime? Besides, with my knowledge of astrology, it had already been clear from my chart that I was most unlikely to live to 35.

Poor Hardy was absolutely devastated when he received the news, but by the time the letter containing it had completed its long trek across the seas to him, my etheric body was of course luxuriating in some wonderful healing. Then, when he himself died, over 27 years later, I knew that, as a convinced atheist, he would have some trouble waking up to the reality of the non-existence of 'death', but I also knew that (like Bertrand Russell, who'd been at Trinity College while I was) his being such a good person would help his crossing over. I further enlisted the support over here of his parents, who had during their last lives been good Christians. They in turn prompted some of their son's believer friends and colleagues who'd outlived him to do their bit with prayer, and the combined effort didn't take too long to work.

The Hardy seniors, with whom I'd already had some interaction, fully appreciated my desire to be among the first to greet him, and so now I'll record the conversation we had the moment that he 'regained consciousness', as it was really quite amusing:

"Goodness me, where am I? I thought I'd died, but here I am still seemingly looking just the same, except a bit younger and fitter. And who's that young Indian just waiting over there with open arms...? No, no, it can't be, it can't *possibly* be...!"

"Yes, my esteemed Harold — I'm permitted to call you that now, rather than 'Sir', am I not? — you'll now gradually be coming to see that perhaps we Indians do know and understand a few things besides mathematics. For yes, I am indeed your fellow Fellow of Trinity College, the renowned, the unforgettable Ramanujan, whom you saved from almost literal starvation and had written down in history as a true genius."

"How *can* that be? Was that letter I received from India, which so broke my (admittedly rather closed) heart, a fake, a joke…? Surely there couldn't be anyone so vile as to play such a trick on me? Oh and yes, *do* call me by the name my parents chose… Good Lord, isn't that them just over there, smiling at me?"

"Yes, Harold," said his mother, "so you still use the word 'Lord', the one strictly used only for the God whose existence you denied, upsetting us many years ago by telling us so! But don't worry, dear, we all have the occasional life on Earth as non-believers and now that you're Home again you'll remember how right people are in such places as India, where spirituality runs so deep that it's hard to obliterate."

"Yes, Harold," I then interjected, "your good parents and I have been looking forward to welcoming you, but look, here come your guides now to take you for a rest, assist you through your life review and remind you how you and I had planned, before entering our last lives, to work together, you being the best possible person to grasp what I was doing and promote it."

I waved him off; he looked distinctly bewildered, but hopefully was accepting my assurance that our work together wasn't yet ended.

As for me, I'm still working, guiding others, and content in the knowledge that I'd completed my agreed task of restoring my beloved homeland's place on the world mathematical map and that my legacy is universally treasured. You see, it was my destiny to introduce new and valuable concepts which might otherwise have taken decades (if not centuries) to be discovered and besides, the experts were truly delighted when, in 1976, my lost notebook was rediscovered.

Now I'll conclude with a brief note about my biographer, Robert Kanigel, without whom the film about part of my life couldn't have been made. A brilliant American, with a scientific background as well as great talent for writing, he was undoubtedly the ideal person for undertaking such a challenging task. In addition to meeting up with me at night in order to have useful discussions, while back in his body during the daytime he travelled extensively around India for his research, besides making an in-depth study of the traditions (many of them strange, to put it mildly!) of Cambridge University. Inevitably, the film omitted a lot of the details you can find in the book, so, if you are sufficiently interested — and especially if you'd like to have a clearer picture of the mathematics involved — I would urge you to read it as well. Now, still nearly six years younger than our scribe, Robert has retired from a Professorship in Science Writing at the Massachusetts Institute of Technology and is working full time on his writing. So I wish him, besides all of you, the very best for his remaining years on that beautiful (though again, alas, war-torn) planet.

# 27

# An India-Loving Composer

*Musicians express in sound what all men feel.*

Gustav Holst

*You may ask — "Where can we find the Lord?" Well, He has given His address, in Chapter 18, Sloka 61 of the Bhagavad Gita. Turn to it and note it down.* Ishvarah sarvabhutanam hriddeshe — *"O Arjuna, the Lord resides in the heart of all beings." Now, after knowing that, how can you look down on any living being in contempt or how can you revel in hate or indulge in the pastime of ridiculing? Every individual is charged with the Divine Presence, moved by Divine attributes. Love, honour, friendliness — that is what each one deserves from you. Give these in full measure.*

Sathya Sai Baba

"Last but not least," goes the saying, and I feel flattered that our scribe appears to subscribe to this view. Since her friend Michael Trott had produced an excellent illustrated book about the composer Hubert Parry (Director of the Royal College of Music when I was a student there), she did at one point consider bringing him into her book, but then she heard a lecture at a Three Choirs Festival which mentioned my interest in India and so that clinched it and she chose me instead. She also felt it appropriate to have me follow on directly from an Indian genius, and I in fact lived (though somewhat longer) at more or less the same time as Ramanujan did.

Parry was of course a very good composer, and his classes that I attended gave me a vision which I learnt to call 'History', but there turned out to be an additional reason for Ann's selecting me rather than him. This is that, upon hearing that she was intending to include me in her book, her brother John (the most musical of that very diverse Merivale sixsome) informed her that while their maternal grandfather, Albert Cazabon, was studying at the Guildhall, he'd come to me for some tuition in composition!

Like the great Sir Edward Elgar, I was pretty much self-taught, yet that didn't prevent me from being much sought after as a composition teacher. The reason for this seems to be that I regarded teaching not as a master imparting knowledge to a pupil, but rather as a process of mutual discovery in which both can share. For instance, I always endeavoured to draw from my pupils their own ideas, encouraging them to develop these in their own individual and unique ways, never imposing or correcting but simply suggesting. So, now that I can look back from this side upon my life as Gustav Holst, knowing that I was loved for those reasons gives me great joy because, since I was more or less born believing naturally in the Hindu doctrine of *Dharma* (that is, pursuing one's path in life against all odds), I never sought fame. It's consequently never bothered me that my case isn't dissimilar to that of Pachelbel, who is undeservedly renowned almost solely for his much-played *Canon*! For yes, contrary to what most people think, I did actually compose a great deal besides *The Planets*, the one and only work that really and truly brought me fame. (Oh, that's not counting the tune to *I Vow to Thee, My Country*, the words of which go right against everything I stood for, and that of the carol *In the Bleak Midwinter*, whose words, on the other hand, I quite like.)

Going back for a moment, however, to 'Cazzie', as he was always known, at least in the Merivale and Cazabon families, he was a gifted violinist and conductor, and when his daughter, Norah, was 15 years old, he got offered the post of conductor of the Sydney Theatre Orchestra. He held this position for nine years, before returning to England, and there he composed a piece for the opening of the Sydney Harbour Bridge, which took place on 19 March 1932. While never achieving any fame at all, he also composed various other pieces of light music, and I myself have much sympathy with that. In fact I once wrote: "I have something within me that prompts me to write light music now and then … All these are as genuinely part of me as the Veda hymns." Incidentally, it was from Albert Cazabon, as well as from their mother Norah, rather than from the Merivale side of the family, that the siblings inherited an immense love of music. Ann, the eldest, was destined to do other things as a career this time round, but she feels very fortunate to have found a husband whose musical tastes are pretty much identical to her own.

And so it was that, when Ann felt that the time had finally come to go to Cheltenham to visit the Holst Victorian House (named prior to Covid the 'Holst Museum') in preparation for writing this final chapter, I was watching what went on, and David, her equally music-loving husband, was more than happy to accompany her. The chosen day (20 June 2023), however, turned out to be an extremely challenging one for them. David had lost his driving licence at 70 on account of eye problems and Ann, becoming at 83 increasingly nervous on the roads, had already decided that she would shortly give her car to their daughter. Since, however, rain had been forecast, she decided to drive down to Great Malvern station and leave the car there for the day.

That particular day had actually been selected, from a few dates that Ann had suggested, by her Woolger friend, Wendy Ellyatt, who lives in Cheltenham. They'd been on several of his training workshops together, as well as subsequent meetings with other colleagues in France, but hadn't been able to meet again for several years. (Wendy, 20 years Ann's junior, is endlessly busy doing valuable work in children's education, all originally triggered by an extraordinary experience she'd had at the very first Woolger workshop she attended.) They'd agreed to meet for lunch at Cheltenham's renowned Japanese restaurant, and Ann was delighted when Wendy offered to bring along a friend of hers who has similar interests to their own. But the itinerary involved Ann and her husband taking two trains to Cheltenham, as well as three taxis once they were there — all quite challenging with their combined disabilities — and the first train being delayed by an hour naturally added to the difficulties.

Everything went perfectly nevertheless, with the couple being fascinated to see the house in which I was born. (And, by the way, I don't mind at all about the change of name, made with the aim of attracting more visitors, because I only lived there until I was eight, others subsequently inhabited it, and the house itself is of general historical interest anyway.) They found the staff there all extremely helpful, and some of them, after pressing Ann to explain the nature of the book she was writing, even expressed interest in her subject. When she mentioned to the first volunteer they met that her special attention had been triggered by learning about my interest in India, the reply was that *that* had been triggered by the fact that many of the country's ex-colonials had settled in Cheltenham upon retiring.

There is indeed a lot of truth in that, but Ann was already sure that the cause must also run deeper and she was of course quite right there. In fact, now that I'm over here, I can see that she and I have previously known one another in India, but, since she's already written extensively about her own past lives and this book is entirely centred on other people, she has no need to be aware of those details at present. (People might wonder why I never went to India in that lifetime. Well, both time and financial constraints were considerable, but also something deep inside made me feel that I really didn't need to go there, since I knew it well already. That's what gave me an affinity with that amazing country's philosophy, as well as my fascination with its ritual and dance.)

Once the couple had seen all they needed to and made their way to the restaurant, the animated lunch conversation was a treat for all four of them. Real problems only started with the train company messing up the return journey in a ridiculous way, upon which I don't need to elaborate, but, after driving home immensely carefully, Ann subsequently collapsed in a heap on the bed, totally exhausted. Since you're going to find some sadness in the account of my most recent life on Earth — but what great art has ever stemmed from a cushy life? — I'll first tell you about something hilariously funny that happened when they got home.

The previous Sunday had been Father's Day, and there awaiting their return from Cheltenham was a parcel addressed to David from their son Christopher. When he opened it, what should he find but a box of chocolates named 'Planets'! Well, as Ann ascertained the next morning after having laughed herself to sleep, Christopher had never even heard of Gustav Holst, let alone my most celebrated piece of music, and Ann hadn't yet told any of their children about the trip to Cheltenham.

Anyway, it now feels appropriate to start telling you something about my life as that composer and teacher. While my family don't quite rival the Bach dynasty, it already had a strongly musical history. Originating probably in Scandinavia, the Holsts had by the late seventeenth century branches in Poland, Germany and then Russia. My great-grandfather, Matthias, who was of German origin, had served as a musician at the Imperial Court of St Petersburg before seeking refuge in England. His grandson, Adolph von Holst, was my father, but we dropped the 'von' on account of hostility towards Germans during World War I. He was employed as organist and choirmaster at All Saints' Church in Cheltenham and also gave piano recitals. He fell in love with my mother Clara, one of his pupils and a gifted singer and pianist, who had been born in

Cirencester, they were married in Cheltenham in July 1871, and I was born on 21 September 1874.

This means (as I discovered in 1910, thanks to Clifford Bax, brother of Arnold the composer, introducing me to astrology when the three of us were on holiday together in Spain) that I was under the Virgo-Libra Cusp. Such people are influenced by the planets Mercury and Venus, which gives them a vision of balance, perfection and grace, also blessing them with wit and charm. Our scribe feels it unnecessary to mention the downside of being born on this cusp, but it can certainly be said that I had the grounded determination of the Virgo earth sign combined with the grace, charisma, and social ease of the Libra air sign, and all this made me both rational and able to express emotions — useful traits for a composer!

My brother Emil was born two years after me, and he became a successful actor in the West End, New York and Hollywood, working under the name of Ernest Cossart. We lived in a three-storeyed house built in 1822–3, which was then number 4 Pittville Terrace, now renamed Clarence Road, with no garden but just a little backyard. Emil and I shared the nursery on the top floor, and the first great tragedy of our life was that our dear mother, who had never been strong, died when I was only eight. You can well imagine the effect of such a loss on two young boys, and my grief-stricken father soon moved us to another house in Cheltenham, recruiting his sister Nina to look after us.

Recognising my aunt's devotion to the family, I later dedicated some of my early compositions to her, but then, in 1885, my father married Mary, another of his pupils, and with her he had another two sons, Matthias (known as Max) and Evelyn. My stepmother, however, had little interest in domestic matters, being absorbed in Theosophy, and our family home was regularly used as a meeting place for the followers of the Russian medium Helena Blavatsky. (Madame Blavatsky, as she is known, lived in Madras for a while and her cottage is situated in a huge garden there, close to a massive tree under which her fellow Theosophists would gather for meditation.) These Cheltenham meetings no doubt served in the long run as another stimulus to my Indian interests, yet all four of us boys consequently suffered a certain amount of neglect, and I have to say that I felt pretty miserable throughout my childhood.

In addition to that, I had poor eyesight and a weak chest, and I suffered all my life from neuritis in my right arm, which made writing very difficult and painful for me. My father, however, whose piano is now housed in the museum, recognised my musical abilities early on, and I was taught to play the piano and the violin (greatly preferring the former). Then, at the age of 12, he got me started on the trombone, as he felt that it might improve my asthma. This proved useful later, when, though I hated doing it, I was able as a student at the Royal College of Music to supplement my income by playing in seaside bands and theatre orchestras. Prior to that I was educated at Cheltenham Grammar School, where my fellows all looked down upon me for being no good at sport.

On a happier note, it was at the RCM that I met Ralph Vaughan Williams (or RVW, as I'll call him). We both joined its Debating Society and became lifelong friends. He was among those who were really kind to me on account of my health, once giving me a gift of £50 to spend on a trip to Algeria for its warmer climes. I cycled through the desert, was truly fascinated by it and in a strange sort of way felt quite at home there, which surely indicates that I must have at some time had at least one desert life. On another occasion the great Sir Henry Wood (founder of the Promenade Concerts) paid for me to have a week in Margate because he thought I looked so ill!

As you probably know, RVW took a great interest in researching folk song and is renowned (in addition to much else of course) for his many wonderful arrangements of truly beautiful traditional melodies. I shared that love to a great degree (witness the Helios CD of my part songs, entitled *This Have I Done for My True Love*, performed by the Holst Singers under the baton of the well-known conductor Stephen Layton, which Ann has been enjoying since their visit to Cheltenham), but I also put much emphasis on originality. In fact, in the DVD mentioned in the Acknowledgements at the front of this book, Stephen Johnson (jointly with Richard Wigmore, our scribe's favourite musicologist) gives an excellent analysis of some of the innovations to be found in my music, seeing me as quite a forerunner in the contemporary music field. I also greatly appreciated dear Ralph commenting: "It is the blend of visionary with the realist that gives Holst's music its distinctive character."

Now, in case you feel that I'm blowing my own trumpet (or I suppose I should really say 'trombone'!) too much, I need to tell you that the thing I cared about most passionately was 'bringing music to the masses'. Few composers are able to live on earnings from their works and I supplemented my paltry income by teaching both at St Paul's Girls' School and at Morley College in London. Before my appointment, Morley had been founded in 1904 specifically for giving education to the working classes (just my cup of tea!) and in selecting me they were seeking someone 'new and avant-garde'. The College hadn't previously been taking musically seriously, but, with my Virgoan perseverance, I managed gradually to build up a class of dedicated music lovers.

Going back to RVW, whom I first met in 1895, shortly after my twenty-first birthday, in addition to being a lifelong friend he had more influence on my music than did anybody else. Our teacher, Stanford, emphasised the need for his students to be self-critical, but RVW and I became one another's chief critics, with each of us playing our latest composition to the other while still working on it. Ralph later observed that "what one really learns from an Academy or College is not so much from one's official teachers as from one's fellow-students", also commenting that we used to discuss "every subject under the sun from the lowest note of the double bassoon to the philosophy of Jude the Obscure", and I certainly learnt at least as much from his evaluation of my work as he from mine. We were also, in spite of my poor health, both great ramblers (I even on occasion, for financial reasons, walked the entire London to Cheltenham route), and being together in the English countryside gave plenty of opportunity for deepening our friendship still further. I missed him sorely after he'd volunteered for military service upon the outbreak of the First World War (from which my poor health of course precluded me), but we corresponded throughout his time away; now that we've met up again over here, he's told me that he also missed *me* during the 24 years in which he outlived me.

It was of course my interest in astrology — I used to call doing friends' charts for them my "pet vice" — that inspired me to compose *The Planets*. I started on 'Mars' at the beginning of the war and completed the whole work a couple of years later; in it my intention was to portray the *reality* of war, rather than glorifying deeds of heroism. By the way, with regard to the war, since I hated not being able to serve in the army, as Ralph and my brother Emil did in France, I volunteered to do something for the troops, but it was only shortly before Armistice Day that my services were finally accepted by the Young Men's Christian Association (YMCA). The music section of their education department was wanting people to work with troops awaiting demobilisation, and so they sent me to Salonica as musical organiser for the Near East. Morley College and St Paul's Girls' School both gave me a year's leave of absence and a big send-off, which was lovely, and from Salonica I was able to visit Greece, which I found most impressive.

Returning again to the subject of Ralph, he, unlike me, had been born into a well-to-do family and didn't really need to work for a living. But rather than being snobbish, his family had strong moral views and led a progressive social life. He himself, throughout his life, sought to be of service to his fellow citizens, believing (like me) in making music as available as possible to everybody, and he wrote many works for performance by both amateurs and students. He didn't go as far as I did with my strong socialism – a bit more on that later – and I was also, besides becoming a teetotaller, quite a pioneer with vegetarianism (with which I decided initially to experiment in the hope of it helping with my health).

Now I'll say a word or two about how I combined my teaching duties with my composing. In the aforementioned DVD, Stephen Johnson and the others who, in turn, speak about my life and music, are shown actually sitting in 'Mr Holst's Room'. I designed it for myself when the new music wing of St Paul's Girls' School was inaugurated on 1 July 1913; I was thrilled with its soundproofing and that's where I did most of my composing. We consequently moved to just around the corner from it, and the first work I completed there was the 'St Paul's Suite'.

On account of my neuritis, which made playing the piano difficult, I used an instrument with a soft touch. I always composed directly for the orchestra, and there would be a couple of people ready to take each bit of what I'd written and immediately transpose it for four hands on the piano so that I could hear what it sounded like. I was *so* grateful for that and (having through much of my life regarded myself as a failure) now really appreciate the fact that the school still preserves my name on the door of that room!

With apologies for having jumped the gun somewhat, it's now more than high time for me to tell you about my personal life and my own family. Well, I promised to say more about my socialism: for a while in early life I used to deliver copies of *The Socialist Worker* on my bike and I first met the lovely Isobel (née Harrison and born in Wood Green, North London) in the late 1890s, when we both attended some of the meetings of the Hammersmith Socialist Society; I conducted their Socialist Choir, which she joined as a soprano. She was a couple of years younger than me and I fell in love with her very quickly. We got married in June 1901 and started our life together in two rented rooms in Shepherd's Bush, with Isobel doing dressmaking to help make ends meet. Our daughter Imogen was born on 12 April 1907, at the time when I was composing my 'Somerset Rhapsody' at the suggestion of the folk music collector Cecil Sharp, and we were by then living in a small house in Richmond, Surrey.

As for Isobel, she stood by me through thick and thin right up until my death, giving me every possible form of support, even at the darkest of times. During World War One she joined other independent-spirited women in volunteering to work for the Green Cross as a part-time driver in the Women's Reserve Ambulance. She had a real flair for home-making and decorating, and she also often gave me a great deal of help by copying out some of my music. At one point we paid a visit to the little town of Thaxted in Essex, immediately fell in love with it and then in 1917 went to live there, in a house named 'The Manse', which was our home until 1925.

In Thaxted Isobel embraced country life, joined the English Folk Dance Society, the Essex Archaeological and the Essex Agricultural societies, and supported the Women's Institute. Even more importantly, however, we became friendly with the Reverend Conrad Noel, known as the 'Red Vicar', who supported the Independent Labour Party and espoused many causes that were unpopular with conservative opinion. He also encouraged the revival of folk-dancing and processionals as part of church ceremonies, innovations which caused controversy among traditionally minded churchgoers.

I became an occasional organist and choirmaster at the Thaxted parish church and also developed quite an interest in bell-ringing. In addition to that, Noel had, in 1916, started an annual music festival at Whitsuntide, and I was able to bring students from both Morley College and St Paul's Girls' School to perform at it, together with local participants. In both 1916 and 1917 we all had a tremendously fun time, with everyone singing and dancing all over the place. My philosophy was that quantity was even more important than quality, and I dedicated my *a cappella* carol *This Have I Done for My True Love* (which I always referred to as 'The Dancing Day') to Noel, in recognition of his interest in the ancient origins of religion. It received its first performance during the Third Whitsun Festival, which took place at Thaxted in May 1918.

Despite the times when I got depressed about the lack of success with some of my works, such as *Sita*, my first Indian opera, I was absolutely thrilled to bits when, just before I went off to Salonica, the great musician Henry Balfour Gardiner gave me a special parting gift of a performance of *The Planets* by the Queen's Hall Orchestra. I asked my friend Adrian Boult to conduct it, thus, I'm very glad to say, really starting him off on his great career, and our dear daughter Imogen, aged 11 at the time, later well remembered sitting in the darkened hall for the performance.

Talking of Imogen, gosh, are we proud of her! Without our in any way pushing her to follow in my footsteps, she showed exceptional musical talent from an early age and at one of our Whitsuntide Festivals when she was 13 the *Morley College Magazine* reported on the "delightful dancing of Mr. Holst's gifted little daughter with her troop of nymphs and swains, the orchestral music for which was composed by the little dancer herself". Later she went straight from St Paul's Girls' School to the Royal College of Music, though here, however, I have to admit to urging her, as she was leaving home for the College, never to open a textbook on harmony! During her time there she developed conducting skills, also winning several prizes for composition, and we really used to love watching her conduct, as she always looked so joyful doing it.

Unlike many of my male contemporaries, I was a great advocate of women being encouraged to succeed in every musical field, and it's a shame that my daughter's own works have never been promoted. She — forever working tirelessly for others — was too modest to do such promotion herself, but now that the BBC has finally woken up to the existence of female composers who were or are just as good at it as are many men, we can live in hope of Imogen Holst one day being Radio 3's 'Composer of the Week'. Besides her many writings (some of them to do with *me*!), she is probably best known nowadays for her educational work at Dartington Hall in the 1940s, as well as for her 20 years as joint artistic director of the Aldeburgh Festival. So, when she joined her mother and me over here in 1984, we were able to have some great discussions about all that she'd achieved.

I think that's enough said about my life and that of my family, but the cause of my death was, to be perfectly honest, quite simply cancer. Even in 1987, when Norah Merivale (née Cazabon) died, nobody liked to use that dreaded word, and my disease was labelled a 'duodenal ulcer'. The doctors imagined that I would recover from the operation they performed, but in fact it all proved to be too much for my heart and, despite considerable pain — a thing I'd had to get used to for a long time anyway with my numerous ailments — I left my body quite easily, on 25 May 1934, with my dear wife at the bedside. My ashes were interred, at my request, close to the memorial to Thomas Weelkes in Chichester Cathedral. This is because, once I'd emerged from under Wagner's spell (a thing to which most composers of my era were subjected!), I developed a great love of early music, and Weelkes was my favourite of the Tudor composers. The service was absolutely lovely, with a memorial oration by Bishop George Bell, and RVW conducting some of my music as well as some of his own.

Upon my arrival over here, who should be the first person to welcome me with open arms but my dear mother, Clara! She said how very sorry she was to have 'abandoned' me at such an early age and then encouraged me to shed some of the tears that the young Gustav had felt obliged to suppress. This was very healing, as was the feeling of freedom from that decidedly weary physical body. I don't need to dwell on my life review, but will just say that my mother, too, insisted that I pat myself on the back for several things, such as my having always been appreciative of others and an inspiration to amateur musicians. Since my particular interests are unlikely to be shared by most readers, I'll refrain from urging you all to seek out my lesser-known works, but I would like to end with something I once said, which our scribe also feels to be a fitting conclusion to this book: "Music, being identical with Heaven, isn't a thing of momentary thrills, or even hourly ones. It's a condition of eternity."

# Epilogue

*That work* [The Planets] *grew in my mind slowly — like a baby in a woman's womb. For two years I had the intention of composing that cycle and during those two years it seemed of itself more and more definitely to be taking form.*

Gustav Holst

Hullo, everybody! This is Susie from the first chapter back again, hoping that you've found the journey as interesting and intriguing as both our scribe and I have. Ann hadn't originally intended to put in another quotation at this juncture, but, while exploring Holst for the final chapter, she happened on this one and decided that she simply had to insert it, since it felt completely analogous to her own two-year journey of writing this book. In fact she has more than once, during her writing career, dreamt that she was having a baby and then realised, upon waking up, that it was symbolic of the book she was working on at the time!

For her, the exploration for this final book of the lives of so many and such very diverse characters has brought immense learning, in addition to numerous challenges. But it is of course for learning that we return to Earth so many times, and overcoming challenges helps us to grow. If you remember, Ann and her husband David (not to mention two of their dogs!) were good friends of mine during my last life on Earth and after I'd crossed over in 2011 I reconnected with my twin soul Peter, so the two of us have been watching this book's progression together with interest over the last couple of years. Ann's had a lot of help from her spirit guide Amos, but it's also been a pleasure to put my oar in now and again, especially when we've met up at night during her hours of sleep (a thing that we over here fortunately no longer need).

When Ann has mentioned to people that she was busy working on her final book, some of them have asked "Why stop?" To this her response is threefold: firstly, this is her ninth book and, nine being the divine number, it seems a good one with which to complete the list. (Hence the 27 chapters, since it quickly became apparent that neither 9 nor 18 would suffice for covering a really wide variety of possible post-death scenarios.) Secondly, 'Death' is surely a good topic with which to finish. Thirdly — and most cogently of all — she doesn't feel that she has another book inside her. When, way back in 1990, her practitioner Mark Young (who, as mentioned in the Introduction, got the idea for this topic simultaneously with her) said that she should write a book, her reply was: "I don't think I've got a book inside me." Now, nine books later, whereas with each of the eight previous ones there was always another lurking in the back of her mind, this is no longer the case. Besides, 84 seems a reasonable age at which to retire!

Now for a few comments on the substance of the book and some of the challenges. The Cathar chapter (describing an actual *meeting* with one of them) was one of the most amazing experiences of our scribe's life and also of great interest to the renowned David Lorimer, who lives in the area and whom Ann had also met (but in the flesh!) that very day. The chapter she was dreading the most was the 'Suicide' one, which was based on a personal experience of hers, though of course she had to invent the story behind it. When, however, she sat down at her computer, she was pleased to find that what came through had a happy ending. Catherine Gascoigne, on the other hand, came through to her when she was meditating in the chapel built around the cell of Julian of Norwich, so you can imagine the delight when Ann googled her and found that such a person was written down in history! (Not that the *full* name had come into her head, just the Christian name and the fact that she'd grown up in Yorkshire.)

Alma Mahler was a very big challenge and when reading about her 'Purgatory', Ann found herself becoming excessively caught up in it all. After that, therefore, she decided to protect herself better, and so each time that she investigated a character, for instance when she was about to open one of the volumes of Van Gogh's letters, she visualised golden light encircling her. But, when it came to embarking upon the Van Gogh chapter, some very interesting things happened. Her late therapy teacher, Dr Roger Woolger, had always stressed to his students the importance of learning to trust whatever came into their heads — a thing that Ann wasn't alone in finding difficult. As mentioned in the Introduction to this book, she had for a long time been in the habit of using a drumming CD to help with journeying to meet a deceased character, but on this occasion firstly her CD player appeared to have suddenly stopped working, and secondly the disc was inside neither its box nor the machine, and there is nowhere else that she ever keeps it. Besides that, the professional artist friend upon whom she'd been relying for having a chat about Van Gogh told her that she felt unable to contribute anything. So all this served as reinforcement to what Ann had been told many times: to go inside *herself* for answers. A useful lesson, perhaps, for many of us!

When, in between Alma Mahler and Van Gogh, it came to Betty Corrigal, something happened that should be of interest for those who like *proof* of what came through during the writing! While Ann and her husband were on the island of Hoy during a tour in Orkney, she herself was unable to climb the tricky slope right up to the Dwarfie Stane, so, with David's visual impairment making him unable to use the camera, their guide kindly offered to take a couple of photos for them. Ann found, however, that the picture of the inside wasn't at all clear and so, when she got home and started writing up Betty's story, she was very intrigued by the bit about the "stone bed" inside the huge stone. Then, *after* writing that paragraph, she thought about searching for a book on the Orkney Islands, the Malvern library had one on all the Scottish Islands and, lo and behold, what should she find therein but a description which exactly matched Betty's own words!

Both Ann's beloved Kathleen Ferrier and the newly discovered (by her, that is) César Manrique were delights to write about, but both Ramanujan and Holst proved to be further challenges, not because they weren't very lovable, too, but simply because she found herself a bit overwhelmed by what felt like a surfeit of material and it was obviously necessary to be selective. This, however, is probably enough said about the non-fictional characters, of whom you will no doubt each have your individual favourites, and I don't think that the fictional ones require any comment.

Now, on the subject of retirement at 84 (the age that Ann will certainly have reached by the time this book appears in print), it's the year of the Uranus Return and while the Saturn Return normally brings major changes in one's life, Uranus offers 'greater freedom and the permission to do new and perhaps crazy things'. So Ann is already planning a change of wardrobe, bringing in colours that are new to her, and also another big decluttering in order to lighten the load left to her children after she and her husband have both departed.

Apart from that, she is quite confident of not being idle. David's Alzheimer's, mixed with vascular dementia (things now afflicting at least one in four people in their age group), is likely to get worse rather than better, which will inevitably increase the amount of care he'll be needing. Related to that, she's keen to start a bereavement/dementia support group in their retirement village and in fact already has three other people eager to join it. Anyway, living in a community such as that in their retirement village, there are always people around wanting advice or simply company.

As for Ann herself, with the inevitable health problems and aches and pains pertaining to that age group, and with all that she feels she has learnt about the 'hereafter', a big bit of her is yearning to get here! Yet she thinks it important to outlive David, who would clearly cope less well on his own than she would, and, with dementia being a comparatively new disease, now that so many of us are living longer, Ann sees it as something she still needed to learn about before being able to clear off for good. (You may remember that I myself had Alzheimer's at the end of my life, so I can empathise with what they're both going through, and it was truly wonderful to be freed of it once I'd left that 85-year-old body.)

Then finally, since apart from her family and her work, Ann's spiritual life is the most important thing to her, she sees the end of life as a good opportunity for focusing on that more fully. David, though a naturally spiritual rather than materialistic person, has never fully shared her beliefs, so she feels that, if widowed, she will have no excuse for not increasing her prayer and meditation time still further, in addition to playing discs of *bhajans* (Indian devotional songs) as well as classical music. Because, after all, what are we here for but to become more fully aware of each and everyone's innate divinity and our ultimate goal of finally returning to the 'place' (for want of a better word) whence we originally came? If this book has in any way helped its readers along this vital path, its aim will have been achieved. So now both our scribe and I wish you all the very best, and we look forward to meeting at least some of you over here.

6TH
BOOKS

## ALL THINGS PARANORMAL

Investigations, explanations and deliberations on the
paranormal, supernatural, explainable or unexplainable.
6th Books seeks to give answers while nourishing the soul:
whether making use of the scientific model or anecdotal and
fun, but always beautifully written.
Titles cover everything within parapsychology: how to,
lifestyles, alternative medicine, beliefs, myths and theories.
If you have enjoyed this book, why not tell other readers by
posting a review on your preferred book site?

Recent bestsellers from 6th Books are:

## The Scars of Eden
Paul Wallis
How do we distinguish between our ancestors' ideas of
God and close encounters of an extraterrestrial kind?
Paperback: 978-1-78904-852-0 ebook: 978-1-78904-853-7

## The Afterlife Unveiled
What the dead are telling us about their world!
Stafford Betty
What happens after we die? Spirits speaking through
mediums know, and they want us to know.
This book unveils their world...
Paperback: 978-1-84694-496-3 ebook: 978-1-84694-926-5

## Harvest: The True Story of Alien Abduction
G.L. Davies
G.L. Davies's most-terrifying investigation yet reveals one
woman's terrifying ordeal of alien visitation, nightmarish
visions and a prophecy of destruction on a scale never
before seen in Pembrokeshire's peaceful history.
Paperback: 978-1-78904-385-3 ebook: 978-1-78904-386-0

## Wisdom from the Spirit World
Carole J. Obley
What can those in spirit teach us about the enduring bond
of love, the immense power of forgiveness, discovering our
life's purpose and finding peace in a frantic world?
Paperback: 978-1-78904-302-0 ebook: 978-1-78904-303-7

## Spirit Release
Sue Allen
A guide to psychic attack, curses, witchcraft, spirit attachment, possession, soul retrieval, haunting, deliverance, exorcism and more, as taught at the College of Psychic Studies.
Paperback: 978-1-84694-033-0 ebook: 978-1-84694-651-6

## Advanced Psychic Development
Becky Walsh
Learn how to practise as a professional, contemporary spiritual medium.
Paperback: 978-1-84694-062-0 ebook: 978-1-78099-941-8

## Where After
Mariel Forde Clarke
A journey that will compel readers to view life after death in a completely different way.
Paperback: 978-1-78904-617-5 ebook: 978-1-78904-618-2

## Poltergeist! A New Investigation into Destructive Haunting
John Fraser
Is the Poltergeist "syndrome" the only type of paranormal phenomena that can really be proven?
Paperback: 978-1-78904-397-6 ebook: 978-1-78904-398-3

### A Little Bigfoot: On the Hunt in Sumatra
Pat Spain
Pat Spain lost a layer of skin, pulled leeches off his nether
regions, and was violated by an Orangutan for this book.
Paperback: 978-1-78904-605-2 ebook: 978-1-78904-606-9

### Astral Projection Made Easy
### and overcoming the fear of death
Stephanie June Sorrell
From the popular Made Easy series, Astral Projection
Made Easy helps to eliminate the fear of death through
discussion of life beyond the physical body.
Paperback: 978-1-84694-611-0 ebook: 978-1-78099-225-9

### Haunted: Horror of Haverfordwest
G.L. Davies
Blissful beginnings for a young couple turn into a nightmare
after purchasing their dream home in Wales in 1989.
Paperback: 978-1-78535-843-2 ebook: 978-1-78535-844-9

Readers of ebooks can buy or view any of these bestsellers
by clicking on the live link in the title. Most titles are
published in paperback and as an ebook. Paperbacks are
available in traditional bookshops. Both print and ebook
formats are available online.

Find more titles and sign up to our readers' newsletter at
**www.6th-books.com**

Join the 6th books Facebook group at
**6th Books The world of the Paranormal**